To Mike,
Living well is indeed
the best revenge.
With sincere appreciation,
Don

WHO WROTE THAT?

AUTHORSHIP CONTROVERSIES FROM MOSES TO SHOLOKHOV

DONALD OSTROWSKI

NORTHERN ILLINOIS UNIVERSITY PRESS
AN IMPRINT OF CORNELL UNIVERSITY PRESS
Ithaca and London

First published 2020 by Cornell University Press

Library of Congress Cataloging-in-Publication Data

Names: Ostrowski, Donald G., author.
Title: Who wrote that? : authorship controversies from Moses to Sholokhov / Donald Ostrowski.
Description: Ithaca : Northern Illinois University Press, an imprint of Cornell University Press, 2020. | Series: NIU series in Slavic, East European, and Eurasian studies | Includes bibliographical references and index.
Identifiers: LCCN 2019042085 (print) | LCCN 2019042086 (ebook) | ISBN 9781501749704 (hardcover) | ISBN 9781501750823 (paperback) | ISBN 9781501749728 (ebook) | ISBN 9781501749711 (pdf)
Subjects: LCSH: Authorship. | Literary forgeries and mystifications.
Classification: LCC PN145 .O78 2020 (print) | LCC PN145 (ebook) | DDC 098/.3—dc23
LC record available at https://lccn.loc.gov/2019042085
LC ebook record available at https://lccn.loc.gov/2019042086

To the memory of Hannah Rose
(2008–2018)
"The light of our life"

Contents

Acknowledgments

The book manuscript that I originally submitted to Northern Illinois University Press for consideration was a comparison of the William Shakespeare and Andrei Kurbskii authorship controversies. I half expected it to be turned down because university presses in general have tended to steer clear of any whiff of the Shakespeare controversy. To my surprise, acquisitions editor Amy Farranto and series editor Christine Worobec did not reject the manuscript out of hand but wondered about the potential market. With their concern in mind, I proposed increasing the number of controversies discussed while abridging the Shakespeare and Kurbskii sections to chapter length. I owe a huge debt of gratitude to both of them for agreeing to my unusual idea for this book in the first place.

I also have to single out Amy for special praise for allowing and obtaining leeway in time while I worked out some of the methodological issues. She understood that I had no direct model as such on which to base this book and that I wanted to make sure that I did it the right way. Thank you, Amy, for your confidence in me.

I am also indebted to the following people for their sound advice.

Peter Stearns (George Mason University) and Kevin Gilvary (Brunel University, London) read the entire typescript at a late stage in its development and provided incisive and much needed constructive criticism.

Gary Goldstein (editor, *The Oxfordian*) read the chapter on Shakespeare and "nagged" me to get it published. I needed the nagging.

Jan Ziolkowski (Harvard University) read and commented on the chapter on Abelard and Heloise.

Paul van Els (Leiden University) allowed me to consult with him throughout, and he read, commented on, and corrected a draft of the chapter about Confucius and the *Analects*.

Brian Boeck (DePaul University) allowed me to consult with him, and he read, commented on, and corrected a draft of the chapter about Mikhail Sholokhov and *The Quiet Don*.

Timothy May (University of Northern Georgia) and Gene R. Garthwaite (Dartmouth College) read and commented on the chapter on Rashid al-Din.

Gail Lenhoff (UCLA) allowed me to make a presentation about the book at her UCLA winter workshop in 2018. I received valuable feedback from the participants in the workshop, especially from Robert Roman-chuk (Florida State University).

Russell E. Martin (Westminster College) and I discussed the book at an early stage, and he provided encouragement to pursue the project.

Hugh Olmsted (Harvard University) crucially asked whether I would be including a chapter on Ossian, which led directly to its inclusion in the final version.

None of these fine scholars should be held accountable for any mistakes that remain or that I inadvertently put it after they read their respective chapter drafts.

Katarina Wronka provided valuable assistance with the index.

An especial thanks goes to Mary Ribesky for skillfully shepherding this project into print.

Finally, there are not enough words for me to express my gratitude to Wren Collé, my long-suffering wife, for being supportive during the entire project and for allowing me to spend many, many hours at the computer and doing research for this book. I promise that I will make it up to you.

Tables

WHO WROTE THAT?

Introduction

Why This Book? Why These Controversies?

I am going to ask you, the reader, if you have not already done so, to look at the table of contents of this book and take note of your initial reaction to the choice of authorship controversies there. Perhaps you will have no reaction to some of the choices. I expect that many readers of this book will not have heard of Rashid al-Din (chapter 5) or Andrei Kurbskii (chapter 7), so they would probably have no opinion about whether these should be included (unless they think that only controversies about people they have heard of should be included). Other controversies listed there may interest you because you have heard of the people involved and might find a discussion of a controversy about their authorship to be worthwhile reading. I expect that most readers will have heard of Confucius (chapter 2) as well as Abelard and Heloise (chapter 4) although they might not be aware there is an authorship controversy involving them.

Then there could be one or more controversies listed that you do not think should be there. Your initial reaction might be that there is no controversy or that only cranks contest that person's authorship. Some people of faith could find the question of Moses's authorship of the Pentateuch (chapter 1) or the question of who wrote the Shakespearean canon (chapter 6) to be out of bounds of legitimate questioning. To be sure, I have similar feelings concerning the question of whether Morton Smith forged a letter by Clement of Alexandria, including passages that the letter writer says are from a Secret Gospel of Mark (chapter 3). My visceral feeling is only cranks have contended that Smith is a forger, although my rational self struggles to understand there are individuals who are not cranks who have legitimate doubts about the authenticity of the letter. Nonetheless, I include it here. Why?

The answer has to do with the aims of this book. One of those aims is to draw attention to the arguments and methods in various fields of historical study that have been used to deal with issues of authorship attribution. In the 1970s, I became interested in the authorship question pertaining to Tsar Ivan IV (1533–1584) and his erstwhile servitor Prince Andrei Kurbskii (d. 1583). The two of them supposedly had a correspondence with each other, but their authorship of those letters, as well as other works attributed to them, was challenged in 1971 by a specialist on early modern Russian history. The mainstream scholarship in the field of Russian studies has generally rejected that challenge and continues to hold the traditional attribution to be correct. In the process of the back and forth between the contending sides, however, one has seen a great deal of new research being done, new discoveries made, and new interpretations advanced, all instigated to a greater or lesser extent by that one historian's detailed expression of skepticism.

In the 1990s, I found myself becoming more and more interested in the challenge to the attribution of the Shakespearean canon to Kurbskii and Ivan's contemporary William Shakespere (1564–1616). Likewise, this challenge has been rejected by mainstream English literature scholarship. Yet, the accusations back and forth also motivated new research, discoveries, and interpretations, despite the efforts of those in the mainstream scholarship to deny there was any controversy.

But then I also noticed two other things. First, there were similarities in the types of arguments used by the defenders of the traditional attributions to Ivan IV, Andrei Kurbskii, and William Shakespere, on one hand, and the arguments used by those who challenged the traditional attributions to those individuals, on the other. Second, no one involved in either the Shakespeare authorship controversy or the Ivan IV–Kurbskii authorship controversy seemed to be aware they were arguing in parallel, often using the same techniques to advance their respective positions. As I looked into other authorship controversies, I found, with only a few exceptions, what appears to be silo scholarship.[1]

---

1. I take my cue here from the American historian of British history J. H. (Jack) Hexter (1910–1996), who in 1963 published an essay in which he castigated historians for the tendency to focus only on social history or political history and so forth to the detriment of finding common ground with those who are in a different "tunnel." J. H. Hexter, *Reappraisals in History: New Views on History and*

By that I mean there is virtually no citation of similar work being done on topics of authorship attribution in other historical periods or in other areas of the world. The scholars who discuss these issues seem intent, for the most part, on trying to reinvent the wheel (or methods of ascertaining authorship) within their own field of expertise. Yet, one cannot fault them for this, for there is no field of study or even textbook on authorship attribution in general and nothing for them to refer to.

So I thought it might be worthwhile to write a book about a limited number of such controversies (nine in this case) that would provide an introduction to anyone interested in reading more about other authorship controversies or in trying to understand what these controversies are all about. In this respect, I must acknowledge the influence of my mentor, Sergei Vasil'evich Utechin (1921–2004). One day in University Park, Pennsylvania, in the early 1970s, he held a session of his seminar outdoors. It was a beautiful late spring day. One of the students raised the question of a controversy that had been going on for some decades in Russian and Ukrainian studies concerning the authenticity of a Rus' epic poem called *The Tale of Igor's Campaign* (*Slovo o polku Igoreve*). Utechin proceeded to outline in some detail the arguments and evidence pro and con. He made no attempt to take sides or steer us toward a particular conclusion. He probably figured that we could do that on our own. Obviously his off-the-cuff remarks some forty-five years ago on a fine spring day made an impression on me. So much so that when it came time to write the chapters of this book, I took them as my model. Instead of trying to convince the reader of the rightness of one side or the other, I took my task to present the parameters of each controversy, as well as the arguments and evidence used by the contending sides. My analyses of these contestations is intended to provide the reader with an introduction to each controversy, not to declare a definitive answer or to steer the reader to accept my own view in each case. Nonetheless, I do point out fallacious arguments and express criticism of faulty use of evidence as well as the lack of evidence for specific assertions. I express my own conclusions but try to do so in such a way that explains what led me to them. That way, the reader is better able to understand my thought processes and is then better able to evaluate my conclusions.

Society in Early Modern Europe (New York: Harper & Row, 1963), 194–196. While tunnel history involves the ignoring within a field of study of other scholarship in that field, silo scholarship, as I am using the term, is the tendency of those within a field of study to ignore neighboring fields of study.

Confirmation Bias

I am asking the reader to approach these chapters with an open mind. Be aware of the very human visceral inclination to reject any arguments or evidence that goes against our initial view and concomitantly to consider only that evidence, argument, and interpretation that support it. This inclination is called "confirmation bias." Refusal to look at the arguments and evidence that go against our initial understanding bespeaks a phenomenon that has been called "premature cognitive closure."[2] When we think that we already know the answer, we tend to look for and find only that which supports it. We look no further. In that way we do not have to deal with evidence, argument, or interpretation that may be stronger or more compelling than what we already have and that might require us to modify or abandon them. By closing our minds to anything that differs from our presently existing views, we never have to admit that we are wrong. We can be assured that we are right, have always been right, and will forever continue to be right. But that is not how scientific study advances. And it is a surefire method to end up being wrong.

I tell my graduate students before they begin their research papers that whatever they think the case to be about their particular topic, they are wrong. When we do research, we learn things that we did not know before, some of it countering what we thought we knew when we began the research. If we engage in premature cognitive closure, then it is clear we are interested only in building a bulwark to defend our existing views, not in gaining a better understanding of the matter. If we are interested in increasing our understanding, then we challenge our own views. We set them up as hypotheses to be tested. This practice corresponds to the dictum of the philosopher of science Karl Popper that theories cannot be proved, they can only be disproved. We hold a theory until it has been disproved. Then we should abandon it rather than try to continue supporting it with increasingly faulty and improbable arguments. Thus I include the Secret Gospel controversy as a way of revisiting an issue so as not to engage in premature cognitive closure about it. As long as there are reputable scholars who doubt the authenticity of the letter Smith claimed to have found at Mar Saba monastery, then I am obligated to give their arguments and evidence due respect and good-faith reconsideration (although I might still come to the same conclusion as I did before).

---

2. See, for example, Robert Jervis, *Perception and Misperception in International Politics*, new ed. (Princeton, NJ: Princeton University Press, 2017 [1st ed., 1976]), xxxv, 187–191.

Choice of Cases

Explaining how I arrived at choosing each controversy to include may be help-ful to the reader. I wanted to avoid simple forgeries, where someone tries to deceive by passing off their own work as someone else's, and cases of plagia-rism, when someone passes off someone else's work as their own. Instead, I wanted to concentrate on issues of attribution and misattribution. Some of the cases I have chosen do involve accusations of forgery (chapters 3, 5, and 8) and plagiarism (chapters 8 and 9), but my main focus of the discussion in each case (with the exception of chapter 8) is devoted to the question of who the author was. In this regard, I was also guided by Utechin when he wrote that we can divide sources into three categories: "(1) genuine, that is, words or ac-tions which are what they appear to be; (2) genuinely deceptive, that is, those which are not what they appear to be but were meant to be taken for what they appear to be; and (3) apparently deceptive, that is, those that are not what they appear to be and were not intended to be taken as such."[3] In the first category are sources that were not intended to deceive by their authors and have not re-sulted in anyone's being deceived. In the second category are those sources that were intended to deceive and succeeded in doing so. In the third category are those sources where the author did not intend to deceive, but the work none-theless unintentionally has misled people.

I included the question of whether Moses wrote the Pentateuch because that controversy is the first of the "modern" controversies—that is, one that used historical methodology as it was developed in the eighteenth and nine-teenth centuries, mainly by German scholars. Yet, in doing the research for the chapter, I found that the seventeenth-century English political philosopher Thomas Hobbes (1588–1679) had been the first to provide a coherent argu-ment against the Mosaic authorship and in doing so thereby anticipated some of the same arguments of modern biblical scholarship.

I chose Confucius and the *Analects* because the controversy deals with the question of how much text an author needs to have written to be considered the author of the entire text. I became aware of the controversy in preparing lectures on ancient China for my world history courses. I assigned the *Ana-lects* to students to read and began to do more research on it. That is when I came across the Brookses' book *The Original Analects*, which took a rather extreme view of limited Confucian authorship.[4] In doing the research for this

---

3. S. V. Utechin, *Russian Political Thought: A Concise History* (New York: Praeger, 1963) x.

4. E. Bruce Brooks and A. Taeko Brooks, *The Original Analects: Sayings of Confucius and His Succes-sors* (New York: Columbia University Press, 1998).

chapter, I found that the "successive layers" view of how the *Analects* was created has a long history in Chinese scholarship.

I chose the question of whether Morton Smith forged the letter of Clement of Alexandria because just as I ask the reader to temporarily suspend any preexisting notions about all the controversies discussed herein, whether or not they are well informed about them, I wanted to include a controversy concerning which I have a similar preexisting notion to at least temporarily suspend. To a greater or lesser extent, my inclusion of the Kurbskii controversy fits that bill as well. In any case, it is a good thing from time to time to challenge one's already existing conceptions. Either those conceptions are wrong, in which case one is better off dropping them, or they could be right and thereby strengthened through the challenge by one's learning something that one did not know before.

I chose the Abelard and Heloise controversy because I had written on Abelard for another book and was interested in finding out more concerning this controversy that I had not had time to investigate earlier. What I found was an intensely argued but for the most part courteously and professionally waged academic debate. The methodological issues discussed connected integrally with a number of other authorship controversies in the book. I chose Rashid al-Din because I had used his *Compendium of Chronicles (Jami al-Tawarik)* when I was writing about the Mongol influence on Russia. Only later did I find that questions had been raised about how much of it Rashid al-Din had actually written. And that brought me to the question of the collection of letters attributed to him but contested.

I became interested in the Shakespeare authorship question while preparing a lecture on Tudor and Stuart England for my world history course. I had used Michael H. Hart's *The 100: A Ranking of the Most Influential Persons in History* (first edition, 1978) while preparing a similar lecture for my history courses. Although Hart's book is written for a popular audience, and the mini-biographies he wrote of each of the one hundred individuals touches on only the most salient points of their life, I was impressed by Hart's thoughtfulness and analytical skill in his explanations of how he ranked them. It was his declaration that he had changed his mind about who the author of the Shakespeare canon was. In the preface to the second edition, he admitted to having made an error when he "followed the crowd" and did not "carefully check the facts" when he attributed the canon to "the Stratford man." When he did carefully check the facts, he found that "the weight of the evidence is heavily against the Stratford man, and in favor of [Edward] de Vere, the 17th Earl of Oxford."[5] At that point, I real-

---

5. Michael H. Hart, *The 100: A Ranking of the Most Influential Persons in History* (New York: Citadel, 1992), xxiii–xxiv.

ized that I had to stop following the crowd on this matter and look at the evidence myself.

My interest in authorship questions involving Andrei Kurbskii dates to my reading of Edward L. Keenan's *The Kurbskii-Groznyi Apocrypha* shortly after it came out in 1971. What I found was a carefully researched, well-argued treatise questioning almost every attribution to either Andrei Kurbskii or Tsar Ivan IV.[6] The Shakespeare and Kurbskii chapters herein reflect the beginnings of my own investigation of authorship controversies.

Initially I did not include the controversy over the Ossian cycle of the late eighteenth and early nineteenth centuries. The Scottish poet James Macpherson claimed he had found ancient manuscript fragments in Gaelic and had translated them into English. Although it was the major authorship controversy of the time and had a huge impact on other national literatures, it seemed to have been resolved in the scholarship. Then I found there have been recent attempts to reevaluate how much Macpherson made up and how much he may have drawn on Scottish Gaelic traditions.

Finally, I included the controversy over whether Mikhail Sholokhov wrote the novel *The Quiet Don* because, as a result of my study of Russian history and culture, I was familiar with the controversy from the political side and was aware of the computer stylistic analysis of the question, but I wanted to delve deeper into it. From the very beginning of the appearance of the novel in serial form in 1928, accusations of plagiarism were rife. But Sholokhov had his supporters both within and outside the Soviet Union. Although he won the Nobel Prize in Literature in 1965, dispute over how much of the novel is actually his still rages.

I could have included for consideration a large number of other authorship controversies, from the aforementioned *Tale of Igor's Campaign* to the six plays attributed to Publius Terentius Afer (c. 195 / 185—c. 159 BC), better known as Terence, or the identity of B. Traven (a pseudonym), author of the novel *The Treasure of the Sierra Madre* and other novels and short stories. I chose not to do so because I wanted a relatively short book that would be useful in the classroom as well. This book makes no claim of trying to be comprehensive of authorship controversies in general; there are plenty more out there. Nor does it make any claim of comprehensiveness within each controversy; there is plenty more to be said about each one. It is intended instead to be merely introductory to the issues involved and to lay the groundwork for eventually having a field of authorship studies.

---

6. Edward L. Keenan, *The Kurbskii Groznyi Apocrypha: The Seventeenth-Century Genesis of the "Correspondence" Attributed to Prince A. M. Kurbskii and Tsar Ivan IV*, with an appendix by Daniel C. Waugh (Cambridge, MA: Harvard University Press, 1971).

In each chapter I provide a brief introduction situating the persons and works being discussed in world history—essentially a *mise-en-scène*. Then follows a "Context of the Controversy" section in which I focus more on the background of that particular authorship controversy. Invariably I need to get into some specifics and the arguments and evidence used by the contending sides. That section I call "Into the Thicket," appropriately enough. It is the most detailed section of each chapter. I am well aware that not everyone finds the give and take of the debates as interesting as I do. Yet it is precisely in those arguments and in that presentation of evidence where the scientific study of each controversy lies. Besides, if we are ever going to have a field of authorship studies that crosses fields of study, then knowing what arguments have been made and the types of evidence that have been used will be the foundation of that field. As the medievalist John Benton wrote in regard to the Abelard and Heloise authorship controversy: "If we are ever to settle the major issue of the authorship of these letters, it will not be through discussions of what might be plausible behavior for people of either the twelfth century or today, but on the basis of the most technical and indeed unemotional issues, questions of style, dating, sources and so on."[7] In other words, the science is in the details. Nonetheless, in presenting those details, I have tried to keep my focus sharply on the most significant aspects of the wrangles.

The final section of each chapter is "The Takeaway," in which I highlight the facets of that particular controversy that involve discussion of methodological issues in general, some of which might be applicable to other authorship questions. Throughout the nine chapters, I look at these controversies as perhaps helping to lay the basis for establishing the principles of authorship attribution across time periods and areas of the world. The reader will most likely notice that the chapters are of unequal length, some being twice as long as others. I had thought about trying to make the chapters of roughly equal length, which works fine for a book such as Raymond Aron's *Unsolved Mysteries of History* (2000), which I use in my course on historical controversies. But trying to impose an arbitrary page length or word count on these attribution controversies seemed to defeat my purpose of laying the foundation for establishing the principles of authorship attribution. Some of the controversies required more exposition than others. I did, believe it or not, exercise restraint as a result of considering readers' patience before delving too deeply into the labyrinth of each controversy.

---

7. John F. Benton, "The Correspondence of Abelard and Heloise," in *Fälschungen im Mittelalter. Internationaler Kongress der Monumenta Germaniae Historica, München, 16.–19. September 1986*, vol. 5: *Fingierte Briefe, Frömmigkeit und Fälschung, Realien fälschungen*, Monumentat Germaniae Historica Schriften, vol. 33, part 5 (Hanover: Hahnsche Buchhandlung, 1988), 97.

What Are the Principles of Attributing a Text to a Particular Author?

Little has been written on the principles of attribution in general terms. The literary scholar Dmitrii S. Likhachev wrote that attribution of texts "in Old Rus' literature [*v drevnerusskoi literature*] is much more complicated than in literature of modern times."[8] After discussing the problems of delimiting Rus' texts and of separating author from redactor, Likhachev provided a number of examples of attributions. He was critical of V. P. Zubov's attempt to distinguish between the contributions of Epifanii Premudryi (d. ca. 1420) and Pakhomii the Serb (d. 1484) to *The Life of Sergii of Radonezh*.[9] He acknowledged: "The history of old Russian literature knows very many examples of insufficient bases of attribution."[10] He warned against the practice of attributing any work from a particular period to the most prominent writer of that period. His main cautionary example is N. V. Vodovozov's attribution of *The Tale concerning Alexander Nevskii* (*Povest' Aleksandra Nevskogo*) and the *Oration about the Ruin of the Rus' Land*, as well as the *Prayer* (*Molenie*) *of Daniil Zatochnik* to Daniil Zatochnik (twelve or thirteenth century). Likhachev was particularly critical of Vodovozov's basis for attributing the *Tale concerning Alexander Nevskii* to Daniil Zatochnik because Vodovozov's sole argument is that Zatochnik could not have let the life of such a great hero as Alexander not be written about.[11]

Likhachev also has much to say concerning the relationship of attribution of modern texts with those of Rus' texts. Modern texts often have documentation in the form of draft copies in the author's handwriting and possession, references by the author and others to the text as it is being written, and records of contracts with publishers, payment of royalties, and so forth. With medieval and early modern texts, we rarely have such information. Medieval writers were not necessarily supposed to identify themselves, and they often borrowed verbatim from other writers without compunction. Rarely do medievalists have manuscript drafts written in the author's hand.

As pertinent as Likhachev's comments are, they provide very little in regard to general principles of attribution. When legitimate questions about authorship are raised, what are the principles that we use to decide the issue?

---

8. D. S. Likhachev, *Tekstologiia. Na materiale russkoi literatury X–XVII vv.*, 1st ed. (Moscow and Leningrad: Akademiia nauk SSSR, 1962), 287; 2nd ed. (Leningrad: Nauka, 1983), 304–344; 3rd ed. (St. Petersburg: Aleteiia, 2001), 299–337.

9. Likhachev, *Tekstologiia*, 288 (1st ed.), 305 (2nd ed.), 300 (3rd ed.).

10. Likhachev, *Tekstologiia*, 289 (1st ed.), 306 (2nd ed.), 301 (3rd ed.).

11. Likhachev, *Tekstologiia*, 291–292 (1st ed.), 308 (2nd ed.), 302 (3rd ed.).

In my preliminary research on each of these authorship controversies (i.e., before I ever thought of writing this book), I came across arguments pro and con that were author specific. That is, arguments were being used by one or more scholars that seemed to me could not be used to establish general principles of authorship—for example, the claim by Stratfordians that those who challenge the Stratford man's authorship of the Shakespearian canon are elitist snobs because they do not think a commoner could write the plays. This is an ad hominem attack that is not only inappropriate for Shakespearian studies but even more so as a general principle of authorship studies.

On the other hand, I also came across arguments that seemed to have broader validity than just to the particular controversy being discussed. For example, were those scholars who claimed that Abelard wrote the letters attributed to Heloise engaging in gender bias because they thought, either consciously or subconsciously, that a woman could not write in such a well-reasoned way? I decided to test those arguments to see if indeed they had broader applicability by studying these nine authorship controversies. I asked which of the arguments used in a particular controversy could be applied to the others and could these then be the basis for establishing a field of authorship attribution.

The human proclivity to seek certainty has led, whenever a particular attribution is challenged, to sides being taken, positions staked out, and conclusions drawn. Scholars writing books and articles about related topics—not specifically about the text or texts in question—will either steer clear of mentioning there is any controversy or resort to some sort of assertion that "most scholars believe" a certain way. To be sure, the authors of those books and articles have not polled all scholars. Even if they meant to include only the limited number of scholars who have done more or less in-depth research on the disputed attribution, scholarship is not a majority rule type of endeavor. The truth is that even those scholars who specialize in an area of study do not usually get into the nitty-gritty of disputes. In some cases, those who do get into that nitty-gritty are only a very small number of researchers in the field. Other times, it can be a fairly large number both in the field and outside of it. Then there are those who have studied an issue but not published on it, in which case it is difficult to say what they think, unless one has asked them directly or heard them speak on the matter.

What I am proposing to do here is to suspend, at least temporarily, our proclivity to reach a cognitive conclusion, premature or otherwise, and instead to examine the types of evidence and argumentation anew with the idea of evaluating the quality of the evidence and of each argument on its own terms. An underlying assumption here is that good arguments, sound use of evidence, and well-formulated interpretations can be made even when the scholarly consensus is opposed to what those uses of evidence, arguments, and interpretations are for.

Part of that evaluation involves comparing each attribution controversy with other attribution controversies. We can ask ourselves whether this particular type of evidence or this particular type of argument can be used for other controversies. For example, statistical analysis of style (sentence length, turns of phrase, use of filler words, and so forth) has been developed in regard to one authorship question and then has been applied to another. That is an easy one. But what about the argument that to deny Heloise wrote the letters attributed to her is to continue to deny women's voice in the Middle Ages? Does it mean that whenever a work is attributed to a woman, it has to be accepted because to do otherwise is to deny women their voice? I think not, but those who support the view that Heloise wrote the letters attributed to her come close to making that argument in favor of accepting that attribution. If so, then can it be made only about Heloise and not about any other women writers? Or is it purely circumstantial? That is, if I think Heloise wrote the letters attributed to her, then can I invoke the "you're denying women's voice" argument against those who doubt she did, while not invoking it against myself when I doubt a particular attribution that involves another woman?

What constitutes a legitimate controversy? John Marenbon, in addressing the "ideologies that underlie the different positions" taken by scholars, asserted that only "one ideological distinction counts: between those scholars who respect evidence and the burdens of argument based on it and those who do not."[12] In a footnote, he does address the possible "objection that this distinction is not ideological at all, but methodological." He overruled that objection on the basis that "if by ideology one means a set of ideas (in the broadest sense . . .) . . . , then the distinction I make is, clearly, ideological as well as methodological."[13] It seems to me that *ideology* is too grand a term for the mishmash of ideas, biases, misconceptions, preconceptions, and half-baked understandings that we all carry around with us. One does not necessarily have to agree with Sunstein and Vermeule's assertion that "In some domains, people suffer from a 'crippled epistemology,' in the sense that they know very few things, and what they know is wrong"[14] to realize that our own personal

---

12. John Marenbon, "Authenticity Revisited," in *Listening to Heloise: The Voice of a Twelfth-Century Woman*, ed. Bonnie Wheeler (New York: St. Martin's, 2000), 21.

13. Marenbon, "Authenticity Revisited," 31, n. 18.

14. Cass R. Sunstein and Adrian Vermeule, "Conspiracy Theories," Harvard University Law School Public Law and Legal Theory Research Paper Series (2008), 10.

epistemologies are not all that perfect. So I prefer to think of Marenbon's distinction "between those scholars who respect evidence and the burdens of argument based on it and those who do not" as mostly a methodological one. As long as there is at least one scholar in Marenbon's first category who continues to contest the consensus view and who also subscribes to the principle of respecting the evidence and arguments based on it, then the controversy is legitimate. If those who contest the consensus view do not "respect evidence and the burdens of argument based on it" (i.e., Marenbon's second category), then there is not a legitimate controversy. The problem, of course, is to determine whether a scholar "respect[s] evidence and the burdens of argument based on it." One would hope that all scholars do, but as I will suggest in my discussion of some of the following controversies in this book, there may be scholars who respect evidence and argument in general and who have manifested that respect in regard to other issues in their field, but in regard to the particular issue in question, such as who wrote a particular text, one can encounter a blind spot in these scholars' general respect for evidence and argument. In other words, I might change Marenbon's distinction to be between "assertions that are based on all the relevant evidence and sound analysis of that evidence and assertions that are not." It is possible for someone who does not respect evidence and nonfallacious argument, because of a particular mindset that person might have, to make a statement that in fact conforms to scholarly standards. It happens rarely, but it does happen. It is also possible for someone who has respect for evidence and argument to, because of meta-scholarly considerations, make unacceptable statements. So rather than reject or accept everything a person says or writes, based on their general respect for evidence and argument, I would prefer to judge each individual assertion on its own merits regardless of who the person is making that assertion, remembering that even a stopped clock is right twice a day.

The question of authorship always matters. I teach history courses in which I require students to submit written assignments. Sometimes a student will hand in written work that he or she did not write. If that student were to say, "Oh, it doesn't matter who wrote it because the ideas are so profound and transcendent that they are meant for the ages," I would not accept that as a legitimate defense. The student would fail the course and be rusticated from the university for a year or more. Why should I accept the assertion that it does not matter who wrote any other text? Is there some elite group of people for whom it does not matter whether they are credited with writing something they did not while students who do the same get punished? I don't think so, or, at least, it should not be.

Besides, one gains a greater appreciation of a text knowing who the author or likely author is. Knowing about the life of Mikhail Bulgakov brings an added dimension to reading *The Master and Margarita*. And knowing that Tolstoy, not Dostoevsky, wrote *War and Peace* increases one's understanding of the ideas contained therein. Authorship is important, even for texts hundreds or thousands of years old. Besides, there are sound reasons why neither Tolstoy nor Dostoevsky could have authored *The Master and Margarita* and why neither Dostoevsky nor Bulgakov could have authored *War and Peace*. To assert otherwise and say that it does not matter who wrote those novels does not even make good nonsense.

Well, now that I have got that off my chest, I just would like to say that I hope you enjoy this book despite any flaws you might find in it and that you learn from reading it as I did in researching it.

CHAPTER 1

Did Moses Write the Pentateuch?

The Pentateuch is the first five books of the Hebrew Bible as well as of the Christian Old Testament. The designation "Pentateuch" derives from Greek *penta* (five) plus *teûchos* (vessel, in the sense of a case for scrolls). These five books are Genesis, Exodus, Leviticus, Numbers, and Deuteronomy. They are also collectively called the Torah. Until the late nineteenth century, the consensus view of biblical scholars was that Moses wrote these first five books of the Bible. The Church father Jerome (AD 340–427), however, suggested that Ezra the Priest wrote the Pentateuch in the fifth century BC based on notes made by Moses. Since the sixth century AD, doubts have been expressed about whether Moses was the author of all the Pentateuch. But it was only in the mid-seventeenth century that the first relatively systematic discussion of the issue appeared. By the late nineteenth century, the scholarly consensus began to turn against Moses being the author of any part of it. Yet in the Bible are references to the Pentateuch's being "the book [*sephar*] of Moses" (Ezra 6:18 and Neh. 13:1) and to Moses's knowing how to write (Exod. 17:14, 24:4, 34:27–28; Num. 33:2). It would then seem to require an explanation for the rejection of Mosaic authorship that is now the standard view in the scholarship.

Context of the Controversy

The first book, Genesis, besides describing the creation of the world, also tells the story of how a Hebrew slave, Joseph, rises to become the vizier (prime minister) of Egypt. His brothers, who had sold him into slavery in Canaan, bring their families to join him in Egypt. The second book, Exodus, picks up the story many years later when the Hebrews have become numerous ("the descendants of Israel were fruitful and increased greatly" [Ex. 1:7]). The new pharaoh perceived their numbers as a threat and enslaved them, but their numbers kept growing. So he ordered the killing of every newly born Hebrew male. A daughter of Levi gave birth to a male child and hid it for three months. When she could no longer hide it, she set it in a basket among some reeds on the shore of the Nile River. The daughter of Pharaoh found the baby and raised it as her own son. She named him Moses "because I drew him out [Hebrew: *mashah*] of the water" (Ex. 2:10).

When Moses had become an adult "he saw an Egyptian beating a Hebrew, one of his people" (Ex. 2:11), so he killed the Egyptian. As a result, he had to flee Egypt and spent forty years in exile in Midian,[1] where he married Zipporah. God, hearing the complaints of the people of Israel in Egypt, appeared to Moses in a burning bush and tells him to go back to Egypt and free his people. After a number of tribulations, Moses led the Hebrews out of Egypt. According to the fourth book, Numbers, there were 603,550 adult males (Num. 1:45). If we count on average 3.5 wives and children for each male, we arrive at a figure in excess of 2 million. At the time, according to demographic estimates, Egypt had a total population of no more than 3 million people. Such a mass out-migration, if both estimates are accurate, would have depleted the Egyptian population. The book of Exodus says that the Moses-led Hebrews wandered forty years in the desert of Sinai and then they reached the land of Canaan, the promised land of milk and honey, where they settled down. Moses, however, dies en route.

Into the Thicket

One discrepancy that struck scholars early on was the question of what alphabet Moses would have used to write down the text. The earliest evidence of Hebrew lettering dates to the tenth century BC as it derived from Phoenician

---

1. Midian is thought to have been on the Arabian peninsula across the Red Sea from Egypt and includes part of present-day southern Israel.

script, which the Hebrews in Egypt would have come into contact with only after the return from slavery in Egypt to the land of Canaan. Since the book of Exodus says that Moses did not enter the promised land, it seems unlikely he would have written the text in Hebrew. It is unlikely that Moses learned to write Hebrew when he was in exile in Midian for forty years because that was again before the Hebrew alphabet was invented, as far as we know. Of course, one could also suggest that he wrote in Egyptian demotic, which he presumably knew and which would have been translated later into Hebrew. Again, we have no evidence either physical or linguistic for that hypothesis, and thus far no one has found any evidence in the text of Egyptian linguistic influence.

Finally, as Biblical scholar John H. Hayes (1934–2013) described it, the absence of "external frames of reference makes it impossible to connect any of the events depicted about Moses with the history of other cultures."[2] Not even the pharaoh of the Exodus from Egypt is given a name. Nor is Moses mentioned in any contemporary source outside the Bible.

Moses: Historical Person or Mythical Figure?

Another problem is that some scholars began to question whether Moses was a historical person or a mythical figure of Hebrew folklore instead. And if he was a historical person, what can we say about him? The historian Ernest Renan (1823–1892) asserted that although Moses "very probably existed," he "is completely buried by the legends which have grown up over him."[3] It was the Biblical scholar Julius Wellhausen (1844–1918) who first argued that the Moses of the Bible is a later fiction of the priests who wrote the Bible.[4] Hayes mentions that "many of the stories [associated with Moses] are legendary in character and are built on folktale motifs found in various cultures."[5] Even the name "Moses" has raised questions. It is doubtful that the daughter of Pharaoh would have given a foundling a name derived from Hebrew, because in the context of a Hebrew-male-killing pharaoh, giving the infant a Hebrew name would have signaled its origins. The biblical scholar Richard Elliott Friedman (b. 1946) compares the name Moses to the English name Drew (as in "I

2. John H. Hayes, "Moses," in *The Oxford Companion to the Bible*, ed. Bruce M. Metzger and Michael D. Coogan (Oxford: Oxford University Press, 1993), 530.

3. Ernest Renan, *History of the People of Israel*, 5 vols., vol. 1, *Till the Time of King David* (London: Chapman and Hall, 1888), 135.

4. Julius Wellhausen, *Prolegomena to the History of Ancient Israel*, trans. J. Sutherland Black and Allan Menzies (Edinburgh: Adam and Charles Black, 1885), 135.

5. Hayes, "Moses," 530.

drew him out").[6] If, say, the dictator of Tyrranistan ordered all male English infants killed in his country, someone in the dictator's family naming a foundling Drew would not have been such a wise thing to do.

The name Moses, however, does mean "child" in ancient Egyptian and can be found, for example, in the names of pharaohs—Ra-m(o)ses, where *Ra* represents his patron god. Friedman pointed out that seven other of the Israelites in Egypt mentioned in the Pentateuch have Egyptian names, all from the house of Levi,[7] so it is not out of the ordinary for Hebrews in Egypt mentioned in the Pentateuch to have Egyptian names. If Moses was such an Egyptian name, then the story provided in Exodus of its having a Hebrew origin could have been to give the person who led the Hebrews out of Egypt more bona fide Hebrew credentials.

To be sure, the existence of Moses as a historical person has its defenders. The popular historian Paul Johnson, for example, mounted an energetic defense:

He [Moses] illustrates the fact, which great historians have always recognized, that mankind does not invariably progress by imperceptible steps but sometimes takes a giant leap, often under the dynamic propulsion of a solitary, outsize personality. That is why the contention of Wellhausen and his school that Moses was a later fiction and the Mosaic code a fabrication of the post-Exilic priests in the second half of the first millennium BC—a view still held by some historians today—is scepticism carried to the point of fanaticism, a vandalizing of the human record. Moses was beyond the power of the human mind to invent, and his power leaps out from the page of the Bible narrative, as it once imposed itself on a difficult and divided people, often little better than a frightened mob.[8]

Moses may have been a real person in the historical past, but Johnson's argument is not a good one in favor of it. First, Wellhausen's skepticism about the reliability of the Bible as a historical source for the events being described has been a legitimate way of studying the Bible since the nineteenth century. Both Johnson's hyperbole and his attempt to denigrate approaches other than his own smacks more of fanaticism than Wellhausen's methodical discussion does. Second, Johnson uses the argument that the human mind is incapable of inventing someone of the power of the Moses character in the Bible. Yet it would

---

6. Richard Elliott Friedman, *The Exodus: How It Happened and Why It Matters* (New York: HarperOne, 2017), 34.

7. Friedman, *The Exodus*, 32.

8. Paul Johnson, *A History of the Jews* (New York: Harper & Row, 1987), 27.

appear that the Moses of the Bible is a composite character who is presented sometimes favorably and sometimes unfavorably in the text. To argue that a character is beyond the power of the human mind to create is not a good criterion for deciding the historicity of an individual. How many fictional characters are equally if not more powerful than the evidence indicates for those who are presented as being real, historical people? Does not Raskolnikov in *Crime and Punishment* or even Sherlock Holmes come across as more powerful personalities, more real than say Narmer or even Hammurabi about whom claims have been made that they changed history? Is the Moses of the Bible more powerful as a character than Raskolnikov or Sherlock Holmes? The only difference would seem to be that characters in novels are presented as fictional whereas Moses is presented as having existed in the real, historical past. But would a historian one thousand years from now understand that Sherlock Holmes was meant to be understood as a fictional character? Finally, Johnson seemed to be practicing a brand of exemplar historical writing here. He seems to be saying historians know that larger-than-life personalities change the course of history, and Moses was one of those. Therefore, he must have existed because history was changed. Again, Johnson's argument can be faulted on the basis that he assumes Moses's existence as part of his argument. In other words, his argument is circular. Besides, there are any number of comic book superheroes whose exploits have changed the course of history in fiction, but Johnson would not argue that they have to exist thereby.

For our purposes, we can assign Moses a place in the virtual past because it is easier to explain the evidence that way. If we posit that Moses was a completely mythical character, then we would have to explain why the writers of the Bible created him. If the stories are fictional, then it would seem a better way to get people to believe them would be by wrapping them around a real person, such as George Washington and the cherry tree or the Hitler diaries. From the style of it, we can conclude that the writers of the Bible were hoping people would believe their stories, no matter how fantastic the events described in them may be. Therefore, it is probable that Moses was a real, historical individual. Whether he did all the things attributed to him is altogether another matter. Even the archaeologist William G. Dever (b. 1933), who is among those who consider Moses to be "a mythical figure,"[9] has suggested that "a Moses-like figure may have existed somewhere in the southern Transjordan in the mid-late thirteenth century B.C."[10] To be sure, the distinction

---

9. "The overwhelming scholarly consensus today is that Moses is a mythical figure." William G. Dever, "What Remains of the House That Albright Built?" *Biblical Archaeologist* 56, no. 1 (March 1993): 33.

10. William G. Dever, *What Did the Biblical Writers Know and When Did They Know It?* (Grand Rapids, MI: Eerdmans, 2002), 98–99.

between a "Moses" and a "Moses-like figure" may be a little too fine for some people who would prefer to merge the two. In any case, it brings us back to Renan's position of over 130 years ago.

Another reason scholars are dubious of a Mosaic authorship is there is so much evidence in the text that is difficult to explain if we assume Moses (or a Moses-like figure) is the author or even that there is a single author. The historian J. Kenneth Kuntz (b. 1934) has categorized this evidence into five types:

(1) duplication of narrative accounts;
(2) internal contradictions;
(3) anachronisms and other problems of chronology;
(4) presence of diverse literary styles; and
(5) shifts and interruptions in the narrative.[11]

These categories are significant for testing not only the authorship of the Pentateuch but also the authorship of other texts where a single-author versus multiple-authors dispute exists. One or two examples from each category in the Old Testament should be sufficient to demonstrate that evidence.

Duplication of Narrative Accounts

An example of the same event being reported twice, as though the author "forgot" he had already narrated it, is Yahweh revealing his name to Moses at two different times, first at the burning bush:

> Then Moses said to God [*Elohim*], "If I come to the people of Israel and say to them, 'The god of your fathers has sent me to you,' and they ask me, 'What is his name?' what shall I say to them?" God [*Elohim*] said to Moses, "I am [*hayah*] who I am." And he said, "Say this to the people of Israel, 'I am [*hayah*] has sent me to you.'" God [*Elohim*] also said to Moses, "Say this to the people of Israel, 'Yahweh, the god of your fathers, the god of Abraham, the god of Isaac, and the god of Jacob has sent me to you': this is my name for ever, and thus I am to be remembered throughout all generations. Go and gather the elders of Israel together, and say to them, 'Yahweh, the god of your fathers, the god of Abraham, of Isaac, and of Jacob has appeared to me saying, 'I have observed you and what has been done to you in Egypt; and I promise that I will bring you up out of the affliction of Egypt, to the land of the Canaanites, the

---

11. J. Kenneth Kuntz, *The People of Ancient Israel: An Introduction to Old Testament Literature, History, and Thought* (New York: Harper & Row, 1974), 42–46.

Hittites, the Amorites, the Perizzites, the Hivites, and the Jebusites, a land flowing with milk and honey.'" (Exod. 3:13–17)

Here God seems to be making a pun on the Hebrew verb *hayah*, meaning "to be," in telling Moses that his name is Yahweh. Then, after Moses has returned to Egypt and first confronted Pharaoh and Pharaoh responds by ordering the Hebrews to gather their own straw to make bricks, Moses confronts God again, wanting to know why he is doing harm to the Hebrews. God repeats his former declaration:

> And God [*Elohim*] said to Moses, "I am Yahweh. I appeared to Abraham, to Isaac, and to Jacob, as El Shaddai [the almighty god], but I did not make myself known to them by my name Yahweh. I also established my covenant with them to give them the land of Canaan, the land in which they dwelt as sojourners. Moreover, I have heard the groaning of the people of Israel whom the Egyptians hold in bondage and I have remembered my covenant. Say, therefore, to the people of Israel, 'I am Yahweh, and I will bring you out from under the burdens of the Egyptians and I will deliver you from their bondage, and I will redeem you with an out-stretched arm and with great acts of judgment, and I will take you for my people, and I will be your god; and you will know that I am Yahweh, your god, who has brought you out from under the burdens of the Egyptians. And I will bring you into the land that I swore to give to Abraham, to Isaac, and to Jacob; I will give it to you for a possession. I am Yahweh.'" (Exod. 6:2–8)

One might suppose this to be a very strange god who forgets he had already revealed his name to Moses in Midian, or he figures Moses was forgetful and had to be reminded, or the author of the passage forgot he had just described it a few passages earlier. A fourth possible explanation, which we will discuss in more detail later in this chapter, is that a compiler combined two stories, one in which God (*Elohim*) revealed his name in Midian, the other in which he revealed his name in Egypt. The compiler could not or did not wish to decide between the two accounts, so he included both.

Of the other examples of duplication of narrative, one in particular stands out in my mind as dispositive of the problem. Genesis 12:10–19 tells the story of Abram (Abraham) and his wife Sarai (Sarah) taking a detour into Egypt because there was a famine in the land of Negeb, their intended destination. Just as they are about to cross the border into Egypt, Abram says to Sarai,

> "I know that you are a woman beautiful to behold; and when the Egyptians see you, they will say, 'This is his wife'; then they will kill me but

they will let you live. Say you are my sister, that it may go well with me because of you and that my life may be spared on your account." (Gen. 12:11–13)

After seeing how beautiful Sarai is and thinking she is Abram's sister, the princes of Pharaoh tell Pharaoh about her. Sarai is taken into the royal palace and Abram is given "sheep, oxen, he-asses, men-servants, maidservants, she-asses, and camels" in return "for her sake" (Gen. 12:16). But "the Lord [YHWH] afflicted Pharaoh and his house with great plagues because of Sarai, Abram's wife" (Gen. 12:17). Somehow Pharaoh finds out that Sarai is Abram's wife and asks Abram why he did not tell him that she was his wife. Instead of killing Abram (as Abram had feared), Pharaoh sends him on his way with Sarai "and all that he had" (Gen. 12:19).

Eight chapters later, Abram (now called Abraham) and his wife Sarai (now called Sarah) go to the land of Negeb and stay in Gerar, where Abimelech rules. Here Genesis tells a story similar to the one about Abram and Sarai in Egypt. Abraham says that Sarah is his sister, and Abimelech "took Sarah" (Gen. 20:2). Then "God [Elohim] came to Abimelech in a dream by night" and told him, "You are a dead man, because of the woman whom you have taken; for she is a man's wife" (Gen. 20:3). God tells Abimelech to "restore the man's wife; for he is a prophet, and he will pray for you, and you shall live." (Gen. 20:7). As Pharaoh did in Egypt, Abimelech asks Abraham, "What have you done to us? What were you thinking of, that you did this thing?' (Gen. 20:9–10). Abraham answered that he thought he would be killed because of his wife and "Besides she is indeed my sister, the daughter of my father but not the daughter of my mother and she became my wife" (Gen. 20:12). In other words, she was his half-sister. Abraham further explained that he told Sarah, "This is the kindness you must do me: at every place to which we come, say of me, 'He is my brother'" (Gen. 20:13). Again, as in Egypt, Abraham benefits materially from the misunderstanding as Abimelech gives him "sheep and oxen and male and female slaves" as well as "a thousand pieces of silver" (Gen. 20:14, 16). Abimelech also tells Abraham that he could reside anywhere in Abimelech's land that it pleased him. As a result, "Abraham prayed to God [Elohim]; and God healed Abimelech, and also healed his wife and female slaves so that they bore children. For the Lord had closed all the wombs of the house of Abimelech because of Sarah, Abraham's wife" (Gen. 20:17–18). The narrative does not explain what affliction Abimelech was healed of.

A number of Biblical scholars have taken the position that the narrative about Abimelech's encounter with Abraham and Sarah presupposes knowledge and fills in the gaps of the story about Pharaoh's encounter with Abram and Sarai earlier. It explains that Abram/Abraham was not lying when he said that Sarai/Sarah was his sister (same father, different mothers), how Pharaoh found out she was his wife (through a dream), and why Abram/Abraham would use the same ploy (neglecting to say she was his wife) for the same reason (fear of being killed because of the desire for her in the lands into which they went). It also implicitly answers the question whether Pharaoh had sexual relations with Sarai/Sarah by explicitly stating that Abimelech did not. It does not attempt, however, to justify the legality of a man marrying his half-sister.

In ancient Egypt, the practice of brother-sister marriages spread gradually from the royal family to other layers of the population. In Pharaonic Egypt (to 323 BC), we have evidence of royal marriages between brother and sister of the royal family. Some scholars think that marriage between full brother and sister was forbidden and only half-siblings allowed. The evidence for brother-sister marriage among commoners during that time is sparse. During Ptolemaic times (323–30 BC), the evidence for brother-sister marriages among commoners increases. In Roman Egypt (30 BC to AD 324), such marriages spread among commoners to the point that, based on the extant Roman census returns, between 15 and 21 percent of all marriages were between brother and sister.[12]

Yet, Genesis is not done with the story. Six chapters later, we find a similar tale told about Abraham's son Isaac and his wife Rebekah who go into Gerar, the same land ruled by the same Abimelech. The text begins by alluding to the famine that sent Abram and Sarai into Egypt: "There was a famine in the land, besides the former famine that was in the days of Abraham" (Gen. 26:1). But instead of telling Isaac to go to Egypt, "The Lord [YHWH, Yahweh] appeared to him, and said, 'Do not go down to Egypt; dwell in the land of which I shall tell you'" (Gen. 26:2). Subsequently when the men of Gerar "asked him about his wife, he said, 'She is my sister'; for he feared to say, 'My wife,' thinking, 'lest the men of the place should kill me for the sake of Rebekah; because she was fair to look upon" (Gen. 26:7). This time Abimelech finds out that Rebekah is Isaac's wife not through a dream but when he "looked out of a window and saw Isaac fondling Rebekah his wife" (Gen. 26:8). As both Pharaoh and Abimelech had previously asked Isaac's father, Abimelech asks Isaac why he said that his wife was his sister. Isaac answered, "Lest I die because of her" (Gen. 26:9). Abimelech is concerned that any of his people could have "lain with" her and "brought guilt upon us" (Gen. 26:10). In contrast, in the second

---

12. Keith Hopkins, "Brother-Sister Marriage in Roman Egypt," *Comparative Studies in Society and History* 22, no. 3 (July 1980): 304.

story, Abimelech was concerned more about his own innocence than that of his people. In this version of the story, we find no divine intervention, warning, or infliction of illness. Abimelech does not give Isaac any gifts, but Isaac "reaped in the same year a hundredfold" and "The Lord [YHWH] blessed him, and the man became rich and gained more and more until he became very wealthy" (Gen. 26:13). Finally, Abimelech tells him to leave "for you are much mightier than we" (Gen. 26:16), which is in contrast to what Abimelech told Abraham in chapter 20 (but is closer to Pharaoh's requiring Abram to leave Egypt in chapter 12). The narrative of chapter 26 does not say whether Isaac knew that Abraham used the same ploy in Egypt with Pharaoh and in Gerar with Abimelech. Nor does it try to provide some justification as the second tale does in regard to Abraham and Sarah for Isaac's referring to Rebekah as his sister.

It seems highly unlikely that these three stories and all the other narrative pairs are the result of a single author. One or two cases of narrative pairs might be attributed to author error in a long text, but the weight of the evidence in terms of numbers and types of narrative pairs bends more probably to the conclusion that they are the result of different authors (or oral traditions) reporting the same folk tale in different ways. In the case of these three sister/wife tales, each tale seems to have a decidedly different viewpoint. The teller of the second tale (of Abraham and Sarah in Gerar) seems to have presumptive knowledge of the first tale of Abram and Sarai in Egypt and seems to be trying to answer questions about it. The reference to the earlier famine in Gerar could have been a later editorial addition. The third tale—about Isaac and Rebekah—still awaits a satisfactory explanation, for there is no indication in it of the teller's knowing about the previous two tales.

The German scholar Klaus Koch considers the stories to be oral variants that were subsequently written down.[13] The American scholars John Van Seters, Claus Westermann, Martin Noth, and Siegfried Hermann consider stories two and three to be literary compositions riffing on and responding to story one, which they see as folklore.[14] In contrast, T. D[esmond] Alexander concludes that all three stories were written by one author who drew on various traditions "with a clear knowledge of what he had already written earlier." I find that Alexander's conclusion does not derive from his otherwise excellent

13. Klaus Koch, *The Growth of the Biblical Tradition: The Form-Critical Method* (New York: Scribner, 1969), 111–132; Koch, *Was ist Formgeschichte? Neue Wege de Bibelexegese* (Neukirchen-Vluyn: Neukirchener Verlag des Erziehungsvereins, 1964), 121–148.

14. T. D[esmond] Alexander, "Are the Wife/Sister Incidents of Genesis Literary Compositional Variants?" *Vetus Testamentum* 42, no. 2 (1992): 152.

analysis. But it is in keeping with his stated position that "Moses' literary activities" should not be rejected.[15]

I will discuss the parallel Flood narratives further on in this chapter.

Internal Contradictions

We can take the theme of God's revealing his name as an example of an internal contradiction. The first quotation above (Exod. 3:13–17) seems to suggest that God thought up the name Yahweh on the spot based on the phrase "I am what I am." In the second quotation (Exod. 6:2–8), God explicitly states that he did not make himself known as Yahweh to Abraham, Isaac, and Jacob. Yet, in at least three places Abraham (Abram) seems to know the name of Yahweh:

> Then Yahweh appeared to Abram, and said, "To your descendants I will give this land." So he built there an altar to Yahweh, who had appeared to him. Thence he removed to the mountain on the east of Bethel, and pitched his tent, with Bethel on the west and Ai on the east; and there he built an altar to Yahweh and called on the name of Yahweh (Gen. 12:7–9).
>
> And the king of Sodom said to Abram, "Give me the persons, but take the goods for yourself." But Abram said to the king of Sodom, "I have sworn to Yahweh, the most high god, maker of heaven and earth, that I would not take a thread or a sandal-thong or anything that is yours, lest you should say, 'I have made Abram rich'" (Gen. 14:21–23).
>
> And Abraham said to his servant, the oldest of his house, who had charge of all that he had, "Put your hand under my thigh, and I will make you swear by Yahweh, God of heaven and earth, that you will not take a wife for my son from the daughters of the Canaanites, among whom I dwell . . . ." (Gen. 24:2–4)

So, it would appear either that Yahweh is intentionally deceiving Moses or these quotations are part of yet another narrative different from the two in Exodus where Yahweh reveals his name.

Anachronisms

Among the anachronisms in the Pentateuch are the references to the Philistines being in Canaan before the Israelites returned from Egypt:

---

15. See T. Desmond Alexander and David W. Baker, *Dictionary of the Old Testament: Pentateuch* (Downers Grove, IL: InterVarsity, 2003), 70.

When Pharaoh let the people go, God [*Elohim*] did not lead them by way
of the land of the Philistines, although that was near . . . . (Exod. 13:17)

Even if we allow the possibility that the Philistines may have arrived shortly
before the Israelites' return, that would not explain why Genesis has passages
in which Abraham and Isaac have direct dealings with them centuries before
the Hebrews even went to Egypt:

And Abraham sojourned many days in the land of the Philistines. (Gen.
21:34)

Now there was a famine in the land, besides the former famine that
was in the days of Abraham. And Isaac went to Gerar, to Abimelech king
of the Philistines. (Gen. 26:1)

Now the Philistines had stopped and filled with earth all of the well
that his [Isaac's] father's servants had dug in the days of Abraham his
father. (Gen. 26:15)

Archaeological evidence, however, points to the Philistines arriving in Canaan
in the twelfth century BC, either after or around the time of the Israelites' return from Egypt.[16] The Philistines were extremely important during much of
the time that is covered in the biblical narrative. They occupied the coastline
and gave their name in Latinized form to the land—Palestine. But the placing
of their presence by the authors of the Bible back in the time of Abraham and
Isaac can most likely be explained by an attempt to use them in some morality tale of the "lessons-of-the-past" type.

Diverse Styles

Diversity of style is difficult to demonstrate without extensive quotations, but
I think one will be able to detect a definite difference in the relationship between Abraham and Yahweh in the following two passages, both of which deal
with similar themes. In the first, Yahweh is kindly and reassuring, and a dialogue occurs between them. The style is direct:

After these things the word of Yahweh came to Abram in a vision, "Fear
not, Abram, I am your shield; your reward will be very great." But Abram
said, "O Yahweh god, what will thou give me, for I continue childless,

---

16. Trude Krakauer Dothan and Moshe Dothan, *People of the Sea: The Search for the Philistines*
(New York: Macmillan, 1992); Manuel Robbins, *Collapse of the Bronze Age: The Story of Greece, Troy, Israel, Egypt, and the Peoples of the Sea* (iUniverse.com, 2001), 315–336.

and the heir of my house is Eliezer of Damascus?" And Abram said, "Behold, thou has given me no offspring; and a slave born in my house will be my heir." And behold, the word of Yahweh came to him, "This man shall not be your heir; your son will be your heir.' And he brought him outside and said, "Look toward heaven, and number the stars, if you are able to number them." Then he said to him, "So shall your descendants be." And he believed Yahweh; and he reckoned it to him as righteousness. (Gen. 15:1–6)

In this second passage, no dialogue occurs, only instructions from Yahweh, who speaks in an elevated style:

When Abram was ninety-nine years old Yahweh appeared to Abram, and said to him, "I am El Shaddai; walk before me, and be blameless. And I will make my covenant between me and you, and will multiply you exceedingly." Then Abram fell on his face; and God [*Elohim*] said to him, "Behold, my covenant is with you, and you will be the father of a multitude of nations. No longer will your name be Abram, but your name will be Abraham; for I have made you the father of a multitude of nations" . . . . And God [*Elohim*] said to Abraham, "As for you, you will keep my covenant, you and your descendants after you throughout their generations. This is my covenant, which you will keep, between me and you and your descendants after you: Every male among you shall be circumcised. You shall be circumcised in the flesh of your foreskins, and it shall be a sign of the covenant between me and you . . . ." (Gen. 17:1–5, 9–11)

The repetition of the phrase "covenant between me and you" is meant to add a ritualistic air to the speech. It is not meant to be reassuring but didactic. It is possible that Yahweh would speak in different ways to Abram / Abraham at different times, but when one multiplies these cases, one begins to suspect more than one hand at work here.

Sudden Shifts in Narrative

A number of intrusions into the narrative flow occur in the Pentateuch. These intrusions appear to be fragments of some other narrative that was left over and never fully edited out, yet not completely included. Perhaps one of the most jarring occurs in Exodus after Yahweh convinces Moses to return to Egypt to lead the Israelites out. After much pleading on Moses's part for Yahweh to choose someone else, Yahweh gets angry. Only then does Moses agree to do Yahweh's bidding. Yet, while Moses is on his way to Egypt with his wife Zipporah and sons, the following passage intrudes itself:

> At a lodging on the way Yahweh met him and sought to kill him. Then Zipporah took a flint and cut off her son's foreskin and touched Moses' feet with it, and said, "Surely you are a bridegroom of blood to me!" So he let him alone. Then it was that she said, "You are a bridegroom of blood," because of the circumcision. (Exod. 4:24–26)

The narrative continues with Yahweh's telling Aaron to meet Moses. The fragment about Yahweh's wanting to kill Moses is left dangling. Did Yahweh want to kill Moses because Moses had previously been recalcitrant about being chosen as the one to save the Israelites? No, that is not likely because in the narrative up to that point, Yahweh seems not to have been angry anymore. Did Yahweh want to kill Moses because he had not circumcised his son? Possibly, but there is no indication that Yahweh required that of Moses—that is, it is not clear that Moses was disobeying Yahweh or breaking one of his laws. Did Yahweh want to kill Moses because he was not "a bridegroom of blood" to Zipporah? Again, it is possible, if we knew what "a bridegroom of blood" was as opposed to a bridegroom of any other type. Nor is it clear why his wife's circumcising his son and touching his feet with the foreskin would make Moses one of the acceptable kinds of bridegrooms.

This passage, dubbed "Zipporah at the Inn," has exercised scholars' imaginations to come up with a plausible explanation. I cannot begin to go into the wide range of conjectures, here, but I will discuss one of the more imaginative. The German historian of religion Walter Beltz (1935–2006) suggested that, because there is no mention of Moses in the previous passage, the personal masculine pronoun in "Yahweh met him and sought to kill him" can refer only to Moses's son. Beltz went on to argue that the term "Moses' feet" is a euphemistic translation for "his genitals," in this case, referring to Yahweh's genitals. Thus, according to Beltz, Zipporah "is initiating Moses' child into a marriage with Yahweh, and he becomes Yahweh's child."[17] Beltz claimed that the name "Moses" was inserted because "devout readers were always scandalized by anthropomorphic treatment of Yahweh, and tried to smooth over the offensive reference to his genitals."[18] Such an interpretation seems strained to say the least. For starters, it depends on both an interpolation and a euphemism

---

17. Walter Beltz, *God and the Gods: Myths of the Bible*, trans. Peter Heinegg (New York: Penguin, 1983), 55–56.

18. Beltz, *God and the Gods*, 56.

to make it work as well as the abstract notion that Yahweh was entitled to the lives of the firstborn as well as the notion that readers would be scandalized by mention of Yahweh's genitals when they were not scandalized by a mention of his buttocks (Exod. 33:23).

Since the text beginning with verse 24 seems clearly to be a continuation from verse 20: "So Moses took his wife and his sons and set them on an ass, and went back to the land of Egypt; and in his hand Moses took the rod of God." Thus, in the narrative as it is now, Moses is the likely object of Yahweh's destructive desire. Also, it is not clear why Zipporah touching Yahweh's genitals with the foreskin of Moses's son would make Yahweh her bridegroom of blood. Finally, one would think that if Yahweh wanted to kill someone, it would happen immediately. That is, thought and act would follow so fast that no time lapse would have occurred, certainly not enough time for Zipporah to circumcise her son, then touch the feet of Moses (or genitals of Yahweh) with the foreskin, and say anything about one or the other being a bridegroom of blood. No condition is set. The narrator does not say that Yahweh threatens to kill Moses unless he does something. It is a very straightforward "[he] sought to kill him." Clearly, something essential for understanding the narrative is missing here, and it seems likely the missing piece is an entire other narrative of which only this fragment remained. Perhaps it was a duplicate of the burning bush story that the editor tried to expunge but missed this fragment. Or perhaps the editor had only this fragment of another story and inserted it where it seemed to make the most sense.

The Samaritan Pentateuch provides another explanation. The Samaritans believe that their version of the Pentateuch is primary in relation to the Hebrew Masoretic text. And, indeed, some of the readings of the Samaritan Pentateuch are closer to the second-century BC Greek Septuagint version. But, in general, text critical scholars consider the readings of the Samaritan Pentateuch to be secondary in relation to the Masoretic Bible. If so, then the account in the Samaritan Pentateuch confirms that the editor of it thought something was amiss in the version that the Masoretic derives from. Instead of trying to kill Moses, Yahweh only wants to stun him. The Samaritan text places the focus on Zipporah as the one causing the problem: "Seebbooraa took a flint and she circumcised her blocked heart, and she brought herself to his feet. And she said, You are indeed a bridegroom of blood to me. And he let her go. Then she said, A bridegroom of blood, to be circumcised."[19] Leaving aside the issue of how one circumcises one's heart, the refocus of the blame onto Zipporah's

---

19. *The Israelite Samaritan Version of the Torah: First English Translation Compared with the Masoretic Version*, ed. Benyamin Tsedaka and Sharon Sullivan (Grand Rapids, MI: Eerdmans, 2013), 132–133.

blocked heart seems to be an attempt to explain what follows twelve chapters later where we find out that Zipporah and her two sons do not go into Egypt with Moses but stay with her father, Jethro. For some reason, even after circumcising her heart, she was not supposed to go into Egypt. And that leaves us back where we started—that is, with a mysterious fragment.

The Problem with the Single-Author Theory

In 1987, Friedman provided an extensive argument against the attribution of the Pentateuch to Moses. Friedman pointed out that

> the tradition that one person, Moses, alone wrote these books presented problems. People observed contradictions in the text. It would report events in a particular order, and later it would say that those same events happened in a different order. It would say there were two of something, and elsewhere it would say that there were fourteen of that same thing. It would say that the Moabites did something, and later it would say that it was the Midianites who did it. It would describe Moses as going to a Tabernacle in a chapter before Moses builds the Tabernacle.[20]

But people are contradictory by nature. We sometimes say and write things that contradict what we have just said or written. So the presence in itself of contradictions in the text would not seem to be a strong argument against single-person authorship. After all, Moses could have gone to a tabernacle that was not the Tabernacle. But it does raise the question why subsequent editors, if the Bible went through any kind of editing process, would not have straightened out these contradictions. Friedman went on to point out examples that really seem to eliminate Moses as the author:

> People also noticed that the Five Books of Moses included things that Moses could not have known or was not likely to have said. The text, after all, gave an account of Moses' death. It also said that Moses was the humblest man on earth; and normally one would not expect the humblest man on earth to point out that he is the humblest man on earth.[21]

Those who believed that Moses wrote the Pentateuch were not about to give up so easily. Whenever someone pointed out a passage that mentions something Moses could not have known, such as a list of Edomite kings

---

20. Richard Elliott Friedman, *Who Wrote the Bible?* (New York: Harper & Row, 1987), 17–18.
21. Friedman, *Who Wrote the Bible?*, 18.

who lived after Moses died, they would argue that this passage was a later interpolation or addition by someone else. Thus, so their argument goes, those passages that could have been written by Moses were written by Moses, whereas those passages that could not have been written by Moses were written by someone else later. This argument was made by the philosopher Thomas Hobbes (1588–1679), the first modern scholar to discuss in a systematic way the question of Moses's authorship of the Pentateuch as we have it:

> It is therefore sufficiently evident, that the five Books of Moses were written after his time, though how long after it be not so manifest. But though Moses did not compile those Books entirely, and in the form we have them; yet he wrote all that which hee is there said to have written: as for example, the Volume of the Law, which is contained, as it seemeth in the 11 of Deuteronomie, and the following Chapters to the 27. which was also commanded to be written on stones, in their entry into the land of Canaan. (Deut. 31. 9) And this did Moses himself write, and deliver to the Priests and Elders of Israel, to be read every seventh year to all Israel, at their assembling in the feast of Tabernacles.[22]

Such a theory of authorship, however, seems designed merely to save Moses as the author of something. It, as well as the entire attribution of the Pentateuch to Moses, may be based solely on a one-sided interpretation of the phrase "the Book of Moses." In the Middle Ages, for example, manuscripts were strewn about higgledy-piggledy in the monastery's library. To identify the manuscripts, sometimes a designation such as "Sermones Bonaventurae" was marked. The problem, as James Burke explained, "It could mean the Sermons of St. Bonaventure or it could mean sermons written by an ordinary bloke called Bonaventure or sermons owned by a Bonaventure or preached or copied, or sermons owned by a church of St. Bonaventure, or worst of all, none of that. The sermons of St. Bonaventure might be just the first things in this book."[23] In this sense, "the book of Moses" could and more likely does means the book ("roll" is more accurate since books were invented later) about the time of Moses rather than written by Moses.

So, how have Biblical scholars tried to explain the characteristics of this narrative evidence if a single author seems unlikely to account for them?

---

22. Thomas Hobbes, *Leviathan* (1651), chap. 33 (spelling and punctuation of the 1651 text).

23. James Burke, *The Day the Universe Changed*, episode 4: "Matter of Fact: Printing Transforms Knowledge," discussing a codex titled *Sermones Bonaventurae.*

The Challenge of Biblical Criticism

If Moses was not the author, then that brings into question the Pentateuch's reliability for the events it describes. Among the nineteenth-century scholars who doubted the reliability of the Bible as a historical source was the historian Ernest Renan. While being trained as a priest, Renan left the Catholic Church over what he perceived to be the incompatibility of modern scholarship with the teaching of the Church. Renan suggested that the "narratives of the Exodus, into which fable has penetrated so deeply, may be even more mythical than is generally supposed, and that the only fact that can be depended upon out of them all is the departure from Egypt of Israel and its entry into the peninsula of Sinai."[24] Renan based his arguments on Biblical criticism as it had developed by his time, which was moving in the direction of arguing that if the Pentateuch was not providing reliable historical evidence, then it is unlikely Moses or any eyewitness wrote it.

Documentary Hypothesis

Scholars began to notice that in some of the duplicate stories, one of the stories referred to God as *Elohim*, while the other story referred to God as Yahweh (which the observant reader may have noticed I was indicating in the quoted passages from the Bible). This observation led to the supposition that a large part of the Pentateuch was made up of two equal narratives that had been stitched together—the J (Yahwist) and the E (Elohist) narratives. But J and E did not account for all of the Pentateuch, so a P (Priestly) narrative and a D (Deutoronomy) narrative were also supposed.

The German philologist and theologian Hermann Hupfeld (1796–1866) proposed in 1853 that the Pentateuch is made up of at least four narratives: (1) a J narrative in which God is referred to as Yahweh throughout (the J is for *Jahve*, the German form of the name, and was first identified by Wellhausen); (2) an E narrative, in which God is initially referred to as *Elohim* and only later in the narrative from the burning bush as Yahweh; (3) a P narrative, which emphasizes the role of the priests; and (4) a D narrative associated mostly with the book of Deuteronomy.[25] Positing four separate narratives that were later combined into one canonical text seems to be a better explanation to many scholars for duplications in the final product than arguing that one author

---

24. Renan, *History of the People of Israel*, vol. 1, 137.

25. Hermann Hupfeld, *Die Quellen der Genesis und die Art ihrer Zusammensetzung von neuem untersucht* (Berlin: Wiegandt und Grieben, 1853).

forgot what he had already written. It also helps to explain the apparent stitching together of two Flood stories. In Genesis 6:19, God [*Elohim*] tells Noah, "And of every living things of all flesh, you shall bring two of every sort into the ark, to keep them alive with you; they shall be males and female." But in Genesis 7:2, Yahweh [YHWH] tells Noah, "Take with you seven pairs of all clean animals, the male and his mate; and a pair of the animals that are not clean, the male and his mate." Likewise, the Flood lasts both for forty days and forty nights (Gen. 7:4, 7:12, 8:6, J narrative) and for 150 days (Gen. 7:24, 8:3, E narrative). The rain begins both on the seventh day after Noah and his family enter the ark (Gen. 7:7, J narrative) and on the day Noah and his family enter the ark (Gen. 7:11–13, E narrative). After the ark settles on Mt. Ararat, Moses releases both a series of three doves, each one seven days apart until one returned with an olive branch (Gen. 8:8–12), and a raven once, which flew around "until the waters were dried up from the earth" (Gen. 8:7). One might wonder, however, why the editor who stitched the narratives together did not edit out the duplications or try to combine two duplicate stories into one. The answer that Friedman has proposed is that there were factions among the Israelites who did not want their particular story changed (see below). Besides, we do have evidence that there were some stories or parts of stories edited out.

Nonetheless, other scholars found the documentary hypothesis, while on the right track, did not adequately explain the text we have. A number of other proposals were made. Two of the most prominent were the supplementary hypothesis and the fragmentary hypothesis. The supplementary hypothesis posits a basic core text, usually D (composed ca. 700 BC), to which J was added (ca. 600 BC) followed by P (ca. 400 BC). Thus, D is pre-exile, J is during the exile, and P is post-exile.[26] Those who hold the Supplementary Hypothesis do not recognize an E text. Those who hold the Fragmentary hypothesis posit no core text as such, merely fragments from various traditions.

Bible Reflects the Time When It Was Written

Friedman provided an interpretation of the composition of the Bible, in particular the Pentateuch, that depends less on the view that the Bible reflects earlier oral traditions and more that it reflects the social and religious conditions that existed when the words were written down. Friedman's explanation, which he says better accounts for the textual evidence, asserts that other people

---

26. The exile occurred from 597 BC (when Nebuchadnezzar II captured Jerusalem and began to take Israeli elites to Babylonia) to 538 BC (when Babylonia was captured by Cyrus II of Persia, who allowed the Hebrews to return to Jerusalem).

(not Moses) compiled the books of the Pentateuch at a later time, sometime between the years 722 and 400 BC.

In his book *The Exodus: How It Happened and Why It Matters* (2017), which explicates further his theory, Friedman proposed the numbers of Hebrews who fled Egypt under Moses given in the book of Numbers were much fewer than the 603,550 adult males. But he then asked why the author of the narrative felt the need to inflate the numbers. Friedman saw a kernel of historicity in this story but only insofar as it is about Levites. He pointed to the archaeological evidence that Hebrews (or the people we call the Hebrews) lived continuously in Canaan throughout this period. In Friedman's scenario, they were then joined by the Levites from Egypt. The inflated number of adult males during the Exodus was meant to enhance the position of the Levites later.[27] In general terms, there is still a conformity to the biblical narrative for, when Joseph's brothers and their families joined Joseph in Egypt, presumably the other Hebrews who were not sibling-related to Joseph stayed behind. If they did not disappear during the ensuing years after Joseph's brothers left for Egypt, then the returning Hebrews were in a position to rejoin them.

As an example of Friedman's method, I focus here on his analysis in *Who Wrote the Bible?* of the story of the golden calf. In the story contained in chapter 32 of Exodus, while Moses is on Mount Sinai receiving the tablets of stone from Yahweh, his brother Aaron has the Israelites give him their gold (rings and earrings) from which he manufactures a statue of a calf. He says to them, "These are your gods [*Elohim*], O Israel, who brought you up out of the land of Egypt!" (Exod. 32:4). Then he builds an altar and declares, "Tomorrow shall be a feast to Yahweh" (Exod. 32:5). When Moses returns down the mountain, Joshua is with him and tells him that he thinks he hears the noise of war in the camp. Moses tells him it is singing. Upon seeing what the Israelites have done in his absence, Moses gets angry and breaks the tablets.[28] When Moses asks Aaron what happened, Aaron prevaricates with the explanation that the people demanded that he make them gods. So, according to Aaron, he took their gold, threw it into the fire, and a calf came out apparently all by itself. Moses then asks, "Who is on Yahweh's side? Come to me" (Exod. 32:26). The sons of Levi (the Levites) went over to him. Moses then tells them to "slay every man his brother, and every man his companion, and every man his neighbor" (Exod. 32:27).[29] As a result, they killed "three thousand men" (Exod. 32:28).

---

27. Friedman, *The Exodus*, 25–83.

28. Some scholars see this act as symbolically breaking the covenant with God, and thus allows Moses to do what follows.

29. In breaking the tablets, Moses would not have to obey the Ten Commandments, specifically the one about "Thou shalt not kill."

When Friedman looked at this story he saw only questions:

Why did the person who wrote this story depict his people as rebellious at the very time of their liberation and their receiving the covenant? Why did he picture *Aaron* as leader of the heresy? Why does Aaron not suffer any punishment for it in the end? Why did the author picture a *golden calf*? Why do the people say *"These* are your *gods,* Israel . . . ,"* when there is only one calf there? And why do they say *". . . that brought you up from the land of Egypt"* when the calf obviously was not made until after they were out of Egypt? Why does Aaron say *"A* holiday to *Yahweh* tomorrow" when he is presenting the calf as a rival to Yahweh? Why is the calf treated as a god in this story, when the calf was *not* a god in the ancient Near East? Why did the writer picture Moses as smashing the tablets of the Ten Commandments? Why picture the Levites as acting in bloody zeal? Why include Joshua in the story? Why depict Joshua as dissociated from the golden calf event? [italics in original][30]

In attempting to answer these questions, Friedman posited a theory in which one of the Levite priests from Shiloh is the author of this story around the year 700 BC. The Levite priests at the time were not the main priests in Israel; the Aaronids, or descendants of Aaron, were the main priests. That would explain why Aaron is not punished in the story for perpetrating the heresy. If Aaron had been punished for heresy to Yahweh, then his descendants could not have been priests. Note that Aaron disclaims any responsibility for what happened because he was doing only what the people asked. If a Levite was the author of the story, then that would also explain why Aaron is depicted as enabling the heresy, for the Levites were in opposition to the Aaronids after Solomon. Friedman saw the making of the golden calf as referring not to some actual event that occurred during the Israelites leaving Egypt but instead a reference to two golden statues of calves (more correctly bullocks) that the king of the northern kingdom, Jeroboam, had made in opposition to the golden cherubs of Solomon kept in the Ark of the Covenant in Jerusalem, then under the control of the southern kingdom. The northern kingdom was destroyed by Assyria in 722 BC, so the implication of the story is that the northern kingdom was punished by Yahweh for making golden calves (bullocks) in the same way the Israelites who worshiped the golden calf were punished by Moses and the Levites in Exodus. Friedman, thus, interpreted the story as the Levites being critical of two opponents: the religious opponents—the Aaronid priesthood—and the political opponents—the kings of the northern kingdom.

---

30. Friedman, *Who Wrote the Bible?*, 71.

Joshua is inserted into the story because he is the successor to Moses, and the Levite priests wanted to clear him of any connection with heresy.

Friedman went on to suggest that the Levite priests from Shiloh who wrote their contribution, E in this case, must have written it in the time of King Hezekiah (715–687 BC) because it was then that the Levites were replaced by the Aaronids as chief priests. It was also after the Assyrians had captured the northern kingdom. At about the same time, an advocate of the house of David from the southern kingdom, Judah, wrote a different version of Hebrew history (J). Then the Aaronid priests, dissatisfied with both versions, wrote their own account (P) as an alternative to both E and J. Finally, Friedman saw Jeremiah as the one responsible for writing the legalistic book Deuteronomy (D). Subsequently, according to Friedman, in the late fifth or early fourth century BC, an Aaronid priest and scribe, Ezra, combined the four narratives—J, E, P, and D—into the Pentateuch. Ezra's compilation was, thereby, the canonical compilation of the first Bible. That would explain, according to Friedman, why we have no complete copies of the Old Testament before the Septuagint, a Greek translation from the third century BC.

Friedman looked to the political and religious conditions of the time that the books of the Bible were being written down and edited into the Pentateuch for an explanation of what is included and how it is being described. Thus, in his analysis, Friedman placed very little importance on the actual events of the historical past that the biblical narratives are ostensibly about. In his view, it would be futile to try to find some residual remnants of beliefs of the earlier Israelites in the Bible from the time they left Egypt. Any beliefs so depicted, according to Friedman's scheme, would reflect the period after the eighth century BC.

The literary critic Harold Bloom suggested another possible consideration—that the author of J was a woman who wrote the narrative as a work of fiction during the time of Solomon.[31] Then priests, according to Bloom, subsequently revised her narrative and combined it with other narratives to create the Pentateuch. For his evidence that the author of J was a woman, Bloom pointed out that women described in the narrative, such as Tamar and Rebekah, are stronger characters than the male figures, such as Abraham and Moses.[32] In addition, the story of Adam's creation occupies only one-sixth as much narrative space as the story of Eve's creation. Friedman in turn criticized Bloom for erroneously attributing passages from other narratives to J and took the translator David Rosenberg to task for translating more than the passages are able to support.

---

31. Harold Bloom, *The Book of J*, trans. David Rosenberg (New York: Grove, Weidenfeld, 1990).
32. Bloom, *The Book of J*, 220.

A present-day exponent of the view that at least some parts of the Pentateuch relate events as described by eyewitnesses is the American archaeologist Baruch Halpern (b. 1953). He argued that parts of the book of Exodus, in particular the songs, can be dated to the period 1125–1100 BC. He accepted the conclusion of the Austrian Egyptologist Manfred Bietak (b. 1940) that the actual leaving of the Israelites from Egypt occurred around 1150 BC. Bietak based that date on the archaeological evidence of the post holes and trenches of reed huts near Luxor in Egypt. The floor plan constructed by archaeologists of these huts is consistent with the floor plan of houses the Israelites in Canaan lived in—the so-called four-room house.[33] Bietak dates the construction of these reed huts to the time when the temple of Rameses III (1187–1153 BC) still existed because of their relationship to a temple constructed during Rameses's reign. That temple, according to Bietak, was most likely demolished under his successor Rameses IV (1153–1147 BC), and he proposed that the reed huts were built to house Israelite workers (perhaps slaves) whose job it was to destroy the temple of Rameses III.[34] Bietak concluded that because Israelites were still working in Egypt around 1150 BC, the Exodus from Egypt could not have occurred earlier than that.

The traditional scholarly date for the Exodus has been approximately one hundred years earlier, somewhere between 1250 and 1200 BC, proposed by the dean of Biblical archaeology William F. Albright (1891–1971).[35] Bietak did acknowledge that the evidence for four-room houses found at Luxor show buildings that differ slightly from most of the four-room houses in Canaan. He also acknowledged that evidence for such four-room houses that have been called "Israelite houses" have been found outside of the traditional area of residence of the Israelites. We have no evidence that Israelite workers or slaves resided in the four-room houses near Luxor or that they helped demolish the temple of Rameses III. Nonetheless, Halpern concluded that those parts of Exodus that can be dated to the last quarter of the twelfth century BC could have been composed at a time when "people who had participated in the Exodus" were still alive.[36] The present general view of the scholarship was expressed by Anne E. Killebrew in 2005 when she argued that one cannot attach

---

33. Manfred Bietak, "Israelites Found in Egypt," *Biblical Archaeology Review* 29 (September/October 2003): 40.

34. Bietak, "Israelites Found in Egypt," 44–45.

35. William F. Albright, "Archaeology and the Date of the Hebrew Conquest of Palestine," *Bulletin of the American Schools of Oriental Research* 58 (April 1935): 10–18.

36. Baruch Halpern, "Eyewitness Testimony: Parts of Exodus Written within Living Memory of the Event," *Biblical Archaeology Review* 29 (September/October 2003): 57.

any particular date or even date range to the Exodus because of lack of sufficient evidence.[37]

Traditional Literal and Figurative Criticism

The view of a number of Christian fundamentalists that every word of the Bible is literally true dates back only as far as the Reformation. At that time, reformers like John Calvin argued that "Any man . . . who would profit by the Scriptures, must hold first of all and firmly that the teaching of the law and the prophets came to us not by the will of man, but as dictated by the Holy Spirit."[38] Thus, as this argument has been continued by others, even the marks of punctuation in the Bible are sacred and inspired by God, while the human authors were merely mechanical recording secretaries. Previously, as long ago as the early third century, the Christian theologian Origen (ca. 185–254) had rejected such an interpretation. While accepting the proposition that much of the history and the law given in the Bible is to be accepted at face value, Origen recognized that "since there are certain passages of scripture [that] . . . have no bodily [literal] sense at all, there are occasions when we must seek only for the soul and the spirit, as it were, of the passage."[39]

This idea of seeking for the spirit of a passage led to extreme forms of symbolic interpretations. The passage where Moses throws down the tablets of the Ten Commandments when he sees the Israelites worshipping the golden calf has been interpreted, for example, as his symbolically breaking the covenant between the Israelites and Yahweh. Likewise, in regard to the passage cited above of Zipporah circumcising their son, the symbolists argue that because Moses was already circumcised (since he was raised as an Egyptian), she circumcised their son as a symbol of the renewal of the covenant with Yahweh. Thus, the bridegroom of blood has renewed the "marriage" contract between Yahweh and his people, just as Moses and Zipporah have renewed their contract by circumcising their son.[40]

---

37. Ann E. Killebrew, *Biblical Peoples and Ethnicity: An Archaeological Study of Egyptians, Canaanites Philistines, and Early Israel, 1300–1100 B.C.E.* (Atlanta: Society of Biblical Literature, 2005), 151–152.

38. *Calvin: Commentary*, trans. Joseph Haroutunian and Louise P. Smith (Philadelphia: Westminster, 1958), 84.

39. *Origen on First Principles*, trans. G. W. Butterworth (London: Society for Promoting Christian Knowledge, 1936), 277.

40. Jack M. Sasson, "Circumcision," in *Harper's Bible Dictionary*, ed. Paul J. Achtemeier (New York: HarperCollins, 2000), 185.

The Takeaway

While some reject the Bible as a reliable historical source, there are others who accept it but do so differently. For those who believe that the Bible can be used as a reliable historical source, there are at least three ways of approaching it: (1) it describes the events either figuratively or literally as they happened (Origen, Calvin); (2) it describes the events in an encoded form, so that the historian has to decode it by figuring out the natural phenomena that are underneath the apparently supernatural events being described (Freud, Barthel); and (3) it can be used as a reliable historical source for the time when it was written down but not for the events being described (Friedman, Bloom).

Although one still finds proponents of the idea that Moses authored the Pentateuch (Johnson) or at least that the idea should not be rejected that Moses was a possible author (Alexander), the evidence of the text, it seems to me, is better explained by different parts of it being composed by different authors over a long period (several hundred years) of time and long after the events being described occurred. Indeed, if one approached the text of the Pentateuch unaware of the long tradition of a single author, one would be hard put to come to that conclusion independently.

A number of the types of arguments in regard to the question of Moses's authorship of the Pentateuch appear in other controversies (as we will see). One notices, in particular, the close reading of the text to extract the last ounce of meaning out of it. One of the common characteristics of this ongoing debate is the non-acceptance of the traditional attribution based on someone at some time putting a name on the text—in this case, "book of Moses."

We will also see (in chapter 7 on Andrei Kurbskii) the argument that whatever the presumed author of the text could have written, he or she did. Whatever he or she could not have written merely represents a later interpolation and should not be used to determine authorship of the main text. In addition, establishing the date of the text is crucial for discussing authorship. Here one has to guard against dating the text to fit the life of a particular individual in order to claim that person is the author, which concern we will see in chapter 6 on William Shakespeare. In other words, one should not assume that because one thinks one knows who the author is, one can then use that assumption to date the text or any part of it. It is, of course, another matter if the identity of the author of a text is not in dispute.

CHAPTER 2

Who Wrote the *Analects*?

> "It is possible, of course, to pick up and read the
> *Analects* without concern for its pedigree, historical
> significance, or authorship . . . . Yet for many *Analects*
> readers past and present, both the authority and
> import of the text are tied to specific claims about its
> authorship and structure."
>
> —Tae Hyun Kim and Mark Csikszentmihalyi[1]

Chinese civilization developed along three main
river systems: Huanghe (Yellow River), Changjiang (Yangtze River), and Hsi-
jiang (West River). Until 221 BC, there were separate societies, cultures, and
political entities in the area drained by these rivers. This was not China as we
know it today. These societies had their own practices, customs, and religious
beliefs. Common to them, however, may have been some kind of abstract creation myth.

We have no reliable chronology before 827 BC. The dates of the various dynasties before then, some of which were thought to be mythical, are approximate (see table 2.1).

Nor do we have much in terms of historical narrative. *The Spring and Autumn Annals* covered only the state of Lu, one of the many separate political
entities of the time, and then only for 241 years, from 722 to 481 BC. The most
extensive narrative of early Chinese history belongs to the court historian Sima
Qian (Ssu-ma Ch'ien) (ca. 145–86 BC), who wrote *Records of the Grand Historian (Shiji)*. It covers a 2,500-year period down to 94 BC. According to Endymion Wilkinson's calculations, it has around 526,000 ideograms (Chinese
characters) originally written on bamboo strips (called slips) with 24 to 36

---

1. Tae Hyun Kim and Mark Csikszentmihalyi, "History and Formation of the *Analects*," in *Dao
Companion to the Analects*, ed. Amy Olberding (Dordrecht: Springer, 2013), 21.

Table 2.1   Early Chinese Dynasties

1. Xia (Hsia) (2205 [or 2005 or 1989] BC to 1766 [or 1784 or 1557] BC)

2. Shang (sometimes called Yin) (1557 [or 1784 or 1766 or 1523] BC to 1050 [or 1028 or 1022] BC)

3. Zhou (Chou) (1050 [or 1028 or 1022] BC to 256 BC)
    a. Early (or Western) Period (to 771 BC)
    b. Later (or Eastern) Period (771 to 256 [or 221] BC)
    (1) Spring and Autumn Period (771 to 481 [or 475 or 403] BC)
    (2) Age of Warring States (481 [or 475 or 403] to 221 BC)

4. Qin (Ch'in) (221 to 206 BC)

5. Han (206 BC to 221 BC)

    a. Western (or Former) Han (202 BC to A.D. 9)

    b. Eastern (or Later) Han (AD 23 to 220/1)

6. Xin (Hsin): Wang Mang (AD 9 to 23), "The Usurper"

ideograms per slip that were bound into between 466 and 700 bundles depending on how many characters were on a slip. The entire text of the *Records* is slightly longer than the translation of the Old Testament into Chinese (503,663 ideograms) by the London Missionary Society.[2]

Context of the Controversy

In contrast to Moses, little doubt has been expressed about whether Confucius (K'ung Fu-tzu or Kongzi) (551–479 BC) was a real person. In fact, according to the Guinness World Records, Confucius has the distinction of having the longest family tree of descendants, now reaching to eighty-six generations. Confucius was a philosopher during the time of Chinese history called "the Spring and Autumn period" (approximately 771–476 BC). This term derives from *The Spring and Autumn Annals*. During Confucius's time, the unity of the Zhou dynasty began to break down into competing warlord dominions, setting the stage for the "Warring States" period (475–221 BC) to follow. Confucius died at the end of the Spring and Autumn period and just before the beginning of the Warring States period.

The *Analects* (*Lunyu*) is a collection of 512 passages arranged in twenty chapters.[3] Around 80 percent of the passages describe what Confucius (the Master) said. For example, passage 1 of chapter 1: "The Master said, 'To learn and

---

2. Endymion Wilkinson, *Chinese History: A New Manual*, 5th ed. (Cambridge, MA: Harvard University Asia Center, 2012), 708.

3. Cheng Shude (程樹德), *Lunyu Jishi* (論語集釋) 4 vols. (1943; Beijing: Zhonghua Shuju,1990), is, according to Paul van Els, "probably the most complete modern, critical edition of the Analects" and is the edition that Edward Slingerland, among others, used to translate from the Chinese text. E-mail communication, September 12, 2019.

then have occasion to practice what you have learned—is this not satisfying? To have friends arrive from afar—is this not a joy? To be patient even when others do not understand—is this not the mark of a gentleman?'"[4] Other passages state they are by someone other than Confucius. For example, the very next passage, number 2, begins: "Master You said, 'A young person who is filial and respectful of his elders, rarely becomes the kind of person who is inclined to defy his superiors . . . .'" Master You (or You Ruo) (ca. 518–457 BC) was a disciple of Confucius, so it is unlikely here that Confucius was quoting from a scholar who lived earlier than him.

The *Analects* is one of the Four Books selected by the rationalist neo-Confucian philosopher Zhu Xi (1130–1200) during the Song dynasty (960–1279) for aspiring scholars to read in order to understand Confucian teachings better than the Five Classics. The other three books that Zhu Xi chose were: the *Great Learning*, a chapter from the *Book of Rites* and nine chapters of commentary by Zengzi (505–435 BC), a disciple of Confucius; the *Doctrine of the Mean*, attributed to Zisi (481–402 BC), the grandson of Confucius; and the *Mencius*, which contains lengthy discussions the philosopher Mencius (Mengzi; 385–303/2 BC or 372–289 BC) had with contemporary rulers. According to the American historian Daniel K. Gardner (b. 1950): "It was Zhu who was primarily responsible for giving the Four Books precedence over the once authoritative Five Classics."[5]

The Five Classics of Confucianism were traditionally ascribed to Confucius in the sense that he wrote some and edited others. The Five Classics are *Classic of Poetry* (a collection of poems, songs hymns, and eulogies), *Book of Documents* (official works and speeches attributed to rulers and officials of the early Zhou period), *Book of Rites* (court ceremonies and rituals), *I Ching* (*The Book of Changes*, a system of divination), and *The Spring and Autumn Annals* (thought at the time the Five Classics list was compiled to have been written by Confucius). Sometimes a lost sixth Classic, *Music*, is added to the list.

These texts became the basis for the famous Chinese examination system, which was established under the Sui dynasty (581–618) and ended only by the overthrow of the Qing dynasty (1644–1912). By any measure, these works had an enormous impact on Chinese history as well as on those countries (such as Korea) that adopted Confucianism from China. Since these texts influence Chinese society and culture, the question is, how much can any of their ideas

---

4. *Confucius Analects: With Selections from Traditional Commentaries*, trans. Edward Slingerland (Indianapolis: Hackett, 2003), 1, All quotations herein from the *Analects* use Slingerland's translation.

5. Daniel K. Gardner, *Zhu Xi's Reading of the* Analects: *Canon, Commentary, and the Classical Tradition* (New York: Columbia University Press, 2003), 2.

be dated back to Confucius himself? Here we look at only one of these texts in regard to this question.

In comparison with the *Records of the Grand Historian*, the received text of the *Analects* has only 3 percent as many ideographs, or around 16,000. The historian and politician Liu Xiang (77–6 BC) wrote that at the beginning of the Western Han dynasty two versions of the *Analects* were in existence of unequal length—the Lu version had twenty chapters and the Qi version had twenty-two chapters. Of those twenty chapters the two versions had in common, the Lu had more passages. The "received" text of the *Analects* is based on the twenty-chapter Lu version.

The standard narrative for how Confucianism became the state ideology of China is a remarkable story. In brief, it begins with virtual silence for hundreds of years following the death of Confucius. We have no evidence about Confucius or Confucianism until the Western Han dynasty, although Arthur Waley does mention one possible pre-Han reference, in the *Fang Chi*, to a text it calls the *Analects*.[6] The thinking is that the Confucianists suffered the same fate as other philosophical groups under the Qin dynasty (221–206 BC) with the infamous burning of the books in 213 BC. Shihuangdi (r. 221–210 BC), the first emperor, on the recommendation of his chief minister Li Si (280–208 BC), attempted to squash independent learning by destroying unauthorized treatises and killing those who refused to give them up.[7] After being almost wiped out, the Confucianists decided to modify their doctrine to emphasize obedience to the emperor as one of the Confucian relationships developing from filial piety (devotion to one's parents, elders, and ancestors). That decision eventually led to Confucianism becoming the state doctrine. Whether that was how it happened or not, the question all this raises for us is, how much of the Confucian literature was lost in the burning of the books of 213 BC? Some scholars have conjectured that only the sixth Classic, on music, was lost at that time. *The Book of Changes* was thought to have survived mostly intact because books of divination were exempted from the book burning. How did the book burning affect our version of the *Analects*? How much of it was written by that time? How much of it is accrual over the centuries? Was the *Analects* as we know it even in existence at that time to be burned?

---

6. Arthur Waley, "Introduction," *The Analects of Confucius*, ed. and annot. Arthur Waley (New York: Macmillan, 1938), 22–23. That involves the citation of only one passage, 2:11, from the *Analects*.

7. Li Si, "Memorial on the Burning of the Books," in *Sources of Chinese Tradition*, 2 vols., vol. 1 (New York: Columbia University Press, 1964), 140–141.

Into the Thicket

The oldest copies (albeit incomplete) of the *Analects* are two handwritten versions made on bamboo strips dated to the half century before Christ. The earliest known extant written copy of the *Analects*, the Dingzhou, has been dated to around 50 BC. It was discovered in 1973 in the tomb of a ruler of Zhongshan. The strips were damaged by a tomb fire, and this copy has only 7,576 ideographs on 620 bamboo strips or a little under half of the received text.[8] The second oldest written copy, the P'yŏngyang (also known as Lelang) *Analects*, was discovered in the early 1990s in North Korea. It dates to 45 BC when it was entombed with an official of the Lelang commandery. It could be older than that depending on how long it existed before then.[9] Neither a description nor publication of it has been made. What scholars outside of North Korea have are photos of thirty-nine bamboo strips. Before the discovery of the Dingzhou copy, the oldest known version was a carved stone copy written around AD 175 in Luoyang, the capital of the Eastern Han dynasty. The received text of the *Analects* is made up of 512 passages divided into twenty chapters (often called books in the scholarly literature). It seems unlikely that Confucius wrote these himself since most of them begin with (or have within them) the phrase "the Master said" or "the Master asked." Although it is not impossible that Confucius would have referred to himself in the third person, it seems more likely that someone else who recognized him as master wrote down the passages that are attributed to him. Of these passages, scholars have differed for almost 2,000 years on how many can be traced back to the time of Confucius himself.

Ban Gu (AD 32–92) was a Chinese politician, poet, and co-compiler of *The Book of Han* (*Hanshu*), a history of the early Han dynasty. He provided the seminal narrative for how it was thought the *Analects* was compiled. According to Ban, Confucius's disciples kept individual records of conversations each one had with Confucius. After Confucius's death, his disciples gathered the notes of their individual conversations together and jointly edited the resulting compilation.[10] The second-century Confucian scholar Zheng Xuan (AD 127–200) agreed with this opinion and specified the Confucian disciples Zhonggong (Ran Yong; 522 BC–?), Ziyou (Ran Qiu; 522 BC–?), and Zixia (Bu Shang; 507–420 BC) as the ones principally involved in the compilation.

---

8. Paul van Els, "Confucius's Sayings Entombed: On Two Han Dynasty Bamboo *Analects* Manuscripts," in *Confucius and the Analects Revisited: New Perspectives on the Dating on Dating, Composition, and Authorship*, ed. Michael Hunter and Martin Kern (Leiden: Brill, 2018), 158.

9. Van Els, "Confucius's Sayings Entombed," 165.

10. Andrew Zhongyu Yan, *An Existential Reading of the Confucian Analects* (Amherst, NY: Cambria, 2011), 10.

We do not have any evidence that Ban Gu's narrative was challenged until the Tang dynasty, when the poet and politician Liu Zongyuan (773–819) expressed the opinion that disciples of Zengzi compiled the *Analects*. The *Analects* has passages attributed to Zengzi shortly before his death, forty-four years after the death of Confucius. Liu Zongyuan argued that the *Analects* "must have been produced well after Confucius's time."[11] He doubted that any of the direct disciples of Confucius were still alive when the *Analects* was compiled. As part of his evidence, he pointed to the use of "style names" (courtesy names) for Confucius's disciples with the exception of Zengzi and Ziyou, who are addressed in the *Analects* as their own disciples would have addressed them. Indeed, more passages (twelve) are attributed to Zengzi in the *Analects* than to any other disciple of Confucius. Among the recent specialists on the *Analects* who have accepted Liu's argument for a date of compilation after Confucius's disciples had died are Roger T. Ames and Henry Rosemont Jr.,[12] Yang Bojun, Chen Daqi, and Benjamin Schwartz, while Andrew Zhonghu Yan has generally accepted the argument of Ban that Confucius's disciples compiled it.

During the Song dynasty (960–1279), the rationalist neo-Confucian philosopher Zhu Xi, following the theory of Ban Gu, asserted that the compilation of the *Analects* was the result of Confucius's pupils, who wrote his words down.[13] During the Qing dynasty (1644–1911), the writer and politician Cui Shu (1740–1816) accepted that chapters 1 through 15 were written down by Confucius's direct disciples, but proposed on a philological basis that the last five chapters that make up the *Analects* were written much later.[14] The Chinese sinologist and translator D. C. Lau (1921–2010) accepted Cui Shu's proposed division.[15] The Japanese Confucian scholar Itō Jinsai (1627–1705) proposed that chapters 11 through 20 were added later to the core of chapters 1 through 10. He did so, according to the American sinologist Michael Hunter, on the basis of a "different argumentative style, the relative length of its entries, and the inclusion of several numbered lists."[16]

---

11. Yan, *An Existential Reading*, 11.

12. Roger T. Ames and Henry Rosemont Jr., "Introduction," in *The Analects of Confucius: A Philosophical Translation* (New York: Random House, 1998).

13. Kim and Csikszentmihalyi, "History and Formation of the *Analects*," 26.

14. Bryan W. Van Norden, "Introduction," in *Confucius and the Analects: New Essays*, ed. Bryan W. Van Norden (Oxford: Oxford University Press, 2002), 13; Edward Slingerland, *Analects: With Selections from Traditional Commentaries* (Indianapolis: Hackett, 2003), xiii–xiv.

15. D. C. Lau, "Introduction," in *Confucius: The Analects (Lun yü)*, trans. D. C. Lau (London: Penguin, 1979), 12, 36.

16. Michael Hunter, *Confucius beyond the* Analects (Leiden: Brill, 2017), 6.

The British sinologist Arthur Waley (1889–1966), in the introduction to his translation of the *Analects*, wrote: "The contents of the book [the *Analects*] itself make clear that the compilation took place long after the Master's death."[17] He pointed out that chapter 8 has passages (numbers 3–7) of Zengzi "well into the second half of the fifth century,"[18] some forty-four years after Confucius died. Waley found that chapters 3 through 9 were more of a unit than chapters 1 and 2 and 10 through 20, which seemed to him to contain more miscellaneous content. According to him, chapters 10 ("a compilation of maxims from works on ritual") and 20 ("stray sentences from works of the *Shu Ching* type") "certainly have no intrinsic connexion with the rest." Chapter 19 "consists entirely of sayings by disciples." He considered all of chapter 18 and parts of chapters 14 and 17 to be "not Confucian in their origin, but have filtered into the book from the outside world, and from a world hostile to Confucius."

The idea that parts of the *Analects* are "hostile to Confucius" may seem paradoxical, but a comparison of those parts that Waley referred to with the rest of the *Analects* seems to bear him out on this point. In Waley's view, chapter 16 "contains nothing characteristic of the milieu that produced" his preferred core section, chapters 3 through 9. Because of this perception that various chapters of the *Analects* are "late," Waley accepted what he called "the ordinarily accepted date of the book," by which he meant "accepted by scholars as the date of the material contained in the book," not "the date of its compilation [which] may well be later."[19] That "accepted by scholars" date is the middle of the fourth century BC. He did single out one passage, 13:3, which he considered even later than that—namely, the end of the fourth century BC.[20] For Waley, it was those middle chapters that he supposed "represent[ed] the oldest stratum."[21] In writing about the historical Confucius, Waley focused on what he called "the Confucius of the *Analects*" although he acknowledged that "one could construct half a dozen other Confuciuses by tapping the legend at different stages of its evolution."[22]

In 1997, Lionel M. Jensen raised the question whether the image of Confucius the man that has been the standard view for the last four or five centuries accurately represents the historical figure who is connected with the *Analects*. He decided that the image bears no relationship to that historical figure.[23]

---

17. Waley, "Introduction," 21.
18. Waley, "Introduction," 21.
19. Waley, "Introduction," 21, n. 2.
20. Waley, "Introduction," 21–22.
21. Waley, "Introduction," 21.
22. Waley, "Introduction," 13.
23. Lionel M. Jensen, *Manufacturing Confucianism: Chinese Traditions and Universal Civilization* (Durham, NC: Duke University Press, 1997).

The Chinese-American scholar Alice M. Cheang contrasted the view expressed by Jensen with that of E. Bruce Brooks. I quote it here at some length to make a point:

> Jensen . . . states the even more radical position that (irrespective of whether there was an historical Confucius, whose existence Jensen does not contest but regards as beside the point) the Confucius we know—as reconstituted in the minds of posterity—is a trope, a rhetorical figure over which successive generations have hung the drapery of their own fabrications. But finally there is a world of difference between their two positions. Brooks holds that there is not much of the historical Confucius in the *Analects*, not that there is none, nor by any means that the historical Confucius is irrelevant to the study of the formation of Confucianism. Far from it, Confucius of Book IV—Brooks's "real" Confucius—determines the form and sets the moral tone of the whole text of the *Analects*.[24]

But Cheang's comparison may be a faulty one since Jensen is referring to how the view of Confucius has changed as the result of European influence, not when the text was written or how much of it can be attributed to Confucius.

In 1998, E. Bruce Brooks and A. Taeko Brooks published a book on the *Analects*, which, although it found little support for the theory proposed in it, did receive praise for the scholarship on display in it. It also raised the discussion of the composition of the *Analects* to a deeper level of intensity. We will encounter a similar phenomenon in subsequent chapters on other authorship controversies.

Brooks and Brooks are the most parsimonious in attributing parts of the *Analects* to Confucius, citing only 16 (IV.1–14 and IV.16–17) passages of chapter 4 as his. They assert that the *Analects* is "a series of texts of different date," and that it is best to read the *Analects* as a "history of early Confucianism, compiled from year to year by the Confucians of Lǔ," a Confucian school.[25] They present the following chronological arrangement of chapters: 4–11, 3, 12–13, 2, 14–15, 1, 16–20. The suggested dates of composition range from 479 to 249 BC.

The Brookses point out that the library catalog of the Han palace lists three copies of the *Analects*: the Lu copy with twenty chapters, the Qi copy with twenty-two chapters, and the old-script copy with twenty-one chapters. They infer that there was no extra material in the old-script version, just a division

---

24. Alice M. Cheang, "'The Master's Voice: On Reading, Translating and Interpreting the *Analects* of Confucius," *Review of Politics* 62, no. 3 (Summer 2000): 575–576, n. 12.

25. E. Bruce Brooks and A. Taeo Brooks, *The Original Analects: Sayings of Confucius and His Successors* (New York: Columbia University Press, 1998), 1.

of chapter 19 into two chapters.[26] For them, the Qi copy probably did contain two extra chapters because the titles of those two chapters in the catalog ("Asking about Kingship" and "Knowing the Way") do not have a correspondence to the material in the Lu copy. The two extra chapters are for them additional evidence that the *Analects* was continuing to be added to. That may be so, but it leaves unanswered the question why those two chapters did not become part of the received text of the *Analects*.

The Brookses take a structuralist approach in discussing the text and which passages were interpolations and which were original with each chapter. They accepted the observation of previous scholars that there seem to be "close relations between specific pairs of Analects sayings" such that "each saying relates through one link to the preceding saying, and through another to the following saying."[27] They elevated the presence of such pairs as a central feature that "characterizes *the entire text*" [italics in original].[28] As such, the passages where the Brookses perceived those pairs constitute the background matrix of the text; where they perceive no linkage with the passage that precedes or follows it, those passages constitute "disruptive interpolated sayings." They do acknowledge, however, that the linkage of a pair can "often be based on trivial features."[29]

Interpolations within each chapter would seem to undercut the Brookses' theory that accretions to the *Analects* occurred only by chapter on average every so-many years. They do not see that as a problem because of their positing of the "twenty-four passage" norm. According to them, every chapter (except for chapters 4, 8, and 20) initially had twenty-four passages, each passage linked to the one preceding it and to the one following it. Chapters 4 and 8, which initially had fewer than twenty-four passages, experienced interpolations designed to reach the twenty-four-passage norm. In the case of chapters 1 and 16, which have only sixteen and fourteen passages, respectively, they hypothesize that originally, each contained only twelve passages and that "they may be an intentional halving of the then normal 24 passage form."[30]

In evaluating what the Brookses have proposed, Cheang wrote:

> The implications of their initial premise are radical: if it can be shown that practically all of the *Analects*—as many as nineteen books out of twenty—do not actually come from Confucius himself, then the persona

26. Brooks and Brooks, *The Original Analects*, 202.
27. Brooks and Brooks, *The Original Analects*, 201.
28. Brooks and Brooks, *The Original Analects*, 207.
29. Brooks and Brooks, *The Original Analects*, 207.
30. Brooks and Brooks, *The Original Analects*, 248.

of Confucius in the text is . . . a literary invention, a device in whose mouth the thoughts of others have been put in order to give them greater authority. *Tuoyan*—attribution to a well-known figure—is a common practice in early Chinese texts, so the supposition is not intrinsically unreasonable. What this means, however, is the relation between the historical and the literary Confucius, as revealed by the reconstructive work of Brooks, is so attenuated as to be virtually nonexistent.[31]

The question can as a result be asked: if what the Brookses propose and others to a lesser extent have surmised, then were the accretions intended to deceive the reader into thinking they were spoken by Confucius? Apparently not, since care seems to be taken to attribute the author of each passage. Should the author of the *Analects* be designated the "school of Confucius" similar to the way much of European late medieval and Renaissance art is attributed to "the school of . . ."? But doing so may be not entirely accurate since we do not know if there was any such school in a unified sense before the Han dynasty. Even if there were such a school, would the members of that school be scrupulous about guarding against oral transmissions getting into the text?

In a review of *The Original Analects*, the specialist on ancient comparative literature David C. Schaberg raised a number of methodological points that might be pertinent for the field of authorship studies in general. He attacked as "faulty" what he saw as six premises that the Brookses base their claims on: "To be shown what Brooks and Brooks have promised to show, one must accept the following premises, all of them faulty." I will discuss only five of those premises here as relevant for our concerns in this chapter. Those premises, according to Schaberg, are: (1) "that ancient Chinese texts grew like trees, and can be dated by a variety of textual dendrochronology"; (2) "the use of evidence—linguistic, statistical, historical, and other—as symptom, with the most sweeping diagnoses made on the basis of near invisible or nonexistent evidence"; (3) "that every saying in the *Lunyu* was invented, transcribed, and incorporated into the work in the time it took to add one chapter"; (4) "a novel view of the internal structuring of *Lunyu* chapters"; and (5) "tendentious, largely unsupported dating of other early Chinese texts."[32]

The first premise that Schaberg described—the dendrochronology one—may or may not be faulty in regard to Chinese texts in general but could be so for a particular Chinese text such as the *Analects*. My own work with Rus'

---

31. Cheang, "The Master's Voice," 575.

32. David Schaberg, "'Sell It! Sell It!': Recent Translations of *Lunyu*," *Chinese Literature: Essays, Articles, Reviews* 23 (2001): 133–137. The sixth premise that Schaberg cited concerns transliterating from Chinese into the Latin alphabet.

chronicles and saints' lives does lead me to think that a tree-ring-like accretion in these texts occurred, and that one can approximately date when an addition was made to their base narratives. And, in many cases, spoken words attributed to a historical figure are part of these accretions.

But not all texts lend themselves to the same kind of dating technique. As Schaberg stated elsewhere in the same review, instead of treating the text "as a timeless medium, Brooks and Brooks make historicizing the *Lunyu* an end in itself, and far surpass any previous scholar in the minuteness and confidence with which they date individual books and individual passages of the work."[33] Their doing so is not inherently faulty, and in fact challenges other scholars to refute their claims with equal erudition. The Asianist Edward Slingerland wrote that even though their book "fails to substantiate most of its more radical claims, it performs an invaluable service by forcing scholars of the text to take seriously the fact that the *Analects* is a heterogeneous collection of writings representing different time periods and a variety of concerns." He went on to write that those who study Confucianism have known of the heterogeneous nature of the *Analects* but have tended to pay it only lip service as they go on to present its text as a unified whole.[34] What Slingerland is referring to is a phenomenon that one encounters by those who would like to discount authorship studies—that it does not matter who wrote any particular text because of its "timeless" nature (see the introduction).

The second premise that Schaberg cited—the use of evidence as symptom—is shown, according to him, in their discussion of "linguistic features" that indicate whether a passage derived from the time of Confucius or was an interpolation made later. Among their assertions is that *si* (in *pinyin* transcription), the Chinese word for *then*, is a sign of antiquity of a passage. Thus, it does not appear in 4:18–25, which along with other historical linguistic features, "tends to confirm a later date for 4:18–25, leaving the sixteen sayings of 4:1–14 plus 4:16–17 as the probable nucleus."[35] But, as Schaberg pointed out, it does appear twice in the passage 4:26, which is attributed to Ziyou, and which the Brookses have declared a later accretion. In short, Schaberg suggested that their formulations of Chinese historical linguistics are to a certain extent manufactured to reach certain conclusions about the various accretions and when they occurred.

The third premise—that accretions were made on a chapter-by-chapter basis—also involves the assumption, according to Schaberg, that those chapters

---

33. Schaberg, "Sell It! Sell It!" 131.

34. Edward Slingerland, "Why Philosophy Is Not 'Extra' in Understanding the *Analects*," *Philosophy East and West* 50, no. 1 (January 2000): 137.

35. Brooks and Brooks, *The Original Analects*, 204.

were added by "the 'head' of the unitary 'school,' whose views are supposed to be represented in the chapters dated to his tenure."[36] This assumption excludes "oral transmission" and "like some other assumptions, this one is neither acknowledged nor discussed, and in several respects defies logic." In Schaberg's view, "the structure of the school(s) is not nearly as well understood as Brooks and Brooks imply, and if there ever was a single paramount leader, it is by no means certain that he exercised the authority to alter the putative proto-*Lunyu* at will." The implication of Schaberg's criticism, like his criticism of their use of historical linguistics, is that the Brookses misrepresent the contextual evidence to appear more certain than it is in order to support their theory about how the *Analects* was compiled: "Since much of the point of *The Original Analects* is to identify 'interpolations' (usually on the basis of the faintest hint of external historical evidence, or on the basis of the faulty assumptions already examined), the notion that one generation might write down a saying learned from a previous generation is fatal to the whole project."[37]

In discussing the fourth premise—an unusual understanding of the *Analects'* internal structure—Schaberg referenced a review article by the intellectual historian John Makeham. In that article, Makeham provided a list of what he considered to be questionable pairings by the Brookses. Makeham concluded: "[T]heir rigid commitment to pairing as a pervasive structural feature compels them to make forced and subjective links between passages." He found "no consistency in the way pairing is used to structure the *Lun yu* text . . . . [and that,] as a general principle, pairing per se cannot be appealed to as justification for identifying interpolation."[38] Schaberg questioned "the silent continuation of a compositional practice over nine generations and 19 very diverse" chapters. Not wishing to go as far as Makeham in denying pairings altogether as a structural practice throughout the *Analects*, Schaberg wondered why the Brookses did not just state where they think they found such pairings and leave the rest of the text as indeterminate in that regard. The answer is the Brookses' structuralist approach requires a structure. That structure can be an ideal type that mostly explains the bulk of the evidence but not necessarily all the evidence.

For the fifth premise—tendentious dating of early Chinese texts—Schaberg criticized their "checklist of texts" for "not bother[ing] to cite alternative views, or even to hint at the complexities of dating issues."[39] The result, according

36. Schaberg, "Sell It! Sell It!" 136.

37. Schaberg, "Sell It! Sell It!" 136.

38. John Makeham, review of *The Original Analects: Sayings of Confucius and His Successors*, by E. Bruce Brooks and A. Takeo Brooks, in *China Review International* 6, no. 1 (1999): 9.

39. Schaberg, "Sell It! Sell It!" 137.

to Schaberg, is that readers will think either that these issues were resolved long ago or that the Brookses have resolved them themselves, neither of which is the case. At the very least, they could have supplied more evidence for their datings. Insofar as that is the case, the Brookses, and any scholars that do so, leave themselves open to questioning whether they assigned dates to the texts that are convenient for their argument.

Paul van Els, noting that the earliest copies of the *Analects* date to around 50 BC and also noting similarities in the calligraphic style of other manuscripts from roughly the same period, questioned the assertion that "the *Analects* was created within a hundred years after Confucius' death" because such "claims . . . are scarcely ever supported by evidence, let alone evidence from archaeological finds."[40] His point is an important one because if sayings can be misattributed to Confucius, they can also be misattributed to his disciples. In other words, one would have to take, to a certain extent, the text of the *Analects* at face value in terms what disciples like Zengzi said. But those sayings could have been added at any time before the archaeographic evidence of the earliest extant copies. The Zengzi sayings do not necessarily need to have been added by his disciples, as Liu Zongyuan proposed. They could have been added or even the entire text composed anytime between 445 and 50 BC. The rest is mostly conjecture.

The scholarship seems to be in agreement that the *Analects* is an accretion text, but what exactly does that mean? The American sinologist Robert Eno (b. 1949), in discussing the *Analects* as an accretion text, defined *accretion* as "texts that are the products both of multiple authors and of multistage redaction processes."[41] Eno based his definition on the Bible, which he called "the classic model of an accretion text." In particular, he noted the documentary hypothesis as applied to the Pentateuch, which posits "a network of interwoven passages from a variety of sources, thus explaining a variety of inconsistencies and redundancies that had long puzzled close readers of the Hebrew Bible."[42] Technically, what Eno is describing is closer to the fragmentary hypothesis, but the point he is making is an important one for authorship studies in general. As Eno pointed out, there are different types of accretion texts—one in which a single author adds over the course of time to a text he or she wrote earlier, another in which a second author adds to another author's text. A third type of accretion text is the Rus' chronicles, in which scribal editors add on to a text to create a new redaction. In contrast to the Pentateuch

---

40. Van Els, "Confucius's Sayings Entombed," 173.

41. Robert Eno, "The *Lunyu* as an Accretion Text," in *Confucius and the* Analects *Revisited*, ed. Michael Hunter and Martin Kern (Leiden: Brill, 2018), 40.

42. Eno, "The *Lunyu* as an Accretion Text," 41.

and the *Analects*, however, previous redactions continue to exist, so that the investigator can see the various stages of the accretion process.[43] In the case of the Pentateuch and the *Analects*, we have more or less only the end product—that is, the final redaction. We do not have the luxury of being able to consult the earlier versions of the text during the process of accretion.

Let us return to the questions I raised at the end of the "Context of the Controversy" section. If the *Analects* is an accretion text in the sense of being added to over the course of time by multiple individuals, then at what point did it assume more or less the received text that we now have? When did it become a stand-alone text in its own right in contrast to a bunch of random sayings attached in one way or another to Confucius? The present scholarship opts for the period of the Western (or Former) Han dynasty (202 BC–9 AD) as when that coalescing occurred. The earliest copy of what is presumed at one time to have been a complete version of the *Analects* dates to 50 BC. Is there compelling evidence of a complete version before then? The answer, somewhat surprisingly, seems to be no.

Makeham provides an example, which I cite here to indicate to the reader some of the complexity of trying to establish any pre-Han dynasty references that would indicate a familiarity with any text or oral tradition that we could consider to be the sayings of Confucius. One extended passage in *Mencius* has been seen as providing evidence of familiarity with the *Analects*:

> Kongzi said, "I hate things that appear to be something but are not. I hate the false millet, because I fear it could confound the sprouts. I hate the flatterers, because I fear they could confound duty. I hate the sharp-tongued, because I fear they could confound trustworthiness. I hate the tune of Zheng, because I fear they could confound the music. I hate the lilac, because I fear it could confound the vermillion. I hate the honest countryman, because I fear he could confound virtue."

This passage seems to correspond in part to four different sayings in the *Analects*:

> 9:22 "The Master said, 'Surely there are some sprouts that fail to flower, just as surely as there are some flowers that fail to bear fruit.'"
> 9:25 "The Master said, 'Let your actions be governed by dutifulness and trustworthiness, and do not accept as a friend one who is not your

---

43. I discuss the layers of accretion in the Rus' chronicles in regard to the battle at Lake Chud in 1242. See Donald Ostrowski, "Alexander Nevskii's 'Battle on the Ice': The Creation of a Legend," *Russian History* 33, nos. 2, 3, 4 (Summer/Fall/Winter 2006): 289–312.

equal. If you have committed a transgression, do not be afraid to change your ways.'"

17:18 "The Master said, 'I hate that purple has usurped the place of vermillion, that the tunes of Zheng have been confused with classical music, and that the clever of tongue have undermined both state and family.'"

17:13 "The Master said, 'The village worthy are thieves of virtue.'"

Makeham questioned the "very large leap of faith" that sees the sayings in the *Mencius* as deriving from a complete *Analects*: "We simply have no idea what sort of Confucius sayings the editors/authors of the *Mencius* had at their disposable; what was the provenance and format of those sayings; or even if they were written or orally transmitted." Instead, he laid out two other possibilities that he sees as "just as plausible: that the received *Lunyu* drew on the *Mencius* or that both the received *Lunyu* and *Mencius* drew from a third source of Confucius sayings."[44] Makeham noted Hunter's proposing "a third possibility: that some *Lunyu* parallels were added to the *Mengzi* at some point in the Han after the compilation and circulation of the *Lunyu*."[45]

Recently, the consensus view that the *Analects* is an accretion text received a scholarly challenge. In 2017, after an exhaustive search for and analysis of pre-Han parallel passages and references to a possible *Analects* (*Lunyu*) text, Hunter concluded that the *Analects* "as a bounded collection of Kongzi [Confucius] material took the stage no earlier than the reign of Emperor Wu [r. 156–87 BC] or thereabouts."[46] Earlier, in his PhD dissertation completed in 2012, Hunter was a bit more specific within that time frame: "Based on a reverse chronological survey of Confucius quotation practice in the early period. I conclude the chapter with the argument that the Analects was compiled between the 150s and 130s BC."[47] He found no attestation to a *Lunyu* text before the Western Han, although some attestations were constructed to appear that there was a pre-Han "backstory."[48] Hunter rejected the accretion theory for the compilation of the text: "Accretion models have to jump through too many methodological hoops to furnish reliable evidence of the *Lunyu's* chronology."[49]

---

44. Makeham, "Chinese Perspectives," 22.

45. Makeham, "Chinese Perspectives," 22, n. 11, citing Michael Hunter, "Did Mencius Know the *Analects*?" *T'oung Pao* 100, nos. 1, 3 (2014): 38–42.

46. Hunter, *Confucius beyond the* Analects, 245.

47. Michael Hunter, "Sayings of Confucius Deselected" (PhD diss., Princeton University, 2012).

48. Michael Hunter, "Did Mencius Know the *Analects*?" *T'oung Pao* 100, nos. 1, 3 (2014): 12.

49. Michael Hunter, "The Lunyu as a Western Han Text," in *Confucius and the* Analects *Revisited*, ed. Michael Hunter and Martin Kern (Leiden: Brill, 2018), 82.

If Hunter is right, then it means that at the time of the burning of the books in 213 BC, there was probably no *Analects* to burn. One cannot help but notice that this timeline for the compilation of the *Analects* correlates with the narrative construct that Confucianists revamped their ideas to be more emperor-friendly in response to the burning of the books. Finally, the assumption since Ban proposed how it was compiled has been that the *Analects* is an accretion text. Yet if we cannot know when it was compiled before references to it start appearing in the time of Emperor Wu, then there may not have been any text to accrete to. It may have been a text compiled at one time by a single compiler in the latter half of the second century or early half of the first century BC.

The Takeaway

Although it is possible that the sayings of Confucius were at least in part written down or passed on orally by his disciples and/or disciples of his disciples, we do not have direct evidence to make that assertion with any degree of certainty. And we have even a lower degree of probability that the sayings were bundled together into anything that resembles the sayings of Confucius. The extent to which those sayings that appear in the received text of the *Analects* can be directly attributed to Confucius, or even to the time of Confucius, is in dispute.

Cheang mentioned the practice of *tuoyan* (words ascribed to) as a practice that may have occurred in the *Analects*. In response to my e-mail query, van Els wrote: "The usage of this term is at least two thousand years old. For example, Ban Gu uses it in the 'Yiwenzhi' section of his *Hanshu.*" Furthermore, explained van Els, it is not clear whether the ascription in all cases was meant to be believed. Yet, "by the time of the Western Han dynasty, this was an identifiable practice. The *Zhuangzi* has a special term for it, namely, 'imputed words' (yuyan 寓言), which refers to fictional characters 'brought in from outside for the purpose of exposition.'"[50] He then quoted from the *Huainanzi*[51] showing that this practice was to be rejected:

---

50. Paul van Els, *The Wenzi: Creativity and Intertextuality in Early Chinese Philosophy* (Leiden: Brill, 2018), 58. The quotation within van Els's quotation is from *The Complete Works of Chuang Tzu*, trans. Burton Watson (New York: Columbia University Press, 1968), 303.

51. The *Huainanzi* is a collection of essays that derived from debates on various topics held at the court of the king of Huianan (lands south of the Huia). It was probably compiled before 139 BC because the *Hanshu*, written by Ban Gu and Ban Zhao, as well as *The Records of the Grand Historian* by Sima Qian, tell of the giving of a presentation copy of the *Huainanzi* to the Emperor Wu in that year by his uncle Liu An, the king of Huianan.

Men of worldly customs often esteem the past and despise the present. Accordingly, those who expound on the Way must place their theories in the mouth of the Divine Farmer or the Yellow Emperor, before they may enter the discourse. Ignorant rulers in chaotic times are greatly removed from their roots, and they just go along with such texts and honor them. Those engaged in learning are confused by their arguments, as they honor whatever comes to their ears. Sitting down together, they praise such texts.

According to van Els: "This passage suggests that texts ascribed to others must be of mediocre quality. They are not praised because of an inherent quality, but because they were supposedly written by ancient luminaries. This passage shows that the practice indeed existed and that, even though the *Huainanzi* realized what was going on, less intelligent readers (at least according to the *Huainanzi*) believed the texts to have been actually written by their ascribed authors."[52]

The question is, in regard to the *Analects* (no matter whether one accepts the Brookses' stringent limitation of sayings in part of chapter 4 of the *Analects* to the time of Confucius), how much was the ascription of other passages to Confucius in the sense of someone's trying to pass off their own thoughts as those of Confucius (intent to deceive)? And how much did that person believe that Confucius had actually said those things or felt it was understood that Confucius did not really say those things but that they were in the spirit of his teachings (with no intention to deceive)? If one concludes that it was probably a mixture of both—that is, some passages were attributed to Confucius with intent to deceive, while others were not intended to deceive—then how does one determine which is which? To provide a sense of the problem, the number of passages ascribed directly to "the Master" or to "Confucius" in each chapter of the *Analects* is:

Chapter 1: 9 passages (of 16)
Chapter 2: 24 passages (of 24)
Chapter 3: 25 passages (of 26)
Chapter 4: 25 passages (of 26) [16 of those are the Brookses's core Confucius]
Chapter 5: 26 passages (of 28)
Chapter 6: 27 passages (of 30)
Chapter 7: 28 passages (of 38)
Chapter 8: 16 passages (of 21)

---

52. Paul van Els, e-mail, January 14, 2019.

Chapter 9: 29 passages (of 31)
Chapter 10: 4 passages (of 27)
Chapter 11: 23 passages (of 26)
Chapter 12: 20 passages (of 24)
Chapter 13: 30 passages (of 30)
Chapter 14: 42 passages (of 44)
Chapter 15: 42 passages (of 42)
Chapter 16: 12 passages (of 14)
Chapter 17: 25 passages (of 26)
Chapter 18: 4 passages (of 11)
Chapter 19: 0 passages (of 25)
Chapter 20: 2 passages (of 3)
Total = 413 passages (of 512)

That means a little over 80.7 percent of the passages have sayings attributed directly to Confucius. Other sayings in the *Analects* are attributed to other masters who had been disciples of Confucius. For example, chapter 1, passage 9 reads: "Master Zeng said, 'Take great care in seeing off the deceased and sedulously maintain the sacrifices to your distant ancestors, and the common people will sincerely return to Virtue.'" Still other passages just describe what Confucius did or was like. For example, chapter 7, passage 38 reads: "The Master was affable yet firm, awe-inspiring without being severe, simultaneously respectful and relaxed." These passages were presumably not spoken or written by Confucius. In addition, the Brookses conclude that only 16, or 3.9 percent, of those 413 sayings attributed to Confucius can be dated to the time of Confucius (or 3.1 percent of the overall text of the *Analects*).

Unlike with Muhammad whose pronouncements were written down (or at least gathered) after his death, to no one else other than Allah are the *sura* of the Qur'an attributed. There are, however, *hadith* that are supposedly statements that Muhammad could have made, but they are given varying degrees of authenticity depending on the chain of attribution (*silsillah*). With the *Analects* it is possible and certainly has been claimed that sayings attributed to Confucius were not his. If Confucius were alive today, he would no doubt have echoed Yogi Berra's comment, "I really didn't say all the things I said." The sayings of Jesus (called "Q" by biblical scholars) do show up in the Gospels, or at least there are direct quotations that are attributed to him. But none of the Gospels can be demonstrated to have been written down by the disciple whose name is attached to it. Nonetheless, the leaders of the early Christian Church, by declaring certain works canonical, affirmed their belief that Jesus indeed said those words ascribed to him.

If there was an oral tradition of Jesus's sayings, we can suppose there probably was a similar tradition of oral sayings attributed to Confucius and Muhammad. Then the writing down of this oral tradition was done following different paths in regard to Confucius, Jesus, and Muhammad. With Confucius, what were regarded as his sayings become the core of a work, the *Analects*, which includes the sayings of other masters as well as descriptions about him. The question in the scholarship now is, was there was a process of gradual accretion, whether in a discernible dendrochronological way or not, over centuries or was the entire text composed at a discrete point in time. With Jesus, the Church's establishing an official canon by the third century sealed the words attributed to Jesus in the Gospels of Matthew, Mark, Luke, and John as canonical, while words attributed to Jesus in other texts, such as the Gnostic Gospels, were not. With Muhammad, the *sura* of the Qur'an are canonical words spoken by Muhammad but only in the sense that he was channeling Allah. Other words attributed to Muhammad are given varying degrees of probability in the *hadith* of actually having been spoken by him.

These issues of intentionality arise in other authorship controversies further along in this book.

CHAPTER 3

Who Wrote the Secret Gospel of Mark?

> "The labyrinth of the 'Secret' Mark debate, a maze into which many have ventured and few returned."[1]
>
> —Robert Conner

A brief introduction to New Testament studies will help us get to the controversy that is involved here. The four Gospels of the New Testament—Matthew, Mark, Luke, and John—have an intertwined textual relationship to each other. Both Matthew and Luke are textually close to Mark. As a result of the similarity (containing the same stories in generally the same order), these three have been designated the synoptic (Greek: σύν [syn., "together"] and ὄψις [opsis, "view"]). The Gospel of John appears to pick up information from Matthew and Luke and tells many of the same stories, but it is more different from each of them than they are from each other. The current thinking is that the Gospels with the names Matthew, Mark, Luke, and John attached to them were not actually written by the respective apostles Matthew, Mark, Luke, and John, but were written in a tradition that whether true or not was attributed to that particular apostle. They are associated with places where those apostles had been. For example, the Gospel of Matthew is associated with Rome; the Gospel of Mark, with Alexandria; and the Gospel of Luke, with Damascus. For centuries, biblical scholars considered Matthew to be the earliest of the Gospels, in part because it seemed the fullest. Over the course of the last 250 years, scholars, with few exceptions,

---

1. Robert Conner, *The Secret Gospel of Mark: Morton Smith, Clement of Alexandria and Four Decades of Academic Burlesque* (Oxford: Mandrake of Oxford, 2015), 7.

have come to the realization that Mark is the earliest of the four canonical Gospels, that Matthew and Luke derive from it, and that John derives from Matthew and Luke. That growing realization coincided with the growing acceptance in textual criticism that the shorter readings tend to be earlier.

Scholars noticed that about 600 of the 661 verses of Mark also appear in Matthew, not always in the exact same wording but similar enough in form. Luke shares 350 of the 661 verses of Mark. One could say that Matthew has a closer textual relationship with Mark than Luke does. But Matthew and Luke contain 200 verses in common that are not found in Mark. So where did the writers of Matthew and Luke get these in-common verses from if they did not get them from Mark or from one another? If the canonical Gospels are written forms of an oral tradition that had developed during the forty or so years after the death of Jesus (ca. AD 32) and the probable date that Mark was written down (ca. AD 75), then the minor differences in the form of the verses they have in common could be explained. That thinking led to the positing of a source that no longer exists and might never have been written down, called *Quelle* (which means *source* in German because German scholars first proposed it). It is usually abbreviated to Q. The scholarship then diverges. In one view (the "two-source hypothesis"), both Q and Mark were the basis for Luke and Matthew independently. In another view (the "three-source hypothesis"), Mark also drew on Q. Some scholars have disputed whether Q was a single source or several sources that contained the sayings of Jesus. The view that it was a single source has led some scholars to attempt to reconstruct it, whereas other scholars consider such attempts to be futile since they understand Q to represent an oral tradition that was not unified.

In addition, the early Christian Church considered a substantial number of writings by early Christians to be noncanonical. The noncanonical Christian writings can be divided into two categories—those the Church considered useful or instructive and those it did not. Early churchmen called the first category "apocryphal," which derives from the Greek word ἀπόκρυφος (from ἀπο "away" and κρυπτειν "to hide"). Although one finds that Gnostic gospels are now often referred to in the scholarly literature as "apocryphal" in the sense of being of doubtful authenticity, early churchmen would not have called them that. Apocryphal Christian writings include Infancy gospels (those written from the second century on about the childhood of Jesus), Jewish-Christian gospels (which are known only from quotations excerpted from them by Church fathers), noncanonical gospels (which date from the mid-second century to the third century), sayings of Jesus gospels (which have no narrative, such as the Gospel of Thomas), Passion gospels (which focus on the events immediately surrounding the crucifixion of Jesus), acts of specific apostles (such as Andrew, Barnabas, Paul, and Peter), Gnostic texts (considered to be non-Orthodox by the early Church), and so forth. The relationship between these noncanonical Christian writings and the canonical ones is not always clear, since an otherwise member in good standing of the early Church might still hold the ideas expressed in these apocrypha as legitimate expressions of orthodox belief.

Into this mix comes a letter purportedly written by Clement of Alexandria (d. 150–ca. 215) but not known to the scholarly community until 1958. In that letter Clement includes two excerpts from the Gospel of Mark that are not in the canonical Gospel. If this letter is authentic and the quotation extracts in it are authentic as well, then the question becomes, how does it affect the scholarly understanding of the relationship of early Christian texts in general and of the Gospels in particular? If it is not authentic (i.e., not written by Clement), then is it a forgery (i.e., intended to deceive) or merely a textbook exercise (i.e., not intended to deceive)? If it is a forgery, then what does it tell us about who forged it? Those who believe that the letter is a forgery have focused on the person who says he discovered the letter in 1958—Morton Smith (1915–1991), professor of ancient history at Columbia University.

Context

As Smith described it, when he was a graduate student in 1941 he first visited the Mar Saba monastery, nineteen kilometers to the southeast of Jerusalem. He spent some three months there living the life of the monks. World War II marooned him in Palestine, so he used the time to study at the Hebrew University in Jerusalem, receiving his PhD in Hebrew in 1948. Ten years later, he returned to Mar Saba looking for manuscripts in the library. At that time, again according to his own account, he found on the endpapers of a seventeenth-century printed edition of the letters of Ignatius of Antioch (ca. 35–ca. 108) two-and-a-half pages of a handwritten text in Greek. The handwriting appeared to be of the eighteenth century. The heading of the letter claims that it was "From the letters of the Most Holy Clement of the *Stromateis*."[2] The work *Stromateis* (*Miscellanies*) is the third volume of the three-volume work

---

2. I am using here the translation by Robert Connor rather than the one given by Smith, for two reasons: (1) in Connor's version the phrasing is more accessible to the general reader and (2) doing so will help to neutralize any notions that I am merely accepting Smith's interpretation of the Greek. "The Letter to Theodore," in Connor, *The Secret Gospel of Mark*, 21–29 (I have eliminated the italics that Connor added); cf. "Transcription of Text," in Morton Smith, *Clement of Alexandria and a Secret Gospel of Mark* (Cambridge, MA: Harvard University Press, 1973), 446–447.

of Church father Clement of Alexandria (Titus Flavus Clemens) on the Christian life and the proper observance of it. The next line of the letter provides the salutation "To Theodore," who appears to be a disciple of Clement.

In the letter, Clement tells Theodore that there are secret parts of the Gospel of Mark, but the information that the Carpocratians told him about those secret parts is incorrect. Clement then cites two of the passages from the Secret Gospel. Clement tells Theodore that he "did well to silence the unmentionable teachings of the Carpocratians" for they have "stray[ed] from the narrow path of the commandments toward the bottomless pit of sins of the flesh embodied . . . ."[3] In regard to what the Carpocratians say about the Gospel of Mark, Clement writes that "some are complete lies, and others, even if they contain some truth, are not accurately represented, for the truth, having been mixed up with inventions, is thereby falsified so that—as the saying goes—even the salt loses its flavor."[4] Clement then describes how when Mark was in Rome during the time Peter was there, Mark recounted in written form what Jesus had done during his ministry, "not, however, revealing everything, much less hinting at the mysteries, but selecting what he considered advantageous for increasing the faith of those being instructed."[5] After Peter was martyred, the letter goes on to say, Mark traveled to Alexandria, bringing what he had written along with Peter's notes, which he incorporated into his written text "what was suitable for those progressing step by step toward knowledge."[6] According to Smith, Mark then composed "a more spiritual gospel for the use of those having attained perfection." That Gospel "contained or indicated more of the hidden sense of Jesus' teachings and actions."[7] In the letter, Clement quickly assured Theodore that Mark "never betrayed the ineffable, nor did he write down the hierophantic teaching of the Lord" but "added" stories and "still other sayings, the interpretation with which he was familiar, to initiate the hearers into the forbidden sanctuary of the truth seven times veiled."[8]

Here we can unpack the language a bit. In the context of this passage, the word *hierophantic* refers to the explaining of mysteries and rituals. According to Clement, Mark did not write down all the things that Jesus taught but only those teachings of Jesus that he thought would be helpful for the initiates into the "forbidden sanctuary," the one concealed by seven veils. The implication

---

3. "The Letter to Theodore," 21–22.
4. "The Letter to Theodore," 22–23. Note that here Smith translates the Greek as "the salt loses its savor." "Transcription of Text," in Smith, *Clement of Alexandria and a Secret Gospel*, 446.
5. "The Letter to Theodore," 23.
6. "The Letter to Theodore," 24.
7. Smith, *Clement of Alexandria and a Secret Gospel*, 33.
8. "The Letter to Theodore," 24–25.

is that there were two books—one "for those progressing step by step toward knowledge," the other for those ready to attain that knowledge. It was a copy of this second book—the mystical gospel (μυστικόυ ευαγγέιον)[9]—that Carpocrates, the leader of the Carpocratians, had acquired by deception. The letter goes on to say that Carpocrates proceeded to misinterpret "according to his blasphemous and carnal opinion" and to mix in his own "shameless lies."[10] Clement knew what the mystical gospel said because when Mark was near death, "he bequeathed his writing to the church in Alexandria, where even now it is most carefully guarded, being read only before those who have been initiated into the great mysteries."[11] Clement instructed Theodore to deny, even under oath, that what the Carpocratians were citing (even if they were doing so correctly) was the mystical gospel of Mark because "everything that is true is not spoken to all men" and "let the fool walk in darkness."[12] The letter itself is incomplete, breaking off at a crucial point just where Clement is about to tell Theodore "the true philosophical explanation."[13]

Clement tells Theodore that "to the clean, everything is clean" so it appears that he does not hesitate to tell him in the nonextant part of the letter what is in the mystical gospel in order to expose the lies of the Carpocratians. Apparently, Theodore is not one of those who had been initiated into the great mysteries for otherwise he would have already had the mystical gospel read to him. Clement then provides an excerpt from the Secret Gospel, one that the Carpocratians were misrepresenting. The excerpt that Clement includes is similar to the Lazarus story that appears in the Gospel of John, but it does not reveal the name of the young man who is raised from the dead by Jesus. Similar to Lazarus, this young man is from Bethany, but whereas Lazarus has two sisters—Mary and Martha—only one sister is identified as that of the unnamed deceased man. In John, both sisters say that if Jesus had been there earlier, their brother would not have died, whereas in the mystical gospel version, the sister says only, "Son of David, have mercy on me." None of them explicitly asks Jesus to revivify their brother. Both descriptions have the body in a cave tomb with a rock that can be rolled away in front of the entrance. In the Secret Gospel version, one finds no mention of Jews looking on as there is in John's version. Also, John's version states explicitly that Lazarus had been dead for four

---

9. The Greek word μυστικος can mean either "secret" or "having to do with the mysteries." In the context of the letter, Connor asserted that it means "more spiritual" rather than "secret." Thus, he translates it as "mystical." Connor, *The Secret Gospel of Mark*, 26, fn. 51.

10. "The Letter to Theodore," 26.

11. "The Letter to Theodore," 25–26.

12. "The Letter to Theodore," 26–27. The last statement is an allusion to Ecclesiastes 2:14: "the fool walks in darkness."

13. "The Letter to Theodore," 29: "According to the true philosophical explanation . . . ."

days, whereas the Secret Gospel version does not specify how long the young man had been dead. In addition, the Secret Gospel version says the young man is wealthy, whereas John's version only implies that to be the case. Otherwise, the similarity of the stories in which Jesus revivifies a young dead man is striking, more so because that story does not appear in either Matthew or Luke.

Smith also pointed out that the location in the narrative of Mark coincides with the location of the Lazarus story in John in relation to the itinerary of Jesus's ministry: "Jesus has gone up from Galilee to Judea, and thence to Transjordan."[14] It also follows the sequence of events described in both Mark and John:

The feeding of the five thousand	Mark 6:31–44	John 6.1
The walking on the sea	Mark 6:47–52	John 6:15–25
Peter's confession	Mark 8:27–30	John 6:66–69
Jesus's prophecy of his resurrection	Mark 10:32–34	John 10:17–18
Lazarus story [omitted]	John 11:1–44	
Anointing in Bethany	Mark 14:3–9	John 12:1–8

Smith concluded: "This coincidence in order of so many events can hardly be accidental."[15] To be sure, it is not a perfect matchup, but the sequencing seems to indicate that if longer Mark had a Lazarus story in it, it would have occupied a similar place in the sequence of events in both Mark and John. On the other hand, a forger would presumably be aware of that relationship between the two Gospels as well and design his story to fit that niche.

Perhaps the most significant difference between the Secret Gospel narrative of the story and that in John is what happens after Jesus raises the deceased man. The Gospel of John ends the story with the words "Jesus said to them, 'Take off the grave clothes and let him go'" (John 11:43). The Secret Gospel version does not have these words, but it does describe more interaction between the youth and Jesus. I quote it here in full because of the controversial nature of it, which I will discuss below:

Approaching, Jesus rolled away the stone from the door of the tomb and immediately going into where the young man was, he stretched out his hand and raised him, holding his hand. And gazing at him the young man loved him and began to plead with him that he might be with him. And going from the tomb, they went into the young man's house, for he was rich. After six days, Jesus summoned him and when evening

---

14. Smith, *Clement of Alexandria and a Secret Gospel*, 149.
15. Smith, *Clement of Alexandria and a Secret Gospel*, 161.

came, the young man went to him wearing a linen cloth over his naked body and he stayed with him that night for Jesus taught him the mystery of the kingdom of God.

The canonical Gospel of Mark also uses the phrase "the mystery [singular] of the kingdom of God" (Mark 4:11), whereas the other synoptic Gospels use "the mysteries [plural] of the kingdom of God." Once again, a forger might be aware of the singular/plural difference.

Smith says that he was concerned that the letter he had found may have been forged. The eighteenth century was a notable time for forgeries.[16] It was the century when James Macpherson's *Ossian* was created and had a significant impact (see chapter 8). The English teenager Thomas Chatterton (1752–1770) forged fifteenth-century poetry. Forgery of works connected with biblical figures are also well known. Perhaps the most notorious occurred in the nineteenth century when Denis Vrain-Lucas (1818–1882) forged around 27,000 autographic letters and documents, a number of which he attributed to Jesus, Judas, Mary Magdalene, and Pontius Pilate. Thus, Smith was careful to couch the significance of his find in the subjunctive: "if Clement . . . really was its author the consequences for the history of the early Christian Church and for New Testament criticism are revolutionary."[17] He devoted much of the analysis in his book to the question of authenticity. The first chapter deals solely with the "manuscript"—that is, the two-and-a-half pages on the flyleaves of the printed book on which the letter was written. Smith found ten paleographic experts to estimate the time of the handwriting. They placed it around 1750. The second chapter analyzed the content and style of the letter with "the commonly acknowledged works of Clement."[18] That chapter concludes that the attribution in the heading of the letter to Clement is correct. The third chapter similarly analyzed the excerpts from what is described in the letter as "the mystical gospel" of Mark in relation to the stylistic characteristics and structure of the canonical Gospel of Mark. The fourth chapter discusses the significance of the evidence that the letter provides regarding the secret side of early Christianity, including "the magical and libertine elements . . . and of the practices of secrecy they entailed . . . ."[19] The final chapter discusses the history of the text of both the Gospel of Mark and the letter attributed to Clement.

---

16. See, for example, Robert Folkenflik, "Macpherson, Chatterton, Blake and the Great Age of Literary Forgery," *Centennial Review* 18, no. 4 (1974): 378–391.

17. Smith, *Clement of Alexandria and a Secret Gospel*, ix.

18. Smith, *Clement of Alexandria and a Secret Gospel*, x.

19. Smith, *Clement of Alexandria and a Secret Gospel*, 279.

This letter is remarkable for a number of reasons, not the least of which is that we have no other extant letters written by Clement. We do have evidence that the Syrian monk John of Damascus (ca. 675–749) quoted three passages from a collection of letters of Clement that he used at Mar Saba monastery in the early eighth century. John of Damascus quoted from letter 21, so we know that there were at least twenty-one letters, all of which are now lost except possibly for this one.

Smith took photos of the pages on which the handwritten text appeared, but the book remained at Mar Saba when he left to return to the United States. Subsequently, the two pages of endpaper with the letter written on them were separated from the printed book and then lost, destroyed, or hidden. The present whereabouts of those pages is unknown.

Between 1958 and 1973, Smith analyzed the contents of the letter and consulted with experts on Greek handwriting and early Christian literature. He compared the style of the writing with the style of Clement's other known writings, as well as with the writings of others from the first and second century. He also compared the style of passages that purport to be quotations from secret passages of Mark with the style of canonical Mark. He proposed that the canonical Gospel of Mark had been "reworked at least four times—by the author of secret Mark, by Matthew, by Luke, and by the Carpocratians (who are said to have used secret Mark)."[20]

As Smith completed chapters for his scholarly study, he sent drafts to various New Testament and patristics scholars, sixteen of whose comments (many of which expressed doubt) he included in the book. Smith published the book in 1973 with Harvard University Press. In the same year Smith published a popular narrative about the letter and his discovery of it. In the popular narrative, he described his understanding that the early Christian movement was divided into three groups. One was "the observant wing, centered in Jerusalem, [which] never had much appeal outside Palestine and was hard hit in Palestine by the great Jewish revolts of 66–73 and 132–135."[21] A second was "the center, represented not only by Paul but also by many of the observant who were willing to compromise, gradually coalesced and gave rise, by the middle of the third century, to a clear majority that claimed to be 'orthodox.'"[22] The third was a "libertine wing [that] gave rise to many of the Gnostic heresies, but also persisted in esoteric groups, like that of Clement, within the 'orthodox'

20. Morton Smith, *The Secret Gospel: The Discovery and Interpretation of the Secret Gospel According to Mark* (Clearlake, CA: Dawn Horse, 1973), 142.

21. Smith, *The Secret Gospel: Discovery and Interpretation*, 141.

22. Smith, *The Secret Gospel: Discovery and Interpretation*, 141–142.

communities."[23] Therefore, in Smith's view, just as some of the observant wing compromised with the center, so too did some of the libertine wing. He conjectured: "It was probably the libertine wing that both produced and preserved the secret Gospel of Mark." It was a member or members of this libertine wing he saw as expanding on canonical Mark by in part drawing on material from an older Aramaic gospel, which had also been used by canonical Mark and the author of the Gospel of John. It was from this Aramaic gospel that "the Greek text of secret Mark was produced by a translation that was made after canonical Mark had been written (c. 75)." In other words, according to Smith: "The translator took canonical Mark as his model and imitated [it] closely." The resulting Secret Gospel, in Smith's opinion, "was used by Matthew about A.D. 90" as well as by Luke, but not by John. Thus, the Lazarus story, which appears in both the Secret Gospel and John, Smith hypothesized as deriving independently from that no longer existing Aramaic gospel.

The scholarly reaction to Smith's book was mixed. Those who liked the book were quite enthusiastic about it. Those who opposed the conclusions expressed their belief that the letter was not written by Clement but was forged at the time it was copied on the endpapers of the typeset book.

Into the Thicket

The first problem to consider is a conceptual one. If one concludes that the fragments reported in the letter of Clement that Smith claimed to have found are authentic and they represent a version of the Greek gospel of Mark that is different from the canonical Gospel we have, then what is the relationship of it to that canonical Gospel? Is it a version that derives from the canonical Gospel and had text added (as Helmut Koester proposed)? Is it a version that predates the canonical gospel, which eliminated these and other parts (as Connor and Brown proposed)? Do they both derive from a no longer existing Aramaic version of Mark (as Smith proposed)? Or are the "Markian" excerpts in the Clementine letter forged and there is no other version of Mark (as the skeptics claim)?

The biblical scholar Scott Brown (b. 1966) prefers the term "longer Mark" in place of "Secret Gospel" so as to avoid passing preliminary judgment on whether one can accept the letter's characterization of it.[24] Connor argues

---

23. Smith, *The Secret Gospel: Discovery and Interpretation*, 142.

24. Scott G. Brown, *Mark's Other Gospel: Rethinking Morton Smith's Controversial Discovery* (Waterloo, Ont.: Canadian Corporation for Studies in Religion, 2005), 121–135.

that, contrary to Smith's view that longer Mark represents a reworking of canonical Mark, in reality canonical Mark is a shortened version of longer Mark. He agrees with Smith that the Gospels of Matthew and Luke derive from canonical Mark, not longer (or secret) Mark.[25]

A number of scholars and popular writers, including though not limited to college professors Bart Ehrman (University of North Carolina), Craig Evans (Acadia Divinity College), Birger Pearson (University of California), and Adela Yarbro (Yale University), have expressed their belief that Smith forged Clement's letter.[26] In 2009, Hershel Shanks, the editor of *Biblical Archaeology Review (BAR)*, asked three senior scholars who doubted the authenticity of the Clement letter to take part in a forum discussion in the pages of *BAR*. All three declined when they found out the identity of the scholars who, favoring its authenticity, were slated to take part on the other side. As a result of their refusal to participate in the forum, Shanks took it upon himself to summarize their arguments. I have based much of the following representation on Shanks's summary. He stated that he found "essentially two" arguments that support a claim of forgery: "1. Morton Smith had the scholarly expertise required to create the forgery. 2. The document itself contains flaws and anachronisms that affirmatively show that it is a forgery."[27] As for motive—why Smith would forge such a letter—the doubters are not agreed. Three possible motives keep reappearing in their writings. One is that he was upset that Brown University had denied him tenure. Since he was not up for tenure at Brown, that is a particularly difficult motive to argue. A second possible motive is the claim that Smith was a homosexual and was concocting scriptural justification for his homosexuality. According to Birger Pearson, an American scholar of early Christianity, Smith felt guilt and "had come to hate the Christian religion that he had once served as an Episcopal priest"[28] Pearson provides no evidence for his conjecture that Smith was homosexual or about Smith's feeling guilt or hating Christianity. A third possible motive that has been proposed was his wanting to see if he could do it. As biblical scholar Bart Ehrman (b. 1955) wrote: "It is not at all inconceivable that sometimes one would forge a document both to see if he could get away with it and to see if he could make experts in his field look foolish."[29] Again, there is no indication in any of Smith's written

25. Conner, *The Secret Gospel of Mark*, 20.

26. Shanks provides a partial list of the doubters. Hershel Shanks, "'Secret Mark': Morton Smith – Forger," *BAR* 35, no. 6 (2009): 49.

27. Shanks, "'Secret Mark': Morton Smith – Forger," 50.

28. Birger A. Pearson, "The Secret Gospel of Mark: A 20th Century Forgery," *Journal of Research on Religion* 4, art. 6 (2008): 11.

29. Bart Ehrman, quoted in Shanks, "'Secret Mark': Morton Smith – Forger," 50.

work or letters that he had any inclination to see if he could get away with it or to make experts in his field look foolish. In a Bayesian sense, these possible motives have to be given a very low probability indeed.

Not only do the proposers of these possible motives offer no evidence in support of their accusations but in fact there is evidence in opposition to each one of them. As Shanks pointed out, Smith had a non-tenure-track contract to teach at Brown for a specific period of time, which he fulfilled. Whether he expected to be offered a tenure-track position at the end of the non-tenure-track contract is another matter, but we have no evidence either way on it. In any case, by the time his book *Clement of Alexandria and a Secret Gospel of Mark* was published, he had already been granted tenure at Columbia University.[30] Presumably whatever anger he supposedly felt against Brown would have been dissipated by the lapse of fifteen years and his new tenured position.

Likewise, there is no evidence that Smith was a homosexual or that he tried to promote homosexual views. He was a lifelong bachelor, but no evidence has come to the fore concerning his sexual orientation. Those who see a homosexual message in the Secret Gospel passage concerning the young man raised from the dead overlook a number of obvious points. Canonical Mark also describes a "young man . . . with nothing but a linen cloth about his body." When Jesus was arrested at Gethsemane, this young man "left the linen cloth and ran away naked" (Mark 14:52–53). The same reasoning that led them to posit that Smith was homosexual should have led them to conclude that the author of the canonical Gospel of Mark was homosexual, but it does not seem to have done so. Elsewhere in the letter, Clement declares that the Carpocratians are wrong when they say that the Secret Gospel says "naked man with naked man" and refers to "the unspeakable teachings of the Carpocratians," who were associated with sexual libertarianism. Someone who was trying to proffer a pro-homosexual message, it seems, would be more likely to write a forgery that embraced the Carpocratian teachings than rejected them.

Likewise, just because someone has the skill and the opportunity to forge a work does not mean that the work is forged. If that were the case, then one would have to conclude that any discovery by any competent scholar of a previously unknown work means the work was forged, whereas the discovery of the same work by someone who did not have the skill means that it was not forged. In both cases, the argument is a non sequitur—one part of it does not follow from the other. Whether a work is forged is not dependent on the expertise of the person who claims to have discovered it, since someone else could have faked the work.

---

30. Shanks, "'Secret Mark': Morton Smith – Forger," 50.

The two main arguments that the doubters make—that Smith had the expertise and that he made mistakes when he forged the document—are at a certain level contradictory. If he had the expertise, then how is it he made mistakes, unless he introduced the mistakes intentionally? This line of reasoning depends first on the doubters' establishing Smith's expertise. They point to his having two PhD degrees, one from the Hebrew University in Jerusalem in Greek manuscript studies, the other from Harvard University in New Testament studies. Studying for these degrees, they say, would have given him the expertise to forge passages from the Gospel of Mark. They also point out that Smith had an interest in patristics (study of writings of the Church fathers). In a letter that he wrote in 1948, Smith said that for a period of six months, he was devoting half his time "to the early Fathers, especially to Clement."[31] In one of Smith's scholarly articles before the publication of his *Clement of Alexandria and a Secret Gospel of Mark*, he cited Clement four times. The implication is that Smith, as Peter Jeffery expressed it, "constructed" the forged Clementine letter "using the vocabulary of Clement's genuine writings."[32]

In regard to his ability to forge eighteenth-century Greek handwriting, the doubters cite another letter of Smith's in which he stated that he intended to study paleography. Ehrman opined that it would not have been difficult for Smith to forge such handwriting: "with some knowledge of paleography, a few dated specimens, any skill at all, and a little practice, it could be done easily enough."[33] Elsewhere, Ehrman stated: "Morton Smith's text is nothing if not brilliant."[34] And Stephen Carlson, another staunch critic of Smith, wrote that he had "one of the most brilliant minds of the twentieth century."[35] In contrast, a third doubter, Peter Jeffery, criticized Smith for his ignorance: "For someone who wrote as much as he did about early Christian worship, it is remarkable how little he read, even of what was considered required reading in his time."[36] It is not clear, however, what exactly Jeffery was referring to that he thought Smith had not read since he does not say.

---

31. *Morton Smith and Gershom Scholem, Correspondence 1945–1982*, ed. Guy C. Stroumsa (Leiden: Brill, 2008), 28.

32. Peter Jeffery, *The Secret Gospel of Mark Unveiled: Imagined Rituals of Sex, Death, and Madness in a Biblical Forgery* (New Haven, CT: Yale University Press, 2007), 121.

33. Bart Ehrman, "Response to Charles Hedrick's Stalemate," *Journal of Early Christian Studies* 11 (2003): 160.

34. Bart Ehrman, "Response to Papers on Secret Mark," Society of Biblical Literature annual meeting, November 24, 2008, quoted in Shanks, "'Secret Mark': Morton Smith – Forger," 50.

35. Stephen C. Carlson, "Can the Academy Protect Itself From One of Its Own? The Case of Secret Mark," Society of Biblical Literature annual meeting, November 24, 2008, quoted in Shanks, "'Secret Mark': Morton Smith – Forger," 50.

36. Jeffery, *The Secret Gospel of Mark Unveiled*, 59.

Among the features of the Clementine letter that the doubters call flaws is the statement that the Carpocratians have mixed falsehood with truth, thus diminishing the truth, "even as salt loses its flavor" when adulterated. Carlson claimed the simile is anachronistic because the method for mixing another substance with salt was developed only in modern times. The problem with salt is that loose salt particles would absorb moisture from the atmosphere and clump together. The result was that it could not be mixed with anything else because it was not free flowing. Granulated salt, as Carlson stated, was invented by the Morton Salt Company in 1910. Thus, Carlson saw the simile as a clue indicating a forgery because the salt company's name "Morton" was also Smith's first name. In response, Shanks pointed out that Carlson cited no evidence for his claim that loose salt did not exist in antiquity. Shanks cited two examples "from the Mishnah, the earliest rabbinic code, dating to about 200 C.E., that flatly contradict the 'anachronistic' salt argument:" The first reference states that one is permitted to "scatter salt on the Ramp [of the Temple altar] so that [the priests] will not slip."[37] The second reference states the Jews are not permitted to buy salt made by gentiles. The Talmud explains that sometimes gentile salt is unkosher because it is *mixed* with fish (i.e., fish without scales).[38]

Carlson picked up on what he considered more evidence of forgery—quality of the handwriting. Quite rightly, Carlson pointed out that forgers can unintentionally reveal the forgery through telltale signs such as making slow pen strokes to make sure they imitate the original correctly, lifting the pen in the middle of a stroke, and the "forger's tremor" or shaky quality of some lines. Carlson cites the book *Questioned Documents*, by noted forger detector Albert S. Osborne (1858–1946), on the methods he used to detect forgeries. Carlson then applied Osborne's methods to analyzing the writing of the letter to Theodore. Sure enough, Carlson finds those very characteristics in the handwriting of the letter. The problem with Carlson's procedure is twofold. First, he assumes that because he has read Osborne's book on detection of handwritten forgeries it is enough to qualify him to do such an analysis. Second, he wants to find evidence of forgery in the handwriting of the letter to bolster his argument. In other words, anyone who has a preconceived notion of what they want to find should probably not be the one doing the analy-

---

37. Hershel Shanks, "'Secret Mark': Restoring a Dead Scholar's Reputation," *BAR* 35, no. 6 (2009): 60, citing Mishnah, Tractate *Eruvin* 10, 14, *The Mishnah*, Danby translation (Oxford: Oxford University Press, 1933), 136.

38. Shanks, "'Secret Mark': Restoring a Dead Scholar's Reputation," 60, citing Jacob Neusner, trans., *The Mishnah, Avodah Zara* 2, 6 (New Haven, CT: Yale University Press, 1988), 664, and the Talmud (b. *Avodah Zarah* 39b).

sis. Carlson could not ask Osborn to do the analysis since he had died decades earlier, but he did ask one person who admitted she was not familiar with Greek. He could have asked one or more of the many handwriting experts around today who are familiar with Greek for an unbiased assessment of the handwriting of the letter, as Smith did, but he did not.

As a result of this lapse on Carlson's part, Shanks enlisted two Greek paleographic experts to analyze the handwriting in the photos of the letter. They agreed that the handwriting was authentically eighteenth century and not a modern forgery and that it significantly differed from Smith's own handwriting in Greek.[39]

The skeptics also cite a detective story published in 1940 by the evangelical Christian James H. Hunter titled *The Mystery of Mar Saba*.[40] In the story, a document is found at Mar Saba monastery, the same monastery from which the letter to Theodore derives. The document in the detective story has significance in that it provides new evidence about the removal of Jesus's body from the tomb. The problem is that the document is a forgery, planted by the Nazis to bring about the downfall of Christianity. The 1947 reprint of the novel even included the text of the forged Greek document used in the novel. Those who claim Smith forged the letter to Theodore believe that the existence of the detective story focused on a forgery from Mar Saba provides conclusive evidence that Smith forged the letter, but it also creates a conundrum. As skeptic Philip Jenkins described it: "The fact that Secret Mark came from Mar Saba is either strong proof of the text's authenticity in that nobody would have dared to invent such a thing in the 1950s or else it is a tribute to the unabashed *chutzpah* of a forger."[41] There is a third possibility, that the existence of the detective story, notwithstanding certain similarities to the context of the letter to Theodore discovery, is entirely coincidental. For if the letter to Theodore is authentic, then the main similarity to the detective story (i.e., a forgery) is lost. If the letter is a forgery, then one should be able to show that the forger got the idea from or at least knew of the detective story. Again, the evidence for any such claim is lacking.

The phenomenon of real life replicating fiction is well known. For example, the Russian poet Alexander Pushkin (1799–1837) wrote in his novel in verse, *Eugene Onegin* (published serially from 1825 to 1832), about a fictional poet named Lensky who was killed in a duel with someone who had been flirting with his fiancée, Olga. Pushkin himself was then killed in a duel in

---

39. Shanks, "'Secret Mark': Restoring a Dead Scholar's Reputation."

40. James H. Hunter, *The Mystery of Mar Saba* (1940; reprint 1947 with text of Greek forgery).

41. Philip Jenkins, *Hidden Gospels: How the Search for Jesus Lost Its Way* (Oxford: Oxford University Press, 2001), 102.

1837 with someone who had been flirting with his wife, Natasha. Similarly Jules Verne published a novel, *From the Earth to the Moon* (1865), in which a capsule containing three men is shot into space to the moon from Florida. The trip to the moon takes three days, exactly the same as the Apollo 11 mission that first landed men on the moon 104 years later. Presumably those who consider the moon landing to be a hoax could use these similarities as evidence to support their contention.

In 2010, the English theologian Francis Watson (b. 1956) claimed to have discovered evidence of a connection between Morton Smith and the Mar Saba detective story. He conjectured that Smith must have read the novel because it was available after the war when Smith returned to the United States. After re-enunciating the skeptics' previously made arguments, including the Morton Salt one, Watson offered what he saw as another clue supposedly seeded by Smith in the letter to Theodore to indicate that it was a forgery. The clue is the Greek word παραχαράσσεται, "falsified," which can be found in the passage "the truth, having been mixed up with inventions, is thereby falsified." Watson connects the Greek word with the English word *forge*, which derives from the Latin *fabricare* through French. All three—English, French, and Latin—also have the sense of manufacturing something, such as at a forge (which the Greek does not), and the person who does that is the *smith* (as in blacksmith). Therefore, according to Watson, by using the Greek word that means falsified, Smith was identifying himself as the forger.[42] Watson's argument here, as with his other arguments in general, is specious. Applying the contrapositive ($\neg Q \rightarrow \neg P$), we can ask: if the Greek word for falsified were not in the letter, then would that mean that someone named Smith was not the forger? Does any letter that has the Greek word for falsified mean that someone named Smith forged it? Watson needed first to establish that the letter was forged, which would at least presume a forger. Instead, he relied on the phrase "the long-standing *suspicion* of forgery"[43] as the foundation on which to build his case against Smith. After all, there is also a long-standing *acceptance* that the letter is genuine, but Watson chose to ignore that circumstance.

Watson also wrote that he found similarity in the description by the fictional character Sir William Bracebridge in the detective story and by Morton Smith in *Clement of Alexandria and a Secret Gospel* in regard to their stated reason for going to Mar Saba—because, although most manuscripts have been removed

---

42. Francis Watson, "Beyond Suspicion: On the Authorship of the Mar Saba Letter and Secret Gospel of Mark," *Journal of Theological Studies* 61 (2010): 152–154.

43. Watson, "Beyond Suspicion," 128 [italics in the original].

from it, they expected they might find a previously unknown manuscript there, and they do.[44] Yet, Mar Saba, like St. Catherine's in the Sinai, is one of the monasteries in the Middle East that over the years has turned up previously unknown manuscripts unexpectedly. Smith did not have to get the idea from a detective novel. It was well known in the scholarly community.

Watson expressed his main concern about the letter to Theodore: "If any newly discovered text could ever bring about 'the downfall of Christianity', the letter to Theodore is that text—at least if interpreted along the lines proposed by its discoverer."[45] It is possible that Watson sees himself as one of the British heroes of the novel who save Christianity by showing the discovered manuscript to be a forgery, and Watson does so by publishing an article in an academic journal. One cannot help but think that if the downfall of Christianity can be brought about by a few lines of text found (or forged) on the endpapers of a seventeenth-century printed edition of the letters of Ignatius, then Christianity is in a lot more fragile condition than anyone else seems to be aware of. And a letter that confirms the miracle of Christ's resurrecting someone from the dead would not seem to be exactly intended to bring about the downfall of Christianity.

Shanks expressed frustration at the continued arguments of the skeptics and likened it to how James Shapiro feels about the arguments of the Oxfordians in regard to the Shakespeare authorship controversy. If Shanks had read a little further in the anti-Stratfordian literature, he would have found the same sense of frustration being expressed at the proponents of the Stratfordian position (more about this in chapter 6). Connor was not so kind in dismissing the arguments of the skeptics: "It is, I believe, no coincidence that opposition to Smith's discovery has mainly come from staunchly evangelical and Catholic quarters . . . . If there is one thing that Bible colleges have taught to perfection, it is contempt for normal canons of evidence. Among evangelicals, belief in the improbable is a mark of faith, the more improbable, the more pure the faith."[46] But this comment veers off into the realm of ad hominem attack, as it tars with the same brush all evangelicals and Catholics as not being concerned with evidence and logical argument, which is clearly not the case. Connor does have a point, however, about defense of the traditional. Since the

---

44. Watson, "Beyond Suspicion," 166–167.

45. Watson, "Beyond Suspicion," 163.

46. Connor, *The Secret Gospel of Mark*, 144. He went on to speak of "the artless mendacity typical of evangelical casuistry," 145. Smith himself could not always maintain his professional restraint in regard to the arguments of some of his theological colleagues, saying about one such critic that his name, Fitzmyer, rhymes with liar.

establishment of the New Testament canon in the third century,[47] churchmen have been assiduous in defending that canon against any additions, deletions, or modifications. If the letter of Clement is authentic, then we have to give serious consideration to the two Markian passages contained in the letter and how they relate to the canonical Gospel of Mark.

The Takeaway

The question being discussed here is who is the author of a copied letter found handwritten on the endpapers of a seventeenth-century edition of the letters of Ignatius. Was it Clement of Alexandria, Morton Smith, or an eighteenth-century forger? Is it genuine or a forgery? A secondary but no less important question is who was the author of the purported excerpts from the Gospel of Mark in the letter. Was the author the same person as the rest of the Markian text or do they represent a reworking of the Markian text by someone else? If the first case, then the excerpts in the letter represent a fuller original text of Mark. If the latter, then the excerpts represent a revised version. Or was it Morton Smith or someone in the eighteenth century who forged the excerpts from Mark as well?

Connor's argument that canonical Mark must be an abridgement of Secret (or longer) Mark is strong. The idea is that those parts of the original Gospel that might be confusing to initiates were expunged but kept in a secret version for those who have reached a sufficient level of spiritual development. If the passages that Clement cited were interpolated into an already existing version of Mark's Gospel, it is unlikely the interpolator would have attempted to imitate Mark's style. No one would be likely to notice a shift in style with the added passages, and we have no evidence that interpolators or forgers at the time were aware of the need for stylistic verisimilitude. There would be a good chance that present-day stylistic analysis would have picked up discrepancies. This point was made about a possible thirteenth-century forging of the letters of Abelard and Heloise (see chapter 4). Since the style of the excerpts from Secret Mark that appear in the letter of Clement is so close to that of canonical Mark, it is more likely that canonical Mark and the excerpts in the letter of Clement were written by the same person.

---

47. R. M. Grant, "The New Testament Canon," in *The Cambridge History of the Bible*, vol. 1, *From the Beginnings to Jerome*, ed. Peter R. Ackroyd and C. F. Evans (Cambridge: Cambridge University Press, 1970), 308.

CHAPTER 4

Did Abelard and Heloise Write the Letters Attributed to Them?

"The authorship of the letters between Abelard and Heloise has been the most controversial question in Abelardian scholarship for over a century."[1]

—John Marenbon

Twelfth-century Paris was a hotbed of theological disputes. Such was the intellectual milieu in which Abelard and Heloise lived and worked. Abelard entered into this conflict and was a participant for decades. But for the first seven hundred years after his death, he was not remembered as a major figure in those disputes. Mark Twain even went so far as to claim: "He died a nobody."[2] Instead, as a result of the thirteenth-century poem *Roman de la Rose* (*Romance of the Rose*) by Jean de Meun and of the discovery by the same person of a set of letters that Abelard and Heloise presumably wrote, they became icons of French and European cultural history as illicit lovers who suffered the consequences. Only in the eighteenth century, during the time of the Enlightenment, when reason was being given priority of approach in intellectual matters, were Abelard's theological and dialectical writings "rediscovered." Scholars then began to see him as a precursor for the Age of Reason and modernity, as he is seen today. It took another two hundred years, until the end of the twentieth century, for scholars to begin to study Heloise as a significant writer herself.

---

1. John Marenbon, *The Philosophy of Peter Abelard* (Cambridge: Cambridge University Press, 1997), 82.

2. Mark Twain, *The Innocents Abroad* (Hartford, CT: American Publishing, 1869), 146.

Context of the Controversy

During the Carolingian Renaissance of the ninth century, an intellectual renewal began to occur in medieval Latin Europe. This intellectual renewal involved recovery of the seven liberal arts[3] as the basis of the school curriculum. Charlemagne's "minister of education" Alcuin of York (735–804) wrote treatises on each of those liberal arts, although the quality of his discourses was still on a relatively low level. In the late tenth century, the monk Gerbert of Aurillac (ca. 945–1003) went to Spain and North Africa to study mathematics, astronomy, and, among other things, dialectic with both Christian and Muslim scholars, some of whom were probably familiar with the writings of ancient Greek thinkers in Arabic translation. When Gerbert returned north, he began teaching what he had learned. He became pope in 999 as Sylvester II. So right around the period of the 990s to 1000s there was a definite although limited influx into Europe of ideas associated with Aristotle and Plato, if not yet their actual works.

Throughout the eleventh and twelfth centuries, we find the introduction of Plato's works in Latin translation into Catholic Europe. Very little of Plato's own writings had been available until that time. We know of only a fragment of one portion of one dialogue, the *Timaeus*, that had existed in Latin.

During the same period, a theological conflict arose between the defenders of the Church's theology, which was based on a Neoplatonic epistemology,[4] and some of the practitioners of ancient Greek methods of dialectic. Dialectic is usually translated as "logic," but ancient and medieval dialectic meant analyzing a proposition and counterpropositions through logical arguments and counterarguments. The idea, going back to ancient Greece, was to try to defeat one's opponent by having the better argument. Dialectic is thus often called "the closed fist." One figuratively pummels one's opponent by pointing out contradictions in their arguments so that there is no way for him or her to get out of it. This compulsory aspect of dialectic juxtaposes with rhetoric, which is called the open fist, where one persuades through the beauty of the words and expressions, and convinces the other person of its correctness.

Toledo in present-day Spain played an important role in terms of the influx of Platonic and Aristotelian texts into Europe. It was a center of learning

---

3. The trivium (grammar, rhetoric, dialectic) and the quadrivium (arithmetic, geometry, astronomy, and music) together make up the seven liberal arts.

4. Christian Neoplatonism posits a God that is unknowable. Emanating from God is the divine mind, where the archetypal forms reside. Emanating from the divine mind is the divine soul. Knowledge of the divine soul, which is real knowledge, can be attained only through each person's individual soul.

under the rulers of Al-Andalus (Andalusia).[5] After the takeover of Toledo by Christian forces in 1085, Latin translations from the Arabic crossed the Pyrenees. French academics began to apply Aristotelian dialectic to theological matters and led some Church theologians to review the Church's synthesis of Neoplatonism with Christian doctrine. Church leaders were not always pleased with the resulting new analyses and attempted to shut them down by condemning the views expressed by such dialecticians as Berengar of Tours (at the Council of Vercelli in 1050) and by questioning the views of Roscelin of Compiègne (at the Council of Soissons in 1092–93).[6] Both Berengar (ca. 999–1088) and Roscelin (ca. 1045 or 1050–1120) raised questions concerning what happens during the Mass—in particular, the Eucharist part of the Church service. Church doctrine was clear. The bread and wine changed into the body and blood of Christ (transubstantiation), although they still appeared outwardly to be bread and wine. Clerics like Berengar, Roscelin, and Abelard were subjecting such theological matters to logical inquiry, which certainly made the traditional theologians suspicious of their motives.

There were those who defended the Church's theology with logical argument, such as Lanfranc of Bec (1010–1089) and Anselm of Canterbury (1033–1109). Anselm's ontological proof presented in his *The Address* (*Proslogion*) (1078) uses dialectic to formulate "a proof" for the existence of God. His argument provoked an almost immediate dialectical counterargument by Gaunilo of Marmoutiers (fl. eleventh century) in his *In Behalf of the Fool* (*Liber pro Insipiente*). Anselm answered in a *Response* (*Responsio*) or *Defense* (*Liber apologeticus*). This exchange, for all intents and purposes, indicates that dialectic had arrived on the theological scene in France and England.

The Church's theology, nonetheless, continued to be defended by using Neoplatonic epistemology, according to which real knowledge can be found only in one's heart, the center of one's soul. Bernard of Clairvaux (1090–1153) roundly criticized Abelard and his views and called him a "new theologian." "New" in this context meant "bad." From Bernard's point of view and from the point of view of many people in medieval times, anything new was immediately suspect because all of truth had already been revealed. Anything new was by definition not true. What Bernard preached was that the way to understanding is not through reason but through suffering and tears, through

---

5. The term Al-Andalus (which possibly derived from Vandals) refers to those parts of the Iberian peninsula that were under Muslim rule between the years 711 and 1492.

6. When the Catholic Church condemns a writing or teaching, it usually orders the person who expressed the condemned view to desist and gives the person a chance to recant. If the person resumes expression of that condemned view or refuses to recant, they could leave themselves open to being declared a heretic.

the heart. This formulation is the standard one of the Christian Neoplatonic view, so it is understandable why he would not like Abelard, who from his perspective was using his reason too much and his heart not enough.

A number of works on theology and logic are attributed to Abelard, including *Yes and No* (*Sic et non*), *Glosses on Porphyry*, *Dialectic* (*Dialectica*), *Commentary on Paul's Letter to the Romans*, as well as an autobiography and letters. His views were questioned at the Council of Soissons (1121) but do not seem to have been formally condemned at that time. Nineteen years later, at the Council of Sens (1140), his doctrines were again apparently not condemned. Nonetheless, Pope Innocent II imposed a punishment of silence upon him for heresy and threatened with excommunication anyone who defended or followed him. As a result of the papal pronouncement, others probably were hesitant to discuss Abelard's works for fear that doing so could get them into trouble too.

Although we do have a few mentions of Abelard in sources from the early twelfth century, much of the information that we have about his life comes from one source—the *Letter of Consolation to a Friend: The Story of My Calamities* (*Historia calamitatum*; hereafter *Calamities*). In it the author boasts of his ability to defeat his opponents in open disputation through logical reasoning. The disputation, a form of academic and, at times, public debate, was becoming more widespread during that time.[7] The technique of dialectic was ideally suited for the disputation format. Although telling us little about Abelard's theological and philosophical views, *Calamities* goes into some detail about his life.

Calamities is one of the works whose authorship has been contested. We have little other evidence about Abelard's life, so we cannot easily confirm or refute most of the statements therein. If Abelard did not write *Calamities*, then who did? And how reliable is the information thereby provided? Was it someone who either knew Abelard personally or had access to reliable information about him? Or was it written over a hundred years later by someone who was drawing on authentic writings and hearsay for some things and making up other things?

If Abelard did write *Calamities*, then the question of reliability remains but on a different level. For information of a matter-of-fact nature—such as where he was born and when he went to Paris—one can assume probable reliability

---

7. For an overview of disputation in medieval Europe, see Alex J. Novikoff, *The Medieval Culture of Disputation: Pedagogy, Practice, and Performance* (Philadelphia: University of Pennsylvania Press, 2013). For a brief survey of disputations throughout Eurasia, see Donald Ostrowski, "The *Debate with Iosif* (*Prenie s Iosifom*) as a Fictive Disputation," in *Iosif Volotskii and Eastern Christianity: Essays across Seventeen Centuries*, ed. David Goldfrank, Valeria Nollan, and Jennifer Spock (Washington, DC: New Academia, 2017), esp. 184–199.

(unless one has other evidence challenging it). For information of a subjective nature—such as that he bested in disputation his teacher William of Champeaux, who as a result became hostile toward him, then one needs to be a bit cautious about acceptance. William might have a different version to tell had he written his own account of these events.

According to *Calamities*, Abelard was born in the village of Le Pellet near Nantes in Brittany. In 1100, he went to Paris, where he attended the cathedral school of Notre-Dame de Paris. That school is where the philosopher and theologian William of Champeaux (ca. 1070–1121) served as his teacher. Around this time, Peter chose Abelard as his surname. The name derives from Old German *Adalhard* and means "noble strength." In Paris, he wrote songs and became known for his intellectual skills. In 1116 or so, he convinced the secular canon Fulbert to allow him to live in the canon's house in return for which he would tutor Fulbert's niece Heloise, whose renown for learning was widespread. Heloise may have been illegitimate, for we have no record of who her father was. The Necrology (List of Deaths) of the Paraclete Oratory tells us that Heloise's mother was named Hersindis.[8] The German medievalist Werner Robl identified her with the Hersindis who was the prioress of Fontevrault and daughter of Hubert III of Champagne.[9] The Necrology also tells us when Heloise's uncle "Canon Hubert" died, which Robl pointed out was the same timeframe as the death of "subdeacon Fulbert" of the cathedral of Notre-Dame. The Hubert/Fulbert name interchange suggests that Fulbert was Heloise's maternal uncle.

The date of Heloise's birth is unknown. Because she is referred to as "a young girl" (*adolescentula*) in *Calamities*, the thinking has been that she could not have been more than seventeen (possibly as young as fifteen) when Abelard moved into Fulbert's house. That would place her birth year around 1100. The abbot of Cluny Abbey, Peter the Venerable, on the other hand, in a letter says that he remembers her as a woman when he was a young man. Since he was born in 1092, it could mean that she was around his age and may have been born ten years earlier than previously thought, in 1090 or 1091.[10] If so, she would have been in her mid-twenties when she met Abelard. The point is that someone who was between fifteen and seventeen would not have attained the intellectual renown that Abelard mentions in his *Calamities*.[11] On the other

8. J. T. Muckle, "Abelard's Letter of Consolation to a Friend (*Historia Calamitatum*)," *Mediaeval Studies* 12, no. 1 (1950): 182, n. 3.

9. Werner Robl, *Heloisas Herkunft: Hersindis Mater* (Munich: Olzog, 2001), 30.

10. Michael Clanchy, *Abelard: A Medieval Life* (Oxford: Blackwell, 1997), 173–174.

11. Constantine Mews, *Abelard and Heloise* (Oxford: Oxford University Press, 2005), 59.

hand, if she had mastered Latin and the classics and possibly Greek and Hebrew as a teenager,[12] then that in itself would have been cause for renown.

Calamities goes on to tell how Abelard and Heloise became romantically
involved. When Fulbert discovered that involvement, Abelard moved out of
Fulbert's house but continued the affair with Heloise. When she became preg-
nant, Abelard had her go to his family in Brittany to have the baby, whom
Heloise named Astrolabe. We find the name Peter Astrolabe recorded in the
Necrology of the Paraclete, so for that bit of testimony in *Calamities* we do
have independent confirmation. Also Peter the Venerable mentions her son
Astrolabe in a letter to Heloise. He is not mentioned by name in any of the
extant letters attributed to Heloise. Besides the statement in *Calamities*, the
only mention of a son in a work attributed to Abelard is the *Poem to Astrolabe*
(*Carmen ad Astralabium*), the verses of advice addressed to him.

Abelard then married Heloise with Fulbert present at the ceremony but
with the understanding that the marriage was to be kept secret so as not to
affect Abelard's career. Nonetheless, according to *Calamities*, Fulbert breached
the secret and started to abuse Heloise. Abelard had her move out of Fulbert's
house into a monastery at Argenteuil, northwest of Paris, whereupon Fulbert
took revenge by sending his henchmen to castrate Abelard. We find testimony
to a limited degree corroborating these events in a letter written by Roscelin—
namely, that Abelard had seduced Heloise ("introduced her to fornication")
and "that part of you by which you had sinned" was removed—but it tells us
nothing about the affair itself or who removed "that part" (except that it was
God's "vengeance").[13] We also have a letter written by Fulk, the prior of
Deuil, telling Abelard that he should consider his castration an act of provi-
dence.[14]

Abelard, in the narrative of *Calamities*, subsequently had Heloise move to
a monastery named the Oratory (place of prayer) of the Paraclete, southeast
of Paris. Around 1135, Abelard returned to be master of a school at the church
of St. Geneviève in Paris. Five years later, Bernard of Clairvaux accused Abelard of heresy at the Council of Sens. After Pope Innocent II sentenced Abelard to silence, Peter the Venerable took Abelard under his protection at Cluny.

On April 21, 1142, Abelard died at the Cluniac priory of St. Marcellus near
Chalon-sur-Saône, where he was initially buried. On November 16, 1144, his

---

12. Jan M. Ziolkowski, *Letters of Peter Abelard: Beyond the Personal* (Washington, DC: Catholic University Press of America, 2008), 8.

13. Roscelin de Compiègne, *Epistola ad Abaelardum*, ed. Joseph Reiners, in *Der Nominalismus in der
Frühscholastik. Ein Beitrag zur Geschichte der Universalienfrage im Mittelalter*, Beiträge zur Geschichte der
Philosophie des Mittelalters, Bd. 8.5 (Munster: Aschendorff, 1910), 63–80.

14. "Quae est Fulconis prioris de Diogilo, ad Petrum Abaelardum," *P.L.*, 178: cols. 371–376.

corpse was secretly reburied at the Paraclete. On May 16, 1163 or 1164, Heloise died and was buried next to Abelard at the Paraclete. Their bones were moved several times after that, including to Père Lachaise cemetery in eastern Paris. By the nineteenth century, that gravesite had become a popular tourist attraction. Mark Twain visited the gravesite in the 1860s and wrote that it "has been more revered, more widely known, more written and sung about and wept over, for seven hundred years, than any other in Christendom, save only that of the Saviour."[15] That popularity derived primarily from the *Roman de la Rose* started by Guillame de Lorris around 1230 and completed by Jean de Meun around 1275. Of the poem's 21,782 lines, only 72 are devoted to telling their story, but that was enough.

Into the Thicket

Two sets of letters are in question here. The first set has fifteen letters. Nine are attributed to Abelard, four of which are addressed to Heloise, and six attributed to Heloise (three addressed to Abelard and one to Peter the Venerable), which Jean de Meun claimed he found and used in the 1280s to translate the letters into French. The second set of 113 anonymous letters was transcribed in the late fifteenth century by the monk Johannes de Vepria (ca. 1445–ca. 1515), prior of Clairvaux from 1480 to 1499. This set has been referred to in the scholarship as *Epistles of Two Lovers* (*Epistolae duorum amantium*). To keep the two sets distinct, I will refer to the first set of letters as AH-1 and the second set as AH-2.

AH-1

One can define four general positions in regard to authorship of AH-1.

(1) Abelard and Heloise wrote the letters respectively attributed to them. This position is the standard view, most fully explicated by Etienne Gilson (1938).

(2) Abelard wrote both his and Heloise's letters. This position was first fully argued by Bernhard Schmeidler (1913). Later D. W. Robertson (1972) and John Benton (1980), among others, adopted it.

(3) A third person wrote the correspondence. This position was held by John Caspar Orelli (1844), John Benton (1972), Hubert Silvestre (1988),

---

15. Twain, *The Innocents Abroad*, 140.

and Deborah Fraioli (1988), although each had different candidates for whom the author might be. Benton (1972) suggested an "anti-feminist at the Paraclete in the thirteenth century might have concocted the correspondence from both authentic and inauthentic materials in an attempt to change the traditional administrative structure of the abbey."[16] Orelli, in contrast, suggested a "friendly monk" (i.e., sympathetic to Abelard and Heloise). Silvestre claimed Jean de Meun, the author of *Roman de la Rose*, did it. Fraioli posited an adversary of Abelard's wrote them as a satire to mock Abelard and Heloise.

(4) Heloise wrote both her and Abelard's letters. This is a hypothetical position since no one has argued it systematically. The closest anyone has come is Tore Janson in 1988, who averred the possibility parenthetically: "In view of the very great similarities in prose rhythm between the letters to Heloise and those to Abelard, . . . I propose that one of them edited the whole collection (or conceivably wrote it all) rather than that each of them wrote quite independently."[17]

Of the fifteen letters of AH-1, seven represent a direct correspondence between Abelard and Heloise (four addressed to Heloise from Abelard; three addressed to Abelard from Heloise). In 1129, when Heloise and her nuns were evicted from the convent of Argenteuil because the Abbey of St. Denis took it over, Abelard, according to *Calamities*, arranged for them to move to the Oratory of the Paraclete, some 120 kilometers to the southeast of Paris. He had founded it as a Benedictine monastery in 1121 in Ferreaux-Quincey, but it was deserted by 1129. The exchange of this first set of letters occurred presumably when Heloise was at the Paraclete. The second letter of the set, which is the first letter attributed to her, refers to the first letter, *The Story of My Calamities*. That work mentions the confirmation by Pope Innocent II in November 28, 1131, of the takeover by Heloise and her nuns of the Oratory of the Paraclete,[18] which seems to provide the earliest possible date (*terminus ante*

---

16. John F. Benton, "A Reconsideration of the Authenticity of the Correspondence of Abelard and Heloise," in *Petrus Abaelardus, 1079–1142: Person, Werk und Wirkung*, ed. Rudolf Thomas (Trier: Paulinus-Verlag, 1980), 41–42. These words are how Benton in 1980 summarized the argument that he made in 1972.

17. Tore Janson, "Schools of Cursus in the Twelfth Century and the *Letters* of Heloise and Abelard," in *Retorica e poetica tra i secoli XII e XIV*, ed. Claudio Leonardi and Enrico Menestò (Florence: La nuova Italia, 1988), 195–196.

18. An oratory is a place of prayer. The word *paraclete* derives from the Greek *paraklētos*, meaning "called in aid" and is used to designate the Holy Spirit. Heloise was prioress at the oratory until she died.

quem non[19]) for the composition of *Calamities*. Thus, the items of AH-1, if they are what they appear to be and if they are placed in the manuscript copies in some kind of chronological order, would have been written most likely during the 1130s. No twelfth-century manuscripts of the letters exist. Nor are there any copies from the Oratory of the Paraclete, where Heloise was prioress when the letters were supposedly written and exchanged.[20] The earliest manuscripts of the first set of letters date to over one hundred years after that. In itself, such a gap between time written and earliest extant copy for twelfth-century French texts is not unusual, but it does leave the door open a little wider for those who wish to argue that the letters were forged in the late thirteenth century. It was against them that Constant J. Mews has countered: "The absence of any twelfth-century manuscript . . . is not an argument against their [the letters'] authenticity."[21] True enough, but it is not an argument in favor of it either.

The allegorical poem *Roman de la Rose*, which, among other things, tells the story of Abelard and Heloise, was written in two parts. The first (shorter) part was written around 1230 by the poet and scholar Guillaume de Lorris (ca. 1200–ca. 1240). The second (longer) part was written possibly between 1268 and 1285 by the poet and song writer Jean de Meun (ca. 1240–ca. 1305). The section that tells the story of Abelard and Heloise is in the second part, so it is easy for a skeptic to propose that all or part of the letters were forged to satisfy the newly found interest in the love affair between Abelard and Heloise. The connecting link in this scenario is Jean de Meun, who also claimed to have translated the letters of Abelard and Heloise from Latin into French.

A basic principle of textual criticism is that the earliest manuscripts do not necessarily contain the best readings. A later manuscript could have been copied from a no longer extant manuscript copy close to the archetype or even the archetype itself, defined as the author's final version (authorial text). Nonetheless, coincident readings from manuscripts distributed over a wide area tend to be better than those from a central location. All of these considerations come into play in regard to the places where the manuscript copies of AH-1 were found.

---

19. A standard Latin term used in textual criticism and codicology to mean "latest possible date" (literally, "end after which not").

20. A prioress is a female head of a priory, and a priory is a small monastery or convent. At the time, priories were usually associated with the Benedictines of Cluny. Benedictines are monks and nuns who follow the monastic Rule of Saint Benedict of Nursia (ca. 480–563). Cluny was a monastery where the Cluniac reform movement began.

21. Constant J. Mews, *The Lost Love Letters of Heloise and Abelard: Perceptions of Dialogue in Twelfth-Century France* (New York: Palgrave, 2001), 41.

Although we have contemporary references to the Abelard-Heloise relationship in the twelfth century,[22] we do not have any contemporary references by others to letters exchanged between them before the discovery of the manuscript copies in the late thirteenth century. We do not have evidence that anyone knew of the letters in the twelfth century. Two of the five earliest manuscripts come from Paris. The third comes from the College of the Oratory at Troyes in Champagne, some 50 kilometers east-southeast of the Paraclete. The fourth comes from Reims, 160 kilometers north-northeast of Paris. The fifth comes from Douai, some 200 kilometers north-northeast of Paris. This circumstance has led to the following proposed reconstruction. Heloise kept a copy of the letters or even the letters themselves at the Paraclete.[23] That copy or the letters themselves remained there until the late thirteenth century. A copy of AH-1 was transferred to Paris, where it was copied several times.[24] The letters themselves were lost or destroyed at some point after the first copy was made. One of the new copies supposedly became the basis for Jean de Meun's writing about Abelard and Heloise in his addition to the *Roman de la Rose*. The Troyes manuscript copy may have been kept at the Paraclete, again copied from the originals, until transferred to the Troyes cathedral. The Reims and Douai copies provide inferior readings, at least according to the medievalist J. T. Muckle. Seven of the nine manuscript copies of the letters have attributions to Abelard and Heloise within them.[25]

For over four hundred years after the discovery of the manuscript copies of the letters, the traditional attribution was accepted (or at least we have no evidence that anyone questioned it). The first publication of the letters appeared in 1616. In the nineteenth and early twentieth centuries, a number of scholars expressed suspicions about the authenticity of the letters.[26] But none of these scholars backed their suspicions with sustained arguments or evidence.

---

22. William Godel (fl. 1145–1173), Walter Map (1140–ca.1210), and Roscelin.

23. R. W. Southern, "The Letters of Heloise and Abelard," in Southern, *Medieval Humanism and Other Studies* (Oxford: Basil Blackwell, 1970), 103. In his novel *The Cloister*, James Carroll has Peter the Venerable, the abbot primate of Cluny, hand over to Heloise upon the death of Abelard the portion of the correspondence that was in Abelard's possession. James Carroll, *The Cloister: A Novel* (New York: Random House, 2017), 7.

24. Betty C. Radice, "Introduction," in *The Letters of Abelard and Héloïse*, trans. Betty C. Radice (Hammondsworth: Penguin, 1974), 47.

25. *Historia calamitatum. Texte critique*, ed. Jacques Monfrin (Paris: J. Vrin, 1959), 9–28, manuscripts T, B, D, Y, C, E, and F.

26. In 1806, Ignatius (Ignaz) Martinianus Fessler raised questions about their authenticity. Ignatius Aurelius Fessler, *Abälard und Heloise*, 2 vols., vol. 2 (Berlin: Friedrich Maurer, 1806–1807), 352 [623]. In 1844, John Caspar Orelli of Turici renewed Fessler's questions of authenticity. In 1855, Ludovic Lalanne suggested that Heloise herself revised her original letters. Ludovic Lalanne, "Quelques doutes sur l'authenticité de la correspondence amoureuse d'Héloïse et d'Abailard," *La Correspondance littéraire* 1, no. 2 (November 1856–October 1857): 27–33. E. D. Petrella, "Sull'autenticità

Beginning in 1913, in a series of three articles, the German historian and diplomat Bernhard Schmeidler (1879–1959) became the first scholar to question in a sustained way the authenticity of the extant texts as a genuine exchange of letters. He claimed (based on stylistic homogeneity of the two subsets of AH-1) that Abelard wrote both his own and Heloise's letters. Schmeidler called them a "literary fiction," although he did allow that they may have been based on a real exchange of no longer extant letters.[27]

In 1933, the French scholar Charlotte Charrier wrote that Abelard edited Heloise's letters.[28] She did not think that Heloise learned her style of writing from Abelard and therefore did not share what she called his "laborious way" (*laborieuse manière*).[29] According to Benton, "anything she [Charrier] liked in the letters attributed to Heloise was probably authentic and anything she did not like was a self-serving interpolation by Abelard."[30] In 1938, the French historian Étienne Gilson (1884–1978) defended the attributions that occur in the letters, although he did acknowledge the possibility that Heloise may have edited them somewhat at the Paraclete. Gilson's defense of the traditional attributions so convinced scholars that no substantial challenge was raised for thirty-four years.

Although the authenticity of the letters, which, as Marenbon states in the epigraph to this chapter, had been in question for quite a while before 1972, doubts were for the most part quietly bubbling below the surface. Most scholars who used the letters as sources in their own works during that time tended not to mention any attribution issue, or if they did, it was in passing and with a quick dismissal as they proceeded to assume the reliability of the letters and the traditional attributions.

In 1972, D. W. Robertson, Jr., seemed to accept the traditional attributions in his biography of Abelard and Heloise, writing: "Each age has made the lovers over in its own image, using Heloise especially as a vehicle for its ideals."[31] But then he took issue with Gilson's arguments in favor of that traditional attribution. He did not go into the specifics of his disagreements because "the

delle lettere d'Abelardo e Eloisa," *Rendiconti del Reale Istituto Lombardo de scienze e lettere,* 2nd ser., 44 (1911): 554–561, 606–618.

27. Bernhard Schmeidler, "Der Briefwechsel zwischen Abalard und Heloise eine Fälschung," *Archiv für Kulturgeschichte* 11 (1913): 1–30; Schmeidler, "Der Briefwechsel zwischen Abaelard und Heloise als eine literarische Fiktion Abaelards," *Zeitschrift für Kirchengeschichte* 54 (1935): 323–338; and Schmeidler, "Der Briefwechsel zwischen Abaelard und Heloise dennoch eine literarische Fiction Abaelards," *Revue Benedictine* 52 (1940): 85–95.

28. Charlotte Charrier, *Héloïse dans l'histoire et dans la légende* (Paris: H. Champion, 1933).

29. Charrier, *Héloïse dans l'histoire,* 22, n. 7.

30. Benton, "A Reconsideration," 41.

31. D. W. Robertson, Jr., *Abelard and Heloise* (New York: Dial, 1972), 223.

authenticity of the correspondence may be questioned on other grounds entirely."[32] In essence, Robertson revived the arguments of Schmiedler from 1913 that, on the basis of similarity of style between the letters attributed to Abelard and those to Heloise, Abelard wrote both his and her letters. Robertson did allow that Heloise may have added some phrases later.

But the scholar who really stirred up the hornet's nest was John F. Benton (1931–1988), an American medieval historian. In a paper delivered at a conference at Cluny Abbey, an event that has been dubbed "Cluny 1972," and subsequently published as an article in the conference proceedings, Benton argued "that sometime in the thirteenth century a forger or forgers, motivated by a desire to modify the institutions of the Paraclete, compiled and reworked the eight letters we can read today in ms. T, making use of both authentic writings of Abelard . . . and a twelfth-century 'autobiographical' letter which was itself a work of imaginative fiction, produced perhaps by some skilled student of the *ars dictaminis* [art of writing letters]."[33] This person or persons used some authentic texts of Abelard's and added fictitious ones to create a forged pastiche.

Benton based his argument on the apparent fact that the monastic rule that Abelard wrote for the Paraclete was not implemented. Benton began his article with a chiding of Abelard scholars for being "strikingly inactive" in light of the subject's significance:

> We have no history of the Paraclet, no archeological exploration of its site, no edition of the unusually detailed thirteenth-century service book (B.N. ms. fr. 14410) which reveals the liturgical program of the Paraclet, no edition or critique of the charters of the Paraclet since the century-old and careless publication of Abbé Charles Lalore, and no study of the correspondence itself which systematically compares its assertions with all other known evidence about Abelard, Heloise, and their monastery.[34]

He lamented that present-day scholars "commonly accept the authenticity of the correspondence either on grounds of style, which has not yet been studied in depth, or on the authority of Monsieur Gilson, who conceived the problem in learned but overly-narrow terms, or because it 'feels' genuine."[35]

---

32. Robertson, *Abelard and Heloise*, 222.

33. John F. Benton, "Fraud, Fiction and Borrowing in the Correspondence of Abelard and Heloise," in *Pierre Abélard, Pierre le Vénérable: les courants philosophiques, littéraires et artistiques en Occident au milieu du XIIe siècle* [actes et mémoires du colloque international], Abbaye de Cluny, 2 au 9 juillet 1972 (Paris: Éditions du Centre national de la recherché scientifique, 1975), 472.

34. Benton, "Fraud, Fiction and Borrowing," 471–472.

35. Benton, "Fraud, Fiction and Borrowing," 471–472.

What Benton is focusing on here is the context in which the texts were produced. He questioned whether anything in the letters compellingly identifies them as twelfth-century creations (as opposed to thirteenth). He saw the request in the third letter attributed to Heloise for Abelard to write a rule for a women's monastery and the appearance of such a rule in a subsequent letter attributed to Abelard as a literary device by the thirteenth-century author or authors to give credence to the rule that they wrote. Benton asked why, if Abelard wrote the rule for the Paraclete in the twelfth century, it was not implemented at that time. Since the Rule of Benedict of Nursia (which was the standard rule for monasteries) was not entirely appropriate for a female monastery, it makes sense that Abelard would make modifications of that rule for a monastery he had founded. And it would seem likely that Heloise, being the prioress of the Paraclete, would have implemented the monastic rule that Abelard had just written especially for the Paraclete. Since it was not implemented, Benton concluded that it must not have been written in the twelfth century.

A major reason that Benton's paper (and subsequent article) had such an impact on Abelardian and Heloisian scholarship is the reputation Benton had built up for himself as a careful, meticulous scholar. He was a scholarly insider and could not be dismissed as some zealous skeptic who did not understand medieval France. He was very much part of traditional scholarship and occupied a named chair at the California Institute of Technology. Also, he was making legitimate criticism of that scholarship—namely, that research on the thirteenth-century history of the Paraclete had been neglected.

Benton's challenge to the traditionally accepted authorship of the letters of Abelard and Heloise "created a furor" (Barbara Newman's words)[36] not only in the scholarly community but also in the public at large. His challenge has been described as "ominous" (Peter von Moos's word)[37] because a great deal of the understanding of the intellectual climate of the twelfth century in France was dependent on the first letter, *The Story of My Calamities*.

If the letters are what they appear to be—that is, Abelard wrote the letters attributed to Abelard, and Heloise wrote the letters attributed to Heloise— then there is no need for concern over the matters that Benton cited. If, on the other hand, they are not what they appear to be, either as forgeries or as thoroughly reworked texts, then there is need for in-depth study of those matters—the thirteenth-century context of the Paraclete. The question is

---

36. Barbara Newman, "Authority, Authenticity, and the Repression of Heloise," *Journal of Medieval and Renaissance Studies* 22 (1992): 123.

37. Peter von Moos, "*Post festum*—Was kommt nach der Authentizitätsdebatte über die Briefe Abaelards und Heloises?" in *Petrus Abaelardus*, 81.

whether the letters can be accepted as twelfth-century texts written by Abelard and Heloise without doing the investigation of their being a thirteenth-century "work of imaginative fiction." The thirteenth-century case would lose by default without a credible context for them to have been written then, but the twelfth-century case is vulnerable because much of the context depends on the scholarly construct of twelfth-century intellectual life, which itself has been so heavily influenced by the testimony of *Calamities*.

In 1974, Peter von Moos surveyed the controversy to that point and pointed out that the state of Abelard studies had changed significantly as a result of Benton's challenge. Before then, according to von Moos, the field was one dominated by the "Schmeidler-Gilson 'complex'"—either Abelard wrote both his and Heloise's letters (position 2 above) or they each wrote their own (position 1).[38] Benton threw open the door to other possibilities.

Yet the furor as well as the ominousness of Benton's challenge was relieved when Benton himself recanted somewhat in 1980. For an individual who challenged the authenticity of a famous text to backtrack is not without precedent. The nineteenth-century German theologian David Friedrich Strauss (1808–1874), for example, retracted much of his challenge to the genuineness of the Gospels, in particular the Gospel of John, in the third edition of his *The Life of Jesus Critically Examined (Das Leben Jesu, kritisch bearbeitet)* only to retract the retraction in the fourth edition.[39] But it is relatively rare for a skeptic to do so. Either skeptics continue to defend their challenge against the criticisms or they keep quiet, perhaps hoping that future scholarship will vindicate them.

In 1980, Benton claimed that his position expressed in 1972—that the letters were written in the thirteenth century—was weakened as the result of a discovery by Fr. Crysogonus Waddell. That discovery was in the manuscript copy of the Diurnal (Daybook) of the Paraclete, containing prayers built on the structure *"Deus, qui . . . te quaesumus ut . . ."* ("God, whom . . . we pray you are . . ."), which was unique to the Paraclete. It was this very structure that letter 3 in AH-1 recommended for the Paraclete. Yet, according to Benton, that structure was already in use by the Paraclete when Abelard came for visits. It was merely carried over into the recommendation of letter 3. If so, then it seems that would still allow for a thirteenth-century author to do the same.

---

38. Peter von Moos, *Mittelalterforschung und Ideologiekritik. Der Gelehrtenstreit um Heloise*, Kritische Information, 15 (Munich: Wilhelm Fink, 1974), 102.

39. Albert Schweitzer, *The Quest of the Historical Jesus: A Critical Study of Its Progress from Reimarus to Wrede*, trans. W. Montgomery (London: Adam and Charles Black, 1910), 119. In words that Benton himself might have written, Strauss remarked in regard to the Gospel of John: "Not that I am convinced of its genuineness, but I am no longer convinced that it is not genuine."

Benton also found the phrase "by your slave" (*per servulum tuum*) in the first prayer "suggests so well the arrogant humility with which Abelard was afflicted that we must think it the work either of the Master or of someone who knew his mentality extremely well."[40] Benton did suggest Heloise as that "someone" but then proceeded without discussing that suggestion further. Yet, any author brazen enough to write letters in the name of Abelard and Heloise might be exhibiting some element of "arrogant humility" himself or herself.

Benton noted that no "new *historical* evidence to support the hypothesis of a thirteenth-century fraud" had been found since he raised the issue of historical inaccuracies in 1972. That fact was a surprise to him because he assumed that evidence would be easily forthcoming. Instead, the new evidence that was coming to the fore was not in support of a thirteenth-century fraud. It gave him pause and caused him to reconsider what he thought were historical inaccuracies: "I can demonstrate no historical errors which by themselves would place the authenticity of the work in doubt."[41] Yet he still thought the letters were a literary fiction in the sense that possibly Abelard himself wrote both the letters attributed to him as well as those attributed to Heloise. Thus, he reverted to the Schmeidler-Robertson view (position 2 above). His reconsideration also restored *Calamities* to its former prestigious status as a fundamental source for twelfth-century French intellectual and religious life.

Defenders of the traditional attribution expressed relief that Benton had retracted his initial claim of a thirteenth-century provenance for the letters, often not noting that he was still not accepting the traditional attribution. They did express some frustration, however, that other scholars seemed to be energized by Benton's initial skepticism that he expressed in 1972 to continue arguing against authenticity. Also in 1980, the British medieval historian David Luscombe remarked, "Since 1972 the appearance of unanimity [in regard to authorship of the letters] has evaporated. The pluralistic society has invaded medieval scholarship; California came to Cluny," and that "there is now a wide range of positions to compare."[42]

Benton made a significant methodological point in regard to medieval writing that torpedoed his earlier claim of a thirteenth-century creation—that is, the notion of anachronisms in a text is a Renaissance discovery. If someone forged a medieval text that was supposed to have been written at the time the forger was writing, then one would not encounter historical or linguistic anachronisms. But if someone forged a medieval text that was supposed to have

---

40. Benton, "A Reconsideration," 45.

41. Benton, "A Reconsideration," 48.

42. D. E. Luscombe, "The *Letters* of Abelard and Heloise since 'Cluny 1972,'" in *Petrus Abaelardus*, 19–20.

been written a substantial amount of time earlier, then that pre-Renaissance forger would not be aware that he or she was supposed to cover their tracks by eliminating historical or linguistic anachronisms. For us to think otherwise, according to Benton, "is itself a thought that is anachronistic."[43] If Benton's hypothesis was correct that the letters were written 150 years after they purport themselves to have been written, then we should expect to find some blatant anachronisms in the AH-1 set of letter. Benton followed up by looking at the two passages that in 1972 he considered anachronistic. He acknowledged that the first of the two passages—the absence of confirmation in twelfth-century texts that the decision of a Church council would result in "a compulsory preventive censorship"—relied too much on interpretation to be considered a genuine anachronism. The second passage involved a quotation from Deuteronomy, which was cited not as "ch. CVII" as in twelfth-century Bibles but as "ch. XXI," which, according to Benton, is "strikingly close to the ch. XXIII which would be the correct number in the thirteenth-century Bible of Stephen Langton."[44] Here Benton was decidedly stretching the evidence. Numbers are often transmitted faultily in manuscript copies, so "XXIII" could have been copied as "XXI." But to base any conclusions about authorship on the faulty transcribing of one number in a manuscript copied 150 years after the text it is transmitting was presumably written and without other solid evidence of anachronisms in that text seems thin in terms of constituting evidence of a work's having been composed later. A copyist could have made the error in trying to update the reference.

Benton cited an earlier article that he and Fiorella Prosperetti Ercoli did in 1975 on word analysis of *Calamities*. In that article they described finding six words as markers. Benton emphasized that six is a "number far too low to be in any way probative." The reader might then be excused for experiencing a "Huh?" moment by the next statement that, nonetheless, "the frequencies of the six words . . . do individually have statistical significance and they all point in the same direction." He left it to the reader to figure out how six words together are not "probative" but individually are statistically significant. He continued that their study of these six words "has shown that all earlier demonstrations of Abelardian authorship based on the frequency of vocabulary have no statistical significance and are in fact contradicted by a controlled investigation."[45] Benton then stated a conclusion that seems to support his earlier nonprobative statement: "Though statistical studies avoid the dangers

43. Benton, "A Reconsideration," 42.
44. Benton, "A Reconsideration," 43.
45. Benton, "A Reconsideration," 44.

of fastening in an impressionistic fashion on a few words, turns of phrase or concepts which might be imitated by an extremely shrewd forger, attention to particular instances of stylistic peculiarities can have value in determining authorship."[46] In a subsequent article, Benton rejected the statistical analysis that he and Prosperetti Ercoli had done in 1975 as faulty, and presented a new statistical analysis, which he asserted "accords with the conclusion that Abelard was the author of . . . all of the letters in the correspondence, including those supposedly written by Heloise."[47]

In 1988, three articles questioning the authorships of AH-1 came out in a six-volume collection on falsifications in the Middle Ages (*Fälschungen in Mittelalter*). Benton published his last article on the topic. In it he broadened the literary fictions to possibly include *The Questions of Heloise* (*Problemata Heloissae*), in which she raised forty-two questions that were answered by Abelard, although Benton could "think of no way to establish with certainty who wrote it."[48] He returned to the question of the similarity in style between the Abelard letters and the Heloise letters in AH-1 by drawing on the findings of Janson in regard to organization of the text. Latin philologists have been aware of and studying patterns of prose rhythms, which they call *cursus*. A *cursus* is a cadence of accented and unaccented syllables that end clauses. These cadences apparently change over time to the degree that philologists have tried to date the time of writing of Latin texts according to these changes. Their pattern of use can also help to identify the author of a text. An example of prose rhythm cadence is:

Non possum lacrimas ipse tenere me**as**.

Sucipias igi**tur**, sua qui delicta fate**tur**.

Janson identified thirteen types of *cursus* plus one category of "others" in the letters of AH-1 and found very little difference in the cadence patterns.[49] Benton interpreted this finding to mean that one person, Abelard, wrote both his and Heloise's letters and asked "the champions of dual authorship" to provide some means of distinguishing their writing from each other.[50]

Hubert Silvestre posited that AH-1 was forged and that the forger was Jean de Meun, the author of the *Roman de la Rose* and the very person who claimed

---

46. Benton, "A Reconsideration," 44.

47. John F. Benton, "The Correspondence of Abelard and Heloise," in *Fälschungen im Mittelalter. Internationaler Kongress der Monumenta Germaniae Historica, München, 16.–19. September 1986*, vol. 5: *Fingierte Briefe, Frömmigkeit und Fälschung, Realienfälschungen*, MGH Schriften, Bd. 33, V (Hannover: Hahnsche Buchhandlung, 1988), 98.

48. Benton, "The Correspondence of Abelard and Heloise," 109 fn. 38.

49. Janson, "Schools of Cursus," 187–195.

50. Benton, "The Correspondence of Abelard and Heloise," 110.

to be the first to find a manuscript that contained AH-1.[51] According to Silvestre, Jean de Meun imitated Abelard's style on the basis of some authentic works of Abelard that he had available to him, which would explain why the style of Abelard's letters and Heloise's letters are so similar. Jean de Meun's motivation for doing so, according to Silvestre, was to argue in favor of clerics having concubines by placing that argument in the words of a learned woman. Silvestre continued to defend this claim in the face of subsequent opposition. In the third article, Deborah Fraioli posited that a contemporary enemy of Abelard and Heloise forged the correspondence as a satire to ridicule them.[52] Fraioli's imaginative reading of AH-1 as a satire is a difficult sell when everyone else is reading the letters as serious and straightforward, no matter whether they think the letters are authentic, forgeries, or imaginative fictions.

In 1989, Luscombe defended the authenticity AH-1 on the basis that "the letters accompanying and prefacing the books of hymns and sequences, the Biblical problems, the *Hexameron* commentary and the sermons," which he sees as "the additional correspondence," "must be considered together [with the set of eight letters] and cannot be considered apart, for they constitute in their entirety a single achievement, that of providing the abbey in effect with a corporate strategic and operational plan."[53] This point is an interesting one because part of Benton's argument against authenticity was precisely that the letters were not being considered in a wider context and that the plan for the monastery in letter 5 was not implemented.

In 1992, Barbara Newman added another dimension to the entire discussion, a dimension that was to have ramifications at the end of the decade concerning the attributions of AH-2. She asserted that claims that either Abelard or someone else wrote the letters attributed to Heloise have no scholarly legitimacy. She argued that those claims are merely attempts to suppress Heloise's voice. She found "an uncanny resemblance" between the scholarly controversies over whether Heloise wrote the three letters of the correspondence attributed to her and "the questions that most vexed Heloise herself"— namely, the suppression of the female voice.[54]

---

51. Hubert Silvestre, "Die Liebesgischichte zwischen Abaelard und Heloise: der Anteil des Romans," in *Fälschungen im Mittelalter. Internationaler Kongress der Monumenta Germaniae Historica, München, 16.-19. September 1986*, vol. 5: *Fingierte Briefe, Frömmigkeit und Fälschung, Realien fälschungen*, MGH Schriften, Bd. 33, V (Hannover: Hahnsche Buchhandlung, 1988), 121–165.

52. Deborah Fraioli, "The Importance of Satire in Jerome's *Adversus Jovinianum* as an Argument against the Authenticity of the *Historica calamitatum*," in *Fälschungen im Mittelalter*, vol. 5, 167–200.

53. Luscombe, "The Letters of Heloise and Abelard since 'Cluny 1972,'" 270.

54. Newman, "Authority, Authenticity, and the Repression of Heloise," 121.

Newman viewed the questioning of Heloise's authorship as sexist male attempts to deny that medieval women could make such well-informed, reasoned arguments. She singled out Benton's use of *cursus* analysis in his 1980 article: "The use of such methods as *cursus* analysis and word counts assumes the opposite, since these techniques would not be employed if the letters had not previously been held suspect on other grounds." She went on to write that "these methods have not been sufficiently refined and tested on works of known authorship to be held reliable for use on doubtful texts."[55] While acknowledging that Benton was "a stimulating, careful, and versatile scholar," she detected a pattern in his scholarly work of gender bias, "an anti-feminist slant" that involved "minimizing the influence of female patrons like Eleanor of Aquitaine and Marie of Champagne" as well as "demonstrating . . . that the physician Trotula could not have written the medical works ascribed to her."[56] Newman added parenthetically that she found the latter demonstration of his convincing, which raises the question whether her acceptance of it should be cited as evidence indicating an anti-feminist slant or whether this shows an absence of a pro-feminist slant on her part. She also focused attention on the language male scholars like Robertson were using to describe Heloise, in particular his use of the words "little" and "poor." That way Newman seems to avoid the charge of making a circular argument—that is, that the arguments of those who questioned whether Heloise wrote the letters are by that very fact questionable because they began with the presupposition that she could not have written those letters. Instead, Newman concluded on scholarly grounds that their arguments were specious and then sought a reason for why they were all specious. A legitimate question can, however, be raised concerning how impartial her analysis of the skeptics' arguments was in the first place. What would the evidence have to look like for Newman to conclude that Heloise did not write the letters attributed to her?

Also in 1992, Peter Dronke subjected the three articles—Benton's, Silvestre's, and Fraioli's—in the 1988 collection *Fälschungen in Mittelalter* to critical analysis. He characterized them as "stronger in ingenuity than in logical rigour" and declared that they "display insufficient stringency of method and argument."[57] Dronke took Benton to task for "computer-aided frequency count of 24 words in the correspondence" in which he shows that "only one word (*etiam*) differs by as much as one standard deviation" and thus that the style of both the set of letters 2, 4, and 6 (attributed to Heloise) and letters 3,

---

55. Newman, "Authority, Authenticity, and the Repression of Heloise," 131, n. 43.

56. Newman, "Authority, Authenticity, and the Repression of Heloise," 125, n. 15.

57. Peter Dronke, "Heloise, Abelard, and Some Recent Discussions," in his *Intellectuals and Poets in Medieval Europe* (Rome: Edizioni di storia e letteratura, 1992), 325.

5, and 7 (attributed to Abelard) "is virtually identical."[58] Thus, Benton claimed that he had found computer-assisted statistical support for his contention that one person, Abelard, wrote both his and Heloise's letters of AH-1. Dronke "strongly suspect[ed]" that a similar choosing of twenty-four words from the writings of any teacher and student of the time would have shown the same frequency. He questioned what he saw as Benton's assumption that Heloise was a passive stylistic receiver of Abelard's style whereas, citing an earlier article of his, Dronke declared that "stylistically Heloise was as much a giver as a taker"—that is, she influenced Abelard's style as much as he influenced hers.[59] One would think that since Heloise was renowned for her learning when Abelard met her, she might have already developed a style of her own. In response to Benton's claim that Heloise adopted her Latin cadence patterns from Abelard, Dronke interpreted Janson's evidence differently: "Apart from the question of rhyme, both Heloise's practice of *cursus* and Abelard's can be seen in relation to a specific current of prose rhythm which is traceable in France from the time of Odilo of Cluny (d. 1049) to Guibert of Nogent (1053–1124), and which includes the epistolary prose of Abelard's teacher Roscelin (ca. 1050–ca. 1125)" and that Heloise could have adopted the "rhythmic style of a renowned Benedictine abbot such as Odilo" when she was at the Benedictine monastery of Argentueil.[60]

This question of Heloise's style is why the issue of Heloise's age at the time of meeting Abelard becomes an issue. If she were an adolescent, as *Calamities* has it, then her Latin style might be more open to influence from Abelard's style. If, on the other hand, she were a woman, as Peter the Venerable's letter says, she might have developed a style that was less susceptible to Abelard's influence. Of course, there is nothing to prevent a precocious adolescent from developing a writing style of their own or an adult from having their style influenced by a charismatic teacher.

Dronke claimed that "the reasoning behind Benton's use of evidence shows a confusion between a necessary condition for identity and a sufficient one." These criteria that Dronke put forth are important to take note of for the goal of this study, which is to see whether principles of authorship attribution can be established across different academic fields of research. He went on to state that any study of the type Benton undertook requires:

---

58. Benton, "The Correspondence of Abelard and Heloise," in *Fälschungen*, vol. 5, 101–102.
59. Dronke, "Heloise, Abelard," 326.
60. Dronke, "Heloise, Abelard," 339–340.

1) an investigation (on the basis of a fair range of authors) of which frequently-used words are statistically *significant* for establishing distinct or identical authorship;

2) detailed data of the comparative frequencies of these words in the writings of *other* masters and their disciples, as well as of authors who are closely linked by belonging to the same school;

3) a discussion of the literary conditions under which we can distinguish close affinity from identity;

4) a discussion of the statistical conditions—where are similar frequencies similar enough to suggest not close affinity but identity?[61]

Significantly, Dronke's criteria fit closely the method that Morton Smith used to establish the authenticity of Clement's letter. On the other hand, one wishes Dronke had applied those criteria to his suggestion that any teacher and student of the time would have written in a style similar to each other.

Yet, seeming to contradict himself, Dronke took on the claim of stylistic homogeneity and argued against it, citing small but significant differences between the style of the letters attributed to Abelard and those attributed to Heloise. Dronke responded to Silvestre's claim that Jean de Meun was the forger by analyzing de Meun's French translation from the Latin of AH-1. Dronke analyzed four significant errors in the French text that indicate the translator misunderstood the Latin source text. If de Meun forged the Latin text of the letters, he would not have misunderstood his own forgery when translating it into French.[62] It is clear from the nature of the errors that the direction of translation was from the Latin to the French, thereby excluding the possibility that de Meun or anyone else used the French version as the basis to back-translate into Latin.

Muckle, among others, although acknowledging the similarity in style, did say that he detected differences: "That of Heloise's letter is more compact and involved . . . . Her style too is more vivid and forceful than that of the *Historia* and of Abelard's letters." Yet, he cautioned that "the difference of content may account for this in part."[63] Mark Twain also claimed to have detected a difference in style,[64] but maybe he wrote that for the sake of his story line. The comparison of style is one I will return to below when I discuss AH-2.

---

61. Dronke, "Heloise, Abelard," 325–326 (italics in original).

62. Dronke, "Heloise, Abelard," 326–330.

63. J. T. Muckle, "The Personal Letters between Abelard and Heloise," *Mediaeval Studies* 15, no. 1 (1953): 51.

64. Mark Twain, *Innocents Abroad*, 145.

Apparently irked by what he sees as an anti-free-love agenda on Fraioli's part, Dronke criticized her for "a disingenuous attempt to claim wider validity for one's personal prejudice, letting it colour, rather than elucidate, the texts of one's choice."[65] He based this assessment solely on Fraioli's use of the word "infamous" to describe those views expressed in one of Heloise's letters. But unless Dronke had some other evidence that Fraioli had an agenda, her use of "infamous" could merely be in relation to the mores of the time, not necessarily applying her own judgment.

In 2000, John Marenbon surveyed the controversy for the twenty-five years since von Moos's book appeared in 1974 and came down squarely on the side of the traditional attribution—that is, that Abelard wrote the letters attributed to him and Heloise wrote those attributed to her.[66] It was clear that the defenders of the traditional view had been more resourceful in finding evidence and formulating arguments than the skeptics. Thus, by 2001, Dronke felt secure enough that the question of attribution had been resolved in favor of the traditional view to state: "I hope the oft-repeated older claim that these are forgeries no longer needs serious discussion."[67] But just at the point when the Abelardo-Heloisians thought they had vanquished the challenges of the skeptics to AH-1, they found themselves faced with the challenge of the attribution of another set of letters to Abelard and Heloise.

AH-2

When the monk Johannes de Vepria transcribed AH-2 in the late fifteenth century, interest in them remained dormant. The letters are unattributed but most of them, have either a V or an M at the beginning. V is understood to stand for *Vir* (Man) and M for *Mulier* (Woman). The contents of the letters indicate a male teacher and his female student. In addition, it was clear V and M were in some kind of relationship with each other that went beyond the academic, similar to the relationship in which Abelard and Heloise found themselves. It would seem to be an odd topic for a form letter packet unless one conjectures that such relationships were far more widespread in medieval times than we have direct evidence for. Among the issues connected with these letters that were not addressed in the scholarship until recently were when and where they were written, whether or not the epistles were written by one per-

---

65. Dronke, "Heloise, Abelard," 332.
66. John Marenbon, "Authenticity Revisited," in *Listening to Heloise. The Voice of a Twelfth-Century Woman*, ed. Bonnie Wheeler (New York: St. Martin's, 2000), 19–33.
67. Peter Dronke, review of *Listening to Heloise. The Voice of a Twelfth-Century Woman*, ed. Bonnie Wheeler, in *International Journal of Classical Tradition* 8, no. 1 (2001): 135.

son or different people, and whether the collection was meant as a rhetorical exercise (created by a monk or nun on their own perhaps inspired by the Abelard-Heloise story) or a copy of the actual letters exchanged by two individuals.

In 1974, the German medieval philologist Ewald Könsgen published an edition of AH-2 as part of his doctoral dissertation.[68] As the subtitle of the book Könsgen chose the words "Letters of Abelard and Heloise?" with a question mark. Nowhere else in the book does he argue for this possibility, only stating that the letters are from the Île-de-France and written by two people like Abelard and Heloise. Twenty-five years later, in 1999, Constant J. Mews, an Australian medievalist, concluded that the missives of AH-2 were definitely written by Abelard and Heloise. He connected them with the statement in letter 2 of AH-1 (the first letter of Heloise to Abelard) in which one finds the words, "When you sought me out formerly for base pleasures, you would frequent me in repeated letters." Mews claimed that those "repeated letters" referred to in Heloise's letter are the ones in AH-2. Mews asserted, "If these love letters were written by a couple other than Abelard and Heloise, the question remains as to who these individuals could be. I argue for the simplest solution, that they are indeed written by Abelard and Heloise." That in fact is not "the simplest solution" but a logical fallacy known as *ad ignorantiam*—a specific assertion must be true because we don't know that it isn't true.[69]

Earlier, in 1992, Newman had contrasted the collection of 113 anonymous letters of AH-2, which she described as "letters in a model collection," with AH-1, which had attributions on them. She wrote that Könsgen's suggested attribution "has found little favor."[70] Despite these words, Newman's article had profound unintended consequences when, in 1999, Mews accepted Könsgen's suggestion and backed AH-2 as being written by Abelard and Heloise. It created a problem. Newman and C. Stephen Jaeger, among other scholars,[71] immediately accepted Mews's claim, but it put skeptics in a bind—to reject Heloise's authorship of the woman's letters in AH-2 left one open to the charge

---

68. Ewald Könsgen, *Epistolae duorum amantium. Briefe Abaelards und Heloises?* Mittellateinisches Studien und Texte 8 (Leiden: E. J. Brill, 1974).

69. A popular example of the fallacy of *ad ignorantiam* is concluding that UFOs must be spaceships with extraterrestrials in them because these unidentified flying objects have not been identified as anything else.

70. Newman, "Authority, Authenticity, and the Repression of Heloise," 132, n. 46.

71. Barbara Newman, review of *The Lost Love Letters of Abelard and Heloise* by Constant J. Mews, *Medieval Review*, December 25, 2000; C. Stephen Jaeger's *Ennobling Love: In Search of a Lost Sensibility* (Philadelphia: University of Pennsylvania Press, 1999), 160: "We can now accept [this set of love letters] as letters exchanged between Abelard and Heloise in the early days of their love affair, not literary exercises."

of trying to silence Heloise. Two medievalists, Giles Constable and Jan M. Ziolkowski, addressed this problem directly. Ziolkowski described it this way:
"Those who reject or question the attribution of *The Lost Love Letters* to Heloise and Abelard (or Abelard and Heloise) place themselves willy-nilly in the
patriarchal lineage of both past anti-feminist males (from Fulbert and Abelard
on down), who have mistreated her, and modern scholars, who have sought
to silence her by avowing that the correspondence was a literary fiction or that
Abelard composed both sides of the exchange."[72] Could one reject the attribution of the M epistles to Heloise without laying oneself open to the charge
of trying to suppress Heloise's voice? Those who supported the traditional attribution of AH-1 found themselves divided over the attribution of AH-2. In
particular, Dronke and von Moos, two scholars who were among the staunch-
est defenders of the traditional attribution of AH-1 against Bentonian skepticism, rejected Mews's claim and became themselves skeptics of the new
attributions.[73]

I will focus here primarily on Ziolkowski's expressed reasons for his unwill-
ingness to accept the attribution of AH-2 to Abelard and Heloise since he was
particularly sensitive to the problem of gender bias. As the starting point for
his critique, Ziolkowski took the three pillars, as described in Newman's review of *The Lost Love Letters*, that Mew's claim rests on: (1) that "learned women
did exchange Latin poems and letters with their male admirers in the early
twelfth century," (2) that "the fragmentary narrative that emerges from the
recently discovered letters is consistent in all particulars with what we know
of Abelard and Heloise," and (3) that "most important, the philosophical vocabulary, literary style, classical allusions, and contrasting positions on love apparent in Könsgen's letters are so thoroughly consistent with the known
writings of Heloise and Abelard that the supposition of their authorship is simpler than any alternative hypothesis."[74] Ziolkowski called these pillars "Newman's taxonomy." He accepted the first pillar—men and women in the twelfth

---

72. Jan Ziolkowski, "Lost and Not Yet Found: Heloise, Abelard, and the *Epistolae duorum amantium,*" *Journal of Medieval Latin* 14 (2004): 175–176; cf. Giles Constable, "The Authorship of the *Epistolae duorum amantium:* A Reconsideration," in *Voices in Dialogue: New Problems in Reading Women's
Cultural History,* ed. Linda Olson and Kathryn Kerby-Fulton (Notre Dame, IN: University of Notre
Dame Press, 2005), 174.

73. Dronke, review of *Listening to Heloise*, 139: "I cannot accept the argument of the two essays
on the *Epistolae duorum amantium* [AH-2] . . ."; Peter von Moos, "Die *Epistolae duorum amantium* und
die *säkulare Religion der Liebe*: Methodenkritische Vorüberlegungen zu einem einmaligen Werk mittellateinischer Briefliteratur," *Studi Medievali,* 3rd ser. 44 (2003): 1–115, where he dated AH-2 to the
fourteenth century.

74. Ziolkowski, "Lost and Not Yet Found," 181, quoting Barbara Newman's summary of Mews's
argument that she made in a review of *The Lost Love Letter* in the online journal *Medieval Review,* December 25, 2000.

century exchanged poems and letters—as a given since abundant evidence was available to substantiate it. It was the other two pillars that he disputed.

In regard to the second of the Newman/Mews pillars—the contents of AH-2 are consistent with the Abelard and Heloise story—Ziolkowski addressed the issue that we do not have evidence of any specific cases of teacher-student affairs in the Middle Ages other than the one involving Abelard and Heloise. He argued that absence of evidence is not evidence of absence. He indicated that there is quite a lot about the Middle Ages we do not have direct evidence for but that we know must have existed. By analogy, he argued, "We do not know the names of any of the schoolmasters (or schoolmistresses) who gave either Abelard or Heloise their basic training in Latin." Continuing that line of thought, he asked, "If Heloise was herself a successful role model for the nuns in the Paraclete, what are the names and where are the texts of the young protégées she nurtured? Should we assume they never existed because we do not know them?" He followed up with:

> Must we presume that no other women and men who wrote Latin had affairs or that no others produced letters in the course of them? Would not all involved in such affairs have had cause to keep silent their names? And is it not within the nature of love for lovers to praise each other extravagantly? All of this is merely to suggest why, even if we accept the *Epistolae* as being genuine letters from the early twelfth century (or earlier), there could have been many candidates for their authorship whose names are not and will never be known.[75]

One might add that if the missives of AH-2 are not copies of letters that Abelard and Heloise wrote but by another man and women, then that would mean those who attribute these letters to Abelard and Heloise are suppressing the voice of another as yet unknown medieval woman writer. Even if the letters did date to the twelfth century, to attribute texts to a famous person because one lacks the imagination to consider the possibility that someone not famous could have written them may be just another form of suppression by denying the voice of the person or persons who actually wrote them.

Concerning the third pillar of Newman's taxonomy—the consistency with the style of the other writings of Abelard and Heloise—Ziolkowski pointed out that the number of words in the items attributed to V and M in AH-2 are roughly equal, around 5,500 words each. He explained that he chose to focus his analysis on a comparison of the sixty-seven items attributed to V with the writings of Abelard because it gave him a larger data base to work with. He

---

75. Ziolkowski, "Lost and Not Yet Found," 182.

rejected Mews's claim of six unique words/phrases that appear in both AH-1 and AH-2 testifying to their having been written by the same authors.

Ziolkowski cited Jaeger's assessment of the difference in style between the epistles of V and those of M—namely, that M's is superior: "The woman's style in both prose and poetry is clearly and demonstrably more learned, more elegant, more classical, more complex, and more richly allusive than that of the man."[76] Jaeger characterizes the man's poem as workmanlike, "yeomanly products of verse-making" and "carpented with the sophistication of two sticks nailed together."[77] Ziolkowski does not contest Jaeger's assessment, but he does question whether Abelard, who has been called "one of the most noteworthy poets of the twelfth century," would have written such mediocre verses even when writing casually.[78] To be sure, even great poets have been known at times to write mediocre verses, but given the high quality of the verses V was receiving from M, one would think that V would rise to the challenge of meeting that quality with his own if he were capable of doing so. Given what else we know about Abelard, we can suppose that his competitiveness would have kicked in, and because it apparently did not, it brings into question whether one can attribute V's missives to him.

Ziolkowski analyzed Janson's data regarding occurrence and incidence of rhythmic and rhymed organization of text in *Calamities* and in the *Poem to Astrolabe* as well as in V's letters in AH-2 along with its "expected frequency" in Latin prose. He applied a Pearson's chi-squared test (χ^2) to check against chance results and found "little accord."[79]

In regard to the comparison of M's writing style with that of Heloise's, Ziolkowski cited the finding in Dronke in a review of Mews's *The Lost Love Letters*. In that review, Dronke wrote that the respective styles are sharply contrasting:

> The 49 excerpts attributed to M in the Veprian collection [AH-2] include poems in leonine hexameters (38 b, 49, 66), in unrhymed Classical distichs (82) and in leonine distichs (69, 73). Her [M's] prose passages tend towards consistent rhyming (mainly half-rhymes and assonances) of pairs of phrases. Many of the longer excerpts from her letters leave no

---

76. C. Stephen Jaeger, *"Epistolae duorum amantium* and the Ascription to Heloise and Abelard," in *Voices in Dialogue*, 133.

77. Jaeger, *"Epistolae duorum amantium* and the Ascription to Heloise and Abelard," 136.

78. Ziolkowski, "Lost and Not Yet Found," 187–188. The quotation is from the Joseph Szövérffy, *Secular Latin Lyrics and Minor Poetic Forms of the Middle Ages: A Historical Survey and Literary Repertory from the Tenth to the Late Fifteenth Century*, 4 vols., vol. 2 (Concord, NH: Classical Folia, 1993–1995), 273.

79. Ziolkowski "Lost and Not Yet Found," 194–195.

pairs of phrases unrhymed. By contrast, the known writings of Heloise include no verse, leonine or Classical, and their rhyming is of a different kind: passages that rhyme abundantly, not just in simple pairings, alternate with long stretches that have no rhymes at all.[80]

In sum, Ziolkowski found a lack of stylistic similarity between Abelard of AH-1 and V of AH-2 as well as a lack of stylistic similarity between Heloise of AH-1 and M of AH-2.

In 2009, Sylvain Piron analyzed the content of M's letters in AH-2 and found connections with those of Heloise in AH-1: "The crucial difference between the two women voices we have been discussing is that one was preparing herself for the eventuality of dramatic events, while the other had already been through tragedy."[81] Here then is the fundamental conundrum of AH-2. They are letters written apparently by two individuals who find themselves in the same or similar position that Abelard and Heloise found themselves. There are no noticeable anachronisms in the letters, and there is nothing in the contents of them that would preclude their having been written by Abelard and Heloise. Yet stylistic analysis beyond citing particular words tends not to support the identification of V with Abelard and M with Heloise. That leaves open the possibility, as I mentioned above, that a third party wrote these form letters with the exchange between Abelard and Heloise in mind but was unconcerned about stylistic verisimilitude. The items of AH-2 may simply have been a literary exercise and not intended to be understood as having been written by Abelard and Heloise.

The Takeaway

Benton, in his article from 1980, in which he partially backtracked his claim that the letters of AH-1 were forgeries raised the specter of six words. He seemed to be arguing both that these six words together have no probative value, but individually they are statistically significant. The six words in questions are: *amplius* (more), *autem* (however), *facile* (easily), *penitus* (internally), *ut* (and) plus subjunctive, and *vehementer* (vehemently).

If some scholars attribute a text to a woman, and other scholars attribute that same text to a man, under what circumstances is it legitimate for those

---

80. Dronke, review of *Listening to Heloise*, 137.
81. Sylvain Piron, "Heloise's Literary Self-fashioning and the Epistolae duorum amantium," in *Strategies of Remembrance: From Pindar to Hölderlin*, ed. Lucie Doležalová (Newcastle upon Tyne, UK: Cambridge Scholars, 2009), 50.

who defend the attribution to the woman to claim the suppression of the woman's voice by the man claimers?

In contrast to the Stratfordians in the Shakespeare authorship controversy (chapter 6), the Abelardo-Heloisians (i.e., those who support the traditional attribution of AH-1 letters) have responded in print with scholarly professionalism *ad argumentum* (to the arguments of the skeptics and the evidence they marshal) rather than *ad hominem* ("to the person" by questioning the motives of the skeptics). For the most part, the Abelardo-Heloisians have presented the arguments of the skeptics fairly and accurately. In part, this difference may be the result that the challenges to the traditional attribution of AH-1 have been from within the academic community, while the challenge to the Stratfordian attribution has been from outside.

Other works that are attributed to Abelard are accepted without question that he wrote them. We will see a similar phenomenon in the chapter on attributions to Andrei Kurbskii (chapter 7).

Hubert Silvestre accused the person who said he discovered the manuscript of the AH-1 letters, Jean de Meun, as being the forger of them. We have already seen this type of accusation against Morton Smith as having forged the manuscript that he said he discovered of the letter of Clement of Alexandria (chapter 3). But unlike the accusers of Smith, few others have repeated Silvestre's accusation against Jean de Meun.

In regard to principles of attribution for AH-1, Benton, in the last article he published on the subject, wrote: "If we are ever to settle the major issue of the authorship of these letters, it will not be through discussions of what might be plausible behavior for people of either the twelfth century or today, but on the basis of the most technical and indeed unemotional issues, questions of style, dating, sources and so on."[82] Benton seems to be invoking the principle that one's emotional proclivity of what one wants the outcome to be can, and often does, affect sound analysis. If one decides ahead of time that one wants Abelard and Heloise to be the authors of the letters attributed to them, then the chances are one will conclude that they are the authors and will find evidence to support that conclusion. If one wants someone else to have been the author, then one will find evidence that someone else was the author. Ironically, Benton himself seems to have fallen into that trap himself, because his second position was that Abelard wrote both his and Heloise's letters, so he found "statistical" evidence that Abelard was the author of both sides of the correspondence. In trying to be consistent that the "technical and unemotional" disciplines of codicology, textual criticism, content analysis, chronol-

---

82. Benton, "The Correspondence of Abelard and Heloise," 97.

ogy, and so on provide more reliable analytical tools for determining attribution, then one needs to analyze those disciplines. Benton made that attempt by resorting to computer-assisted stylistic analysis twice. Each time was less than successful. The first time, he rejected the findings some thirteen years later; the second time, other scholars have pointed to his flaws in interpreting the data. Right after the words he wrote about "technical and indeed unemotional issues," he went on to present five types of evidence that Abelard wrote both his letters and the letters attributed to Heloise. Yet it seems that Benton was on the right track.

CHAPTER 5

Who Wrote the *Compendium of Chronicles* (*Jami al-Tawarik*) and the Collection of Letters Attributed to Rashid al-Din?

"Arguably the most distinguished figure in Persia during Mongolian rule."

—Historian Morris Rossabi, about Rashid al-Din[1]

In 1206, in the steppe area north of China, notable men gathered to hold an assembly (*quriltai*), which chose a Mongol chieftain named Temuchin to be ruler (khan) of a confederation of pastoral nomad peoples. Upon being chosen, Temuchin took the name Chinggis Khan and proceeded over the course of the next twenty-one years to lead the steppe people in conquering more territory than any other single person in history. Upon his death in 1227, his empire stretched across Eurasia from central Asia in the west to China in the east. Sometime before his death, he decided to divide the empire among his four eldest sons—Ogodei, Chagatai, Tolui, and Jochi. But Jochi predeceased his father, so Jochi's portion (*ulus*) went instead to Batu, Jochi's son. The three sons and grandson of Chinggis continued to add on territory, mostly in major parts of eastern Europe and the Middle East. Effectively, as William McNeill explained, these conquests united the Eurasian ecumene.[2] It meant that merchants (like Marco Polo and his father and brother), and diplomats (like John of Plano Carpini and William of Rubruck),

---

1. Introduction by Morris Rossabi (City University of New York), "Genghis Khan: World Conqueror?" http://www.blackwellpublishing.com/content/BPL_Images/Content_store/Sample_chapter/9780631189497/GK_sample_chap.pdf.
2. William McNeill, *The Rise of the West: The History of the Human Community* (Chicago: University of Chicago Press, 1963), 317, 572–573.

Table 5.1   House of Hulagu

- Hulagu (1256–1265)
- Abaqa (1265–1282)
- Ahmad Tegüder (1282–1284)
- Arghun (1284–1291)
- Gaikhatu (1291–1295)
- Mahmud Ghazan (1295–1304)
- Oljeitu (Muhammad Khodabandeh) (1304–1316)
- Abu Sa'id Bahadur (1316–1335)

could travel across the Eurasian landmass in safety because the roads were protected by the Mongol authorities.

The four divisions of the empire were Yuan China (ruled by Ogodei), the Chagatai khanate (ruled by Chagatai), Ilkhanate (ruled by Tolui), and the Ulus of Jochi (ruled by Batu). The ruler of Yuan China was the head of the Mongol Empire, and each of the other three khans owed allegiance and tribute to him. The name of the third of these khanates, the Ilkhanate, derives from the granting by Qubilai Khan (the son of Tolui) to his younger brother Hulagu the title of subordinate khan (*il-khan*) in 1256. Hulagu, the first ruler of the house of Hulagu, was followed by seven rulers (see table 5.1) before the Ilkhanate began to break up.

The Ilkhanate, which covered the territory from the eastern part of Anatolia (present-day Turkey) in the west to the western part of present-day Pakistan and most of Afghanistan in the east, is the location of this particular authorship controversy. It involves a man who was court physician to the khan of the Ilkhanate and then became its vizier (prime minister).

Context of the Controversy

The *Compendium of Chronicles (Jami' al-Tawarikh)* is a three-volume work that John A. Boyle described as "the first world history."[3] It is attributed to the Persian statesman, physician, and historian Rashid al-Din Hamadani (1247–1318). At the time it appeared, a writer by the name of Abu al-Qasim 'Abdallah

---

3. John A. Boyle, "Juvayni and Rashīd al-Dīn as Sources on the History of the Mongols," in *Historians of the Middle East*, ed. Bernard Lewis and Peter M. Holt (London: Oxford University Press, 1962), 133–137; Boyle, "Rashīd al-Dīn: The First World Historian," *Iran* 9 (1971): 19; Karl Jahn, "Rashīd al-Dīn as World Historian," in *Yádnáme-ye Jan Rypka: Collection of Articles on Persian and Tajik Literature*, ed. J. Bečka (Prague: Academia, 1967), 79–87; David Morgan, *The Mongols* (Oxford: Basil Blackwell, 1986); 20; 2d ed. (Malden, MA: Blackwell, 2007), 18.

ibn 'Ali Kashani (d. 1324) claimed that he was the author. Kashani was known for having written the *Tarik-e Öljäitü*, an important contemporary source for the reign of Oljeitu Khan (r. 1304–1316). Although scholars are divided over how much of the *Compendium of Chronicles* Rashid actually wrote, there is general acceptance that even if he did not write every word, the entire work was at least accomplished under his direction. In order to explain Kashani's claim that he wrote it, scholars have hypothesized that Kashani was one of those who worked under Rashid's direction.[4] And as *New Yorker* staff writer Tad Friend (1962–) wrote about Hollywood screenwriters: "The problem is that nearly every writer feels chiefly responsible for a script he's worked on."[5] That feeling may or may not be true about Kashani. He may have in fact written or largely written the *Compendium of Chronicles*, but the circumstance that Friend describes is more likely the case.

A different story attends the letters that are attributed to Rashid, *The Collection of Rashid's Letters* (*Mukatibat-i Rashidi*). As with the letters of Abelard and Heloise (see chapter 4), doubts have been raised as to their authenticity—first by the English scholar of Persian literature Reuben Levy (1891–1966) in 1946, then by the British scholar of Persian studies Alexander H. Morton (1942–2011) in 1999. Responses from the defenders were soon in coming—the Soviet historian Il'ia P. Petrushevskii (1898–1977) responded in 1948 to Levy's challenge, and the Iranian museum consultant Abolala Soudavar (1945–) responded in 2003 to Morton's challenge. Other scholars have expressed their opinions in footnotes and asides in their texts about whether the letters are authentic but without adding much in the way of evidence or argument one way or the other. What are the issues of authorship that have been raised in these challenges and responses? And what bearing, if any, do they have on Rashid al-Din's authorship of the *Compendium of Chronicles*? This chapter assesses the evidence and arguments in the four main articles (two for and two against authenticity) that go into some detail on the question of the authorship of *The Collection of Rashid's Letters*.

The generally accepted details of the life of Rashid al-Din are as follows. Rashid was of Jewish descent but converted to Islam around 1277 when he was thirty years old. We first have evidence of him as the physician of Abaqa Khan (r. 1265–1282). No more evidence about him exists until the reign of Ghazan Khan (r. 1295–1304) when he and Sa'id al-Din were appointed co-viziers. Both continued in that position under Ghazan's successor as khan, Oljeitu.

---

4. W. W. Barthold, *Turkestan Down to the Mongol Invasion*, 4th ed. (London: Gibb Memorial Trust, 1977), 47.

5. Tad Friend, "Credit Grab," *New Yorker*, October 20, 2003, 160.

When Sa'id al-Din was assassinated in 1312, 'Alishah, an even more implacable foe of Rashid, became co-vizier. Rashid resigned as co-vizier in 1316 or 1317, and in 1318 he was charged with poisoning Oljeitu Khan and executed. His son Ghiyathu'd-Din ibn Rashid al-Din Fad'lullah served as vizier of the Ilkhanate for a brief time after his father's death.

Into the Thicket

The focus of this chapter is a collection of fifty-four items ostensibly compiled by Muhammed Abarquhi, who served Rashid al-Din perhaps as his secretary. Forty-seven of the items are letters attributed to Rashid, four are letters written to him, one is an introduction to the collection by the compiler, and one is a petition to Rashid at the end. The Soviet scholar A. I. Falina, who translated the letters into Russian, wrote in 1971 that *The Collection of Rashid's Letters* was maintained in whole or in part in thirteen manuscript copies—two in Cambridge, England; one in St. Petersburg, Russia; one in Istanbul; and nine in Iran. The two Cambridge manuscripts (one being a nineteenth-century copy of the other, which is an undated manuscript) are in the collection of Albert Houtum-Schindler and are described by the British Orientalist Edward Granville Browne (1862–1926).[6] According to Falina, the undated Cambridge manuscript was used by the Iranian scholar Muhammad Shafi' to publish his edition in Persian of the letters in 1947.[7] Shafi' dated the manuscript to the end of the fourteenth or beginning of the fifteenth century.[8] In 1971, A. I. Falina published a Russian version of Shafi''s text.[9] As a result of Shafi''s edition being based on faulty manuscripts, there are only fifty-three items in it, one fewer than the complete edition of the collection of letters published by Muhammad Taqi Danishpazhuh in 1980 based on a study of fifteen manuscript copies, apparently using two more than Falina knew about.[10]

The scholarly dispute over authenticity of the letters raises in an acute way a number of issues in regard to determining authenticity in general. Among the issues are: Can showing that one of the letters of a collection is a forgery be enough to bring into question the entire collection or does it require more than

---

6. Edward G. Browne, "The Persian Manuscripts of the Late Sir Albert Houtum-Schindler, K.C.I.E," *Journal of the Royal Asiatic Society* 49, no. 4 (October 1917): 693–694.

7. Rashīd al-Dīn, *Perepiska*, ed. and trans. A. I. Falina (Moscow: Nauka, 1971), 35–37.

8. Rashīd al-Dīn, *Letters*, ed. Muhammad Shafi' (Lahore: University of the Panjab, 1947), 236–237.

9. Rashīd al-Dīn, *Perepiska*, ed. and trans. Falina.

10. Rashīd al-Dīn, *Sawānih al-afkār-i rashīdī*, ed. Muhammad Taqi Dānishpazhūh (Tehran: Intishārāt-i Dānishgāh-i Tihrān, 1980). As a result, the numbers of the letters in Levy's and Petrushevskii's articles is one digit lower than those in Danishpazhuh's edition.

one letter? If so, then how many does it require? At what point do discrepancies in the text bring into question the authenticity of the text itself? Does a wrong date constitute an anachronism? To what extent can faulty copying or hypercorrections by an editor or scribe be used to explain discrepancies and anachronisms?

In 1946, Reuben Levy in a short (just over four pages) article challenged the traditional attribution of those letters.[11] He accepted the attribution of the *Compendium of Chronicles* to Rashid al-Din and compared the style of writing in the letters with that of the *Compendium*. Levy posited that the letters were written in the fifteenth century in India. Although he pointed to three anachronisms in dates and two examples of extravagant rhetoric as well as raising questions concerning a list of pensioners, he did not provide much in the way of evidence that the letters were written over two hundred years after Rashid died or were of Indian provenance. Petrushevskii, for the most part, discussed Levy's argument in a methodical point-by-point rebuttal.[12] That allows us to juxtapose their views directly and to determine the specific issues of contention.

Comparison with the Compendium of Chronicles

In the letters themselves, Levy pointed out instances that he thought constituted anachronisms, examples of "magniloquence" out of place for someone of Rashid's carefulness (again, as indicated by his reading of the *Compendium of Chronicles*), and other oddities. In regard to Levy's argument that the style of the letters does not match that of the *Compendium of Chronicles*, Petrushevskii declared that one really needs a philological comparison in order to make that assertion.[13] Besides, stated Petrushevskii, one should more properly compare the letters with the Arab-language works of Rashid on theology than with the Persian-language *Compendium*, which included large excerpts from other Persian-language works as well as having a collective of writers contributing to it.[14]

Style

Levy noted "the lack of the characteristic marks of Rashid al-Din's style and language, amply displayed in the *Jami' al-Tawarik*."[15] Here Levy is already on

---

11. Reuben Levy, "The Letters of Rashīd al-Dīn Fadl-Allāh," *Journal of the Royal Asiatic Society of Great Britain and Ireland* 1 (April 1946): 74–78.

12. Il'ia P. Petrushevskii, "K voprosu o podlinnosti perepiski Rashid ad-Dina," *Vestnik Leningradskogo universiteta* 39 (1948): 124–130.

13. Petrushevskii, "K voprosu," 125–126.

14. Petrushevskii, "K voprosu," 126.

15. Levy, "The Letters of Rashīd al-Dīn," 74.

thin ice from a methodological viewpoint because he stakes out the *Compendium of Chronicles* as accurately representing Rashid's style. Yet doubts about how much the *Compendium* can be attributed to Rashid have been raised by a number of different scholars. One could just as easily stake out the collection of letters as accurately representing Rashid's style and use it as a basis to question Rashid's contribution to the *Compendium*. In addition, Levy asserted that the letters "are filled with anachronisms and improbabilities and phrased in the vaguest and most palpably exaggerated fashion." He found it to be "a matter passing belief" that "a statesman both cautious and businesslike . . . should have dealt with matters concerning finance and revenue in such inflated and unrestricted terms."[16] Petrushevskii countered Levy's charge that Rashid should have written his letters in a more "cautious and business-like style" by asserting that Rashid "wrote the letters not for future investigators but for his sons, for trusted people and friends well familiar with his affairs, beliefs, and political views."[17] Here Petrushevskii seems to have abandoned his own suggestion that he had just made a few lines earlier that Rashid's secretary Muhammed Abarquhi might have written the letters. Petrushevskii went on in this vein for a few more sentences, but he probably could just have left the entire matter drop after stating that such a comparison should not be made without a philological study of the works attributed to Rashid.

Time of Composition and Provenance

Levy asserted that "the present collection of letters would seem to be of not earlier date than the fifteenth century," fully two hundred to three hundred years after Rashid al-Din lived. He also suggested the letters were not even Iranian but "of Indian provenance."[18] Petrushevskii responded that Levy had no basis for proposing an Indian provenance other than "the fact that in the letters there are reports about relations of Rashid al-Din with Muslim Indians." But, as Petrushevskii pointed out, the letters also mention his contacts "with people living in Asia Minor, Egypt, the Maghreb, and Central Asia," all of which then would seem to have equal basis to proposing a place of composition.[19] As we will see, Morton does provide more substantiation for Levy's Indian provenance theory.

---

16. Levy, "The Letters of Rashīd al-Dīn," 74.
17. Petrushevskii, "K voprosu," 126.
18. Levy, "The Letters of Rashīd al-Dīn," 74.
19. Petrushevskii, "K voprosu," 128.

Anachronisms

In the category of anachronisms, Levy cited Letter 7, which purports to be written in the city of Sultaniyah during the reign of Oljeitu but dated Sha'ban 690 (August 1291). Oljeitu did not become khan until 1304. The city was founded when Arghun was khan (683/1284–690/1291) but according to Levy was not called Sultaniyah until the reign of Oljeitu, "who was the first Mongol prince to be entitled 'Sultan.'"[20] Thus, if it was written in "Sultaniyah," it could not have been written before 1304. If it was written in 1291, it could not have been written in "Sultaniyah." Petrushevskii noted that the letters may not have reached us as they were originally written.[21] The compiler or, alternatively, a copyist could have "updated," in his view, the name of the city in the letter after 1304.

In another letter, dated 670/1272, the writer states that he has been neglectful "because of my great preoccupation with affairs of state and the business of the treasury," but at the time, according to Levy, Rashid was still only the court physician, not the co-vizier.[22] Petrushevskii questioned the willingness of Levy "to so categorically assert that Rashid al-Din did not occupy administrative office before 1298" because the historical evidence about him is so sparse at this point in time.[23] Here we have an instance of the absence-of-evidence-is-not-evidence-of-absence argument.

Letter 29(30) purports to have been written during the reign of Arghun (r. 1284–1291), but refers to "the Kings and Sultans" of India. Levy asserted that the only Indian ruler to fit that status of sultan was Ala al-Din, who became sultan in 1296, at least four or five years after Arghun died.[24] In regard to the ostensible anachronism of calling Ala al-Din a sultan four or five years before he became one, Petrushevskii objected that Ala al-Din "wielded huge factual power, had his own possessions, and independently conducted war with neighbors" during the reign of his uncle, Sultan Firuz (r. 1290–1296). Thus, Ala al-Din was acting like a sultan before he technically became one. According to Petrushevskii, the case is similar to that of the Timurid Baysonqor (1397–1433), whom historians called sultan even though he never ruled as sultan during the reign of his father, Sultan Shahrukh (r. 1405–1447).[25] The difference, of course, is that the reference to Ala al-Din as sultan is not being done by someone act-

---

20. Levy, "The Letters of Rashīd al-Dīn," 75.
21. Petrushevskii, "K voprosu," 129.
22. Levy, "The Letters of Rashīd al-Dīn," 76.
23. Petrushevskii, "K voprosu," 127.
24. Levy, "The Letters of Rashīd al-Dīn," 77.
25. Petrushevskii, "K voprosu," 126.

ing in the capacity of a historian when doing so. Nonetheless, one can find any number of other examples in the historical record of a titular nomenclature that was not being strictly followed. Muscovite grand princes were being called tsar by various people for various reasons and even at times in official documents for decades before the formal adoption of the title in 1547.[26]

Petrushevskii also added a fourth anachronism to the three that Levy pointed out. In Letter 42(43), which claims to be written from Caesarea (Qaysariyya) in 1291 (AH 690), Rashid al-Din writes to the Hamadán officials about maintaining the hospital and pharmacy that he had founded there, and that he is sending a physician named Ibn Mahdi to report about it. Petrushevskii did not think that Rashid had the authority to do this until he became vizier in 1298.[27] Nonetheless, Petrushevskii explained that "these anachronisms do not give us the right to declare all the correspondence of Rashid al-Din as forgeries, as R. Levy had done." Petrushevskii referred to the "anachronisms and clearly incorrect information about contemporaries" in the *Compendium of Chronicles* but "no one got it into their head on that basis to declare this work a later forgery."[28] This argument of Petrushevskii's is a risky one to make because, first, doubts have been expressed about Rashid al-Din's authorship of it, and, second, in other fields of study when someone has made such an argument about the dating and authorship of a particular work (that no one has doubted it), then, sure enough, often one finds someone who then raises doubts about it.

Levy cited Letter 7(8) as an example of exaggeration. According to Levy, the letter writer bestows on Majd al-Din (Rashid's son) provinces that include Egypt: "the provinces of Iran from the Oxus to the furthest limits of Rum, whence to the shores of the Indian Ocean (Darya-i Sind) and all the territories of Egypt." But, as Levy pointed out, Egypt was not under the control of the Ilkhanate.[29] Petrushevskii agreed with Levy's claim that Letter 7's granting to Rashid al-Din's son rule over Egypt was an exaggeration since Egypt was not under Ilkhanate control but countered that it was an official exaggeration, not limited to Rashid al-Din. For example, Ghazan Khan made the same claim in a decree. So if one questions the authenticity of the letters on that basis, then, according to Petrushevskii, one must also question the authenticity of that decree.[30] The claim by governments to have territory that they do

26. Donald Ostrowski, *Muscovy and the Mongols: Cross-Cultural Influences on the Steppe Frontier, 1304–1589* (Cambridge: Cambridge University Press, 1998), 178–182.

27. Petrushevskii, "K voprosu," 130.

28. Petrushevskii, "K voprosu," 130.

29. Levy, "The Letters of Rashīd al-Dīn," 75.

30. Petrushevskii, "K voprosu," 126.

not actually rule has been a not infrequent one in the historical record.[31] Here Rashid would then just have been following the official governmental line. Yet there is another possibility. The letter writer was not necessarily asserting that Egypt was under Ilkhanate control but only that Ilkhanate rule goes "up to the borders of Egypt."[32] In that case, it would not be an exaggeration at all.

Another passage grants to Majd al-Din the office of Shaykh al-Islam and that of shaykh of a Sufi hospice (*khanaqah*) in Baghdad, but according to Levy there is no mention to be found in Hamd Allah Mustawfi's *Pleasure of the Hearts* (*Nuzhat al-Qulub*) of a Sufi hospice in Baghdad.[33] In regard to Levy's claim that no Sufi hospice existed in Baghdad, Petrushevskii responded that in the *Compendium of Chronicles*, there is a decree of Ghazan that mentions a *waqf* (donated building usually for religious purposes) in Baghdad.[34] The text of the *Compendium of Chronicles*, however, mentions only a "seat of the judiciary in the City of Peace Baghdad." A few lines further on it does mention a *waqf*, but that was "in the province of Hamadan, in the vicinity of Safed Koh, in the village of Buzinjird," not in Baghdad.[35] Even though Petrushevskii's rejoinder misfires here, Levy's claim in this case depends on the exhaustiveness of Mustawfi's *Pleasure of the Hearts*, which for any number of reasons might not have included a Sufi hospice in Baghdad. Certainly it is not enough in itself to determine the genuineness of a letter.

Levy characterized Letter 43(44) as providing "a ponderous recapitulation of his [the letter writer's] vast and all-embracing powers."[36] Again, he found it totally uncharacteristic for Rashid's style based on the style of the *Compendium of Chronicles*.

In Letter 19(20), Levy detected what he considered several oddities in the list of pensioners that the governor of Baghdad, Rashid's son Amir 'Ali, is sup-

---

31. For example, in the middle of the seventeenth century the Russian tsar when writing to European recipients claimed in his official title that he was "Sovereign of the Iberian lands of the Kartlian and Georgian tsars" but would not include that phrase when writing to central Asian and Middle Eastern recipients. The reason was that the Kartlian and Georgian tsars were under the authority of the shah of Persia, which central Asian and Middle Eastern recipients would know, but European recipients would not be expected to know. Grigorii Kotoshikhin, *O Rossii v tsarstvovanie Aleksei Mikhailovicha: Text and Commentary*, ed. Anne E. Pennington (Oxford: Oxford University Press, 1990), 52–53.

32. For the decree(s), Petrushevskii cites *Jami al-Tawarik* according to the Istanbul manuscript copy and *Sbornik letopisei*, vol. 3, trans. A. K. Arends, ed. A. A. Romaskevich, E. E. Bertel's, and A. Iu. Iakubovskii (Moscow: Akademiia nauk SSSR, 1960), 240, 275, 282. Cf. Rashiduddin Fazlullah [Rashid al-Din], *Jami'u't-Tawarikh: Compendium of Chronicles*, trans. W. M. Thackston (Cambridge, MA: Harvard University Department of Near Eastern Languages, 1999), 694, 725, 731, 732: "from the River Oxus to the borders of Egypt."

33. Levy, "The Letters of Rashīd al-Dīn," 76.

34. Petrushevskii, "K voprosu," 127, citing *Sbornik letopisei*, vol. 3, 233.

35. Rashiduddin Fazlullah, *Jami'u't-Tawarikh*, 688.

36. Levy, "The Letters of Rashīd al-Dīn," 78.

posed to provide for. Levy finds it "peculiar" that Rashid, a follower of the Shafi'i *madhhab* (one of the four Sunni schools of law), should include Shi'a on the list "if it is true that he was at the time very anxious to prove his orthodoxy."[37] To Levy's wondering why the head Shi'a imam of Iraq, Jamal al-Din Mutahhar al-Hilli, was on the list even though Rashid was a member of a Sunni sect, Petrushevskii asserted that al-Hilli had great influence on Oljeitu Khan, so Rashid could not keep him off the list even if he had wanted to.[38]

Levy also questioned the appearance on the list of the names of people who were wealthy (thus, not needing a pension) and too young to receive one. Levy did allow that maybe it was someone else in each case with the same name.[39] Petrushevskii found no problem with the list of pensioners. In each case, where Levy pointed to someone who had died before Rashid's list came out, Petrushevskii could point, with one exception, to another individual with the same name who was still alive. The one exception was Azud al-Din Idzhi, who was born around 1300. Petrushevskii did note that it could be another Azud al-Din Idzhi being referenced about whom we have no evidence.[40] What he found suspicious was that the letter claimed to be sent from Tus to the emir Sutai. That emir is named in the *Compendium of Chronicles* "not earlier than the 1290s."[41]

Levy commented on "the assumed writer's constant references to the elevated status he possessed in India at a time when there had been no Mongol penetration into the country."[42] Levy also pointed out that the "munificent largesse" that the letter writer granted to "certain of his old servants" was slated to begin in the year 780 (1378/9), sixty-two years after he died and the elderly servants would have been long gone. Thus, according to Levy, the falsifier gives himself away.[43] Petrushevskii reaches exactly the opposite conclusion—that it shows the genuineness of the letters because no falsifier would include something "so clearly absurd." Instead there is "only one logical explanation," according to Petrushevskii—the author or perhaps a copyist mistakenly wrote AH 780 (1378) for AH 718 (1318).[44]

Petrushevskii accepted the statement in the introduction that the collection of Rashid's letters was compiled when Rashid's son Ghiyath was vizier (r. 1327–1336). There are dates on only three of the letters so the time of composition

37. Levy, "The Letters of Rashīd al-Dīn," 76.
38. Petrushevskii, "K voprosu," 127.
39. Levy, "The Letters of Rashīd al-Dīn," 76–77.
40. Petrushevskii, "K voprosu," 129, col. 2, n. 5.
41. Petrushevskii, "K voprosu," 129–130.
42. Levy, "The Letters of Rashīd al-Dīn," 77.
43. Levy, "The Letters of Rashīd al-Dīn," 78.
44. Petrushevskii, "K voprosu," 128.

of the rest is often guesswork. Petrushevskii thought that the problematic ones could have been added at the time of compilation. Even if so, that does not preclude, according to Petrushevskii, the collection from being used as a reliable historical source about socioeconomic conditions of the time. Nor does it matter in terms of the representation of Rashid's political ideas since his sons shared those ideas.[45]

We end this round with stronger citation of evidence and marshaling of logical arguments on the side of Petrushevskii and the genuineness of the collection of letters. Between 1948, when Petrushevskii's article appeared, and 1999, when Morton's article appeared, very little scholarship was published that discussed the authenticity of *The Collection of Rashid's Letters* as a whole. If a reference was made at all to the issue, it was done so usually in a footnote where a particular scholar opined their personal view. There were some exceptions, however.

One issue that had been the focus of attention is whether Rashid al-Din traveled to India. In 1971, K. A. Nizami discussed Letter 30(29), which tells of a diplomatic mission that Rashid took to India. Nizami noticed that in Rashid al-Din's *History of India*, which was completed in or after 1303–1304 (AH 703), he states that among his sources were travelers who had returned from India, but he does not mention his having been there.[46] Rather than question the authenticity of the letter, Nizami proposed that Rashid went to India after that date but before 1308 when he writes to his son Mahmud (Letter 44[43]) and tells him to look after his commercial interests as well as his properties there. Presumably these had been bestowed on Rashid during a previous trip. That way, the diplomatic mission of Rashid al-Din to India could have occurred between 1304 and 1308. Thus, according to Nizami, the mention in the letter of Arghun as ilkhan at the time must be a mistake; Oljeitu should have been meant.

In 1975, the British historian Peter Jackson discussed Letter 53, which describes a military expedition from the Ilkhanate that took Lahore and pillaged Sind province. Jackson asserted that "no other source mentions the campaign, and the authenticity of the letter is suspect."[47] In addition, the letter is addressed to Rashid's son Ibrahim as the governor of Shiraz, but according to

---

45. Petrushevskii, "K voprosu," 130.
46. K. A. Nizami, "Rashīd al-Dīn Fazl Allah and India," in *Majmūʿa-yi Khaṭāba-hā-yi Taḥqīqī dar bāra-yi Rashīd al-Dīn Faḍlallāh Hamadānī*, ed. S Naṣr (Tehran: Dānishgāh-i Ṭihrān, 1971/2), 47–48.
47. Peter Jackson, "The Mongols and the Delhi Sultanate in the Reign of Muhammad b. Tughluq (1325–1351)," *Central Asiatic Journal* 19, no. 1/2 (1975): 129–130. Jackson cited Levy's article for his claim that "the authenticity of the letter is suspect," but not Petrushevskii's rejoinder.

Jackson, "Ibn Zarkub, in his *Shiraz-nama*, composed in 744/1343-4, makes no mention of Khwaja Ibrahim as governor of Shiraz in these years."[48]

In 1982, Simon Digby discussed Letter 47(46), which has a list of luxury goods gathered from around Gujarat or transshipped there. He asserted that "some material in the collection in which this document was reproduced is clearly inauthentic." Thus, the list of items is not to be relied upon in regard to quantities: "We cannot therefore take on trust the absolute quantities of the items said to have been dispatched, ranging from diamonds weighing 2.29 and 4.58 g. to 38.52 metric tonnes of teak-wood; but the list provides some guide as to relative quantities." He suggested a date of "before 1400" for "the forgeries or alterations" and wrote that he based this assertion on "current scholarly opinion."[49] Yet the only reference he cited was Levy's article, which he acknowledged proposed a fifteenth-century time of composition. Nonetheless, Digby's assertion does highlight the question of how much of any collection of letters can be used as reliable evidence if some of the collection is acknowledged not to be authentic. Does it change the dynamic in terms of accepting testimony as reliable evidence? Does one accept that testimony as authentic as long as it is not challenged or as long as it fits within a construct that we have? In other words, is whatever fits the construct authentic, and whatever doesn't, isn't? Now we return to the mainline arguments.

In 1999, Morton surveyed the arguments of Levy and Petrushevskii. He expressed bewilderment at Levy's claim that the material in the letters is "vague" since what stands out in reading the letters "is precisely the amount of petty detail many of them contain," especially in regard to the describing of events or the giving of orders.[50] But the events described and the orders given, in Morton's estimation, are not realistic. Instead of the letters being seen as "forgeries," which are meant "to cheat," Morton proposed that they were "playful" and "designed to bamboozle harmlessly."[51] Thus, his assessment is two-stepped. First, he pointed out what he considered to be the unrealistic parts (i.e., those that do not correspond with other contemporary source testimony). Second, he made the case for its being a work of historical fiction.

Morton began by picking up on Jackson's doubts about Letter 53 and came to the conclusion that "[t]he letter is . . . completely fictitious." He reached this

---

48. Jackson, "The Mongols and the Delhi Sultanate," 130, n. 66.

49. Simon Digby, "The Maritime Trade of India," in *The Cambridge Economic History of India*, vol. 1, ed. Tapan Raychauduri and Irfan Habib (Cambridge: Cambridge University Press, 1982), 139–140.

50. A. H. Morton, "The Letters of Rashīd al-Dīn: Īlkhānid Fact or Timurid Fiction?" in *The Mongol Empire and Its Legacy*, ed. Reuven Amitai-Preiss and David O. Morgan (Leiden: Brill, 1999), 157–158.

51. Morton, "The Letters of Rashīd al-Dīn," 196.

conclusion on the basis that the campaign described in the letter of the Ilkhanate against Punjab and Sind never occurred: "Whatever their limitations, the sources are adequate to establish when military operations on such a scale were undertaken by the ruler."[52] Falina had determined, in her translation of the letter, that if the campaign had occurred it would have been during the last few years of the reign of Ghazan or the first years of the reign of Oljeitu, so Morton was able to identify the narrative sources that cover that period, including Rashid al-Din's *Compendium of Chronicles*. It would certainly be odd for Rashid to make up a campaign that never happened, and then to describe it in a letter but not in his world history.

Morton also picked up on Nazami's discussion of Letter 30. He argued that Nazami's "solution" of substituting Oljeitu for Arghun as the name of the khan does not save the letter's authenticity. He found the absence of any evidence that Rashid al-Din had traveled to India during Oljeitu's reign as well to be "adequate in itself to show that the letter is not authentic."[53] But he also proposed what he considered to be additional evidence that the diplomatic mission of Rashid al-Din to India was "pure fiction." He pointed to the account of the contemporary Persian historian Wassaf (fl. 1299–1323) of a diplomatic mission from Oljeitu to Ala al-Din (r. 1296–1316) of Delhi in 1310–1311 (AH 710). That mission presented a decree (*yarligh*) from Oljeitu upbraiding Ala al-Din for not sending a diplomatic mission to Oljeitu that acknowledged his succession to the throne of the Ilkhanate. Morton inferred from the decree, as reported by Wassaf, that no previous mission from Oljeitu had been sent.[54] On the one hand, since Wassaf was a protégé of Rashid al-Din, one might think that he would more readily include mention of Rashid's diplomatic mission to India if there had been one. On the other hand, Wassaf stated in his history that his main goal was "to write in the grand style" and, as Browne described it, "the historical events which he records served merely as the material on which he might embroider the fine flowers of his exuberant rhetoric."[55] So one should not rely too much on what Wassaf does not include.

Morton based the core of his argument on formulating a theoretical principle about authorship attribution in general. He referred to finding "particular items of information in one letter which seem to tally with those in others. At first these signs of consistency may be reassuring, but when the Letters

---

52. Morton, "The Letters of Rashīd al-Dīn," 165.

53. Morton, "The Letters of Rashīd al-Dīn," 168. Soudavar subsequently argued that Rashid's trip to India occurred during the reign of Ghazan (see later in this chapter).

54. Morton, "The Letters of Rashīd al-Dīn," 168–169.

55. Edward G. Browne, "The Historians of the Īl-Khání Period," in Browne, *A Literary History of Persia*, vol. 3 (Cambridge: Cambridge University Press, 1928), 68.

come seriously under suspicion the opposite is true."[56] That is, Morton is asserting that signs of consistency between and among letters about a particular piece of information may become evidence for forgery of those letters once doubts arise about the particular information they are in harmony with. Such a notion, as stated here, when raised to the level of principle for determining authorship is, however, problematic. If internal consistency as well as consistency with other sources is an indication of authenticity when letters are not under suspicion, but an indication of inauthenticity when the letters come under suspicion, then if the suspicion is removed, does that evidence revert to favoring authenticity? If so, then the toggle between authenticity and inauthenticity would seem to depend upon a subjective judgment of how serious one considers the suspicion to be, which does not appear to be a feasible way of proceeding in regard to assessment of the validity of evidence.

Morton went on to argue, however, that it is not suspicion of the work (in this case, a collection of letters) that brings the consistency into question, but suspicion of the validity of the particular piece of testimony that is repeated consistently in other letters of the collection, which brings that testimony into question. The testimony in various letters concerning India, such as an Ilkhanate military campaign against the Delhi Sultanate, Ilkhanate control of territory in India, and Rashid's travels there, not only are not corroborated in other primary sources but also are in direct conflict with the testimony of some of those sources. Morton concluded: "It is a mistake therefore to think that the material on India is marginal to the question of the authenticity of the Letters."[57] Although Levy had proposed that the letters had an Indian provenance, he did not explain in any detail why he thought so. Petrushevskii basically dismissed any such claim of Indian provenance, also without going into any detail. Morton did not make any connection with Levy's proposed Indian provenance, but he did emphasize the importance of the "material on India" in connection with the authorship question.

Instead, Morton discussed "a topic that may be considered more fundamental, that of the problems posed by a number of references to Rashīd al-Dīn's sons."[58] In all, there were fourteen sons and four daughters named in Letter 37.[59] According to Morton, the writer of the letters was not knowledgeable about what his "sons did or could have done, or even how many of them there were."[60] Morton pointed out that we have no evidence other than the letters

56. Morton, "The Letters of Rashīd al-Dīn," 169.
57. Morton, "The Letters of Rashīd al-Dīn," 171.
58. Morton, "The Letters of Rashīd al-Dīn," 172.
59. Browne, "The Historians of the Īl-Khání Period," 84.
60. Morton, "The Letters of Rashīd al-Dīn," 172.

of the existence of a number of the sons whose names appear in the letters. As an example, Morton singled out Saʿid al-Dīn, supposedly the eldest son, whose name appears in Letters 11, 37, and 52. In both Letters 11 and 52, he is described as being the governor of a province. Morton pointed to a "conspicuous problem with both letters," which is that the province he governs is described as covering areas part of which "never formed part of the Ilkhanid empire, part was only briefly under Mongol occupation, and part was never directly administered . . . [such as] Antioch [which] was never a Mongol possession."[61] For Morton, this description and descriptions of other places that were not part of the Ilkhanate show that "it is all invention" and that Letter 37(36), which states that among Rashīd al-Dīn's properties is a quantity of land in Antioch, confirms "[t]hat the person responsible for [writing] it did think that Antioch was part of the Ilkhanid empire . . . ."[62] Morton also pointed to Letter 40 in which the "author thinks that Qinnasrīn and ʿAwāṣim belong to the Īlkhāns," which they never did.[63] Morton concluded that "as with the references to India, so in this area the Letters maintain some consistency, but in a way that argues against rather than for their authenticity."[64] I discussed this problem above in regard to Egypt. The point is that countries do make claims that they rule an area (e.g., Ukraine claims to be governing Crimea; the Republic of China [Taiwan] has claimed off and on to be governing mainland China), and they can appoint governors of those areas either with the intent of acquiring them or as an honorific position. After all, Chinggis Khan assigned areas to his four sons that were not completely part of the Mongol Empire at the time.

A person named Mahmud is addressed in Letters 5, 9, and 43 as governor (emir) of the province of Kirman. According to Browne, this was the Mahmud who was one of Rashid's sons. The problem that Morton saw here is that the year of birth for Rashid's son Mahmud in official documents is 1309. That date, if true, according to Morton, makes it highly unlikely that Mahmud was governor of anything before Rashid's death nine years later in 1318.[65] This issue is different from the one discussed in the previous paragraph—that is, an honorific governorship over a province that is not actually under a government's control, whereas Kirman was a province directly under the control of the Ilkhanate.

61. Morton, "The Letters of Rashīd al-Dīn," 173.
62. Morton, "The Letters of Rashīd al-Dīn," 174.
63. Morton, "The Letters of Rashīd al-Dīn," 175.
64. Morton, "The Letters of Rashīd al-Dīn," 175.
65. Morton, "The Letters of Rashīd al-Dīn," 175–176.

According to Morton, a third son, Jalal, is implied in the letters to be the governor of the province of Rum once or twice during the reign of Ghazan and once or twice during the reign of Oljeitu, as well as being governor of Isfahan or Iraq-i 'Ajam once during the reign of Ghazan and governor of Isfahan or Iraq-i 'Ajam once during the reign of Oljeitu. Morton looked at what he considered to be "relatively good information on the appointment of Governors in the general chronicles, the contemporary local history of Āqsarā'ī." He found that Aqsara'i does mention Jalal but only as *Sahib-Diwan* in 1317, the first year of the reign of Abu Sa'id. No mention is made of any earlier appointments of Jalal in Rum. As a result, Morton concluded: "Jalal was never Governor of Rūm under Ghazan or Öljeitü or even Abū Sa'īd, and the letters that state or imply that he was must be rejected."[66]

Morton concluded his overall argument by returning to the discrepancies in style that Levy brought up between the letters and other writings attributed to Rashid al-Din. He asserted that "the Letters have negative value" in terms of providing reliable "evidence for political and administrative history and for the prosopography of the Ilkhanid period."[67] Instead, Morton sees it as a work of fiction, "something approaching a historical novel, epistolary in form of course." He found the chronology to be "non-linear" as well as no discernible plot, although he did find "some structure":

> At the beginning, No. 1 is a formal introduction, in praise of God and His prophet, No. 2, a moralizing piece, introduces the topic of the just ruler and 3 and 4 alert us to the importance of the role of the vizier. The last piece, No. 54, addressed to an unidentified son, concludes the collection with an exposition of the qualities of the good man.[68]

Through the "manifest protagonist, Rashīd al-Dīn . . . the real author's preoccupations are to some extent revealed."[69] Morton remarked that Rashid "as vizier seems to have remarkable freedom of action." Rashid's sons and other subalterns "lead armies on his instructions." Morton found the world being described to be "simplified and idealized" in that "it bears no resemblance to the dangerous and difficult bureaucratic world revealed by" contemporary writers, including Rashid al-Din in the other writings attributed to him. In Morton's view: "Our hero maintains Islamic values, is free with moral advice, and particularly emphasizes support for the *'ulamā* [the community of religious

---

66. Morton, "The Letters of Rashīd al-Dīn," 181.
67. Morton, "The Letters of Rashīd al-Dīn," 196.
68. Morton, "The Letters of Rashīd al-Dīn," 197.
69. Morton, "The Letters of Rashīd al-Dīn," 197.

scholars."[70] Echoing Levy's observation, Morton reported that this "fictional Rashīd al-Dīn has a very high opinion of himself; his frequent braggart boasting is wholly inappropriate for a royal employee." As a result of what he perceives to be an "offhand attitude displayed toward Mongols and Turks, and the exaggerated powers" attributed to the vizier, Morton deemed it unlikely that the letters were "intended for presentation to the real holders of power in the Timurid world" but instead to the "Tājīk scribes, the bureaucratic administrators . . . who lacked real power."[71] In Morton's opinion, they took "consolation for their unsatisfactory position in the present in nostalgia for an unreal past."[72] Morton considered the differences between the testimony found in the collection of letters and that of other contemporary sources to be so huge that he thought they could be explained only by the author of the collection of letters having intentionally written a fictional work to entertain his fellow scribes. Thus, as Morton proposes it, the author was not attempting to deceive his readership, so it cannot be considered a forgery.

In 1997, two years before Morton published his article, David Morgan (1945–2019), who apparently knew of Morton's arguments through other means, sided with him that the letters are not authentic and that they date to the Timurid period.[73] In 2001, Thomas Allsen (1940–2019) opined that "Morton's contention . . . persuasively argued," but declared that the collection "contains very specific and very accurate data bearing on the issue of West Asian citrus in China."[74] He found that "the writer was well informed on matters of Chinese agriculture" in general and on the sweet lemon (līmū) in particular as his description "is fully consistent with the Chinese accounts . . . and with other remarks of Rashīd al-Dīn."[75]

In Soudavar's article published in 2003, he responded to Morton's article on two levels: thematic (motives for a forgery, rhetorical exaggerations regarding territory controlled by the Ilkhanate, "oddities and omissions," methodological problems, and stylistic analysis) and specific letters (30, 35, 37, 48, and 53). Soudavar challenged Morton's conclusions on the basis that Morton engaged in what we are calling confirmation bias and did not understand the culture of medieval Persian letter writing: "Morton's article suffers . . . from an

70. Morton, "The Letters of Rashīd al-Dīn," 197.

71. Morton, "The Letters of Rashīd al-Dīn," 199.

72. Morton, "The Letters of Rashīd al-Dīn," 199.

73. David Morgan, "Rašid al-din and Ġazan Khan," in *L'Iran face à la domination mongole*, ed. Denise Aigle (Tehran: Institut français de recherché en Iran; Louvain: Diffusion, Peeters, 1997), 182. See also David Morgan, *The Mongols*, 2nd ed. (Malden, MA: Blackwell, 2007), 182.

74. Thomas Allsen, *Culture and Conquest in Mongol Eurasia* (Cambridge: Cambridge University Press, 2001), 123.

75. Allsen, *Culture and Conquest*, 124.

incomprehension of the motives of Persian scribes and history writers, wrong assumptions, and neglect of crucial evidence."[76] Even though Soudavar had "recently warned researchers about the pitfalls of forgeries and semi-fakes . . . . [he is] now . . . in the awkward position of . . . defending the authenticity of a work against allegations of forgeries." Nonetheless, he asserted that "the objective remains the same: that research should not be hampered by unwarranted allegations."[77] He sought to demonstrate the legitimacy of those criticisms in the rest of the article.

Soudavar began with the question of motive. Soudavar dismissed the motive proposed by Morton as the reason the text was written—to entertain fellow scribes—as "such a possibility simply defies common sense."[78]

Although Morton does use the term *forgery*, his proposal that the collection of letters was intended as entertainment for fellow scribes does not indicate a forgery as such. Others might be "bamboozled" by it, but the intention, if Morton is correct, was not to deceive but to entertain. In other words, it may be deceptive but not intentionally so. In addition, declaring that something does not make sense or "defies common sense" is not in itself a refutation. If one can point to a logical fallacy or a misrepresentation of the evidence, then one can declare the argument or assertion incorrect. What makes sense to one person might not make sense to another.

Soudavar ticked Morton on the aim of compiling the collection that Abarquhi made in the introduction to the collection—namely, "to be for the novice-scribe (*mota'allemān*) and the speakers (*motakallemān*), a refined companion in travel and a witty friend at home."[79] In other words, the compiler intended the letters in this collection to serve as form letters for other letter writers to imitate.[80] If so, then one could imagine the fantastical information that Morton thought he discerned in it might be just intended to be entertaining while the collection itself had a serious purpose.[81]

Soudavar pointed to what would otherwise be considered confirmation bias on the part of Morton. For example, in a work written between 1470 and 1486, the author incorporates four of the letters in the collection of letters into his text, copying them verbatim. But he also compares them stylistically with a work by Qazvini composed before 1334. The author of the fifteenth-century

---

76. Abolala Soudavar, "In Defense of Rašid-od-Din and His Letters," *Studica Iranica* 32 (2003): 77–120.

77. Soudavar, "In Defense," 79.

78. Soudavar, "In Defense," 80.

79. Soudavar, "In Defense," 80.

80. Soudavar, "In Defense," 81.

81. An example of such a mix of a serious book with fanciful examples might be Karen Elizabeth Gordon's *The Well-Tempered Sentence: A Punctuation Handbook for the Innocent, the Eager, and the Doomed* (New York: Ticknor and Fields, 1983).

work concludes that Qazvini borrowed from Rashid al-Din. In contrast, Danishpazhuh, the editor of a recent edition of the collection of letters, concludes that Rashid borrowed from Qazvini. Either way, according to Soudavar, Morton should have mentioned this similarity for "it implied a composition date of no later than 1334 and a fatal negation of his [Morton's] Teymurid fabrication thesis."[82] To be sure, Morton could have responded as Benton did in his challenge to the twelfth-century date of the letters of Abelard and Heloise—that they could have been based in part on some authentic materials while still having been written by someone else at a later time.

In regard to Rashid's son Mahmud not being old enough to be governor of a province, Soudavar accused Morton of making the unwarranted assumption that the apparent discrepancy is evidence of fictionalization. A simpler explanation, according to Soudavar, is that the Mahmud being addressed as governor of a province in Letters 6, 10, and 44 is a different Mahmud from the one who is Rashid's son.[83]

Soudavar did not confront specifically Morton's assertion that Antioch and other areas claimed in the letters to be part of the Ilkhanate were, in fact, never part of it. But he explained away the claiming of territory that was not part of the Ilkhanate as standard propaganda, which I discussed earlier in this chapter.

Soudavar pointed to two instances of fabrication in the *Compendium of Chronicles*—concerning the birth of Jochi and that Ghazan had appointed Oljeitu his successor. Both of these fabrications were intended, according to Soudavar, "to enhance the legitimacy of Uljaytu and polish the image of the Mongol dynasty."[84] So fabrication in and of itself does not exclude Rashid al-Din from being the author. In terms of differing claims to particular territories or cities, Soudavar pointed out that Syrian maps show the Golan Heights to be part of Syria whereas Israeli maps show the Golan Heights to be part of Israel.[85] He found that "as a whole, the territorial claims of the Letters are very consistent with the Il-Khānid political ideology."[86]

Toward the end of his article, Soudavar engaged in a method that has been used in other authorship controversies (see chapters 6, 7, and 8), called profiling. Profiling in this context means extracting from the content of the work or works the characteristics of the author. He identified eight characteristics: (1) "a detailed fiscal administrative knowledge of various province[s]," (2) "me-

---

82. Soudavar, "In Defense," 79.
83. Soudavar, "In Defense," 104–108.
84. Soudavar, "In Defense," 82.
85. Soudavar, "In Defense," 83.
86. Soudavar, "In Defense," 84.

dicinal knowledge," (3) "a command of Qorānic verses that only a commentator of the Qorān . . . would have," (4) the ability to "respond to intricate philosophical and religious questions asked by prominent theologians," (5) "a vast knowledge about geography," (6) maintained "contact with so many scholars and learned men," (7) knew "detailed information about agriculture and agricultural products," and (8) "possessed literary skills." Each of these characteristics of the author of the letters, according to Soudavar, corresponded with the known characteristics of Rashid al-Din.[87]

If one takes four items in a collection of fifty-four items as authentic, then is that sufficient to assert (as Soudavar seems to) that all the other items in the collection are authentic? The flip side is claiming that all items in a collection are fake if a few of them are shown to be so. Ideally, I suppose, the authenticity of one item in a collection should not be dependent on the authenticity of any of the other items. Nonetheless, if one or more items in a collection can be shown to be fake, then the researcher cannot help but take that finding into consideration when assessing the authenticity of the others.

In 2013, in his PhD dissertation from the University of Washington, Stefan Kamola briefly critiqued Soudavar's response to Morton. He found that "some of Soudavar's arguments are effective ripostes to Morton's critique," but other arguments depend upon creating "historical scenarios which, though feasible, . . . are not mentioned in other sources." Kamola mentioned in particular the trip that Rashid al-Din supposedly took to India: "Soudavar argues that such an embassy could have occurred . . . in the wake of the failed invasion of Syria in the winter of 1300–1301."[88] Likewise, according to Kamola, Soudavar identified the campaign against India that Letter 53 describes with a campaign that Oljeitu undertook in central Asia against Daud Khwāja (1304–1316). Kamola described Soudavar's method in this particular case as "a sort of analogical historiography that Soudavar has famously applied to other Ilkhanid-era documents."[89] Kamola singled out Soudavar's overlooking what he (Kamola) considered to be "perhaps Morton's most compelling argument for rejecting the letters, namely their literary qualities as a collection" and "chief among these, Morton demonstrates that the letters construct an alternate, ahistorical life for Rashīd al-Dīn's best documented son, Jalāl al-Dīn."[90] In this regard, Soudavar may have done one of the things he criticized in Morton—namely, neglecting crucial evidence.

---

87. Soudavar, "In Defense," 115–116.

88. Stefan T. Kamola, "Rashīd al-Dīn and the Making of History in Mongol Iran" (PhD diss., University of Washington, 2013), 5–6, 14–17.

89. Kamola, "Rashīd al-Dīn," 6.

90. Kamola, "Rashīd al-Dīn," 6.

The Takeaway

The view that Rashid al-Din directed the composition of the *Compendium of Chronicles*, thus perhaps not actually writing it himself, has also been proposed in regard to Andrei Kurbskii and his relationship to the corpus of works attributed to him (see chapter 7).

Levy's and Morton's method includes the principle that mistakes indicate the attributed author (in this case, Rashid al-Din) is not the real author. They assume that the attributed author was knowledgeable and would not make such errors, while the real author was not knowledgeable and, as a result, did make them. The difference, in their views, is a marker that distinguishes the attributed from the real author. It is important then for them and for the skeptic in general to point out errors ("error" defined as something contradicted by reliable evidence), inconsistencies (or even consistent inconsistencies), and anachronisms. Yet, all authors make mistakes. One might argue that there are certain mistakes no author would be expected to make, but that determination also depends upon the researcher correctly understanding the context of what was written. In some cases, it might be the researcher making the mistake.

Morton's proposal that the letters are historical fiction in epistolary form written by a scribe for the entertainment of fellow scribes, if correct, would take it out of the realm of forgery. Similar to *tuoyan* or *ethopoeia*, it was not meant to deceive anyone. We will see a similar claim advanced regarding some of the works attributed to Andrei Kurbskii (see chapter 7).

We can take Soudavar's four general criticisms of Morton's article and see if they work as general criteria to help determine authorship of any particular work. Thus reworded, they become: (1) understand the motives of the person who wrote the text, (2) make correct assumptions, (3) do not neglect crucial evidence, and (4) make only warranted allegations. In regard to criterion 1, Soudavar went on to write that "without a plausible motive, forgery does not make sense."[91] That assertion elevated to a principle of authorship attribution simply does not wash. We can know that something is a fake but have no plausible motive. For example, the bone and tool finds in the Piltdown quarry in the early 1910s were shown forty years later to be faked, but we do not have a good explanation for why they were planted. Or, rather, we have several plausible explanations to choose from, none of which has won out over the others. In any case, the absence of a more or less agreed-upon motive does not diminish one whit the fact that the Piltdown finds were faked.

---

91. Soudavar, "In Defense," 79.

In regard to criteria 2 and 4, there is an element of subjectivity about them. Are "correct assumptions" ones that agree with our own? No doubt, Soudavar did not intend that to be the meaning, and he certainly would not engage in doing so himself. But there is also no doubt there are people out there who automatically assume that any assumption that does not agree with their own is incorrect. Yet one could adopt an assumption that is not initially one's own when seeing the legitimacy of it. Nonetheless, we do not do so in order to explore further the notion of incorrect assumptions and how to judge whether an assumption is correct or not. The same goes for whether an assertion is warranted or not.

The question of what constitutes crucial evidence can at times be a tricky one. What one scholar considers crucial evidence might not be seen so by another scholar. As we will see in the Shakespeare authorship controversy (chapter 6), for anti-Stratfordians, in particular Oxfordians, the accurate detail concerning the cities in the plays set in Italy is crucial evidence, while for Stratfordians it is not. While Soudavar criticized Morton for overlooking what he (Soudavar) considered to be crucial evidence, so Kamola criticized Soudavar on the same basis.

Profiling, as Soudavar did, was also done earlier by Thomas Looney to establish the author of the Shakespeare canon (see chapter 6), by Edward L. Keenan to establish the author of the first letter of Kurbskii to Ivan Groznyi (see chapter 7), and by Roy Medvedev in discussing the authorship of *The Quiet Don* (see chapter 9). It is a practice that a number of literary scholars condemn, but it is a vital part of historical study to analyze written materials for historical evidence, including evidence about the author.

CHAPTER 6

Who Wrote Shakespeare?

> "That's rubbish and I'll fail you if you ask that
> question again."
>
> —James Shapiro, professor of English literature,
> Columbia University, on what he says in the classroom
> to any student who asks about the Shakespeare
> authorship controversy[1]

> "Each of them is more likely to have written the works
> of Shakespeare than William Shakespeare himself."
>
> —Quoted by Keir Cutler, playwright and performer,
> on the number of alternative candidates proposed as
> having been the author[2]

Hundreds of books and thousands of articles
have been written about the Shakespeare authorship controversy, yet it is possible to obtain a PhD in English literature and not have heard of it. Many
(most?) of those (both with and without PhDs) who have heard of it tend to
dismiss it as not worthy of consideration. After all, "Shakespeare wrote Shakespeare" has become one of the pillars of most people's worldview, akin to the
earth is round and $2+2=4$. Anyone who challenges what from their point of
view is obviously true must be a crank or charlatan or someone who is being
argumentative for argument's sake. Yet, is there another way to account for
the persistence of the skeptics?

Let us begin with a thought experiment. Let us say we have a body of literary work comprising forty plays, several narrative poems, and a collection
of sonnets. We do not know who wrote them, but there are two candidates.
Candidate 1 is a playwright and poet, and the date of the works directly attributed to him ends before the first works of our anonymous corpus begins.
Almost all the plays are about the court aristocracy and/or written from an

---

1. James Shapiro, interview with Brooke Gladstone, *On the Media*, WNYC, April 22, 2016.
2. Quoted in Keir Cutler, *The Shakespeare Authorship Question: A Crackpot's View* (Kindle locations
80–82) and cited as "Unknown origin, sometimes attributed to J. M. Barrie."

aristocratic viewpoint, and Candidate 1 is a nobleman of high standing who had access to the court. The works drew on over two hundred written sources, and Candidate 1 had access to one of the finest private libraries in his country. The Geneva Bible was the basis for biblical quotations in the plays and poem, and Candidate 1's Bible has underlinings and marginalia for around 250 verses that appear in the body of works for which we are trying to find the author. Eleven of the plays have their setting in Italian cities, and Candidate 1 spent about ten months in Italy in the same cities. The plays and sonnets describe incidents that are similar to incidents in the life of Candidate 1, including that he was captured by pirates and that he was reconciled with his estranged wife through a "bed trick." The anonymous body of work indicates its author possessed an extensive education, for the author is credited with contributing some 1,700 words to the English language and displays knowledge not only of Latin, Greek, French, and Italian but also accurate information about government, politics, rhetoric, the law, sailing vessels, medicine, falconry, and the classics. Candidate 1 was educated at the two major universities in the country as well as studying at the preeminent graduate law school in the country. He knew Latin, Greek, French, and Italian, and left an extant cache of forty-four letters.

Candidate 2, on the other hand, is a commoner from a provincial area with its own dialect, although none of the plays, poems, or sonnets is about commoners nor has any of the dialect of his area been confirmed in any of the works. We have no evidence, except for six labored signatures,[3] that Candidate 2 received any education or that he was even literate. We have no evidence that his parents, wife, or children were literate. He left no letters, only some litigious court documents. None of the events described in the plays or allusions in the poems and sonnets can be connected with events in his life. We have no evidence he had access to any books or library. We have no evidence he knew any language other than his own nor evidence that he left his home country. None of his contemporaries describes him as a playwright or as a writer of any type. His will makes no mention of his having any books although it is detailed about his worldly possessions in other respects.

So to whom would you attribute the anonymous body of works? If you are an established scholar in the field of English literature, the probability is you would attribute the body of works to Candidate 2, the provincial of questionable literacy. In contrast, those who question the traditional attribution to Candidate 2 tend to be actors, writers, Supreme Court justices, and amateur scholars

---

3. Labored signatures, barring forgery, can be a sign of a number of things, including nervous or muscular impairment or illiteracy. For an example of the former, see the authentic signature of Ronald Reagan shortly after he was shot in 1981; for an example of the latter, see authenticated signatures of Shoeless Joe Jackson, who was illiterate.

or scholars in another discipline. The holding of Candidate 2 as the author seems to be a matter of faith among the adherents, a faith that is based on a similarity in names and reinforced by the academic establishment that has constructed an extensive and impressive superstructure of conjecture. The holding of Candidate 1, the well-educated aristocrat, as the author, however, is not without its obstacles, including the need to resort to conspiracy as an explanation for the absence of evidence directly connecting him to the works in question.

Context of the Controversy

As the reader may have guessed, Candidate 1 is Edward de Vere, the 17th Earl of Oxford (1550–1604) (hereafter Edward de Vere).[4] Candidate 2 is William Shakespeare of Stratford-on-Avon (1564–1616) (hereafter William of Stratford).[5] The descriptions that I have given above are their historical personas. Many people for some time have had a problem correlating the literary persona that is the author of the Shakespearean corpus with the historical persona that is William of Stratford. The inability to correlate the two personas has led to the proposal of over five dozen individuals as the possible author, including Francis Bacon, William Stanley, Christopher Marlowe, and Elizabeth I, whose historical personas better fit the Shakespeare literary persona than does William of Stratford's. Stratfordians tend to dismiss the historical persona argument as unnecessary speculation, since we already know who wrote the works attributed to William Shakespeare; it was, in their view, William Shakespeare. And they point to the plethora of proposed counterclaimants as a sign of the weakness in the anti-Stratfordian position.[6] For this particular analysis, I will focus primarily

---

4. "Edward Oxenford" was the name used in publishing some of his poems.

5. The spelling of William of Stratford's last name varies. The name on his parish record of baptism is "Shakspere." The family name has various spellings: "Shaxpere," "Shakspeyr," "Shagspere," or even "Shaxbere"—none with the middle "e." Therefore, according to anti-Stratfordians, the first syllable was most likely pronounced with a short "a." For understandable reasons, Stratfordians dislike the anti-Stratfordians' using those spellings and prefer the name that appears on the First Folio: Shakespeare. Using "Shakespeare" for William of Stratford allows their joke that the anti-Shakespeareans don't think Shakespeare wrote Shakespeare but that it was someone else with the same name. For purposes of a more neutral designation, I am adopting "William of Stratford" for the person the Stratfordians call "Shakespeare" and the anti-Stratfordians call "Shakspere." To set up an equivalency in name, I will use "Edward de Vere" for his main competitor instead of "the Earl of Oxford" or "Oxford," his usual designations.

6. A Stratfordian is one who believes that William of Stratford wrote the works attributed to William Shakespeare. An anti-Stratfordian is one who disputes that belief. Some anti-Stratfordians have their own candidates for authorship, such as Francis Bacon or Christopher Marlowe, but not all anti-Stratfordians favor a particular counterclaimant. An Oxfordian is an anti-Stratfordian who contends that Edward de Vere is the author of those works.

on one counterclaimant, Edward de Vere, because he embodies all the characteristics that other anti-Stratfordians find separately in their respective candidates, such as knowledge of the court, poetic ability, learning, knowledge of languages besides English, as well as having traveled in the countries (Italy, France, Denmark, and Greece) where fourteen of the plays are set.

During World War I, an English schoolteacher named J. Thomas Looney created a profile of the author of the Shakespearean corpus based on the contents of the plays and poetry, and concluded that their author possessed nine general characteristics:

> 1. A matured man of recognized genius. 2. Apparently eccentric and mysterious. 3. Of intense sensibility—a man apart. 4. Unconventional. 5. Not adequately appreciated. 6. Of pronounced and known literary tastes. 7. An enthusiast in the world of drama. 8. A lyric poet of recognized talent. 9. Of superior education—classical—the habitual associate of educated people.[7]

He also found the author to possess nine special characteristics:

> 1. A man with Feudal connections. 2. A member of the higher aristocracy. 3. Connected with Lancastrian supporters. 4. An enthusiast for Italy. 5. A follower of sport [including falconry]. 6. A lover of music. 7. Loose and improvident in money matters. 8. Doubtful and somewhat conflicting in his attitude to women. 9. Probable Catholic leanings, but touched with scepticism.[8]

Seeking a historical person whose characteristics correlated with the literary persona, in turn, led Looney in 1920 to propose Edward de Vere as the author of the Shakespearean corpus.[9] Such profiling on the basis of the written texts is a methodologically legitimate way to proceed (as we have seen in the chapter on Rashid al-Din and will see in the chapters on Andrei Kurbskii and Mikhail Sholokhov), because it allows other scholars either to replicate or refute the findings based on the evidence.

Stratfordians in general tend to diminish the value of such profiling in determining authorship in favor of what they see as "documentary evidence,"[10]

---

7. J. Thomas Looney, *"Shakespeare" Identified in Edward de Vere, the Seventeenth Earl of Oxford* (London: Palmer, 1920), 92, and 84–92 for a discussion of each characteristic.

8. Looney, *"Shakespeare" Identified*, 103, and 93–104 for a discussion of each characteristic.

9. Looney, *"Shakespeare" Identified*, 105–344.

10. Stuart Hampton-Reeves, "The 'Declaration of Reasonable Doubt,'" in *Shakespeare beyond Doubt: Evidence, Argument, Controversy*, ed. Paul Edmondson and Stanley Wells (Cambridge: Cambridge University Press, 2013), 207.

and some Stratfordians, influenced by the so-called New Criticism, are outright dismissive that any autobiographical evidence can be gleaned from the writings attributed to Shakespeare. The New Criticism is an approach to literature that intentionally ignores authorship or authorial intent as well as social and cultural context in favor of deep readings of the text and an aesthetic appreciation of its structure and perceived meaning. A poem or other literary text is understood to be a self-referential thing unto itself, or as Leroy Searle called it, a "self-sufficient verbal artifact."[11] In her virtuoso commentary on Shakespeare's sonnets, Harvard University professor of English literature Helen Vendler, following the first part of W. H. Auden's famous instruction on reading a poem, analyzed each sonnet as "a verbal contraption."[12] She explains that, like any poet, Auden understood that the first question must be answered first before the second can be correctly answered:

> I believe that the deepest insights into the moral world of the poem, and into its constructive and deconstructive energies, come precisely from understanding it as a contraption made of "words," by which I mean not only the semantic units we call "words" but all the language games in which words can participate. Because many essays on the sonnets attempt moral and ethical discussion without any close understanding of how the poems are put together, I have emphasized in this Commentary the total "contraptionness" of any given sonnet as the first necessary level of understanding."[13]

She does not seem, however, to get to the second part of Auden's instruction— that is, to figure out "what kind of guy inhabits this work."[14] Yet she does leave the door open to possibly figuring out what kind of guy Shakespeare was by providing this tantalizing morsel: "As to what Shakespeare may conceal from the reader, or even from himself, such a supremely conscious writer conceals, it seems to me, very little."[15] The Columbia University professor James Shapiro, in contrast, sees the works of Shakespeare as "pure imagination." In response to the question posed to him whether someone who did not have firsthand knowledge of the things he was writing about could do so correctly, he asserted that one does not have to know animals to write *Animal Farm*. True

---

11. Leroy Searle, "New Criticism," in *The Johns Hopkins Guide to Literary Theory*, 2nd ed. (Baltimore: Johns Hopkins University Press, 2005), 691.

12. Helen Vendler, *The Art of Shakespeare's Sonnets* (Cambridge, MA: Harvard University Press, 1997), 10–11.

13. Vendler, *The Art of Shakespeare's Sonnets*, 11.

14. W. H. Auden, *The Dyer's Hand, and Other Essays* (New York: Vintage, 1968), 50–51.

15. Vendler, *The Art of Shakespeare's Sonnets*, 11.

enough, but one does have to know something about the Russian Revolution to do so. He furthermore stated that the attempt "to read the works [of Shakespeare] as autobiography . . . is the original sin" and "the slipperiest slope that ever a scholar slid down."[16] He was referring specifically to Edmond Malone's attempt to find out information about Shakespeare from the works he was supposed to have written, yet I think it fairly represents Shapiro's position in regard to any attempt to find any such autobiographical evidence.

Such a banning of attempts to extract knowledge about the author from the works that author wrote may work for a type of literary criticism, but it is inappropriate for historical study. The historical level of reading focuses on (at the risk of quoting myself) "what the . . . [work] tells us about the time in which it was written and the attitudes of its author."[17]

Stratfordians in general have also been dismissive of any questioning on historical terms of Stratfordian authorship. The Harvard University professor Marjorie Garber, for example, referred to the authorship question as "a minor wrinkle in Shakespeare studies."[18] Other Stratfordians have at some level taken note of the historical criticisms and acknowledged there are gaps in our source evidence about William of Stratford. They then attempt to fill in the gaps by imagining what he must have been doing during the so-called lost years (1585–1592). Thus, he could have been variously captured by pirates, gone to Italy as a spy for the government, clerked in a law office,[19] served as a tutor in an aristocratic home, or been a medical student, a country schoolmaster, a soldier, a sailor, a printer, a gardener, and so on, all to explain his knowledge of any particular field.[20] In contrast, the *New York Times* editor William S. Niederkorn accused the Stratfordians of a "quasi-religious fervor for biographical dogma" in trying to fit the chronology of the plays to the life of William of Stratford and in trying to imagine a biography for him that would fit the corpus of works attributed to Shakespeare.[21]

---

16. James Shapiro, interview with Brooke Gladstone, *On the Media*, WNYC, April 22, 2016, at 11:14. Shapiro in the same interview (at 6:03) also said, "The whole notion of literature as autobiographical, as self-expression, was not Shakespeare's culture. If we are trying to shoehorn Shakespeare into a confessional writer about his sexual life, about his religious beliefs, we are not going to get closer to who the man was."

17. Donald Ostrowski, "Three Criteria of Historical Study," https://donostrowski2.bitbucket.io/history.pdf.

18. Marjorie Garber, *Shakespeare after All* (New York: Random House, 2004), 20.

19. Stephen Greenblatt, *Will in the World: How Shakespeare Became Shakespeare* (New York: Norton, 2004), 71–72.

20. Diana Price, *Shakespeare's Unorthodox Biography: New Evidence of an Authorship Problem*, paperback ed. (shakespeare-authorship.com, 2012), 262.

21. William S. Niederkorn, "Foreword," in Roger Stritmatter and Lynne Kositsky, *On the Date, Sources and Design of Shakespeare's* The Tempest (Jefferson, NC: McFarland, 2013), 1.

Into the Thicket

One argument used by those who believe the Stratford man wrote the Shakespeare corpus is that the chronology of the plays, some of which have been dated to after 1604, excludes Edward de Vere, who died in that year. The problem with the traditional chronology is that the dating of particular plays has been done so specifically to fit the life span of William of Stratford.[22] This dating argument, thus, is circular. Instead, the dating range (i.e., the earliest possible date and the latest possible date) of each play allows for either candidate to have been the author.

That principle of establishing a date range was used by Kevin Gilvary and his coauthors to review the evidence for the dating of the plays that have been attributed to Shakespeare. They took two approaches to each play—a Stratfordian analysis and an Oxfordian analysis. Table 6.1 shows their results and the date range of when those plays could have been written.[23] The asterisk after a title means that it can be found in the First Folio (1623). The Q before a date means it was first published in quarto; the F, in folio. Table 6.2 represents works other than the plays that are part of the Shakespeare canon. And table 6.3 represents works that have at one time or another been attributed to Shakespeare but are not now (or yet) considered part of the canon.

In addition, as Peter R. Moore pointed out, no play shows any indisputable reference to an event or derives from a source that dates to after 1603.[24] One piece of evidence in regard to dating that has received a great deal of attention is Ariel's reference in *The Tempest* to "still-vexed Bermoothes." Traditional scholarship has pointed to a description in a letter of 1610 written by William Strachey of the crash of the *Sea Venture* in 1609 off the coast of Bermuda. Strachey's letter was not published until 1625. A number of Stratfordians have cited this letter as evidence against the Oxfordians. Yet recent scholarship, both Stratfordian and anti-Stratfordian, has rejected Strachey's letter and its description of a Bermuda shipwreck as a source for the play.[25] A number of scholars

---

22. Kevin Gilvary, "Introduction," in *Dating Shakespeare's Plays: A Critical Review of the Evidence*, ed. Kevin Gilvary (Tunbridge Wells, UK: Parapress, 2010), 3–8. See also my review of *Dating Shakespeare's Plays: A Critical Review of the Evidence*, ed. Kevin Gilvary (Tunbridge Wells, UK: Parapress, 2010) in *Brief Chronicles: An Interdisciplinary Journal of Authorship Studies* 3 (2011): 246–257.

23. The date ranges are taken from *Dating Shakespeare's Plays*, 477.

24. Peter R. Moore, *The Lame Storyteller, Poor and Despised*, ed. Gary Goldstein (Buchholz: Verlag Laugwitz, 2009), 170–171.

25. The chapter in *Dating Shakespeare's Plays* on dating *The Tempest*, co-authored by Philip Johnson and Kevin Gilvary, does a commendable job of summarizing briefly and accurately the issue as well as the evidence and arguments for and against seeing a connection between Strachey's letter and the play (40–44). See also Stritmatter and Kositsky, *On the Date, Sources and Design of Shakespeare's* The Tempest.

Table 6.1   Extant plays generally accepted as having been written by Shakespeare
(according to *Dating Shakespeare's Plays*)

PLAYS	EARLIEST–LATEST POSSIBLE DATE	FIRST PUBLISHED
Comedies		
*All's Well That Ends Well**	1567–1623	F1623 (with Thomas Middleton?)
*As You Like It**	1590–1600	F1623
*The Comedy of Errors**	1566–1594	F1623
*Love's Labour's Lost**	1578–1598	Q1598
*Measure for Measure**	1580–1604	F1623 (adapted by Thomas Middleton)
*The Merchant of Venice**	1558–1598	Q1600
*The Merry Wives of Windsor**	1558–1602	Q1602
*A Midsummer Night's Dream**	1585–1598	Q1600
*Much Ado about Nothing**	1583–1600	Q1600
*The Taming of the Shrew**	1579–1598	Q1594?/F1623
*The Tempest**	1580–1611	F1623
*Twelfth Night**	1580–1611	F1623
*The Two Gentlemen of Verona**	1559–1598	F1623
*The Winter's Tale**	1588–1611	F1623
Histories		
*King John**	1587–1598	Q1591?/F1623
*Richard II**	1587–1597	Q1597, Q1598
*Henry IV, Part 1**	1587–1598	Q1598
*Henry IV, Part 2**	1587–1600	Q1598
*Henry V**	1577–1600	Q1600
*Henry VI, Part 1**	1587–1592	Q1600 (with Marlowe, Nashe, and Anonymous)[1]
*Henry VI, Part 2**	1587–1594	Q1594 (with Marlowe and Anonymous)
*Henry VI, Part 3**	1587–1592	Q1595 (with Marlowe and Anonymous)
*Henry VIII**	1583–1613	F1623 (with John Fletcher)
*Richard III**	1587–1597	Q1597 (with John Fletcher?)
Tragedies		
*Romeo and Juliet**	1562–1597	Q1597
*Coriolanus**	1579–1623	F1623
*Julius Caesar**	1579–1599	F1623
*Macbeth**	1587–1611	F1623 (adapted by Middleton)
*Hamlet**	1586–1602	Q1603
*Troilus and Cressida**	1581–1609	Q1609
*King Lear**	1590–1606	Q1608
*Othello**	1584–1604	Q1622
*Antony and Cleopatra**	1579–1608	F1623
*Cymbeline**	1579–1611	F1623
*Titus Andronicus**	1579–1594	Q1594 (with George Peele)
*Timon of Athens**	1579–1623	F1623 (with Thomas Middleton)

Table 6.1   (continued)

PLAYS	EARLIEST–LATEST POSSIBLE DATE	FIRST PUBLISHED
Other Plays		
Edward III	1577–1595	Q1596 (with Anonymous [Thomas Kyd?]
The Famous Victories of Henry V	1577–1594	Q1598 (stationer's register 1594)[2]
Pericles, Prince of Tyre	1576–1609	Q1609 (with George Wilkins)
The Two Noble Kinsmen	1566–1614	Q1634 (with John Fletcher)

[1] *New Oxford Shakespeare: Complete Works. Critical Edition*, ed. Gary Taylor, John Howett, Terri Bourus, and Gabriel Egan (Oxford: Oxford University Press, 2016).

[2] Slater asserted: "It is nearly certain that he [Oxford] was the author of *The Famous Victories of Henry V*." Gilbert Slater, *Seven Shakespeares: A Discussion of the Evidence for Various Theories with Regard to Shakespeare's Identity* (Oxford: Cecil Palmer, 1931), 29. Jiménez also argues for De Vere's authorship in Ramón Jiménez, "'The Famous Victories of King Henry the Fifth," in *Dating Shakespeare's Plays: A Critical Review of the Evidence*, ed. Kevin Gilvary (Tunbridge Wells, UK: Parapress, 2010), 461–468.

have accepted that Bermoothes refers to a district of London of the time. In his *Dictionary of Slang*, Eric Partridge identified "Bermudas, Bermoothes" as "A London district (Cf. Alsatia, q.v.) privileged against arrest: certain alleys and passages contiguous to Drury Lane, near Covent Garden, and north of the Strand."[26] Thus, the phrase "still-vexed" should be understood as vexed with stills (i.e., distilleries for the production of alcohol).[27]

On what basis is each work attributed, or in the case of the Apocrypha, not attributed to William Shakespeare? The First Folio, in which thirty-six plays appear, is the primary means of attribution. Four other plays (under "Other Plays" in table 6.1) have been attributed to Shakespeare in the scholarship. Three of those, and thirteen altogether, are now thought to have been written in collaboration with someone else. In addition, there are at least ten other plays (listed under "Apocrypha") that have at one time or another been attributed to Shakespeare but are not so accepted in the present scholarship. Two of those plays—*The London Prodigal* (1605) and *A Yorkshire Tragedy* (1608)—were first published in quartos with the name William Shakespeare on the title page. *Sir John Oldcastle* (1600) was republished in 1619 with "written by William Shakespeare" on the title page. Four other plays—*Locrine* (1595), *The Puritan, or The Widow of Watling-Street* (1607), *Thomas Lord Cromwell* (1602), and *The Troublesome Reign of John King of England* (1611)—stated on the title page that they were by "W.S." (three plays) or "W.Sh." (one play). All seven of these plays are generally rejected as part of the canon, apparently for stylistic reasons. Yet,

26. Eric Partridge, *A Dictionary of Slang and Unconventional English* (London: Routledge, 2002), 71.

27. Richard Paul Roe, *The Shakespeare Guide to Italy: Retracing the Bard's Unknown Travels* (New York: HarperCollins, 2011), 290–292.

Table 6.2   Other works generally accepted as being written by Shakespeare

Poems

Sonnets (published in 1609)

A Lover's Complaint (published with *Sonnets* in 1609)

The Phoenix and the Turtle (1601)

The Passionate Pilgrim (1599 "by W. Shakespeare")[1]

The Rape of Lucrece (1594)

Venus and Adonis (1592–1593)

Lost plays

Love's Labour's Won

The History of Cardenio (collaborated with John Fletcher?)

[1] Stratfordian scholars do not accept that all the poems in this collection were written by William Shakespeare. Among the other authors proposed for individual poems are Richard Barnfield, Bartholomew Griffin, Thomas Deloney, Christopher Marlowe, Walter Raleigh, and Anonymous.

the forty plays that are now considered part of the canon also have significant stylistic differences among and within them. As a result, a number of conjectures have ensued in regard to what does or does not constitute one of those styles at any particular time in Shakespeare's supposed playwriting career.

To account for the different styles, Edmond Malone posited in 1778 a chronology of the composition of the plays.[28] Malone warned a number of times in his essay of the tentativeness and the lack of evidence for dating the plays: "In what year our author began to write for the stage, or which was his first performance, has not been hitherto ascertained. And indeed we have so few lights to direct our enquiries, that any speculation on this subject may appear an idle expence of time," and "If the dates here assigned to our author's plays should not, in every instance, bring with them conviction of their propriety, let it be remembered, that is a subject on which conviction cannot at this day be obtained." Nonetheless, Edward Dowden accepted Malone's chronology with only a few minor modifications and proposed the following taxonomy in 1875: (1) "in the workshop," the period of Shakespeare's youth when he is experimenting and reworking other authors' plays, (2) "in the world," the period in which his "imagination began to lay hold of real life" and history in particular, (3) "out of the depths," the period in which the author "ceased to care for the tales of mirth and love; for the stir and movement of history," and began to explore "the great mystery of evil," and (4) "on the heights," the period in

28. Edmond Malone, "An Attempt to Ascertain the Order in Which the Plays Attributed to Shakespeare Were Written," in *The Plays of William Shakespeare in Ten Volumes with the Corrections and Illustrations of Various Commentators*, vol. 1, ed. Samuel Johnson and George Steevens, 2nd ed. (London, 1778), 269–346 (see chronology in front matter).

Table 6.3   Works that have been attributed to Shakespeare but are not generally accepted
as having been written by him

Apocrypha

Arden of Faversham (with Anonymous)

The Birth of Merlin

Locrine (quarto published in 1595 "Newly set foorth, overseene, and corrected, By W.S.")

The London Prodigal (quarto published in 1605 "By William Shakespeare")

The Puritan, or The Widow of Watling-Street (quarto published in 1607 "Written by W.S.")

The Second Maiden's Tragedy

Sir John Oldcastle (quarto published in 1619 "Written by William Shakespeare")[1]

Thomas Lord Cromwell (quarto published in 1602 "Written by W.S.")

A Yorkshire Tragedy (quarto published in 1608 "Written by W. Shakspeare")

Sir Thomas More (with additions by Shakespeare?)

The Troublesome Reign of John King of England (quarto published in 1611 "Written by W. Sh.")[2]

The Paine of Pleasure (co-author with Anthony Munday [1580])[3]

---

[1] Published anonymously in 1600 by Thomas Pavia. In 1619, he added the words "Written by William Shakespeare." Henslowe's diary states that it was written by four authors.

[2] First published anonymously in 1591, then again in 1622 "Written by W. Shakespeare."

[3] Sarah Smith, "A Reattribution of Munday's 'The Paine of Pleasure,'" *The Oxfordian* 5 (2002): 70–99. Smith also incorporated this research find of hers into the plot of her novel *Chasing Shakespeares* (New York: Atria Books, 2003).

which the poet exhibited a "wise, large-hearted, calm-souled" attitude.[29] Most
subsequent attempts to date the plays were influenced by the need to fit
Dowden's chronological phases, although his chronological phases are based
on little more than a creative speculation as applied to an imaginary biography
of William of Stratford. The hypothesis that a writer develops a more sophisticated style as he or she matures, as Dowden proposed for Shakespeare, is un-
tested. Any number of authors from Ayn Rand to Alexander Solzhenitsyn,
from Norman Mailer to Mikhail Sholokhov wrote a stylistically sophisticated
early work followed by somewhat less stylistically sophisticated later works.[30]

The Role of the First Folio (1623)

In the preface to the First Folio, Ben Jonson has a poem in which he refers to
the "sweet swan of Avon":

---

29. Gilvary, "Introduction," in *Dating Shakespeare's Plays*, 5. See Edward Dowden, *Shakespeare: A Critical Study of His Mind and Art* (London: Henry S. King, 1875).

30. Ayn Rand's first published novel, *We the Living* (1936), was undoubtedly her best. In regard to Solzhenitsyn, it is difficult to think of a more perfect stylistic work of his than *One Day in the Life of Ivan Denisovich* (1962). Neither Mailer nor Sholokhov surpassed their first novels, *The Naked and the Dead* (1948) and *Quiet Flows the Don* (1928–1932, 1940), respectively.

"Sweet Swan of Avon! What a sight it were
To see thee in our waters yet appeare,
And make those flights upon the banks of Thames
That so did take Eliza, and our James!"

Stratfordians have pointed to this phrase as conclusive evidence that William of Stratford is Shakespeare because he came from Stratford-on-Avon.

A more likely interpretation is that of Alexander Waugh—namely, "Avon" refers to Hampton Court (sixteen miles west on the Thames River from the Tower of London), where Elizabeth I (Eliza) and James I saw plays.[31] The evidence that Hampton Court was called Avon (previously Avondunum) derives from John Leland's *Genethliacon* (1543) and his *Kykneion asma. Cygnea Cantio* (1545).[32] A Stratfordian response on Oxfraud.com questions Waugh's scholarship ("he hasn't read the book he's citing as evidence") and whether Hampton Court was ever really called Avon.[33] Yet the point is not whether Hampton Court was ever called Avon but whether Ben Jonson might have thought it so. Waugh went on in his article to cite other contemporary sources, no doubt drawing on Leland, that equate Avon with Hampton Court, such as Raphael Holinshed in his *Chronicles* (1587): "We now pronounce Hampton for Avondune."[34] Waugh's conclusion is that "the name 'Avon,' meaning Hampton Court, was a commonly known fact among the educated men and women of Jonson's day."[35] Even if Waugh is correct, it cannot be used as evidence in relation to whether William of Stratford wrote the Shakespearean corpus, but it would provide a better understanding of what Ben Jonson may have meant by the phrase "sweet swan of Avon," which if understood as a swan on the Avon River is a rather meaningless phrase in regard to a writer of plays. If one understands "Avon" to mean Hampton Court and also if one recalls that all swans in England were protected by the monarch since at least

31. Alexander Waugh, "The True Meaning of Ben Jonson's Phrase: 'Sweet Swan of Avon,'" *The Oxfordian* 14 (2014): 99–100, 102.

32. John Leland, *Genethliacon illustrissimi Edduerdi Principis Cambriae, Ducis Coriniæ, et Comitis Palatini* (London: Reyner Wolfe, 1543); Leland, *Kykneion asma. Cygneia cantio* (London: Reyner Wolfe, 1545), 108.

33. "Brave New Avon," Oxfraud.com, http://oxfraud.com/100-braver-new-avon.

34. Raphael Holinshed, *The First and Second Volumes of Chronicles*, augmented by John Hooker (London, 1587), 101. Other contemporary sources are: William Lambarde, *Dictionarium Angliæ topographicum & historicum: An alphabetical description of the chief places in England and Wales; With an account of the most memorable events which have distinguish'd them* (written 1590s; published 1730 by Fletcher Gyles, over-against Gray's-Inn, Holborne); William Camden, *Britannia, siue Florentissimorum regnorum Angliæ, Scotiæ, Hiberniæ, et insularum adiacentium ex intima antiquitate chorographica descriptio: nunc postremò recognita, plurimis locis magna accessione adaucta, & chartis chorographicis illustrata* (London: Eliot's Court Press, 1607); Henry Peacham, *Minerva Britannia* (1612), 185.

35. Waugh, "True Meaning," 100.

the thirteenth century,[36] then a monarch-protected playwright (the swan) writing plays (taking flight) for the court (Avon), which is on the banks of the Thames River, suddenly becomes, in this context, a much more meaningful interpretation of these verses.

Anti-Stratfordians, like Diana Price, point out that fifteen of thirty-three individual editions of the plays that were published before the First Folio, as well as the sonnets and *A Lover's Complaint*, carry as author on the title page a hyphenated name, "Shake-speare." Presence of a hyphenated name in sixteenth- and seventeenth-century English literature could indicate a nom de plume—such as Martin Mar-prelate, "Mar-Martin, Mar-ton, Mar-tother, Trouble-knave, Signior Some-body, Tom Tel-Truth and . . . Cuthbert Curry-knave."[37] In text critical terms, it is more likely "Shake-speare" became conflated to "Shakespeare" than the reverse. Stratfordians Randall McLeod and Gary Taylor have proposed that the printer for layout reasons added a hyphen to keep the rear tail of a swash *s* from making contact with the forward tail of the swash *k* before the *e*. Yet, as Moore responded, we have numerous cases of the hyphenation of Shake-speare even when the font is roman type without any such possible typographic reason to hyphenate.[38]

The Stratford man's baptismal name was Shakspere, and on his marriage certificate was Shaxpere, so a Stratfordian could argue (although to the best of my knowledge none has) that he used Shake-speare as a nom de plume by adding the *e* and hyphen after *k* as well as turning the final syllable "spere" into "speare." Irvin Leigh Matus found examples of Elizabethans whose real names were hyphenated. The publisher Robert Waldegrave decided at a certain point to hyphenate his name as Walde-grave. And the Protestant martyr Sir John Oldcastle's last name is sometimes rendered Old-Castle.[39] Price countered that Waldegrave/Walde-grave is a poor analogy because we have no cases of William of Stratford's hyphenating his own last name. Besides, argued Price, Waldegrave hyphenated his name consistently whereas Shakespeare/Shakespeare was hyphenated inconsistently as were other hyphenated pseudonyms. In addition, it was publishers like Waldegrave who hyphenated author's names, not the author who made the choice.[40] Price's argument cuts both ways because if a publisher (Waldegrave) was willing to hyphenate his own

---

36. Arthur MacGregor, "Swan Rolls and Beak Markings: Husbandry, Exploitation and Regulation of *Cygnus olor* in England, c. 1100–1900," *Anthropozoologica* 22 (1996): 44.

37. A. J. Pointon, "The Man Who Was Never Shakespeare: The Spelling of William Shakspere's Name," in *Shakespeare beyond Doubt? Exposing an Industry in Denial*, ed. John M. Shahan and Alexander Waugh (Tamarac, FL: Llumina, 2013), 26–27; cf. Price, *Shakespeare's Unorthodox Biography*, 57–58.

38. Moore, *The Lame Storyteller*, 208–209.

39. Irvin Leigh Matus, *Shakespeare, in Fact* (New York: Continuum, 1994), 29–30.

40. Price, *Shakespeare's Unorthodox Biography*, 58.

real name, perhaps other publishers were willing to do so with author's real names, like Shake-speare, that could lend themselves to being hyphenated. Yet, even in the prefatory pages of the First Folio, the publisher hyphenated Shake-speare five times and presented it unhyphenated fourteen times.

Imagination vs. Knowledge and Experience

Likewise, the claim has been made that those who point out the relationship between the descriptions in the plays and events in the life of Edward de Vere are giving into a penchant for trying to find biographical or autobiographical information in art. Shapiro wrote: "What I find most disheartening about the claim that Shakespeare of Stratford lacked the life experiences to have written the plays is that it diminishes the very thing that makes him so exceptional: his imagination."[41] Goldstein countered such preoccupation with imagination on the part of Stratfordians by paraphrasing William Faulkner that a successful writer needed three attributes: experience, observation, and imagination.[42] Shapiro could retort with the rest of Faulkner's quotation: "any two of which, at times any one of which, can supply the lack of the others."[43]

There are at least two problems with Shapiro's claim—one specifically in regard to the Shakespeare authorship controversy, the other in raising such a claim to a general principle of attribution. First, there is no outside evidence (i.e., other than the Shakespearean corpus itself) to justify the claim that William of Stratford had such an imagination. In other words, the argument is recursive: William of Stratford wrote the plays, sonnets, and long poems because he had the imagination to do so, and we know he had the imagination to do so because he wrote the plays, sonnets, and long poems. In contrast, we do have such an independent claim for Edward de Vere's imagination from a contemporary source, notably a hostile one. Sir Charles Arundell in his famous "libels" wrote about de Vere's telling of one of his Italian stories: "This lie is verye rife with him and in it he glories greatlie, diverslie hathe he told it, and when he enters into it, he can hardlie owte, whiche hathe made suche sporte as often have I bin driven to rise from his table laugheinge."[44]

---

41. James Shapiro, *Contested Will: Who Wrote Shakespeare?* (New York: Simon & Schuster, 2010), 277.

42. Gary Goldstein, *Reflections on the True Shakespeare* (Buchholz: Laugwitz Verlag, 2016), 34, 207.

43. Quoted in Jean Stein, "William Faulkner: The Art of Fiction, no. 12," *Paris Review*, issue 12 (Spring 1956).

44. "Libels Part 4. Charles Arundel *contra* Oxford: Formal Statement and Three Libels," *PRO SP12/151[/45], ff. 100-2* §1.2, http://www.leadbetter.cc/nelson/oxlets.html.

Second, Shapiro's assertion that all one needs is imagination could be used to justify anyone's writing anything. It could also be used to deny that a person with knowledge and experience could write something accurate about a given topic since, if we follow that logic, anybody with sufficient imagination could write the same thing. For example, the argument could be made that the British intelligence officer David Cornwell (pen name, John le Carré) did not write *The Spy Who Came in from the Cold* because anyone with sufficient imagination could have written that novel and replicated accurately its Cold War espionage techniques. One could use Shapiro's assertion to question James Joyce's authorship of *Dubliners* or Naguib Mahfouz's authorship of the *Cairo Trilogy* on the basis that anyone with sufficient imagination could have imagined Dublin or Cairo, respectively, and that it did not require someone who had firsthand experiential knowledge of these cities. Third, it could be used to argue that William of Stratford was so imaginative that he imagined himself as the 17th Earl of Oxford writing under the pseudonym "Shakespeare." That would save the traditional attribution to William of Stratford and explain the correlation of events in the plays with events in the life of Edward de Vere. It would also explain why the sonnets seem to be written to a male nobleman. William of Stratford was, thereby, just imagining what it would be like to be a nobleman in love with another nobleman. But, again, such unnecessary abstract constructs violate Occam's razor. The simpler explanation is that a nobleman wrote the plays and sonnets with no need for him to imagine he was someone else.

If one cannot use the life of an author as a means to understand their work, then we are eliminating one of the most important scholarly tools at our disposal—namely, historical analysis. Literary criticism uninformed by historical study seems to care little for who wrote a work; what matters is the outward manifestations of that work. For historical investigation, in contrast, the historical context of a literary work is important for understanding the work. In that respect, the claims that the Stratford man wrote those works is a scholarly dead end. No connection has been found between the plays and poems and the life of William of Stratford.[45] The claim that Edward de Vere wrote those works opens up many lines of historical inquiry.

For example, Stratfordians had identified the Geneva Bible text as the one used by the author of the Shakespearean canon. Then it was discovered that a Geneva Bible that belonged to Edward de Vere had underlinings and glosses

---

45. Greenblatt claims a connection between the mentions of gloves and the imagery of leather in the plays with John Shakspere's profession of glover and tanner. Greenblatt, *Will in the World*, 55–56, 168–169.

of 1,028 verses, of which about 25 percent are reflected in the plays.[46] The Stratfordian George French had also identified the character Polonius (advisor to the monarch) in *Hamlet* as based on Lord Burghley. Edward de Vere grew up as a ward of the state in Lord Burghley's household from the age of twelve until his majority at twenty-one. Oxfordians claim that the advice that Polonius delivers to his son Laertes (act 1, scene 3: "To thine own self be true . . .") is similar to precepts in Burghley's privately written advice to his son Robert Cecil in 1584.[47] These letters were not published until 1618 as *Certain Precepts*, while the play *Hamlet* first appeared in print in 1603. Oxfordians argue that de Vere would have had access to those letters from his father-in-law Lord Burghley or through Robert Cecil, his brother-in-law. The Stratfordian Edmund K. Chambers pointed out that when *Certain Precepts* was printed, the accompanying words were: "from a more perfect copie, than ordinarily those pocket manuscripts goe warranted by." Chambers then proposed: "Conceivably Shakespeare knew a pocket manuscript" of the *Precepts*.[48] Stratfordians either downplay the similarity or claim that William of Stratford could have had access by, for example, having been a servant in the house.

E. A. J. Honigmann argued that William of Stratford was a servant during the lost years (1586–1592) but in the home of a wealthy Lancashire Catholic.[49] Other theories, according to J. M. Pressley of the Shakespeare Resource Center, include "Shakespeare leaving Stratford with a traveling troupe of actors, or working as a soldier, law clerk, butcher, glover, scrivener, or merchant. One story even puts a young Shakespeare in London, holding horses outside of theaters for patrons." Pressley added that all these theories are "overwhelmingly

---

46. For an analysis of those markings, see Roger A. Stritmatter, *The Marginalia of Edward De Vere's Geneva Bible: Providential Discovery, Literary Reasoning, and Historical Consequence* (Northampton, MA: Oxenford Press, 2001). The evidence that this was de Vere's Bible derives not only from the coat of arms on the cover but also the recording in 1570 in the royal Court of Wards of the purchase by Edward de Vere of a gilt-edged Geneva Bible along with other works: "To William Seres, stationer, for a Geneva Bible gilt, a Chaucer, Plutarch's works in French, with other books and papers . . . £2/7/10." S.P. Dom. Add. 19/38 cited in B. M. Ward, *The Seventeenth Earl of Oxford, 1550–1604: From Contemporary Documents* (London: John Murray, 1928), 33.

47. The Stratfordian Steve Roth wrote in his book on *Hamlet* that the precepts of the letter are "perhaps mimicked in Polonius's advice to Laertes." Steve Roth, *Hamlet: The Undiscovered Country*, 2nd ed. (Seattle: Open House, 2013), 149. But on his webpage, Roth states that he finds the similarities between the two sets of precepts "not very remarkable." Steve Roth, "Burghley's Precepts to His Son," http://www.princehamlet.com/burghley.html.

48. E[dmund] K[ercheval] Chambers, *William Shakespeare: A Study of Facts and Problems*, 2 vols. (Oxford: Clarendon, 1930), 418.

49. E. A. J. Honigmann, *Shakespeare: The "Lost Years"* (Manchester: Manchester University Press, 1985).

tall tales with roughly the same legitimacy as George Washington chopping down the cherry tree."[50]

In addition, the character of Ophelia had been identified by Stratfordians with Anne Cecil, the daughter of Lord Burghley and wife of Edward de Vere. Like Ophelia, she too died young, but unlike Ophelia her death was not attributed to suicide resulting from depression, at least not officially. Oxfordians point out that, like Hamlet, de Vere was captured by pirates, then released. Like Hamlet, de Vere's father had died early and his mother had remarried quickly. Like Hamlet, de Vere had his own theater troupe (actually, two—a boys' company and a men's company). Like Hamlet, de Vere had accidentally killed a person with a sword under ambiguous circumstances. For de Vere, it was an undercook, Thomas Brinknell, who reportedly ran upon his sword; for Hamlet, it was Polonius (Burghley) himself whom he stabbed with a sword through a tapestry, not knowing who it was. Hamlet entrusts his kinsman Horatio with carrying on his work. De Vere had a cousin named Sir Horatio Vere whom he admired and who survived his own death in 1604. Oxfordians claim that *Hamlet* is the most autobiographical of the Shakespearean plays.[51] Biographer Alan H. Nelson dismissed the similarities and saw only dissimilarities with the life of Edward de Vere: his father was not murdered; Edward was only twelve at the time, "far younger than Hamlet"; his mother did not remarry in a month as Hamlet's mother did but waited more than a year; the man she married was not her deceased husband's brother; de Vere accepted marriage with Burghley's daughter, not rejecting marriage as Hamlet did with Ophelia; his wife did not commit suicide; and "neither [of his wife's brothers] challenged him to a duel or killed him with an empoisoned rapier."[52] Nelson raises an important methodological point, namely in any comparison, considering the differences can be as important as discerning the similarities. Yet, one may well consider the differences in this and the other cases Nelson cites to be covered by the author's poetic license and imaginative elaboration of real-life events within a fictional genre. Fiction does not have to coincide exactly with the autobiographical reality it seeks to portray.

---

50. J. M. Pressley, "Shakespeare's 'Lost Years': The Mystery between Stratford and London," http://www.bardweb.net/content/ac/lostyears.html.

51. Mark Anderson wrote: "The outlines of *Hamlet* are so pronounced within de Vere's life that one invariably illuminates the other." Mark Anderson, *"Shakespeare" by Another Name: The Life of Edward de Vere, Earl of Oxford, the Man Who Was Shakespeare* (New York: Gotham Books, 2005), 190; Robert Sean Brazil claimed: "*Hamlet* tells the story of Oxford's life, down to the details." Robert Sean Brazil, *Edward de Vere and the Shakespeare Printers* (Seattle: Cortical Output, 2010), 19.

52. Alan H. Nelson, "The Life and Theatrical Interests of Edward de Vere, Seventeenth Earl of Oxford," in *Shakespeare beyond Doubt: Evidence, Argument, Controversy*, ed. Paul Edmondson and Stanley Wells (Cambridge: Cambridge University Press, 2013), 44–45.

In contrast, Stratfordians have proposed none of the occurrences in the play can be correlated with events in the life of William of Stratford, with the possible exception that he named one of his sons "Hamnet" (a decidedly odd choice if one claims that it relates to William of Stratford's life). More likely William of Stratford's son was named after Hamnet Sadler, a friend and neighbor in Stratford who in turn named his own son William. In addition, some scholars have mentioned that a certain Katherine Hamlett was known to have drowned in the Avon River around this time. But positing that Katherine Hamlett became Ophelia in a play called *Hamlet* is a stretch. The name "Hamlet" of the play most likely derives from one of the tales in *Les Histoires Tragiques* (1576) by François de Belleforest (1530–1583), who in turn derived it from the Latin version of the Old Danish name "Amleth" found in the *Gesta Danorum* (thirteenth century) history by Saxo Grammaticus.

A second play that the Oxfordians claim has a number of circumstances and events corresponding with the life of Edward de Vere is *All's Well That Ends Well*. The male lead in the play, Bertram, like de Vere, is a young nobleman of an ancient family. He, like de Vere, lost his father and came to court as a royal ward to be brought up under royal supervision. After reaching maturity he, like de Vere, asks to be assigned military service and for permission to travel, but his requests are turned down or deferred. He, like de Vere, leaves anyway without permission. He, like de Vere, is married to a young woman, Helena (in de Vere's case, it is Anne Cecil), with whom he was raised in the same household. Bertram and Helena, like Edward and Anne, have marriage problems of which the salient feature is the husband's refusal to sleep with his wife. Bertram, like de Vere, makes a nocturnal assignation, and their respective wives arrange to substitute themselves for the assignee. In the process Bertram and Helena, like Edward and Anne, become reconciled. To be sure, there are differences between the play and what occurred between Edward de Vere and his wife Anne Cecil. The play takes place in Roussillon, Florence, and Paris, not in London; Helena is most likely based not on Anne Cecil but on Hélène de Tournon, the youngest sister of Just-Louis, Lord Tournon, count of Roussillon, whom Edward de Vere met in the spring of 1576 on his way back from Italy.[53] But to then claim there is no connection between the play and Edward de Vere's life would require resorting to extraordinary coincidences as an explanation.

Another issue that involves dating as well as attribution of such comedies as *The Tempest*, *The Two Gentlemen of Verona*, and *Love's Labours Lost* is the Italian form of theater called *commedia dell'arte*, which was prominent in the sixteenth

---

53. Anderson, *"Shakespeare" by Another Name*, 108.

and seventeenth centuries. *Commedia dell'arte* utilized stock characters, such as Brighella, il Capitano, Colombina, il Dottore, Harlequin (Arlecchino) Innamorati, Pantalone, Pedrolino, Pulcinella, Sandrone, Scaramouche (Scaramuccia), il Somardino, La Signora, Tartaglia, and *zanni* (clowns), as well as stock situations in which the actors often improvised. In addition to the comedies mentioned above, a number of scholars have picked up on influence of the form in at least one of Shakespeare's tragedies, *Othello*.[54] To be able to adapt the form from comedy to tragedy indicates the playwright had thoroughly internalized that form. At the level of literary criticism, it is apparently enough to note the influence of *commedia dell'arte* on a number of Shakespeare's plays but not to consider how the playwright came to be influenced by that Italian form. If those who mention the similarities with *commedia dell'arte* do consider the mechanism of the influence, they speculate that one of the seven Italian play companies that visited England between 1546 and 1578 may have visited Stratford where a young William (b. 1564) may have seen it. The Stratfordian P. S. Skantze proposed that "the vivid oral recounting of travelers, of friends, of actors" was sufficient for William of Stratford to master the form.[55] In contrast, one anti-Stratfordian has asserted: "For a playwright to be influenced by *commedia dell'arte*, he or she would need to have seen such plays performed, and probably more than once."[56]

Richard Paul Roe has pointed to details contained in the Italian plays that are accurate and of such a nature that Roe concluded it is highly unlikely anyone would have acquired knowledge of them other than having been to Italy. Roe found what he considered to be the sycamore grove described in *Romeo and Juliet* outside the walls of Verona that is still there[57]; located the Saint Pe-

54. Barbara Heliodora C. de Mendonça, "*Othello*: A Tragedy Built on a Comic Structure," in *Aspects of* Othello: *Articles Reprinted from* Shakespeare Survey, ed. Kenneth Muir and Philip Edwards (Cambridge: Cambridge University Press, 1977), 92–99; Louise George Clubb, "Italian Stories on the Stage," in *The Cambridge Companion to Shakespearean Comedy*, ed. Alexander Leggatt (Cambridge: Cambridge University Press, 2002), 43–45; Pamela Allen Brown, "*Othello* Italicized: Xenophobia and the Erosion of Tragedy," in *Shakespeare, Italy and Intertextuality*, ed. Michele Marrapodi (Manchester: Manchester University Press, 2004), 145–157; Teresa J. Faherty, "*Othello dell' Arte:* The Presence of *Commedia* in Shakespeare's Tragedy," *Theatre Journal* 43 (1991): 179–194; Irene Musumeci, "Imagining *Othello* as *Commedia dell'arte*" (2002), http://bardolatry.altervista.org/Iago.htm; Ren Draya and Richard F. Whalen, eds., *Othello, the Moor of Venice* (Truro, MA: Horatio Editions-Llumina, 2010); Richard F. Whalen, "*Commedia dell'arte* in *Othello*, a Satiric Comedy Ending in Tragedy," *Brief Chronicles* 3 (2011): 71–106.

55. P. A. Skantze, "Making It Up: Improvisation as Cultural Exchange between Shakespeare and Italy," in *Shakespeare and Intertextuality: The Tradition of Cultures between Italy and England in the Early Modern Period*, ed. Michele Marrapodi (Rome: Bulzoni Editore, 2000), 259.

56. Ostrowski, review of *Dating Shakespeare's Plays*, 251.

57. Roe, *The Shakespeare Guide to Italy*, 7–10. A Stratfordian response is that the grove could have been planted later. See Ros Barber, *Shakespeare the Evidence: The Authorship Question Clarified* (July 28,

ter's church in Verona that is mentioned three times in *Romeo and Juliet*[58]; demonstrated that Milan was a river port and that it was accessible by water from Verona as occurred in *The Two Gentlemen of Verona*[59]; identified Saint Gregory's Well mentioned in *The Two Gentlemen of Verona* (act 4, scene 2) as a plague pit and found its location outside the city walls[60]; identified the landing place where Lucentio's boat docked in Padua for the opening scene of *The Taming of the Shrew*[61]; located the house of the merchant of Venice[62]; determined the location of the Tranect in Venice and Portia's estate "Belmont," which is prominent in act 3, scene 4 of the *The Merchant of Venice*[63]; identified the exact place in Florence (on the corner of Borgo Ognissanti and the Piazza Goldoni near the Saint Francis sign) where Widow and Helena await Bertram in act 3, scene 5 of *All's Well That Ends Well*[64]; identified the island in *The Tempest* as Vulcano, north of Sicily, which had previously been visited by Aeneas in the *Aeneid*[65]; and so forth. Roe corroborated his "suspicions" that "[i]t was his [the playwright's] method, his 'trick' of pointedly naming or describing some obscure or unique place that might look like an invention or mistake but which turns out to be actual. It would be one that is not necessarily a place for a scene, but somewhere that today we might say is 'off-camera,' and with an identity that has little (or nothing) to do with the plot: a one-of-a-kind place which reveals an unusual, intimate, knowledge of Italy."[66] Countless examples exist outside the Shakespearean corpus of a writer, artist, or composer who was inspired by a real-life place or object, such as Richard Wagner's being inspired for the set design of *Parsival* by his visit in 1880 to the Villa Rufo in Ravello, Italy.

Stratfordians, if they address the issue at all, either deny the accuracy of the Italian information in the plays or propose that some Italian visitor to or Italian merchants in England may have provided William of Stratford such detailed information about those places[67] or perhaps he himself was a secret

2015), 315–316, https://leanpub.com/Shakespeare. Actually, not likely. The sycamore trees descendents of the original grove are now scattered throughout the area (personal observation).

58. Roe, *The Shakespeare Guide to Italy*, 29–33.

59. Roe, *The Shakespeare Guide to Italy*, 36–61.

60. Roe, *The Shakespeare Guide to Italy*, 76–84.

61. Roe, *The Shakespeare Guide to Italy*, 96–104.

62. Roe, *The Shakespeare Guide to Italy*, 138–139.

63. Roe, *The Shakespeare Guide to Italy*, 144–152.

64. Roe, *The Shakespeare Guide to Italy*, 209–211.

65. Roe, *The Shakespeare Guide to Italy*, 264–275.

66. Roe, *The Shakespeare Guide to Italy*, 29.

67. Mario Praz, "Shakespeare and Italy," in *The Flaming Heart: Essays on Crashaw, Machiavelli, and Other Studies of the Relation between Italian and English Literature from Chaucer to T. S. Eliot* (New York: Doubleday Anchor, 1958), 165.

agent for the English government, which sent him to France and Italy to spy during his lost years.[68] But the matter again becomes one of having to invoke Occam's razor. The simplest coherent explanation that fits the evidence in regard to the Italian plays is that the author had spent some time in Italy. If Roe is correct, then one thereby gains insights into how the plays were composed. The author went to a place, imagined a scene with dialogue, and wrote it down either there or soon after. Later, he combined the scenes into a play.

One conjecture that Stratfordians make to account for the extraordinary knowledge evident in the plays is that William of Stratford learned it in taverns from merchants or sailors, although we have no evidence of this. Shapiro came up with another conjecture—in addition to the speculation that "he may have owned some [books], borrowed others," the historical William of Stratford may have "browsed in London's bookstalls in search of additional sources of inspiration," going from bookseller to bookseller, reading bits and pieces from different books as he was browsing.[69] Shapiro also proposed ("it may well be") that Elizabethan theater companies "maintained a stock of comparatively inexpensive books" (again a speculation for which we have no evidence). Shapiro's speculations are part of his attempt to explain how it is that Shakespeare had vast book learning while at the same time there is no evidence that William of Stratford owned, borrowed, or had access to any books. But it does not explain why he would not buy books after he became wealthy.

In any case, Shapiro made no attempt to determine whether books at the bookstalls would have had the sources and information found in the plays. For literary criticism, uninformed by historical investigation, the implausibility of such conjectures plays no significant role. The belief that the Stratford man wrote the plays justifies for Stratfordians any historical construct to make it work, no matter how improbable, lacking in evidence, or comparable learning experience by any other human being. Since it is a given proposition, from the literary scholars' point of view, that the Stratford man wrote the Shakespearean corpus, it does not matter overly much to them how he acquired that knowledge. For purposes of historical study, in contrast, these questions of how an author acquired his or her knowledge and the relationship between their life and what is described in their literary works are of significance. The study of the origins of a creative idea is just as important as the study of its impact.

While William of Stratford was known as a grain merchant, he may also have been involved in the theater as an investor. Alan Robinson traced his

---

68. Georges Lambin, *Voyages de Shakespeare en France et en Italie* (Geneva: Droz, 1962), 130.

69. Shapiro, *Contested Will*, 275.

career from Stratford to London and back. Robinson concluded that William of Stratford became a wealthy man after 1596 in London (when he had only £5), but the source of his wealth is not known. We have no record he was ever paid for writing a play, the payment for which was low. The standard fee at the time was between £5 and £10.[70] Yet, if William of Stratford had written a play and not received payment for it, it is likely he would have sued, since in 1604 he sued the apothecary Philip Rogers for a smaller amount, 35s 10d plus 10s damages over the sale of twenty bushels of malt and a loan.[71] Ros Barber, in her MOOC through the University of London, proposed that William of Stratford was a theater broker.[72]

Edward de Vere, in contrast, although a member of the aristocracy and the recipient of a royal stipend of £1,000 a year, was constantly in need of money. What was he using the money for? Oxfordians suspect it was to put on plays[73] and, like Thomas Jefferson, who was also continually in debt, to purchase books. To be sure, one does not have to be in debt to be an author or composer. The poet Wallace Stevens and the composer Charles Ives worked for insurance companies in Connecticut and were financially well off. Yet, the sheer productivity and quality of the Shakespearean output between 1592 and 1604 better fits the lifestyle of someone who does not have to earn a living. It coincides with Edward de Vere adopting a semi-reclusive lifestyle during that same period, first at Stoke Newington and then after 1596 at Hackney.

Stylometrics

From 1987 to 1990, professors Ward Y. Elliott and Robert J. Valenza conducted a study at Claremont McKenna College in which they looked at fifty-eight "full and partial Shakespeare claimants," as listed by *The Reader's Encyclopedia of Shakespeare*.[74] They submitted the verses of the Shakespearean corpus and the

---

70. Alan Robinson, "The Real William Shakespeare," in *Great Oxford: Essays on the Life and Work of Edward de Vere, 17th Earl of Oxford, 1550–1604*, ed. Richard Malim (Tunbridge Wells: Parapress, 2004), 239.

71. "William Shakspere of Stratford," http://fly.hiwaay.net/~paul/shakspere/evidence1.html.

72. Ros Barber, "Introduction to Who Wrote Shakespeare?" MOOC, University of London, Goldsmith's, 2018.

73. Gilbert Slater concluded that the annuity was intended for de Vere to write military plays as propaganda for the dynasty. He calculated that the yearly expenditure of the Exchequer between 1584 and 1602 averaged £428,000, over two-thirds of which went to military matters. Gilbert Slater, *Seven Shakespeares: A Discussion of the Evidence for Various Theories with Regard to Shakespeare's Identity* (Oxford: Cecil Palmer, 1931), 18–20.

74. *The Reader's Encyclopedia of Shakespeare*, ed. Oscar James Campbell, associate editor Edward G. Quinn (New York: Crowell, 1966), 115.

writings of thirty-seven of the claimants to stylometric analysis. Their explanation for not analyzing the verses of all fifty-eight is that "[t]he remaining twenty-one claimants have left no known poems or plays to test."[75] They concluded that no similarity exists between the poetry of Shakespeare and that of his contemporaries, so none of them, including Edward de Vere, could have been the author of Shakespeare's corpus.[76] Somewhat significantly, neither they nor the *Encyclopedia* included William of Stratford among the claimants. If they had, he would have been listed as claimant number 59, and he would have fallen into the category of claimants who "have left no known poems or plays to test." Thus, he would have failed the test to being included. By not including William of Stratford as one of their claimants, but then concluding he was the author, they are committing the fallacy of the circular proof (or assuming the conclusion).[77]

The inadequacies of their analysis are significant. For starters, the Claremont Shakespeare Authorship Clinic ignored the changing nature of English punctuation over time, as Moore noted in *The Lame Storyteller*: "The Clinic feels that one of its best tests is its exclamation mark count; Shakespeare's works show some exclamation marks, and Steven May's edition of Oxford's poems shows none. But, again, the Clinic neglected the time factor." Moore pointed out that: "According to [A. C.] Partridge, the exclamation mark was not used in England until the 1590s, that is, after Oxford's poetry was written."[78] Moore also pointed out that the clinic took their Shakespearean punctuation from the 1974 Riverside edition of Shakespeare's works, overlooking the description of the editor, G. Blackmore Evans of Harvard University, of his idiosyncratic approach to punctuating the texts.[79] What the Claremont clinic in effect may have done was to compare the punctuation styles of publishing houses rather than of authors. As Partridge wrote: "Despite the rationalization of theorists,

---

75. Ward E. Y. Elliott and Robert J. Valenza, "And Then There Were None: Winnowing the Shakespeare Claimants," *Computers and the Humanities* 30 (1996): 191–245; Elliott and Valenza, "Oxford by the Numbers: What Are the Odds That the Earl of Oxford Could Have Written Shakespeare's Poems and Plays?" *Tennessee Law Review* 72, no. 1 (2004): 331, caption to table 1.1.

76. Ward E. Y. Elliott and Robert J. Valenza, "The Shakespeare Clinic and the Oxfordians," *The Oxfordian* 12 (2010): 138–167; Elliott and Valenza, "Oxford by the Numbers," 323–453.

77. An example of circular proof is the popular interpretation given to UFOs. By definition, UFOs (unidentified flying objects) are unidentified. Some people then identify any flying object that is unidentified as a flying saucer flown by extraterrestrials, when all we can say is that the flying object is unidentified.

78. Moore, *The Lame Storyteller*, 284; cf. A. C. Partridge, *Orthography in Shakespeare and Elizabethan Drama: A Study of Colloquial Contractions, Elision, Prosody, and Punctuation* (Lincoln: University of Nebraska Press, 1964), 125–126.

79. Moore, *The Lame Storyteller*, 284; cf. *The Riverside Shakespeare*, ed. G. Blackmore Evans (Boston: Houghton Mifflin, 1974), vi, 39–40.

however, and even the force of literary and theatrical example, printing-houses seem to have called the tune, and to have re-modelled, in varying de-gree, what came to their hands [in regard to dramatic punctuation]. Nowhere does this become clearer than in the quartos of plays printed in the decade 1594–1604."[80]

Moore went on to analyze "the four non-punctuation dependent tests" and pointed out that "[t]he Clinic passed Oxford on Line Beginnings and . . . on Percentage Word Length once the Clinic's faulty data is corrected, but he al-legedly fails on Relative Clauses." The Relative Clauses test has two subtests: Relative Pronouns and Relative Clauses. In regard to the Relative Pronouns subtest, Moore found Edward de Vere to be "within Shakespeare's range and within two deviations of Shakespeare's mean . . . so he passes that subtest." In regard to the Relative Clause subtest, Moore found that Edward de Vere was "well within Shakespeare's range on five of them" and only outside the range on having "two too many 'that's'."[81] As a result of his analysis of the clinic's data, Moore came to a different conclusion—that is, the data show support for the Oxfordian candidate.[82] Since William of Stratford must be eliminated ac-cording to the Claremont clinic's own rules, they in effect succeeded in dem-onstrating stylometrically that Edward de Vere is the most likely author of the Shakespearean canon.

More recently, in 2016, the American statistician and applied linguist Joseph Rudman surveyed the attempts to do a statistical analysis of the Shakespeare canon. After pointing out that valid studies of this type must adhere to the scientific method but thus far have not done so, he concluded "that such a valid study is not attainable with the limits of present-day knowledge."[83]

Nelson disputed the claim that Edward de Vere wrote the plays and po-ems, among other reasons, on the basis of difference in spelling of words between Edward de Vere's handwritten letters of the late sixteenth century and the printed version of the plays and poems from the 1620s.[84] Nelson does not take his analysis to the logical next step, which is to compare the spelling in the plays attributed to Shakespeare with the spelling in the letters of other Elizabethan writers. To compare the spelling in the handwritten letters of just one writer with the spelling in the printed Shakespearean corpus is simply

---

80. Partridge, *Orthography in Shakespeare*, 126.

81. Moore, *The Lame Storyteller*, 286.

82. Moore, *The Lame Storyteller*, 287.

83. Joseph Rudman, "Non-Traditional Authorship Attribution Studies of William Shakespeare's Canon: Some Caveats," *Journal of Early Modern Studies* 5 (2016): 328.

84. Nelson, *Monstrous Adversary*, 62–67.

faulty methodology. Comparison with the spelling in the letters of William of Stratford, of course, cannot be done because there are no such letters.

The lawyer William Plumer Fowler, on the other hand, claimed to have found and provided evidence for 3,000 to 4,000 "parallelisms" between phrases in the known letters of Edward de Vere and the phrasings in the plays, poems, and sonnets attributed to Shakespeare.[85] To be sure it would be easy to isolate any particular parallelism, such as "while the grass grows," and dismiss it as a commonplace. But to do so would be, in the Oxfordian view, to miss the point. It is the weight of the evidence Fowler assembles focused on one individual that, in their view, is determinative. Fowler meant by "parallelism" the same type of expressions that the Oxfordian Eva Turner Clark meant when she wrote: "Oxford's mannerisms of speech are those of Shakespeare." She also wrote that these "expressions . . . are commonly found in Shakespeare, rarely in the writings of contemporary dramatists, who had their own pet phrases."[86] One phrase that is in fact a word-for-word correspondence is Edward de Vere's use of the biblical phrase "I am that I am" in his letter to Lord Burghley of October 30, 1584, and in Sonnet 121.[87] Dismissing this as a biblical commonplace does not quite work here because, if Hank Whittemore is correct, no other Elizabethan writer chose to use it—only Shakespeare and Edward de Vere.[88] Neither Clark nor Fowler, however, did a systematic study of the writings of Shakespeare's contemporaries to demonstrate their proposition.

I am familiar with only two attempts to do a similar parallelism study for a Shakespeare contemporary. One was the online article of Jerome Harner, "Why I Am Not an Oxfordian."[89] Harner listed nine such parallelisms between the writings of Francis Bacon and the Shakespeare corpus. A second attempt was made by John Casson in regard to Sir Henry Neville. Casson randomly selected ten letters by Neville and compared the words in them with words used only once in Shakespeare's plays, such as the word *muttering*, which ap-

---

85. William Plumer Fowler, *Shakespeare Revealed in Oxford's Letters* (Portsmouth, NH: Peter E. Randall, 1986), 1–822. The number 3,000–4,000 I estimated on the basis of 800 pages in Fowler's text devoted to the comparison of phrases in the letters with the works of Shakespeare and four to five parallelisms identified per page. Nelson was either unaware of Fowler's book or chose to ignore it.

86. Eva Turner Clark, "Lord Oxford's Letters Echoed in Shakespeare's Plays," *Shakespeare Fellowship Quarterly* 7, no. 1 (1946): 10.

87. "Oxford's Letter of October 30, 1584, for Help in Postponing His Debt to the Queen," in Fowler, *Shakespeare Revealed*, 321. The phrase is from Exodus 3:14.

88. "Reason No. 9 Why 'Shakespeare' Was Edward de Vere Seventeenth Earl of Oxford: 'I AM THAT I AM,'" *Hank Whittemore's Shakespeare Blog*, https://hankwhittemore.wordpress.com/2011/04/10/reason-no-8-why-shakespeare-was-edward-de-vere-earl-of-oxford-i-am-that-i-am/.

89. Jerome Harner, "Why I Am Not an Oxfordian: Bacon Versus De Vere. A Review of the Evidence" (2000), http://www.sirbacon.org/harneroxford.htm.

pears only in *Othello*. Casson pointed out that *Othello* premiered at the Banqueting House in Whitehall on November 1, 1604, the same day Neville used that word in a letter he wrote from Parliament. Casson claims to have found over eighty such word-usage correlations, none of which he describes.[90] His one described example could be used as evidence instead that Neville saw the premiere and wrote the letter afterward.

The Stratfordians have an easy job of it because they can point out that there is only one direct match in Fowler between letter and play or poem. They do not have to defend the fact that there are no direct matches or parallelisms between the Shakespearean corpus and the letters of William of Stratford because those letters do not exist. Anti-Stratfordians find it strange that the greatest writer in the English language either wrote no letters or that all his letters were destroyed. The former case seems highly unlikely, while the latter would involve a conspiracy much more vast and improbable than the one the Oxfordians claim took place to deny Edward de Vere's status as the author of the works of Shakespeare.

Personal vs. Impersonal Evidence

In regard to contemporary testimony about an individual, Barber made a useful distinction between personal and impersonal evidence. Personal evidence is from someone who was in a position to know the individual personally. Impersonal evidence is from someone who had heard about that individual or read something they had written but had never met or seen them.[91] We find a corresponding bifurcation in the evidence about Shakespeare the writer and businessman William of Stratford. All the contemporary testimony we have about Shakespeare as a writer is impersonal—that is, based solely on his plays and poetry. All the contemporary evidence we have about William of Stratford that is personal never mentions him as a poet or playwright.

Group Theory

Although I have focused in this chapter on the dispute between Stratfordians and Oxfordians, and set aside consideration of other proposed candidates,

---

90. John Casson, *Much Ado about Noting: Henry Neville and Shakespeare's Secret Source* (London: Dolman Scott, 2010).

91. Barber, "Introduction to Who Wrote Shakespeare?"

I would like to discuss briefly one other proposed possibility that has a long history—namely, group authorship. We might term this idea the Shakespeare syndicate. The notion that a group of authors combined to write the works of Shakespeare dates back at least as far as Delia Bacon (1811–1859) in the nineteenth century. She was never clear on who she thought the members of the group were and, instead, focused on Francis Bacon as the leader of the group. The English economist and college professor Gilbert Slater (1864–1938), in his *Seven Shakespeares* (1931), proposed Francis Bacon, Christopher Marlowe, William Stanley, Roger Manners, Edward de Vere, Sir Walter Raleigh, and Lady Mary, Countess of Pembroke as members of the group. But he did so on the basis of external considerations of who might have been the members of such a group, not so much on the evidence of the texts themselves.[92] Positing a group effort would help to account for a number of difficulties in regard to establishing authorship. For example, how could one person coin so many (over 1,700) words? Why does no contemporary mention meeting or seeing the playwright? Why is there no paper trail, evidence of Shakespeare's actually writing the plays or poems, such as a diary entry, correspondence ("I am writing a play about a king with three daughters"), and so forth? Why are there such wide divergences in the styles of the writing? It would also help account for the instances in the plays that relate closely to the life of Edward de Vere. Ironically, the assiduous work of the Stratfordians in detecting collaborators with "Shakespeare" on the plays may be providing evidence not only in favor of the group authorship theory but also for who members of that group may have been. Besides Edward de Vere and William of Stratford (as theater broker), members would have included John Fletcher, Thomas Kyd, Christopher Marlowe, Thomas Middleton, Thomas Nashe, George Peele, George Wilkins, and possible others such as Anthony Munday. It might also help explain why the Droeshout engraving of "William Shakespeare" as the frontispiece of the First Folio appears to be of someone wearing a mask.

The Takeaway

In looking for general principles of attribution, we have a number of possibilities to consider here. The spelling of an author's last name has little or no relevance for attribution. Some of the poems of Edward de Vere when published are attributed to "Edward Oxenford" and he could have used Shake-

---

92. Slater, *Seven Shakespeares*, Bacon (107–126); Marlowe (127–149); Stanley (150–172); Manners (173–175); Pembroke (207–255); de Vere (176–206, 271–276); Raleigh (256–276).

speare as his nom de plume. Likewise, William of Stratford could have used the spelling Shake-speare as his nom de plume. People can spell their names in different ways at different times. The Harvard University history professor Serhii Plokhii sometimes spells his last name as Plokhy. Frederic Pierce wrote about a forbearer of his: "There are in existence autographs by the original Thomas, as being spelled in three different ways—Pierce, Peirce, and Pieirce."[93]

The name on title pages of works attributed to "Shakespeare" has significant relevance but not decisive. The general consensus has been to accept that the thirty-six plays of the First Folio were written by Shakespeare. Of those thirty-six plays, twenty-one were first published in quarto; the other fifteen first appeared in the First Folio. Scholars, however, do not accept all the plays that were originally published in quartos with an attribution to Shakespeare as having been written by Shakespeare. See table 6.3 above, where plays with some possible indication of William Shakespeare on the title pages of seven of the quartos (two attributed to "William Shakespeare"; one to "W. Shakespeare"; one to "Shakespeare"; one to "W.Sh."; and two to "W.S.") have been rejected. In all, nine plays that are not in the First Folio were published with some indication on the title page as having been written by William Shakespeare, but only two of those have been more or less accepted as having been written by him (albeit in collaboration with another playwright). Two other quarto plays that do not appear in the First Folio and do not have any indication on the title page of having been authored by Shakespeare have been widely accepted as his.

Contemporary and near contemporary attributions can be mistaken. A contemporary example occurred in 1578, when the Italian Alessandro Guagnini (1538–1614), who had served in the Polish army, published a work in Latin entitled *A Description of European Sarmatia*. Maciej Stryjkowski (ca. 1547–1593), who was his subordinate in Poland, claimed before the royal court that Guagnini stole the work from him and that he (Guagnini) was illiterate (*literum rudis*). The king, Stefan Batory, upheld Stryjkowski's claim, decreeing the work to be his, yet Guagnini continued to publish the work under his own name. If such an attribution (i.e., on a title page) occurs, then the burden is on those who disagree with that attribution. If no such attribution occurs, then the burden is on those who want to attribute a work to a particular author.

Anti-Stratfordians often point out that William of Stratford came from an illiterate family, including his wife, his son Hamnet, and his daughter Susanna. The literacy of family has some relevance in considering authorship but

---

93. Frederic Beech Pierce, *Pierce Genealogy Being the Record of the Posterity of Thomas Pierce, an Early Inhabitant of Charlestown, and Afterwards Charlestown Village (Woburn), in New England* (Worcester: Chas. Hamilton, 1882).

depends to a great extent on what is being written. Gandhi's wife remained illiterate, but all four of his sons were literate. Gandhi wrote extensively about politics and personal matters but no literary works. Harriet Jacobs's family was illiterate, but she wrote a memoir about personal experiences. In contrast, Bach and Mozart came from musically literate families, which helps to explain their early development as musicians and composers. Bach's second wife, Anna Magdalena Wilcke (1701–1760), was musically literate, as were all his children. Mozart's father, Leopold, (1719–1787) was a concert violinist, conductor, and composer, and his sister Anna Maria (1751–1829) was a musician and composer. His wife, Constanze, (1762–1842) was trained as a singer; both of their sons were musically literate. Sholokhov's mother was illiterate, but she learned to read and write in order to communicate with her son when he was in Moscow.

Personal literacy has significant relevance but depends to a great extent on what is being written. Homer may have been blind, and medieval troubadours depended on their memory. Muhammad was illiterate. Yet someone at some point wrote down their verbal creations. Shakespeare's works were most likely not dictated. In any case, neither the six signatures said to be William of Stratford's is in the Italianate style that writers of the period generally adopted.[94]

We have no direct evidence that William of Stratford went to any school. The Stratfordians argue that William of Stratford could have attended the grammar school near his boyhood home in Stratford. His father was alderman; therefore, it would have been extraordinary if he had not attended the local grammar school. And a grammar school education in those days in England was very good. The anti-Stratfordians argue that grammar schools were for the wealthy, and being an alderman did not necessarily entitle one to send one's son to the school. Even if William did attend the grammar school there, we do not have the curriculum from that grammar school, so it is only surmise as to what was taught. Price took the evidence we have for what texts were taught at other grammar schools anywhere in England and posited that they could have been read at the Stratford grammar school. She then compiled a list of those authors upon whom Shakespeare drew and divided those authors into two lists. The first list has those twenty-five authors drawn upon by Shakespeare that we have evidence of at least excerpts of their works being taught in at least one grammar school in England of the time. These include Aesop, Aristophanes, Julius Caesar, Horace, Juvenal, Livy, Lucan, Ovid,

---

94. See Frank Davis, "Shakspere's Six Accepted Signatures: A Comparison," in *Shakespeare beyond Doubt? Exposing an Industry in Denial*, ed. John M. Shahan and Alexander Waugh (Tamarac, FL: Llumina, 2013), 34–37 for examples of the signatures of 28 writers and 9 actors of the time, all in the Italianate style.

Seneca, Terence, and Virgil. The second list has those 145 authors that Shakespeare drew upon for whom we have no evidence they were taught at any grammar school anywhere in England of the time.[95] This list includes, among others, Alberti, Appian, Marcus Aurelius, Miguel de Cervantes, George Chapman, Chaucer, Geoffrey of Monmouth, Boccaccio, William Camden, Castiglione, Richard Hakluyt, Leo Africanus, Plato, Proclus, and Bernard of Clairvaux. To that list, we can now add George North's *A Brief Discourse on Rebellion and Rebels* (1576).[96] Whoever wrote the Shakespearean corpus had a far wider range of reading than could have been obtained at an English grammar school of the time. The Oxfordians point out that de Vere received his bachelor's degree from Cambridge, his master's degree in law from Oxford, and attended Gray's Inn, a law school. Alan Nelson, however, dismissed the Cambridge and Oxford degrees as "unearned," and claimed that his three years at Gray's Inn were just a "courtesy admission."[97] Nelson provides no evidence for these assertions, leaving open the likely conclusion that they are baseless.

The relevance of education of the author for the principles of authorship depends on what genre is being discussed. Letters and memoirs do not require an education as such. Literary works integrally borrowing from other literary works of the time require that the author be not only literate but have a substantial education.

The anti-Stratfordians claim that the author of the Shakespeare canon had specialized knowledge. The plays, according to them, exhibit depth and range of learning in such specialized and courtly disciplines as classical philosophy, literature, music, law, military strategy, art history, ancient and foreign languages, ancient history, natural history, foreign lands, falconry, government, politics, rhetoric, and medicine—that is, knowledge only a university-educated person of high birth could obtain.

Some of the Stratfordians counter that the allusions to various pursuits and careers are not as arcane as they appear, merely a smattering of lore any artist could have picked up—say, at the local pub or by talking to visitors from Italy or from browsing the bookstalls in London to give the illusion of knowledge— and that it is no big deal.

Oxfordians like to point out that we have direct evidence that De Vere was a university-educated person of high birth. He knew Latin, French, and

---

95. Price, *Shakespeare's Unorthodox Biography*, 250–252; cf. Stuart Gillespie, *Shakespeare's Books: A Dictionary of Shakespeare's Sources* (London: Athlone, 2001).

96. Dennis McCarthy and June Schlueter, *"A Brief Discourse on Rebellion and Rebels" by George North: A Newly Uncovered Manuscript Source for Shakespeare's Plays* (Cambridge: Brewer, 2018).

97. Nelson, *Monstrous Adversary*, 42–43, 45, 46.

Italian,[98] and traveled to the places in Italy in which eleven the plays are set. He studied law and cosmography, engaged in falconry, jousted in tournaments, played tennis, and wrote poetry and plays, all of which we have corroborating evidence for. Stratfordians speculate that William of Stratford may have been a spy, a servant, a law clerk, a holder of horses at the door of the Globe Theater, and so forth, all without any corroborating evidence.

The relevance for establishing principles of attribution depends on the accuracy of the specialized information. An author can imagine and even obtain a high degree of verisimilitude concerning matters about which the author has no personal knowledge, but details in the works that are accurate can provide evidence concerning who the author was. In January 1996, for example, Random House published the novel *Primary Colors*, listing the author as "Anonymous." The insider information contained in the book about the Clinton campaign for the presidency in 1992 narrowed the field of possible authors. Quickly the leading candidate became *Newsweek* columnist Joe Klein, who repeatedly denied being the author. David Kusnet, a Clinton speechwriter, noting that "many episodes . . . reveal a street-level knowledge of politics and policy" and that the views expressed were similar to those Klein had expressed in his columns, concluded the author was Klein. Yet, even when a stylometric analysis by Donald Foster shortly thereafter pegged Klein, he continued to deny it and denounced Foster. A handwriting analysis in July by the *Washington Post* of glosses on an early typescript draft of the novel clinched it and led to Klein's reversal of his denial.[99] For historians, investigating the context as well as cultural, political, social, and autobiographical influences is a valuable method for studying any literary work. Literary critics tend to privilege the display of their own virtuosity in interpreting texts without being overly concerned with who the author of those texts was (see Garber's "a minor wrinkle"). We will revisit the issue of specialized knowledge and how the author acquired it when we discuss the authorship controversy surrounding Mikhail Sholokhov in chapter 9.

The issue of autobiographical details in the writings plays a significant role in the controversy over the author of the Shakespeare canon. Anti-Stratfordians

---

98. Some Stratfordians have asserted that Shakespeare did not know Italian or, if he did know some, he did not know it well. For a discussion, see Benedikt Höttemann, *Shakespeare and Italy* (Berlin: Lit Verlag, 2011), 170–176.

99. Anonymous, *Primary Colors: A Novel about Politics* (New York: Random House, 1996); David Kusnet, "'Primary Colors'—Outside the White House beyond the Beltway," *Baltimore Sun*, February 11, 1996; Donald Foster, "Primary Culprit," *New York*, February 26, 1996: 50–57; David Streitfeld, "'Anonymous' Undone by His Own Hand?" *Washington Post*, July 17, 1996; Todd Lindberg, "The Media's True Colors," *Weekly Standard*, July 29, 1996. Note that Sholokhov's handwriting on drafts of *The Quiet Don* has not clinched Sholokhov's authorship for the skeptics (see chapter 9).

argue that none of the events or allusions in the plays, sonnets, or other works of the Shakespeare canon can be related to events in William of Stratford's life. For example, there is no mention of Stratford, his hometown, and none of the Warwickshire dialect that William of Stratford grew up with appears in the works. Assertions have been made by various Stratfordians to cover this gap by claiming certain wordings in the Shakespeare canon could represent the Warwickshire dialect, but Gary Goldstein evaluated any such claims to be dubious at best.[100]

The Stratfordian position seems to be that the entire Shakespearean corpus is made up of works of pure imagination. The absence of autobiographical details demonstrates what a genius he was. Besides, maybe someone will some day find examples of Warwickshire dialect in the corpus.

Oxfordians delight is detailing events and allusions in the plays and sonnets that can be related to specific events in Edward de Vere's life, as we would expect if he were the author. No other person of the time, according to them, fits as well the probable historical profile that can be drawn from the works attributed to Shakespeare. In Sonnet 37, for example, the author refers to himself as lame. Oxfordians point out that we have de Vere's own testimony that he was lame in a letter dated 1595 in which he offers to visit Lord Burghley "as well as a lame man might."[101] The injury they speculate may have resulted from a Montague-Capulet-type street brawl a dozen years earlier between him and his retinue and that of Sir Thomas Knyvet, the uncle of his mistress Anne Vavasour or that he obtained the injury in one of the jousting tournaments he participated in. We have no evidence that William of Stratford was ever lame.

Autobiographical details are highly relevant for determining authorship. To be sure, authors can write works of pure imagination, but it would be highly unusual for an author not to put at least a few autobiographical elements into some of their works. And we should certainly expect more of such in a corpus of works as extensive as the Shakespeare canon.

The anti-Stratfordians point out that even the Stratfordians say that the plays demonstrate awareness of inner workings of courtly intrigue and politics that William of Stratford could not possibly have had. The Stratfordians resort to ad hominem attack when they say that this argument shows that the anti-Stratfordians are snobs because they think a commoner could not write plays. Have they never heard of Ben Jonson? Besides, Shakespeare could have picked up information about the court when he acted in plays before the court. The

---

100. Gary Goldstein, "Shakespeare's Native Tongue," *Shakespeare Oxford Newsletter,* Fall 1990, 4–8; repr. in *De Vere Society Newsletter,* November 2009, 28–31.

101. Nelson, *Monstrous Adversary,* 357.

Oxfordians counter that Edward de Vere served at the court and knew Elizabeth I personally. Lord Burghley—Elizabeth's secretary of state and then her treasurer—had been his guardian for nine years and later his father-in-law for seventeen years. Finally, as Lord Great Chamberlain, de Vere took part in court ceremonies.

The relevance for principles of attribution is that specialized knowledge of any kind has to be evaluated closely to determine whether it is the kind of knowledge that can be picked up only firsthand or through book learning or can be imagined.

The claim has been frequently made that those who are questioning the Stratford man's authorship of the plays and poetry of Shakespeare are engaging in some kind of class discrimination or just being snobs because they think a commoner could not write plays and poetry. If we were to raise that claim to a principle of attribution, then any time we have a work or body of works and we have two or more possible authors, at least one of whom is an aristocrat and at least one of whom is not, then we should always choose the one who is not an aristocrat. Instead, a better approach in terms of establishing a principle of attribution is to examine the content of a work or body of works and ascertain the point of view that it represents. If a work reflects an aristocratic point of view, then it is a greater likelihood that an aristocrat wrote it than that a commoner imagining an aristocratic point of view wrote it. And if it reflects a non-aristocratic point of view, then it is more likely a non-aristocrat wrote it.

It could be significant that although William of Stratford had a commoner background, none of the plays or poetry is about commoners, unlike Ben Jonson, who was a commoner and who wrote about commoners. All the Shakespearean plays and poetry are about well-born people. Almost all of them are about the court or courtiers. All are written from an aristocratic point of view. The Stratford man did attain the status of "gentleman" in 1596, so that might thereby exclude him right there from being the author of the Shakespeare corpus by those who prefer to think only a commoner could have written the plays. I am aware of some cases, such as that of Harriet Jacobs whose authorship of *Incidents in the Life of a Slave Girl, Written by Herself* (published in 1861 with Linda Brent as author) was challenged because the thinking was that a slave could not write or at least not write that well.[102] Yet the Shakespearean corpus is surely a different case, since Harriet Jacobs had

---

102. See, for example, Jean Fagan Yellin, "Texts and Contexts of Harriet Jacobs's Incidents in the Life of a Slave Girl: Written by Herself," in *The Slave's Narrative*, ed. Charles T. Davis and Henry Louis Gates, Jr. (New York: Oxford University Press, 1985), 262–282; Yellin, *Harriet Jacobs: A Life* (Cambridge, MA: Basic Civitas, 2004), xi–xvii.

been a slave girl, and she wrote about what she knew (i.e., her own experiences). The anti-Stratfordians claim that the author of the Shakespearean corpus wrote about what he knew (not just imagined), but he also drew widely on other authors.

One of the main arguments against de Vere's candidacy is the traditional chronology of the plays, a number of which are thought to have been written after de Vere died in 1603. Oxfordians counter that the traditional chronology was created to fit the life of William of Stratford and thus would explicitly exclude anyone else with a different life span. Unaware of any attempt to codify the bases of establishing the date of a written text, I proposed in 2011 the following principles for establishing the approximate date of an otherwise undated written text:

1. A work cannot have been created before a work from which it borrows.
2. A work cannot have been created after a work that borrows from it.
3. Style, terminology, spelling, punctuation, and grammar can help to date a written work approximately.
4. Codicological dating (for example, according to watermarks and paleography) can establish an earliest possible date for a manuscript or printed copy and thus help to establish a latest possible date of composition.
5. A publication date can establish a latest possible date of composition but not an earliest.
6. The content of a written work can be used to place it in the context of a period in which it was most likely written.
7. References in other works, such as diaries, interviews, letters, marginalia, memoirs, notes, etc., to the work can help establish a latest possible date.
8. Reference to historical events (including a prediction of something that was unlikely to be known to the supposed author—that is, a postdiction) can provide an earliest possible date.[103]

The underlying premise of this list is the ability of establishing two possible dates—the earliest possible date of composition (*teminus post quem*) and the latest possible date of composition (*terminus post quem non*), as was done in *Dating Shakespeare's Plays.*

---

103. Ostrowski, review of *Dating Shakespeare's Plays*, 243.

CHAPTER 7

Who Wrote the Works Attributed to Prince Andrei Kurbskii?

> "If a learned skeptic began to assert that all the 'works' of Ivan [the Terrible] were spurious, it would be difficult to argue with him."
>
> —Sergei Platonov (1923)[1]

The reign of Tsar Ivan IV "the Terrible" (r. 1533–1584) was a turbulent one by any measure. Russia conquered the Kazan' and Astrakhan' khanates (1552 and 1556, respectively), thus expanding its control down the Volga River to the Caspian Sea. Russia also initially (between 1558 and 1578) gained a large amount of territory in the Baltic area during the Livonian War (1558–1583), which was fought against Poland-Lithuania, Sweden, and at times Denmark. After Stefan Batory was elected king of Poland, the tide of war turned against Russia, which by 1582 had to give up all the territory it had earlier gained. In addition, during Ivan's reign Russia began the conquest of Siberia, saw a major part of Moscow burn in 1547, experienced Crimean Tatar attacks, including the sack of the suburbs of Moscow in 1571, while the political elite experienced suppression, torture, and executions, and the populace endured famine and plague.

But it was not all war, death, and mayhem. The governmental administrative system was expanded and reformed. Russia established commercial relations with England. A number of cultural achievements occurred. Among these are: the Stoglav Church Council (1551) codified Russian Church law; the government issued the law code (*Sudebnik*) of 1550, which updated and expanded the law code of 1497; the Great Menology, a comprehensive twelve-

---

1. S. M. Platonov, *Ivan Groznyi* (Peterburg: Brokgauz-Efron, 1923), 7.

volume collection of saints' lives, patristic teachings, and apocrypha arranged according to month; the *Illustrated Chronicle Codex*, a ten-volume work that contains 9,745 folios and 17,774 miniatures and covers history (with some overlaps and gaps) from the creation of the world to 1567; the Book of Degrees, a dynastic history of Rus' arranged according to each generation of the ruling family; and various building projects, including the Church of the Intercession on the Moat (St. Basil's in Red Square).

In 1533, the previous ruler, Vasilii III, the grand prince of Muscovy (r. 1505–1533), died, leaving his wife, Elena Glinskaia, and two sons, the three-year-old Ivan and the one-year-old Iurii. Ivan was declared Vasilii's successor with his mother acting as regent. Five years later, in 1538, Elena died, invoking a period where factional struggles among the boyars came to the fore. With the election of Makarii, archbishop of Novgorod, as metropolitan of Rus', Ivan found a protector and political adviser. In 1547, Ivan was crowned tsar, a title that was a double entendre in that it could mean either emperor in European diplomacy or khan in steppe diplomacy. Poland-Lithuania refused to acknowledge the upgrade in title of the Russian ruler. In December 1564, Ivan left the Moscow Kremlin and took up residence in Alexandrovo Sloboda, a grand princely residence northeast of Moscow. From there, he established and ran the *Oprichnina*, a secret police force that operated as a state with a state. In 1572, he ended the *Oprichnina* and returned to Moscow, where in 1584 he was stricken while playing chess and died.

Prince Andrei Mikhailovich Kurbskii was one of Ivan's top military leaders. He took part in the conquest of Kazan' in 1552. He also led the Russian forces during the Livonian War that captured Dorpat in 1558. In April 1564, he defected to Lithuania, where he lived until his death in 1583. Kurbskii is most famously known for engaging in an exchange of letters with Ivan IV and for a history of Ivan's reign. These two items have been among the important sources of evidence for the reign of Ivan IV. Platonov wrote that "It [*The History*] contains much historical material both valuable and exact."[2] Numerous other works and translations have also been attributed to Kurbskii, all of which he supposedly wrote after he defected.

Context of the Controversy

The completely accepted view in the scholarship had been that the manuscript copies we have of the correspondence represent the letters that Kurbskii and

---

2. Platonov, *Ivan Groznyi*, 8.

Ivan exchanged in the second half of the sixteenth century. Then, in 1971, that "learned skeptic" that Platonov mentioned in 1923 appeared in the person of Edward L. Keenan (1935–2015), a Harvard University professor of Russian history. He challenged the accepted attribution of these letters. Not only did he question whether Kurbskii and Ivan wrote them, he also questioned their basic literacy and whether they wrote anything at all. Keenan's book, titled *The Kurbskii-Groznyi Apocrypha*, was published by Harvard University Press and received the Thomas J. Wilson prize for "the best first book by a young author." The scholarly response, in contrast, was overwhelmingly negative. Keenan had few defenders. Yet the book inspired scholars into doing more research on the sources, if only to refute Keenan's claims. He subsequently wrote three articles responding to critics, only altering his views slightly to be even more skeptical that Kurbskii composed or translated anything, even rejecting Kurbskii's authorship of the so-called Lithuanian letters that he had initially accepted as having been dictated by Kurbskii. Keenan died convinced he was correct. His opponents remain equally convinced he was wrong.

In the Thicket

In the interest of full disclosure, the reader should know that I am among the few scholars who have defended Keenan's views in print. The article on which much of the following description of the points of contention is based is one in which I tried to present the various views as fairly as I could without engaging in overt polemicizing.

The *Miscellany of Kurbskii* (*Sbornik Kurbskogo*)[3]

Just as the First Folio of 1623 has served as the main basis for attributing a core of plays to William Shakespeare, the Kurbskii miscellanies (*sborniki Kurbskogo*), none of which dates earlier than the 1670s, have been the main basis for attributing the core set of works to Andrei Kurbskii. The Russian scholar Konstantin Erusalimskii has extensively studied the extant manuscripts of what he calls collectively the *Miscellany of Kurbskii*.[4] He classified those eighty-five

---

    3. An earlier version of this part of this chapter appeared as "Attributions to Andrei Kurbskii and Inferential (Bayesian) Probability," *Canadian-American Slavic Studies* 49, no. 2–3 (2015): 211–233. My gratitude to Russell E. Martin, the editor of *CASS*, for allowing me to publish a revised version here.
    4. K[onstantin] Iu. Erusalimskii, *Sbornik Kurbskogo. Issledovanie knizhnoi kul'tury*, 2 vols., vol. 1 (Moscow: Znak, 2009), 3.

manuscripts into five groups (recensions) based primarily on their contents.[5] Unlike the First Folio, however, in which it is clear that all the works are meant to be attributed to William Shakespeare, in the Kurbskii miscellanies not all the works are directly attributed to Kurbskii. In the Second Recension, for example, two out of the thirteen "Lithuanian" letters and all of the translations are unattributed. In addition, neither of the two major works that bookend the contents of the Second Recension copies—*The History of the Grand Prince of Moscow* and *The History of the Eighth Council*—has an attribution.

The second component of each of the miscellanies is made up of three letters addressed to the "Muscovite Grand Prince," and those are attributed to Andrei Kurbskii. Clearly scholars felt justified in attributing all the contents of the first two recensions to Kurbskii because fourteen of sixteen letters seem to be attributed to him. One can justifiably ask on what basis, if any, the attributions have been made. We cannot know whether all the works in the Kurbskii miscellanies were meant to be attributed to Andrei Kurbskii. The title *Miscellany of Kurbskii* (*Sbornik Kurbskogo*) does not appear in any of the codices.[6] Recensions Three through Five contain works attributed to Taranovskii, Guagnini, and Stryjkowski, so the principle of attribution regarding the items in the *Miscellany of Kurbskii* is that any unattributed items were written by him.[7]

Let us take a closer look at the works within the *Miscellany of Kurbskii* as published by Erusalimskii.

1. *The History of the Grand Prince of Moscow* (*Istoriia o velikom kniziae Moskovskom*) (proposed dates of composition: 1570s, 1573, 1575–1577, spring and summer of 1581, 1590s onward, or ca. 1675).

We do not know who first attributed *The History of the Grand Prince of Moscow* to Andrei Kurbskii (none of the manuscript copies mentions an author), but already by the time that the Russian historian V. N. Tatishchev (1686–1750) was doing his historical research, *The History of the Grand Prince* (hereafter *The History*) was being identified as "of Kurbskii" (*Kurbskago*).[8] Various views have been expressed regarding when *The History* may have been written. According

---

5. The first volume contains his analysis; the second, his publication of the texts. When citing his publication of *The History of the Grand Prince of Moscow*, I will use the acronym *IVKM*. Erusalimskii adopted the manuscript GIM, sobranie Uvarova, no. 301, of the Second Recension as his base text with variant readings from eleven other manuscripts.

6. Erusalimskii, *Sbornik Kurbskogo*, vol. 1, 3.

7. See Ostrowski, "Attributions to Andrei Kurbskii," 215.

8. Erusalimskii, *Sbornik Kurbskogo*, vol. 1, 154. Some scholars think the gloss "kur istoriia" in several manuscript copies of Andrei I. Lyzlov's *Scythian History* from the 1690s is the earliest attribution

to the Soviet historian A. A. Zimin (1920–1980), *The History* was written shortly after 1573, some nine years after Kurbskii fled to Lithuania, because the last deaths it mentions are those of three individuals who died in 1573.[9] Erusalimskii dated the composition of *The History* to the period 1575–1577 on the basis that it borrowed from a sermon of John Chrysostom (ca. 349–407) found in the *Novyi Margarit* (literally, "New Pearl," a collection of ecclesiastical writings), which he accepted as having been compiled in 1575.[10] The German scholar Inge Auerbach proposed that *The History* was written during the spring and summer of 1581, because it mentions missionary activities "just as now done in India by the king of Spain and Portugal" (*"iako i nyne sodelyvaemo krolem Ishpanskim i Portugal'skim vo Indii"*).[11] Philip II, the king of Spain (r. 1556–1598), inherited the throne of Portugal in late 1580 and united the two kingdoms early the next year in the Iberian Union, which lasted until 1640. Two Russian scholars concluded on different linguistic grounds that *The History* was written before the union of the two kingdoms. The literary scholar Vasilii V. Kalugin (b. 1955) objected that this formulation in the text is elliptical in that it represents an "incomplete construction that was characteristic for Rus' syntax" and that "two rulers of sovereign countries" were meant.[12] Erusalimskii objected that *krolem* (king) here is dative plural ("to the kings"), not instrumental singular ("by the king").[13]

In order to explain other apparent anachronisms, contradictions, and outright errors in *History* and other Kurbskiana in general, Erusalimskii proposed seventeenth-century editing as the culprit and advocated a two-tiered approach: "Recognizing Kurbskii's authorship does not avoid the issue that is resolved with particular difficulty in respect to the manuscript tradition of Kurbskii's works: What in the manuscript tradition is original and what is the result of copying, reading, and editing?"[14] The Russian historian Aleksandr I. Filiushkin (b. 1970) articulated this same argument in 2007 and endorsed Erusalim-

---

of *The History* to Kurbskii. David Hari Das, "History Writing and Late Muscovite Court Culture: A Study of Andrei Lyzlov's *History of the Scythians*" (PhD diss., University of Washington, 1991), 223.

9. A. A. Zimin, "Kogda Kurbskii napisal 'Istoriiu o velikom kniaze Moskovskom'?" *Trudy Otdela drevnerusskoi literatury* 18 (1962): 305–308.

10. K. Iu. Erusalimskii, "Ideal'nyi sovet v 'Istorii o velikom kniaze Moskovskom,'" in *Tekst v gumanitarnom znanii. Materialy mezhvuzovskoi nauchnoi konferentsii 22–24 aprelia 1997 g.*, ed. O. M. Meduzhevskaia, M. Iu. Rumiantseva, K. Iu. Erusalimskii, and V. V. Zvereva (Moscow: Rossiiskii gosudarstvennyi gumanitarnyi universitet, 1997), 79, 86–87.

11. Inge Auerbach, "Gedanken zur Entstehung von A. M. Kurbskijs 'Istorija o velikom knjaze Moskovskom,'" *Canadian-American Slavic Studies* 13, nos. 1–2 (1979): 169, 171.

12. V. V. Kalugin, *Andrei Kurbskii i Ivan Groznyi. Teoreticheskie vzgliady i literaturnaia tekhnika drevnerusskogo pisatelia* (Moscow: Iazyki russkoi kul'tury, 1998), 41.

13. Erusalimskii, *Sbornik Kurbskogo*, vol. 1, 286, n. 253.

14. Erusalimskii, *Sbornik Kurbskogo*, vol. 1, 755.

skii's expression of it in 2012.[15] Proponents of the Kurbskii attributions place a high probability of validity on that argument and think we should start from a default position that Kurbskii was the author of the original form of each of the works attributed to him and peel off only those parts that he could not have written. For skeptics, such an argument has a low probability of validity and appears to be saying that in the works attributed to Kurbskii anything that Kurbskii could have written, he wrote; anything he could not have written was an interpolation or later scribal accretion. The same argument of default acceptance was used by those who favored Moses as the author of the Pentateuch.[16] Skeptics, instead, think we should start from a default position of agnosticism as to who the authors were of the individual items of Kurbskiana and see if we can establish authorship, whether of Andrei Kurbskii or anyone else.

No statement appears in the text of *The History* of its having been written by Andrei Kurbskii or even mentions his name. The text, which is written in the form of a first-person narrative, provides frustratingly little to connect the narrator with Andrei Kurbskii. It does mention a certain "Semen, called Kurbskii from the kin of the princes of Smolensk and Iaroslavl',"[17] whom historians have identified as the great-uncle of Andrei Kurbskii. Yet the narrator does not identify him as such, nor does the narrator claim kinship with the "princes of Smolensk and Iaroslavl'," which is unexpected if the author of the narration was from that princely line. Subsequently, when discussing Prince Iurii Ivanovich Pronskii-Shemiakin (d. 1554) and Prince Fedor Ivanovich Troekurov (d. 1568), whom the author describes as "exceedingly brave young men from the kin of the princes of Iaroslavl',"[18] he again neglects to mention his supposed connection with that princely line as though he were not connected with it at all. On the other hand, toward the end of the text, the narrator twice mentions his connection with the Iaroslavl' line: "my brothers, the princes of Iaroslav" and "to my cousin, the prince of Iaroslavl', whose name was Andrei Alenkin."[19] Proponents of the Kurbskii attribution have not found those differences to be significant. Skeptics, in contrast, find that these differences lend

15. See A. I. Filiushkin, *Andrei Mikhailovich Kurbskii. Prosopograficheskoe issledovanie i germenevticheskii kommentarii k poslaniiam Andreia Kurbskogo Ivanu Groznomu* (St. Petersburg: Izdatel'stvo Sankt-Peterburgskogo universiteta, 2007), 580–581; and Filiushkin, "Putting Kurbskii in His Rightful Place," *Kritika: Explorations in Russian and Eurasian History* 13, no. 4 (Fall 2012): 969.

16. See chapter 1.

17. *IVKM*, 8; *Prince A. M. Kurbsky's History of Ivan IV*, ed. and trans. J. L. I. Fennell (Cambridge: Cambridge University Press, 1965), 6–7.

18. *IVKM*, 33; *Kurbsky's History*, 36–37.

19. *IVKM*, 185, 222; *Kurbsky's History*, 188–189, 226–227. Andrei Alenkin has been identified as Andrei Fedorovich Alenkin-Zheria (d. 1570).

support to their proposition that *The History* was composed in various stages over a period of time.

Proponents have attempted to extrapolate from the contents of *The History*, which they say correspond to events in the life of Kurbskii, but some of the historical information proffered by the narrator seems to be accepted as being about Kurbskii only because it appears in *The History*. For example, the author mentions his brother who fought bravely at the taking of Kazan' in 1552 but does not name him. The Russian historian N. M. Karamzin extrapolated from his conviction that Andrei Kurbskii wrote *The History* to conclude that the reference must be to Andrei's brother Roman and claim, therefore, that Roman was with Andrei at Kazan'.[20] Erusalimskii proposed that Karamzin came to this conclusion based on his misreading of the genealogy books' reference to a "Roman Kurbskii," who it turns out was Roman Fedorovich Kurbskii, the great-uncle of Andrei.[21] Auerbach stated that we have no evidence for Andrei Kurbskii's having a brother other than one named Ivan,[22] nor any evidence that his brother Ivan was at Kazan'. Nonetheless, Auerbach concluded that Ivan is the nameless brother being referred to in *The History*, and she declared on the basis of *The History*, which says "he died in the following year," that he died two years later, in 1554.[23] Likewise, on the basis of *The History* (and his acceptance of Auerbach's conclusion), Filiushkin placed Ivan Kurbskii's death in 1553 or in 1552 in Iaroslavl'.[24]

The traditionally given year of Kurbskii's birth, 1528, is based solely on information provided by the narrator of *The History*. In describing the Kazan' campaign of 1552, the narrator states that he was "about twenty-four years old" (1552 − 24 = 1528).[25] Yet, if Kurbskii did not write *The History*, then one may question how accurate that information is and if it applies to Kurbskii at all. Despite the fact that *The History* has been accepted as autobiographical, no statement in *The History*, as the American historian Brian Boeck (b. 1971)

---

20. N. M. Karamzin, *Istoriia gosudarstva Rossiiskogo*, 2nd ed., 12 vols., vol. 8 (St. Petersburg: Tip. N. Grecha, 1818–1829), 181, nn. 330, 334; see also Fennell in *Kurbsky's History*, 58, n. 1.

21. *Sbornik Kurbskogo*, vol. 1, 179, n. 36.

22. Inge Auerbach, *Andrej Michajlovič Kurbskij. Leben in osteuropäischen Adelsgesellschaften des 16. Jahrhunderts* (Munich: Otto Sagner, 1985), 21, n. 5. A brother Roman is mentioned by the translator in an eighteenth-century preface to a translation of John of Damascus, which has been attributed to Kurbskii. See Juliane Besters-Dilger, *Die Dogmatik des Johannes von Damaskus in der Übersetzung des Fursten Andrej M. Kurbskij (1528–1583)* (Freiburg: U. W. Weiher, 1995), xlviii–xlix.

23. Auerbach, *Andrej Michajlovič Kurbskij*, 70; *IVKM*, 67; *Kurbsky's History*, 70–71.

24. Filiushkin, *Andrei Mikhailovich Kurbskii*, 24, n. 41 (=1553); idem, *Andrei Kurbskii* (Moscow: Molodaia gvardiia, 2008), 284 (=1552 in Iaroslavl').

25. *IVKM*, 35; *Kurbsky's History*, 38–39; cf. Auerbach, *Andrej Michajlovič Kurbskij*, 19; and V. V. Kalugin, "Kogda rodilsia kniaz' Andrei Kurbskii," *Arkhiv russkoi istorii* 6 (1995): 241–242.

pointed out, indicates knowledge of Kurbskii's life in Lithuania.[26] One might expect something more specific than a general castigation of courtier behavior (see below) from someone who had been living there for at minimum almost ten years (or seventeen years if one accepts Auerbach's dating of *The History*).

It is not clear for whom *The History of the Grand Prince of Moscow* was written. For example, it uses the phrase "in their language" several times to identify a particular word or phrase. In narrating Ivan's throwing of animals "from high places [*s stremnin vysokikh*]," the author adds: "but in their language from the roof or terem [*s krylets abo s teremov*]."[27] The editor of an English edition of the text, J. L. I. Fennell (1918–1992), added in a footnote: "Evidently a condescending attempt by Kurbsky to enlighten his ignorant Russian readers by giving as an alternative to the Church Slavonic стремнины the vernacular крыльца and теремы."[28] If so, then it is odd that the author would use "in their language" as though the readers were not Russian. Platonov thought *The History* was written "to influence public opinion in Lithuania." The passage seems to indicate that the reader knows Church Slavonic but not Russian, yet the text is written in Muscovite Slavonic, presumably for a Muscovite Russian audience. Perhaps the language style was meant to convey the patois of the borderlands between Russia and Poland. Although we have examples of works written in that patois, none corresponds with the style of *The History*. Platonov may have been on the right track when he proposed that it was "a lampoon (*pamflet*), not a history."[29]

The text has words of a Polish origin scattered throughout like raisins in a bun.[30] Keenan called it "a parody of the polonized language of Ukrainian emigrants to Muscovy in the later seventeenth century."[31] Most of the occurrences in the text of such words involve the simple homophonic substitution of a Polish word for a Russian word: for example, *mesto* (Polish *miasto*) for *grad*

---

26. Brian J. Boeck, "Miscellanea Attributed to Kurbskii: The 17th Century in Russia Was More Creative than We Like to Admit," *Kritika: Explorations in Russian and Eurasian History* 13, no. 4 (Fall 2012): 959.

27. *IVKM*, 10; *Kurbsky's History*, 10–11. See also "great proud *pans* (or boyars in their tongue)". *IVKM*, 10, *Kurbsky's History*, 8–9.

28. *Kurbsky's History*, 10, fn. 2.

29. Platonov, *Ivan Groznyi*, 8.

30. Ustrialov has a "Glossary of Foreign and Antiquated Words, Which are Found in Kurbskii's Works." N. G. Ustrialov, *Skazaniia kniazia Kurbskogo*, 2 vols., vol. 2 (St. Petersburg: Tipografiia Imperatorskoi Akademii nauk, 1833), 297–309; 2nd ed. (St. Petersburg: Tipografiia Imperatorskoi Akademii nauk, 1842), 475–486; 3rd ed. (St. Petersburg: Tipografiia Imperatorskoi Akademii nauk, 1868), 425–436. Fennell included a list of "Words Borrowed from Other Languages" in an appendix to his *Kurbsky's History*, 296–299.

31. Keenan, *Kurbskii-Groznyi Apocrypha*, 313, n. 42.

(town); *abo* (Polish *albo*) for *ili* (or); *vezha* (Polish *wieża*) for *bashnia* (tower); *rada* (Polish *rada*) for *sobor* (council). There is minimal Polish-Russian verbalizing. The resulting argot in *The History* may have lent a Polish flavor to the text for a Russian audience.

Skeptics consider the probability to be low that this word substitution in *The History* represents a genuine Polish influence on the author.[32] They see the appearance of those words as being consistent with the author's being someone other than Kurbskii but trying to make it appear as though an émigré like Kurbskii wrote it. Proponents, in contrast, think it highly probable that these Polonisms represent genuine Polish influence. Among the latter, Erusalimskii, however, agreed with Keenan's assertion that the macaronic style of *The History* has not found sufficient explanation in the scholarship.[33] Auerbach made an attempt to account for the varying styles found in the works attributed to Kurbskii in general by supposing phases of influence by successive literary advisors.[34]

Likewise, at the beginning of the digression about the corruption of the Polish court, the author uses the word *here* when making reference to the Polish king. It gives the impression that the author is writing in Poland-Lithuania for Polish or Lithuanian readers. Yet the author makes disparaging remarks about those same supposed readers:

> The lords of this land stuff their gullets and bellies with costly buns and almond cakes at incalculable expense and immoderately pour down various kinds of dearest wines, as it were into leaky casks, leaping high and striking the air together with their hangers-on and in their drunkenness praising one another so exceedingly boastfully and proudly that they promise not only [to capture] Moscow or Constantinople, but, even if the Turk were in the sky, to drag him down with their other enemies.

He goes on to say how the Polish-Lithuanian lords sleep to midday and "are slothful and idle," that "they have no care for their fatherland," and "do not care for their own subjects."[35] Such words must have made an odd impression on Polish-Lithuanian readers if that is the audience for whom *The His-*

---

32. A similar type of word substitution, but of Russian for English words, occurs in Anthony Burgess's novel *A Clockwork Orange* (New York: Norton, 1963). See, for example, the first-person narrator's substitution of *moloko* for milk, *droog* for friend, *malchick* for boy, *soomka* for bag, and so forth.

33. Erusalimskii, *Sbornik Kurbskogo*, vol. 1, 311–313.

34. Inge Auerbach, "Identity in Exile: Andrei Mikhailovich Kurbskii and National Consciousness in the Sixteenth Century," in *Culture and Identity in Muscovy, 1389–1584*, ed. A. M. Kleimola and G. D. Lenhoff (Moscow: ITs-Garant, 1997), 17–24.

35. *IVKM*, 118; *Kurbsky's History*, 126–127.

tory was intended. For skeptics, it gives the appearance instead of having been written for Muscovites in Muscovite Slavonic with Polish word substitutions. In addition, there are a number of errors in *The History*, the nature of which prompts doubts concerning whether the author was the historical Andrei Kurbskii. For example, the author writes that Aleksei Adashev (1510–1561) had the rank of *lozhnichy* (from Polish *łożniczy*),[36] the equivalent of the Russian *postel'nichii*, meaning "gentleman of the bedchamber." Fennell pointed out that Adashev held the rank of *spal'nik* at the wedding of Ivan IV and Anastasiia (1530–1560) and that Kurbskii may have confused *spal'nik* with *postel'nik*.[37] While possible, one must question the likelihood that a court rank conscious nobleman would confuse two different ranking positions, although to be fair, one could chalk it up to faulty memory after a lapse of time away from that milieu. *The History* calls the archimandrite Feodorit Kol'skii (1481–1571) "a martyr of the terror of Ivan IV." But as the Finnish medievalist Jukka Korpela (b. 1957) pointed out, the Paterikon of the Solovki Monastery records Feodorit's death without mention of his being killed,[38] and there is no confirming source testimony that Feodorit was martyred. He was ninety years old at the time of his death. Would Kurbskii in Lithuania be under the impression that Feodorit was martyred when he was not?

The author of *The History* states that the German diplomat and writer Sigismund von Herberstein (1486–1566) wrote his *Rerum Moscoviticarum commentarii* in Latin in Milan.[39] No known edition of Herberstein's work was published in Milan during the lifetime of the historical Andrei Kurbskii, although there was one published in Venice in 1550. Did Kurbskii confuse Venice with Milan? Did a later editor add the part about Milan? Or did a seventeenth-century author of *The History* use a Milanese edition that would have been unavailable to the historical Kurbskii? One tends to weight the probability of the answer to each of these questions according to one's view of whether or not Kurbskii was the author of *The History*.

The word *History* (*Istoriia*) in the title coincides with the titles given late seventeenth-century Muscovite works while *Tale* (*Skazaniia* or *Povest'*) was

---

36. *IVKM*, 75; *Kurbsky's History*, 80–81.

37. *Kurbsky's History*, 80–81, n. 1. For the wedding of Ivan IV and Anastasiia Romanovna Iur'eva, see *Drevniaia rossiiskaia vivliofeka*, ed. Nikolai Novikov, 2nd ed., 20 parts (St. Petersburg, 1788–1791), 13: 34. See also Russell E. Martin, *A Bride for the Tsar: Bride-Shows and Marriage Politics in Early Modern Russia* (DeKalb: Northern Illinois University Press, 2012), 113–117.

38. *Solovetskii paterik* (Moscow: Sinodal'naia biblioteka, 1991), 43; Jukka Korpela, "Feodorit (Theodorit) Kol'skii: Missionary and Princely Agent," in *Religion und Integration im Moskauer Russland: Konzepte und Praktiken, Potentiale und Grenzen 14.–17. Jahrhundert*, ed. Ludwig Steindorff (Wiesbaden: Otto Harrassowitz, 2010), 204; cf. Kalugin, *Andrei Kurbskii i Ivan Groznyi*, 201–202.

39. *IVKM*, 8; *Kurbsky's History*, 6–7.

more likely to be used in Russia in the late sixteenth century.[40] The German historian Dietrich Freydank (1928–1999) proposed that Kurbskii used the word *istoriia* in the Latin sense—as an account of contemporary events—in contrast to the Greek sense—as an investigation of long-past events.[41] Such an understanding of *istoriia* would fit the intellectual context either of sixteenth-century Poland or of seventeenth-century Russia, but not of sixteenth-century Russia, when the term *Skazanie* (*Tale*) would have been used. The phrase "of the Muscovite Grand Prince" instead of "of the Tsar and Grand Prince of All Rus'," which was part of Ivan's title after 1547, accurately represents the official policy at the time in the commonwealth against accepting the title "tsar" for Ivan IV, but we find within the text of *The History* itself a number of references to Ivan as tsar and even as "our tsar."[42] Who is the "our" of "our tsar"? Kurbskii was no longer a subject of Ivan's and ceased owing allegiance to him when he defected.

2. Three (or five) letters to Ivan Groznyi (proposed dates of composition: April 1564, 1569, September 1579, or 1620s–1675).

Keenan proposed that the first letter of Andrei Kurbskii to Ivan IV (K1), which he decided was written in the 1620s, should be attributed to Prince Semen Shakhovskoi (d. 1654 or 1655), an ecclesiastical and political figure and writer. Besides his coming to the conclusion that the personal information in K1 matches the biography of Shakhovskoi, Keenan also noted a similarity in style between K1 and letters written by Shakhovskoi.[43]

Proponents of Kurbskii's authorship dismiss Keenan's Shakhovskoi theory for various reasons. Perhaps the most often cited is the Russian historian Boris N. Morozov's article in which he watermark-dated one of the manuscript copies of K1 to 1595. Such a date, if confirmed, would preclude Shakhovskoi as the author. Morozov's analysis of the manuscript in question—RNB, Q.XVII.67—described the watermark on the folios (16v–17) of the K1 copy as "very unclear."[44] Based on the watermarks within other quires in the miscellany, he acknowledged it was put together in the early 1620s. But he argued that the quire (no. 6) in which K1 is found is linked with the surrounding quires

40. Compare to Keenan, *Kurbskii-Groznyi Apocrypha*, 62–63.

41. Dietrich Freydank, "A. M. Kurbskij und die Thorie der antiken Historiographiie," in *Orbis mediaevalis. Festgabe für Anton Blaschka zum 75. Geburtstag am 7. Oktober 1967*, ed. Horst Gericke, Manfred Lemmer, and Walter Zöllner (Weimar: H. Böhlaus Hachfolger, 1970), 57–62.

42. See, for example, *IVKM*, 5, 67, 83, 87; *Kurbsky's History*, 2–3, 72–73, 90–91, 92–93.

43. Keenan, *Kurbskii-Groznyi Apocrypha*, 35–46.

44. B. N. Morozov, "Pervoe poslanie Kurbskogo Ivanu Groznomu v sbornike kontsa XVI–nachala XVII v.," *Arkheograficheskii ezhegodnik za 1986* (Moscow: Nauka, 1987), 282.

(no. 5 and nos. 7–12) because the works being copied in them cross the quire boundaries. He then identified several watermarks in the linked quires as being from the years 1594 to 1595. The problem is that each of these watermarks that he identified has similar counterparts from the 1610s or 1620s.[45] Although Morozov stated in the article that his "present observations are preliminary" and that the miscellany requires a separate work devoted to it, proponents of the Kurbskii attribution give a higher probability to the earliest limit of the date range (i.e., 1594–1595) of his watermark identifications. Skeptics, in contrast, would like to see further exploration of the later limit of the watermark date range (i.e., 1620s), as well as that separate study of the miscellany that Morozov called for.

In what I have termed "the Isaiah conundrum,"[46] the relationship of K1 to a *Complaint* (*Zhaloba*) of the Ruthenian monk Isaiah of Kam'ianets-Podil'sk (fl. second half of sixteenth century) is at issue since these two works coincide over significant portions of their respective texts. If one holds that the traditional date of 1566 for the composition of Isaiah's *Complaint* is correct but that it derives from K1, then one needs to provide an explanation for how Isaiah in a Rostov prison in 1566 had access to K1, a letter presumably written two years earlier in Lithuania to the tsar by a princely émigré. The historian Nikolay Andreyev (1908–1982), himself a Russian émigré, proposed that Ivan IV visited Isaiah in his jail cell in Rostov in 1566 and showed him the letter from Kurbskii,[47] although we have no evidence for such a visit. The Soviet historian Ruslan G. Skrynnikov (1931–2009) accepted the direction of borrowing that Keenan proposed (i.e., *Complaint* to K1) but redated Isaiah's *Complaint* to 1562, which would have allowed Kurbskii to borrow from it in 1564. That redating, however, leads to the need to explain how Kurbskii was able to get a copy of a text in Lithuania that a monk wrote while in prison two years earlier in Vologda. Skrynnikov conjectured that an unknown person from Lithuania, who was in contact with "a secret opposition in Moscow" managed to secretly visit Isaiah in his jail cell in 1562 in Vologda and brought a

---

45. For example, the watermark one-handled pot with the letters PD can be found in Geraklitov's album, nos. 436 (1622) and 649 (1626); the one-handled pot with the letters IH can be found in Likhachev's album, nos. 1965 and 1966 (1611); and the one-handled pot with the letter M can be found in Geraklitov's album, no. 654 (1626). A. A. Geraklitov, *Filigrani XVII veka na bumage rukopisnykh i pechatnykh dokumentov russkogo proiskhozhdeniia* (Moscow: Akademiia nauk SSSR, 1963); N. P. Likhachev, *Paleograficheskoe znachenie bumazhnykh vodianykh znakov*, 3 vols. (St. Petersburg: Tip. V. S. Balamev, 1899).

46. I discuss this issue more extensively in "'Closed Circles': Edward L. Keenan's Early Textual Work and the Semiotics of Response," *Canadian Slavonic Papers / Revue canadienne des slavistes* 48, no. 3–4 (2006): 269–277.

47. Nikolay Andreyev, "The Authenticity of the Correspondence between Ivan IV and Prince Andrey Kurbsky," *Slavonic and East European Review* 53 (1975): 588.

copy of the *Complaint* back with him for Kurbskii to see.[48] For Keenan, the question of access of the author of K1 to Isaiah's *Complaint* is not such a problem, because if Semen Shakhovskoi wrote K1 in the 1620s, then there are any number of possible ways for him to have gained access to a copy of a letter written sixty years earlier.

Likewise, proponents of the view that Andrei Kurbskii wrote K1 assign a high value of probability that two early references concerning a letter from Kurbskii to Ivan IV are to the correspondence.[49] One of these appears in the *Livonian Chronicle* (*Livländische Chronik*) of Franz Nienstädt (1540–1622), which mentions Kurbskii's writing to Ivan after he defected. The second is in an "instruction" of 1581 to the envoy O. M. Pushkin, which says Kurbskii "wrote a rude letter to the sovereign."[50] There is also a reference by Stefan Batory in the *Lithuanian Metrica* to a boastful letter sent by Ivan "to us, Kurbskii, and others."

Skeptics assign a low value of probability that those references are to our K1 because text critical analysis of KI has led them to conclude that the K1 we have could not have been written at the time those references were made and that they must be to an earlier nonextant letter that was dictated by Kurbskii.[51]

3. Thirteen letters to Polish-Lithuanian recipients (proposed date of composition: late sixteenth century). Three letters to Prince Kostiantyn Wasyl Ostroz'skyi (ca. 1524–1608); one letter to Mark, the pupil of Artemii; two letters to Kuzma Mamonich; one letter to Kodian Chaplich; two letters to Pan Fedor; one letter to Princess Czartoryz'ska; one letter to Pan Drevinskii; one letter to Ostafii Trotskii; and one letter to Semen Sedlar.[52]

Initially, in 1971, Keenan considered these Lithuanian letters to be genuinely dictated by Kurbskii, but by 1998 he concluded they were written by a Ruthenian monk named Andrii from Jarosław.[53] Implicit in Keenan's argument

---

48. R. G. Skrynnikov, "On the Authenticity of the Kurbskii-Groznyi Correspondence: A Summary of the Discussion," *Slavic Review* 37 (1978): 114.

49. Charles J. Halperin, "Edward Keenan and the Kurbskii-Groznyi Correspondence in Hindsight," *Jahrbücher für Geschichte Osteuropas* 46, no. 3 (1998): 390; Filiushkin, "Putting Kurbskii in His Rightful Place," 968.

50. Excerpts from the 1581 "instruction" to the envoy O. M. Pushkin were published by B. N. Floria in his "Novoe o Groznom i Kurbskom," *Istoriia SSSR*, no. 3 (1974): 144–145.

51. Keenan, *Kurbskii-Groznyi Apocrypha*, 206, n. 8; and Ostrowski, "Closed Circles," 276–277.

52. Erusalimskii, *Sbornik Kurbskogo*, vol. 2, 351–409.

53. Keenan, *Kurbskii-Groznyi Apocrypha*, 210; Edward L. Keenan, "Response to Halperin, 'Edward Keenan and the Kurbskii-Groznyi Correspondence in Hindsight,'" *Jahrbücher für Geschichte Osteuropas* 46, no. 3 (1998): 412. He wrote that the manuscript attribution of these letters to Kurbskii

is the supposition that someone, perhaps the compiler of the *Miscellany of Kurbskii*, had reassigned the letters to Andrei Kurbskii. In any case, I think it accurate to say that the style in which these letters are written (a combination of plain Slavonic and Ruthenian vernacular [*prosta mova*]) and the subject matter differ markedly from the style and subject matter of the letters addressed to Ivan IV.

4. *The History of the Eighth Council* (*Istoriia o osmom sobore*) (proposed dates of composition: 1581–1583; after 1598).

The nineteenth-century Russian historian Nikolai G. Ustrialov (1805–1870) first attributed *The History of the Eighth Council* to Kurbskii in 1833.[54] The dating of this work has been a point of contention, in particular concerning the relationship of *The History of the Eighth Council* to a work titled *Answer* (*Otpis'*) written by an Ostrih cleric in 1598, more specifically its relationship to an abbreviated version of *The History of the Robber Florentinian Council*, which he included as an addendum.

In 1598, the Uniate bishop (and metropolitan of Kiev and Halych [r. 1599–1613]) Ipatii Potii (1541–1613) wrote to Konstantin Ostroz'skyi to persuade him to join the union established by the Union of Brest in 1596. This union placed a number of Ruthenians under the jurisdiction of the papacy. Bishop Potii asserted that there was nothing new in the Union of Brest over the decisions of the Council of Ferrara-Florence (1437–1439). In response to Potii's letter, an individual identifying himself as "the Ostrih Cleric" wrote to Potii asserting that the Council of Brest was very different from the Council of Ferrara-Florence. He included an abbreviated version of a work titled *The History of the Robber Florentinian Council*, which bears similarities to *The History of the Eighth Council*.[55] We have three possible relationships of these texts to explain these similarities: (1) *The History of the Eighth Council* derives from the Ostrih cleric's version of *The History of the Robber Florentinian Council*; (2) *The History of the Eighth Council* derives independently from an earlier version or versions

---

occurred in "late copies." Keenan also attributed the preface to *Novyi Margarit* to this Andrii. Keenan, "Response," 412.

54. Ustrialov, *Skazaniia kniazia Kurbskogo*, vol. 2, 243–256. See also G. Z. Kuntsevich, *Sochineniia kniazia Kurbskogo*, vol. 1: *Sochineniia original'nye* (St. Petersburg, 1914 [also published as *Russkaia istoricheskaia biblioteka*, vol. 31]), cols. 473–484. S. P. Shevyrev wrote about it: "Novye izvestie o Florentiiskom sobore, izvlecheniie iz Vatikanskoi rukopisi," *Zhurnal Ministerstva narodnogo prosveshchenie*, 1841, bk. 1, 60–78.

55. Klirik Ostrozhskii, "Istoriia o razboinich'em florentiiskom sobore" (in *Pamiatniki polemicheskoi literatury*, vol. 3, 1903) *Russkaia istoricheskaia biblioteka* 19 (1903): 433–476.

of *The History of the Robber Florentinian Council*; or (3) *The History of the Robber Florentinian Council* derives from *The History of the Eighth Council*.

In the nineteenth century, Mikhail O. Koialovich (1828–1891) saw *The History of the Robber Florentinian Council* as having been written in response to certain works that were composed before the Union of Brest (1596) and dated to the period 1586–1591.[56] The church historian Metropolitan Makarii (Bulgakov) (1816–1882) proposed that *The History of the Robber Florentinian Council* was written in response to an apologia for the Council of Florence by Stanisław Radziwiłł (1559–1599) in 1586. Makarii thus argued that the earliest possible date of composition for it was 1586.[57]

The Russian ecclesiastical scholar Fedor I. Delektorskii disagreed with Makarii and asserted instead that the Ostrih cleric indicated *The History of the Robber Florentinian Council* had already been written a long time before the cleric included it in his *Answer*. Delektorskii proposed that it was written in response to the work by the Jesuit Peter Skarga (1536–1612) titled *About the Single Church of God*, which dates to 1577 and which contains chapters on the Council of Florence. Delektorskii placed the latest possible date for composition of *The History of the Robber Florentinian Council* as 1583 because that was the year of death of Kurbskii, who, he argued, had borrowed from it for his *History of the Eighth Council*.[58] Kalugin, citing Delektorskii, dated *The History of the Eighth Council* "probably" to the period 1581–1583, on the basis that it had to have been composed "after completion of the work over the compositions of John of Damascus since references to 'fragments' of his production" are in it.[59] Filiushkin also dated its composition to 1581–1583.[60] Keenan considered it to be a Muscovite revision and translation of the printed text attributed to the Ostrih cleric published in 1598.[61] Valerii Zema subsequently analyzed the relationship between the two works and concluded that *The History of the Eighth Council* abridges and paraphrases the composition of the Ostrih cleric.[62]

The question then becomes whether the work that the Ostrih cleric included in his *Answer* was an original composition of his or another work that had been written earlier and from which the Ostrih cleric and the author of

56. M. O. Koialovich, *Litovskaia tserkovnaia uniia*, 2 vols., vol. 1 (St. Petersburg, 1859–1861), 173.

57. Metropolitan Makarii (Bulgakov), *Istoriia russkoi tserkvi*, 2nd ed., 12 vols., vol. 9 (St. Petersburg: P. Golike, 1883–1903), 422, 426.

58. F. I. Delektorskii, "Kritiko-bibliograficheskii obzor drevnerusskikh skazanii o Florentiiskoi unii," *Zhurnal Ministerstva narodnogo prosveshcheniia* 300 (August 1895): 177.

59. Kalugin, *Andrei Kurbskii i Ivan Groznyi*, 88.

60. Filiushkin, *Andrei Kurbskii*, 286–287.

61. Keenan, *The Kurbskii-Groznyi Apocrypha*, 210.

62. See Valerii Zema, "Sprava viry," *Kyivs'ka starovyna*, no. 3 (2001): 190–199.

The History of the Eighth Council could have independently borrowed. Yet the earlier date of the composition of *The History of the Robber Florentinian Council* is also in dispute depending upon whether one thinks it was in response (1) to polemical works written between 1586 and 1591 (Koliachev); (2) to an apologia for the Council of Florence written in 1586 (Makarii); or (3) to a work by Peter Skarga written in 1577 (Delektorskii). Since Kurbskii died in 1583, a proponent of the view that Kurbskii wrote *The History of the Eighth Council* would tend to assign a high probability to Skarga's work of 1577 as the antecedent text and asymptotically low probabilities to the works from 1586 or 1586–1591 as antecedent texts, whereas a skeptic would tend to opt for the works either from 1586 or the 1586–1591 as having a higher probability as the likely antecedent texts.

In the letter to Mark, "Andrei Kurbskii" wrote that the elder Artemii (d. early 1570s), the former hegumen of the Trinity St. Sergius Monastery, suggested to him the need for translation into Russian of the works of Basil of Caesarea (ca. 329–379).[63] Kurbskii, as a result, supposedly began to learn Latin. His teacher was purportedly a German scholar named Ambrose, whom Auerbach identified as Ambrosius Szadkovius, a graduate of Kraków University in 1569.[64] In addition, Kalugin gave weight to the words of Szymon Okolski (1580–1653) in his *Orbis Polonus*, published in 1641 in Kraków, in which he wrote that Kurbskii "the great genius, in a short time when already advanced in years, learned the Latin language, which until then he had been ignorant."[65] Keenan, in contrast, dismissed Okolski's statement as the "ignorant and partisan speculations" of a "Polish Dominican polemicist."[66] From the point of view of authorship studies, both scholars, it seems to me, missed the point. Kalugin neglects to point out that Okolski was three years old when Kurbskii died, so he was hardly in a position to know whether Kurbskii had actually learned Latin. Okolski may have been all the things Keenan accused him of, but those characteristics are not why Okolski's testimony carries little weight. It is what Ros Barber called "impersonal evidence" in regard to

63. Erusalimskii, *Sbornik Kurbskogo*, vol. 2, 355–357.

64. Auerbach, "Gedanken zur Entstehung von A. M. Kurbskijs 'Istorija o velikom knjaze Moskovskom,'" 170; Auerbach, *Andrej Michajlovič Kurbskij*, 379–380, 399–400; Auerbach, "Ein Analphabet als Schriftsteller? Zur Entstehung und Überlieferug des 'Novyi Margarit,'" in *Andrej Michajlovič Kurbskij Novyj Margarit. Historisch-kritisched Ausgabe auf der Grundlage der Wolfenbütteler Handschrift*, ed. Inge Auerbach, Band 3. Lieferugn 11–15 (Bl. 319–466, S. 1–51) (Giessen: Wilhelm Schmitz, 1987), 17–18.

65. Szymon Okolski, *Orbis Polonvs, splendoribus caeli: Triumphis mundi: pulchritudine animantium: decore aquatilium: naturae excellentia reptilium, condecoratvs*, 3 vols., vol. 1 (Kraków, 1641), 504. See Kalugin, *Andrei Kurbskii i Ivan Groznyi*, 32.

66. Edward L. Keenan, "Was Andrei Kurbskii a Renaissance Intellectual? Some Marginal Notes on a Central Issue," *Harvard Ukrainian Studies* 27, nos. 1–4 (2004–2005): 26.

those statements about Shakespeare by people who did not know him personally (see chapter 6).

Keenan had previously pointed out that Kurbskii's signature in Latin characters on his last will and testament from 1582 displays a notably rudimentary writing ability.[67] One could counter that Kurbskii's years as a warrior may have made his fingers clumsy with a pen, which resulted in script that appears unsteady, or, as has been suggested to explain the shaky signatures of William of Stratford, he was ill at the time.

In order to explain how works in Russian could be written by someone who testified that he could not write in Cyrillic, Auerbach proposed that Kurbskii dictated to scribes.[68] The linguist and historian Francis J. Thomson proposed that Kurbskii himself did not do the actual writing or translating but had people around him who did.[69] If Thomson is correct, then that raises the question to what extent Kurbskii can be considered the author or translator of any of those works. Recognizing the problem, Thomson stated that Kurbskii "had the idea of a translation project" and that he claims to have made the translation "with the aid of assistants trained in Latin."[70]

Kalugin suggested that Kurbskii's statement of inability is merely meant to indicate that he could not write Cyrillic in Lithuanian chancellery style, not that he could not write in Cyrillic at all.[71] Yet, chancellery style of writing in the sixteenth century, both in Lithuania and in Muscovy, was not dissimilar to church style; the two diverge during the course of the seventeenth century.[72] Erusalimskii proposed that Kurbskii's claim was merely some kind of legal ploy and did not reflect his real writing capabilities.[73] Boeck found Erusalimskii's explanation a strained one for a defender of the attribution to Kurbskii to make given that in *The History of the Grand Prince* the author spoke against "perversion of judicial proceedings" and praised "impartial justice."[74] Boeck's

---

67. Keenan, *Kurbskii-Groznyi Apocrypha*, 208–209; Edward L. Keenan, "A Landmark of Kurbskii Studies," *Harvard Ukrainian Studies* 10, nos. 1–2 (1986): 245–246.

68. Auerbach, *Andrej Michajlovič Kurbskij*, 375–379; Auerbach, "Ein Analphabet als Schriftsteller?" 15–51.

69. Francis J. Thomson, "The Corpus of Slavonic Translation Available in Muscovy: The Cause of Old Russia's Intellectual Silence and a Contributory Factor to Muscovite Autarky," in *Christianity and the Eastern Slavs*, vol. 1: *Slavic Cultures in the Middle Ages*, ed. Boris Gasparov and Olga Raevsky-Hughes (Berkeley: University of California Press, 1993), 188–189.

70. Thomson, "Corpus of Slavonic Translation," 208, n. 145.

71. Vasilii Kalugin, "Literaturnoe nasledie kniazia Andreia Kurbskogo (Spornye voprosy istochnikov)," *Palaeoslavica* 5 (1997): 86; Kalugin, *Andrei Kurbskii i Ivan Groznyi*, 17–23.

72. Keenan, "Response," 408, n. 15.

73. Erusalimskii, *Sbornik Kurbskogo*, vol. 1, 79–80.

74. Boeck, "Miscellanea Attributed to Kurbskii," 959.

point is that if Kurbskii was prevaricating in court, that makes it less likely that he wrote *The History*, where judicial prevarication is denounced.

The existence of the declaration in the document from 1571 that he could not write in Cyrillic script apparently lowers the probability that Kurbskii wrote the works attributed to him, all of which are in Cyrillic script. It is evidence for which the proponents need to provide a counterexplanation. In contrast, the existence of a document from 1581 that mentions a "rude letter" from Kurbskii to Groznyi apparently increases the probability that Kurbskii wrote K1. It is evidence for which the skeptics need to provide a counterexplanation. No single point of contention decides the case definitively in favor of the skeptics or the proponents. Each camp has its counterexplanations for the unexpected oddities that arise with their respective hypotheses.

Works Attributed to Kurbskii Not in the *Miscellany of Kurbskii*

Among other works that are attributed to Kurbskii that do not appear in any copies of the *Miscellany of Kurbskii* is the preface to the *Novyi Margarit* (*New Pearl*), proposed dates of composition 1572 or 1575. The *Novyi Margarit* is maintained in two copies. One copy, GPB, Undol'skii 187, is defective, missing the first 111 folios; the other, Wolfenbüttel in the Library of Count August, which dates to the eighteenth century, is the only complete manuscript and thus the only copy of the preface. The Russian historian N. D. Ivanishev (1811–1874) attributed the text to "Prince Andrei Kurbskii" in 1849. The text reads: "Preface of the much sinful Andrei Iaroslavskii."[75] Ivanishev mentioned references to the *Novyi Margarit* in *The History of the Grand Prince* as well as in his letter to Mark, pupil of Artemii, but it is not clear whether Ivanishev was using those references to confirm the attribution of the preface to Kurbskii.[76]

Zimin dated the composition of the preface to "soon after June 1572" because it mentions the Kovel' city official (*namestnik*) Ivan Kelemet, who fled

---

75. The preface was published by N. D. Ivanishev in "Vremennaia Komissiia dlia razbora drevnikh aktov," *Zhizn' kn. Kurbskogo v Litve i na Volyni*, 2 vols., vol. 2 (Kiev: I. K. Val'ner, 1849), 303–316. The attribution occurs in the table of contents of volume 2 as well as in the preface to volume 1. The attribution was accepted by N. G. Ustrialov, *Skazaniia kniazia Kurbskogo*, 3rd ed. (St. Petersburg: Tipografiia Imp. Akademii nauk, 1868), 269–278. From there, it entered the mainstream scholarship. A. S. Arkhangel'skii, *Ocherki iz istorii zapadno-russkoi literatury XVI–XVII vv.* (Moscow, 1888; also published in *Chteniia v Imperatorskom Obshchestve istorii i drevnostei rossiiskikh pri Moskovskom universitete* (*ChIOIDR*), 1888, bk. 1, sec. 1), appendix, 68–72. Ferdinand Liewehr, *Kurbskijs "Novyi Margarit"* (Prague: Taussig & Taussig, 1928).

76. "Vremennaia Komissiia," *Zhizn' kn. Kurbskogo*, vol. 1, XLVI–XLVII.

with Kurbskii. Ivan Kelemet's death occurred on March 9, 1572, and three months later, according to Zimin, Kurbskii gave his property to a servant.[77] Skrynnikov dated the composition of the preface to "not later than July 7, 1572," because that is when Sigismund II, king of Poland (r. 1548–1572), died. Sigismund's death is not mentioned in the preface,[78] which Skrynnikov thought it likely to have been mentioned if the preface had been written later. Kalugin argued that it could not have assumed final form before 1575 because in the text is a reference to Prince Michael Andreae Oboleczki, who returned to Kraków from Italy only in 1575.[79]

In 1998, Keenan attributed the prefaces and postscripts to all the translations, including the preface to the *Novyi Margarit*, to an ecclesiastical writer and translator of the second half of the sixteenth century, Andrii from Jarosław.[80] Indeed, the epithet "much sinful" in the heading is usually associated with ecclesiastical writers. The question then arises whether the autobiographical information provided by the author in the preface coincides with the other biographical information we have about Andrii from Jarosław. For example, the author of the preface states that his mother, wife, and son (his only child) were imprisoned. Also he refers to "my brothers, the princes of Iaroslavl'." The Byzantino-Slavist Ihor Ševčenko (1922–2009), as a result, concluded that Keenan's proposal does not help his case.[81] The report by the author of the preface, referring to the imprisonment of his mother, wife, and son, is not confirmed, however, in any other source about Kurbskii. K1 says only "little have I seen my parents, and my wife I have not known."[82] If he did not "know" his wife, then he could not have had a son (at least not by that wife). Such information in the text does not necessarily coincide, it would seem, with the life of the historical Andrei Kurbskii. The reference in the preface to the Iaroslav princes as being his brothers could apply to either Andrei Kurbskii or to Andrii from Jarosław since the Jarosław that Andrii came from, a market town in what is now southeastern Poland, was known for its connections with the princely Ostroz'skyi family.[83] The preface does refer to Metro-

77. Zimin, "Kogda Kurbskii napisal 'Istoriiu o velikom kniaze Moskovskom'?" 306.

78. R. G. Skrynnikov, *Perepiska Groznogo i Kurbskogo: Paradoksy Edvarda Kinana* (Leningrad: Nauka, 1973), 99.

79. Kalugin, *Andrei Kurbskii i Ivan Groznyi*, 36.

80. Keenan, "Response to Halperin," 412.

81. Early Slavists Seminar, Russian Research Center, Harvard University, Cambridge, Massachusetts, March 12, 1999.

82. *The Correspondence between Prince A. M. Kurbsky and Tsar Ivan IV of Russia 1564–1579*, ed. J. L. I. Fennell (Cambridge: Cambridge University Press, 1963), 6–7.

83. See Krystyna Kieferling, *Jarosław w czasach Anny Ostrogskiej (1594–1635): szkice do portretu miasta i jego właścicielki* (Przemyśl: Archiwum Państwowe: Polskie Towarzystwo Historyczne. Oddział, 2008).

politan Filipp (r. 1566–1568) and his martyrdom, which occurred in 1569. That martyrdom could be of concern either to Andrei Kurbskii or to the cleric Andrii. The entire question remains unresolved.

Other works that are not in the *Miscellany of Kurbskii* that have been attributed to Andrei Kurbskii also require further investigation in regard to that attribution.

1. Three letters to the Elder Vas'ian of the Pskov-Pechersk Monastery (proposed dates of composition: December 1563–April 1564 [Andreyev]; the first two letters before April 1564, the third one after April 1564 [Skrynnikov]; all three after April 1564 [i.e., after Kurbskii fled to Lithuania; Lur'e, Likhachev]; ca. 1570 [Petukhov, Maslennikova]; 1621–1625 [Keenan]).[84] Two of the letters are addressed to a certain "Vas'ian" but provide no indication which Vas'ian. The first and third letters name the author as Prince Andrei Kurbskii. The Russian historian Evgenii V. Petukhov (1863–1948) argued that the addressee is the Elder Vas'ian Muromtsev because he is mentioned in *The History of the Grand Prince*, attributed to Kurbskii.[85]

The time of the writing of the letters to Vas'ian has found no agreement in the scholarship. Andreyev proposed that Kurbskii wrote the letters to Vas'ian before he fled to Lithuania in April 1564 because he says he met the monks of the Pskov-Pecherskii Monastery seven years earlier, which was most likely during the first Livonian War campaign in 1558.[86] Skrynnikov argued that the third letter was written immediately after Kurbskii's flight, probably in May or June.[87] The Russian cultural historians Ia. S. Lur'e (1922–1996) and D. S. Likhachev (1906–1999) proposed that Kurbskii wrote the letters after fleeing to Lithuania (April 1564) but did not provide a *terminus post quem non*. Petukhov proposed

---

84. E. V. Petukhov, "O nekotorykh istoricheskikh i literaturnykh faktakh, sviazannykh s imenem Uspenskogo Pskovo-Pecherskogo monastyria v XVI i XVII vv.," *Trudy X Arkheologicheskogo s"ezda*, vol. 1 (Riga, 1899), 256–263; Ia. S. Lur'e, "Voprosy vneshnei i vnutrennei politik v poslaniiakh Ivana IV," in *Poslaniia Ivan Groznogo*, ed. D. S. Likhachev and Ia. S. Lur'e (Moscow: Akademiia nauk SSSR, 1951), 472 and following; D. S. Likhachev and Ia. S. Lur'e, "Arkheograficheskii obzor posanii Ivana Groznogo," in *Poslaniia Ivan Groznogo*, 540; N. N. Maslennikova, "Ideologicheskaia bor'ba v pskovskoi literature v period obrazovaniia russkogo tsentralizovannogo gosudarstva," *Trudy Otdela drevnerusskoi literatury* 8 (1951): 207–208; Keenan, *Kurbskii-Groznyi Apocrypha*, 29–30, 41–46.

85. E. V. Petukhov, *Russkaia literatura. Istoricheskii obzor glavneishikh literaturnikh iavlenii drevnogo i novogo perioda*, 2 vols., vol. 1, 3rd ed. (Petrograd: Suvorin, 1916), 182; Petukhov, "O nekotorykh istoricheskikh i literaturnykh faktakh," 256–263.

86. Andreyev, "Kurbsky's Letters to Vas'yan Muromtsev," 415.

87. R. G. Skrynnikov, "Kurbskii i ego pis'ma v Pskovo-Pecherskii monastyr'," *Trudy Otdela drevnerusskoi literatury* 18 (1962): 113.

that "the time of writing both letters was around 1570." His reasoning began with the premise that the letters were written one after the other in a short period of time. One of them mentions the books of Frantsysk Skorina (ca. 1490–ca. 1535), which were published 1517–1519, as appearing "about 50 years ago." Depending how many years "around" and "about" are, Petukhov arrived at the year 1570. Keenan proposed a date range of 1621 to 1625. He pointed out that Skorina's *Psalter* first appeared in Vilnius in 1525, significantly fewer than fifty years before the 1564 date that Andreyev proposed, but that another edition of the same *Psalter* was published in Vilnius in 1575, exactly fifty years before the 1625 date that Keenan thought Shakhovskoi wrote the third epistle to Vas'ian (clearly not Muromtsev).[88]

These following works are not attributed to Kurbskii in the works themselves but are done so centuries later by scholars for reasons that are rarely explicitly stated.

2. Preface to the book of John of Damascus, *Dialectica*.[89] Preface to the *Life of Simeon Metaphrastes*.
3. Marginal glosses to translations of John Chrysostom and John of Damascus.[90]
4. Translations
   (a) Completion of translation of the works *Dialectica*[91] and *On Syllogism* of John of Damascus (1579).[92]
   (b) Translated works of John Chrysostom, which entered into *Novyi Margarit* (1575).
   (c) Beginning of work on translation of *Bogosloviia* (*Theology*) of John of Damascus.
   (d) The prefatory note to the sermons of John Chrysostom published in Moscow in 1665 states that Kurbskii translated the sermons 44 through 47. The Russian linguist Alexander Kh. Vostokov (1781–1864), in his catalog of the Russian and Slavonic manuscripts of the Rumiantsev Museum published in 1842, expressed doubt about that attribution to Kurbskii because the manuscript he was describing

---

88. Keenan, *Kurbskii-Groznyi Apocrypha*, 29–30, 41–46.
   89. Published by Mikhail Obolenskii in "O perevode kniazia Kurbskogo sochinenii Ioanna Damaskina," *Bibliograficheskie zapiski* 1858, no. 12, cols. 355–366.
   90. Published by Arkhangel'skii, *Ocherki iz istorii zapadno-russkoi literatury*, "Prilozheniia," 88–128.
   91. Arkhangel'skii, *Ocherki iz istorii zapadno-russkoi literatury*, "Prilozheniia," 155–166.
   92. Filiushkin, *Andrei Kurbskii*, 286.

with those sermons had a translation that differed from the one in the 1665 edition.[93]

(e) The Russian historian-archivist Mikhail A. Obolenskii (1805–1873) attributed some other translations of John of Damascus to Kurbskii seeing similarities with Kurbskii's "known works."[94] Since the "known works" of Kurbskii are not so known, perhaps one should suspend judgment about attributions made on that basis, at least for the time being.

(f) To Kurbskii are attributed the translations of a dialogue of the Patriarch of Constantinople Gennadius Scholarius (r. 1454–1464), several of the works of Pseudo-Dionisius the Areopagite, Gregory of Nazianzus (the Theologian) (ca. 329–390), Basil of Caesarea, and others.

5. The émigré Russianist Élie Denissoff (1893–1871) attributed to Kurbskii a biographical notice concerning Maksim Grek.[95]

Stylometrics

In 1994, G. I. Sarkisovaia wrote an article demonstrating a stylometric analysis of some of the letters attributed to Kurbskii. These were the third letter to Ivan IV and the second letter to Vas'ian. The style of the two letters was compared with the style in *The History of the Grand Prince of Moscow*. Sarkisovaia concluded that the style is the same for the letters and *The History*.[96] Therefore, in her view she had identified the style of Kurbskii. The analysis was faulty for a number of reasons. Part of Keenan's challenge to the authenticity of the works attributed to Kurbskii is his placing the composition of the third letter to Ivan IV and the *History of the Grand Prince* within the same time and milieu— the 1670s in the Ambassadorial Chancellery (*Posol'skii prikaz*). Also notably she did not include any of the so-called Lithuanian letters, which date to the

93. Aleksandr Vostokov, *Opisanie russkikh i slovenskikh rukopisei Rumiantsovskogo muzeuma* (St. Petersburg: V tip. Imp. akademii nauk, 1842), 251.

94. Mikhail Obolenskii, "O perevode kniazia Kurbskogo sochinenii Ioanna Damaskina," *Bibliograficheskie zapiski* 1858, no. 12, cols. 355–366. The manuscripts that contain these translations are described in Vostokov, *Opisanie*, 251, while two other copies (one previously owned by Piskarev; the other indicated as "1619?" by Keenan) are in the Rossiiskaia publichnaia biblioteka (RPB).

95. Élie Denissoff, "Une biographie de Maxime le Grec par Kourbski," *Orientalia Christiana Periodica* 20 (1954): 44–84; Denissoff, "Maxime le Grec et ses vicissitudes au sein de l'Église Russe," *Revue des études slaves* 31, nos. 1–4 (1954): 7–20.

96. G. I. Sarkisova, "Beglyi boiarin Andrei Kurbskii i ego poslaniia," in *Ot Nestora do Fonvizina. Novye metody opredeleniia avtorstva*, ed. L. V. Milov (Moscow: Progress, 1994), 248–270, 408–418.

late sixteenth century. In other words, there seems to have been a selection of certain evidence that would ensure the outcome the researcher wanted.

Comparison of Shakespeare and Kurbskii Controversies

There are a number of similarities between the biographies of Andrei Kurbskii and William of Stratford besides their lives overlapping for nineteen years. We have no evidence that Kurbskii received an education while in Muscovy, no direct evidence that he could read or write, and no evidence that he traveled much except from Muscovy to Kazan' and then to Lithuania, and, as with William of Stratford, his signature is labored.[97] In addition, as with William of Stratford, the literacy of Andrei Kurbskii has been questioned. Although William of Stratford never left a statement saying that he could not write, Kurbskii does leave a court document in which he claims he could not write in Cyrillic (see below).

Nonetheless, one also finds personal similarities between Kurbskii and Edward de Vere. Both were members of the aristocracy who fled from their ruler. Kurbskii fled from Ivan IV to the Lithuanian ruler in 1564. De Vere fled from Elizabeth's court to Calais and then Flanders in 1573. Both were involved in military matters. Kurbskii commanded a regiment in the taking of Kazan' (1552) and served on the Livonian front both for and against the Muscovites and Lithuanians. De Vere briefly commanded a contingent of English cavalry in the Low Countries in the mid-1580s, and later commanded a ship during the attack of the Spanish Armada.[98] One also finds differences. Kurbskii remained in exile until his death nineteen years later. De Vere returned to England when summoned by the queen. Kurbskii was primarily a military man, whereas de Vere was a courtier in the sense of Castiglione's *The Courtier*.

In the previous chapter, I pointed out that Looney used authorial profiling to attempt to derive biographical information about the author of the Shakespearean canon. Keenan used a similar type of profiling in 1971 to draw inferences from the first letter of Prince Andrei Mikhailovich Kurbskii to Ivan Groznyi (K1) in ascertaining characteristics of the author.[99] He identified seven autobiographical characteristics of the writer of K1: (1) "religious tone and

---

97. Auerbach provides a facsimile of Kurbskii's signature, made using the Latin alphabet on his will, in Auerbach, *Andrej Michajlovič Kurbskij*, 377.

98. For the available evidence on de Vere's commanding English cavalry and participation in the battle against the Armada, see Alan H. Nelson, *Monstrous Adversary: The Life of Edward de Vere, 17th Earl of Oxford* (Liverpool: Liverpool University Press, 2003), 296–297, 311–319; and Anderson, *"Shakespeare" by Another Name*, 204–206, 222–229.

99. Keenan, *The Kurbskii-Groznyi Apocrypha*, 35–46.

polished Slavonic"; (2) "tendency toward rhymed prose"; (3) "wrongs committed against the author" by the recipient; (4) "oppression of the writer's family" by the recipient; (5) "preoccupation with death"; (6) "military exploits of the author are central to his plea"; and (7) "complaint about marching to and fro with the tsar's army." Keenan then compared these features of K1 with four possible authors—Isaiah of Kam'ianets'-Podil'sk, Andrei Kurbskii, Ivan Khvorostinin (d. 1625), and Semen Shakhovskoi—and concluded that these characteristics fit the life story of Shakhovskoi best.

Similar to the anti-Stratfordians, who point out that William of Stratford's will does not mention any books and leaves his "second best bed" to his wife, Anne, Keenan pointed out that the will of Andrei Kurbskii does not mention any books and leaves a suit of armor to Prince Konstantin Ostroz'kyi, "the well-known patron of early Ukrainian book publishing."[100] Also similar to the anti-Stratfordians, who consider significant the various spellings of William of Stratford's surname, there is an issue about the spelling of Kurbskii's name (see below). Likewise, Keenan questioned the correlation between the literary persona of the works attributed to Kurbskii and the evidence we have for his historical persona.

Whereas the anti-Stratfordians usually propose a single candidate, whether it be de Vere, Marlow, Bacon, someone else, or even the Shakespeare syndicate, to have been the real author of the entire Shakespearean canon, the anti-Kurbskians have different candidates for different parts of the Kurbskii canon. I will discuss each of the main points of comparison between the two controversies, as I see them.

Spelling of the Surname

Keenan asserted that, although the spelling Kurpski can be found in various texts, one would not expect "the analphabetic phonetic transcription" that is found in his will. Instead, a person of erudition would have known that the spelling of his native village was Kurba.[101] According to the Kurbskii proponents, such as Auerbach, the spelling difference is not significant and does not show that Kurbskii was analphabetic.[102]

---

100. Keenan, *Kurbskii-Groznyi Apocrypha*, 59.
101. Keenan, *Kurbskii-Groznyi Apocrypha*, 209.
102. Auerbach, "Ein Analphabet als Schriftsteller?" 15–51.

Name on Title Page of Works Attributed to Him

Attribution of the letters to Ivan IV first occurs in manuscripts of the 1620s. No attribution occurs in the manuscript copies of *The History of the Grand Prince of Moscow*, *The History of the Eighth Council*, or translations from Eusebius's *Ecclesiastical History* and from Chrysostom. Those attributions to Kurbskii may be the result of their appearance with the letters to Ivan IV in the *Miscellany of Kurbskii*, copies of which date no earlier than the 1670s. Some manuscript copies (earliest, 1690s) of Andrei Lyzlov's *Scythian History* contain the marginal gloss "kur history" *("kur istoriia")*, but this reference, requiring the addition of -bskii's (*-bskago*) to the end of *kur*, is ambiguous at best. The preface to *Novyi Margarit* has an attribution to Kurbskii in one manuscript copy of the early eighteenth century. An attribution of a translation from John of Damascus to Kurbskii dates to the eighteenth century.

Literacy of Family

Skeptics and proponents agree that evidence of the literacy of Andrei Kurbskii's family comes only with his third marriage late in life to Alexandra Petrovna Semashko, who raised their son Dmitrii after his father died when his son was a year old. Dmitrii went on to become a statesman in the grand duchy of Lithuania.

Personal Literacy

We have no works in Kurbskii's hand. Some proponents of the Kurbskii attributions proposed that he dictated his works. Thomson proposed the translations project was Kurbskii's idea and that he supervised those trained in Latin to do the actual translating. Skeptics allow only that he dictated a "rude" letter to Ivan IV but quickly add that whatever was in the letter, it is not the extant letter that we have.

Education

If we accept the court testimony of Kurbskii that he could not write in Cyrillic, then any formal education he had could only have occurred after he defected to Lithuania, where the Latin alphabet was widely used. Yet, the extant copies of works attributed to Kurbskii are in Cyrillic.

Specialized Knowledge

Nothing in the original works attributed to Kurbskii required specialized knowledge of classical philosophy, literature, music, law, military strategy, art history, ancient and foreign languages, ancient history, natural history, foreign lands, falconry, government, politics, rhetoric, or medicine. Translations from Cicero, John of Damascus, Eusebius, and so on required some classical and religious education.

Autobiographical Details

The History of the Grand Prince of Moscow contains very little of what can be called autobiographical information. We find no mention of Kurbskii's life in Lithuania in *The History*.[103] The closest such information is only a generalized denigration of courtiers of the Polish king.[104] The claim that his brother died as a result of wounds during the taking of Kazan' is unconfirmed by any other source. The preface to the *Novyi Margarit* contains autobiographical information, but it could be about a different individual with a similar name, the cleric Andrii from Jarosław.

Knowledge of the Royal Court

Proponents see Kurbskii's description of the Muscovite court to be valuable insider information. Skeptics see his description of the Muscovite court to be questionable and contradicted by other evidence, such as the existence of a chosen council (*Izbrannaia rada*) in Moscow.[105]

One of the problems with the Kurbskiana is that presumably the author (or authors) is writing about what he knows (or what they know), but it is difficult to find confirmation of the evidence in the Kurbskii corpus that connects *The History of the Grand Prince*, *The History of the Eighth Council*, the letters, the preface, and so on with the historical persona that was Andrei Kurbskii.

---

103. Boeck, "Miscellanea Attributed to Kurbskii, 953.

104. Ostrowski, "Attributions to Andrei Kurbskii," 221.

105. Anthony Grobovsky's The *"Chosen Council" of Ivan IV: A Reinterpretation* (Brooklyn: Gaus, 1969). See also A. I. Filiushkin, *Istoriia odnoi mistifikatsii: Ivan Groznyi i "Izbrannaia Rada"* (Moscow: VGU, 1998). Although neither Grobovsky nor Filiushkin considered the problem with the use of the term *izbrannaia rada* in *The History* sufficient to question the attribution to Kurbskii, their thorough investigations of the problem have been used by skeptics as part of their arguments against such an attribution. See, for example, Keenan, *Kurbskii-Groznyi Apocrypha*, 63.

Claim to Have Written the Works Attributed to Him

We have no evidence Kurbskii ever claimed to be the author of the works attributed to him. Kurbskii, like William of Stratford, was litigious, often about small amounts, and like William of Stratford, he makes no mention in any of his lawsuits of being an author or of having rights to anything he had written.

Books

A major point of contention between the proponents and the skeptics concerns whether Andrei Kurbskii could write in Cyrillic. We have a legal document from October 9, 1571, signed "Andrej Kurpski manu proprija" in Latin characters. In the document he stated: "I am unable to write in Cyrillic."[106] On the other hand, insofar as we can believe a seventeenth-century copy of a letter supposedly written by Prince Aleksandr Polubenskii (who commanded Lithuanian forces in the area to which Kurbskii fled), Kurbskii seems to have owned books before he defected. Polubenskii wrote to a certain Iakov Shablikin to "find out about the books" that Kurbskii left behind.[107] In light of the 1571 document, one has four options concerning Polubenskii's letter: (1) disregard the 1571 document and continue to speculate about Kurbskii's literary accomplishments before his fleeing to Lithuania,[108] (2) conclude that, like Charlemagne, Kurbskii could read but not write, (3) posit that Kurbskii could not read and had the codices read to him (as some scholars have suggested was done for the courtiers at medieval courts), or (4) suppose that the codices were not read at all but served merely as objects of veneration.

Contemporary Evidence (Paper Trail)

I insert here a modified version of Diana Price's chart of literary paper trails in sixteenth- and seventeenth-century England. Lines in bold represent information added by me, namely Edward de Vere and Andrei Kurbskii.

---

106. Auerbach, *Andrej Michajlovič Kurbskij*, 375. Keenan translated "по руски" here as "in Ruthenian" rather than "in Russian" to mean "the several literary languages or stylistic registers employed roughly 1500–1700 by non-Muscovite East Slavs of the Dniepr Basin." Keenan, "Response to Halperin," 407, fn. 11. But languages can be written in the Latin alphabet. I take the meaning of the document to be that Kurbskii could not write using the Cyrillic alphabet.

107. "Gramota Polubenskogo," *Russkaia istoricheskaia biblioteka* 31, supplement, no. 3, cols. 495–496. It is located in the manuscript. RNB, Pogodin 1567, fols. 10v–12.

108. See Nikolay Andreyev, "Kurbsky's Letters to Vas'yan Muromtsev," *Slavonic and East European Review* 33 (1955): 417–418.

Table 7.1   Diana Price's chart of literary paper trails (my additions in bold)

	1	2	3	4	5	6	7	8	9	10
Ben Jonson	+	+	+	+	+	+	+	+	+	+
Thomas Nashe	+	+	+	+	+	+	+	+	+	
Edward de Vere	+	+	+	+	+	+	+	+	+	
Samuel Daniel	+	+	+	+	+	+	+	+		+
Edmund Spenser	+	+		+		+	+	+	+	+
Philip Massinger	+	+	+	+	+	+	+	+		
George Peele	+	+	+	+	+	+		+	+	
Gabriel Harvey	+	+		+	+	+	+	+	+	
Michael Drayton		+	+	+		+	+	+		+
George Chapman		+	+	+		+	+	+	+	
William Drummond	+	+			+	+	+	+	+	
John Marston	+	+	+			+	+	+	+	
Anthony Munday		+	+	+	+	+	+	+		+
Robert Greene	+		+	+			+	+		+
John Lyly	+	+		+		+	+	+		
Thomas Heywood		+			+	+	+	+		+
Thomas Lodge	+	+		+			+	+	+	
Thomas Middleton	+		+		+	+		+		
Thomas Dekker		+	+			+	+	+		
Thomas Watson	+			+			+	+		+
Francis Beaumont	+						+	+		+
John Fletcher	+						+	+	+	
Thomas Kyd	+	+		+				+		
Christopher Marlowe	+							+		+
John Webster			+				+	+		
Andrei Kurbskii		+							+	
William of Stratford										

Key

1. Evidence of education

2. Record of correspondence, especially concerning literary matters

3. Evidence of having been paid to write

4. Evidence of a direct relationship with a patron

5. Extant original manuscript

6. Handwritten inscriptions, receipts, letters, etc., touching on literary matters

7. Commendatory verses, epistles, or epigrams contributed or received

8. Referred to personally as a writer (miscellaneous records)

9. Evidence of books owned, written in, borrowed, or given

10. Notice at death as a writer .

Skeptics assert there is no mention by Kurbskii's contemporaries of his being an author or translator. There is, however, documented mention of a letter from Kurbskii to Ivan IV. When we place Andrei Kurbskii's literary trail on the same grid with his contemporaries in England, we find two fulfilled characteristics but then only partial. We do have a record of a correspondence but not about literary matters. And we do have evidence of his owning books but not written in, borrowed, or given. The fulfillment of two of the ten characteristics puts Kurbskii between William of Stratford and John Webster, the two lowest names on the chart, thus decreasing the inferential probability that Andrei Kurbskii was a writer. The evidence for Edward de Vere, in contrast, fulfills nine of the ten characteristics, which places him in the same position on the table as Thomas Nashe and Samuel Daniel, and only behind Ben Jonson in regard to number of literary trail characteristics fulfilled.

Relevance for principles of attribution: A paper trail is highly relevant especially for this period in European history. This absence of contemporary evidence is a correct use of the *argumentum ex silentio* because, if Price is correct in regard to contemporaries of Shakespeare, there is some contemporary evidence about each of them as an author. Such evidence is something we can legitimately expect. Its absence in regard to the greatest of them all, Shakespeare, is not just extremely odd but even bizarre. Its absence is less odd and bizarre for Kurbskii but still significant. Therefore, the absence requires explanation.

Chronology of the Compositions

The proponents argue that all the works attributed to Kurbskii were basically written while he was alive. Any post-1583 elements in them are considered to be later interpolations, which seems intended to make the composition dates of these works conform to the biography of Kurbskii. The skeptics argue that the post-1583 elements are not interpolations but clues to their dates of composition.

Relevance for principles of attribution: A work whose composition date has been fairly solidly established (especially in terms of earliest possible date / latest possible date) can exclude a number of claimants. But when the proposed dates of composition are made to fit the biography of a particular claimant, then that dating is not to be trusted. The Kurbskii proponents' argument that anything attributed to Kurbskii that he could have written, he wrote, and anything in them he couldn't have written is an interpolation was used *mutatis mutandis* by those who argued that Moses wrote the Pentateuch, but it is a weak argument. Interpolations in a writer's work do occur, but one cannot assume that is always the case in order to maintain the case for that writer.

The Takeaway

It is important for us to examine, insofar as possible, authorship claims on the basis of evidence, logic, and elegance of interpretation (parsimony), not just assume that because someone is traditionally seen as the author the likelihood is they are. Attribution is an immature auxiliary historical science, especially in regard to medieval and early modern texts. The studies of the Shakespearean corpus and of Kurbskiana have gone far to advance the practice of attributing texts, although those contributions have yet to be added to the theory of attribution, if one even exists.

The general tendency in the scholarship has been to respond to text critical and linguistic arguments and evidence with arguments and evidence that are in a different register, that is, of a non-text critical and non-linguistic variety.[109] That way a scholar does not need to deal with disciplines that they never studied and with which they are unfamiliar. In any case, such disciplines may be perceived to carry with them a taint of suspicion, as though some kind of trickery is being perpetrated, especially when either linguistic or text critical analysis or both challenge the traditional dating and attribution. It feels safer to fall back on familiar narrative constructs and traditional attributions.

---

109. See, e.g., Isabel de Madariaga's opposition to Keenan's questioning the traditional attributions to Kurbskii and Ivan IV: "I am not qualified in linguistic and textual analysis. But as a practicing historian I cannot accept the validity of Keenan's theories on historical grounds." Isabel de Madariaga, *Ivan the Terrible: The First Tsar of Russia* (New Haven, CT: Yale University Press, 2005), xvi.

CHAPTER 8

How Inauthentic was James Macpherson's "Translation" of Ossian?

"There is no literary controversy of modern times that has for so long a period, and with so deep an interest, attracted the public attention as that on the authenticity of those poems, published about the middle of the last century, by Mr. James Macpherson, under the name of the Poems of Ossian."

—Irish scholar Edward O'Reilly (1830)[1]

"No English author before him, not Shakespeare, Milton, Addison or Pope, had found such hosts of foreign admirers; no one after him except Byron, hardly even Sir Walter Scott and Dickens, has had a greater fame."

—Literary scholar J. S. Semple (1905)[2]

In 1760, the Scottish poet James Macpherson (1736–1796) published *Fragments of Ancient Poetry Collected in the Highlands of Scotland*, which he claimed was his own translation into English from old Gaelic manuscripts he discovered in the Scottish Highlands. In 1762, Macpherson published *Fingal, an Ancient Epic Poem*, a cycle of poetry presumably sung by the legendary Scottish bard Ossian, which he also claimed was a translation from the Gaelic. A year later, in 1763, he published the third part of the cycle, *Temora*. These publications created a sensation for they coincided with the revival of interest in Scotland with medieval literature. It also coincided with

---

1. Edward O'Reilly, "To Investigate the Authenticity of the Poems of Ossian, Both as Given Macpherson's Translation, and as Published in Gaelic, London 1807, under the Sanction of the Highland Society of London; And on the Supposition of Such Poems Not Being of Recent Origin, to Assign the Probable Era and Country of the Original Poet or Poets," *Transactions of the Royal Irish Academy* 16 (1830): 163.

2. J[ohn] S[emple] Smart, *James Macpherson: An Episode in Literature* (London: David Nutt, 1905), 11.

the attempt by the Scots to find a heroic past for Scotland, especially after the Scottish defeats in 1715 and 1745 to the English in battle. At around the same time Macpherson was publishing these works, the English were publishing Celtic and ancient revival works such as Thomas Gray's *The Bard: A Pindaric Ode* (1757), Edward Capell's *Prolusions, or Select Pieces of Ancient Poetry* (1760), and Thomas Percy's *Reliques of Ancient English Poetry* (1765) celebrating the English past. In addition, the Irish were beginning to publish Irish bardic poetry, some of it datable to the sixth century.

The Ossian cycle also stimulated investigations into and searches for ethnic folk literature, in particular for national epics throughout Europe and Russia that represented the mystical spirit of the nation. One still finds the Ossian cycle listed as a Scottish national epic alongside the 14,000 line poem *The Brus* composed by the fourteenth-century Scottish poet John Barbour and the 11,000 line poem *The Wallace* attributed to the fifteenth century *makar* (bard) Blind Harry. In Macpherson's work, Ossian is the name of the bard who, when old and blind, presents the stories of battles and unhappy love affairs through poems or otherwise organized text. Ossian's father Fingal (Fionn mac Cumhaill, Finn Mac Cool, or Finn Mac Coul) was a legendary warrior (*fiann*) as was Ossian himself. His son is Oscar, who by the time of the narration has died. The Ossian cycle tells the story of these Scottish Gaelic warriors in battle fending off the Vikings.

Yet, from early on, skeptics such as Samuel Johnson, David Hume, and Horace Walpole expressed doubt about the authenticity of Macpherson's translations. Those doubts spread as Macpherson refused to produce the Gaelic manuscripts that he said he was translating from. In addition, almost from the beginning, Irish scholars made accusations of plagiarism against Macpherson as they noticed similarities between genuinely Irish Gaelic works and the Ossian cycle. But Macpherson also had his staunch supporters. In 1807, they published his Gaelic "originals," which turned out to be back translations that Macpherson had apparently made himself. By 1830, the plagiarism accusations were cataloged by Edward O'Reilly (1765–1830), who devoted a number of pages of his investigation of the Ossian cycle to detailing them.[3]

Eventually the scholarly opinion swung against Macpherson's claim that he was translating an authentic Scottish Gaelic cycle of medieval poetry. Nonetheless, the poetry itself was taken up during the Romantic era by those who saw in it genuine elements of the origins of a Scottish national identity. Just as the English had *Beowulf*, the French had the *Song of Roland*, and the Germans

---

3. O'Reilly, "To Investigate the Authenticity of the Poems of Ossian," 61–67, 156–165.

had the *Nibelungenlied*, so the Scots had Ossian. Even within the scholarly community an attempt is being made to reassess Macpherson's Ossian cycle and look for elements of an authentic Scottish oral tradition that may have influenced him and that he may have drawn upon.

Context of the Controversy

The eighteenth and early nineteenth centuries in Scotland were a period of vibrant artistic creativity and intellectual and scientific accomplishments to the extent that the name the Scottish Enlightenment has been ascribed to it. The Scottish Enlightenment was an integral part of the general European Enlightenment. There are reasons why Macpherson wrote what he did when he did and why his Ossian cycle was received as positively as it was. To explain how Macpherson's fraud could have such a profound impact on European society, I need to make a digression into the European and Scottish Enlightenments. It will also provide a context for understanding how a work of this type could have arisen in the middle of the Enlightenment.

Phases of the Enlightenment

The Enlightenment was not all homogenous in that not everyone thought the same way. There were a number of currents and crosscurrents, and the framework of thinking evolved through three distinct phases. Of course, it does not work out cleanly in a chronological boundary sense because there are overlaps, and there are people saying contrary things to each other throughout. Yet there was a different dominant mode during each of these phases. One could think of the entire period as a musical composition in three movements, not dissimilar to the sonata form that was so popular during the Enlightenment. Just as a dominant chord in music creates tension, and the return to the tonic chord resolves that tension, so too during the Enlightenment the dominant mode of privileging rationality created tension while resolution to the tonic mode of a balance of emotions with rationality was being sought. And, as in music, where there are subdominant chords that mediate between the dominant and tonic chords, so too one can discern subdominant modes that mediated between dominant and tonic modes, some of them in a minor key. Macpherson's creative imagination might then be seen to be part of one of those subdominant, minor key modes.

RATIONAL AND OPTIMISTIC (CA. 1690–CA. 1750)

The first phase is the "rational and optimistic" phase, which stretches from roughly 1690 to 1750. This phase was initiated in great part by Isaac Newton's figuring out a mathematical description of what gravity does. Newton, in effect, had created a unified field theory for all motion, both on the earth and in the heavens. As soon as that theory began to be popularized by people like Voltaire, the idea developed that one could apply the same kind of scientific method to the study of society and figure out everything at the level of mathematical proof. If we could bring society's laws into conformity with natural laws, the presumption was that doing so would lead to human happiness. As the poet Alexander Pope wrote, "Nature and Nature's laws lay hid in night:/ God said, "Let Newton be!" and all was light." Thus, the driving force of this first phase of the Enlightenment was to figure out the natural laws that governed human activity.

It was during this first phase that interest in what later became folklore studies began as one of the subdominant modes. The French fabulist Charles Perrault (1628–1703) published *Tales of Mother Goose* (*Contes de ma Mere L'Oye*) in 1697, fairy tales that were based on French folk tales. His work led to the creation of the literary genre of the fairy tale. In 1725, the Italian historian Giambattista Vico (1668–1744) published the ambitious *The New Science* (*Scienza Nuova*), a milestone in the development of the idea that each nation has its own "communal conscience." It was the interest in finding the principles of the communal conscience that gave impetus to exploration of the deep past of the nation, where those principles could presumably be found in an uncorrupted natural state. It tied in very well with the notion of the "noble savage." The hope that Macpherson had tapped into that uncorrupted core past of the Scottish people excited many of the Scottish supporters of Macpherson and the authenticity of the Ossian poems.

CHALLENGE TO REASON AND OPTIMISM (CA. 1750–CA. 1775)

The second phase ran from roughly 1750 to 1775. The dominant mode was a questioning of that early rationalism and optimism, as Enlightenment thinkers came more and more to realize that they were not figuring things out and that things were not falling into place. Instead, the inexplicable kept occurring. Like the proverbial candle flame, the larger their knowledge became, the greater the circle of darkness around it grew and the more the *philosophes* became aware of what they did not know. As a subdominant mode during this period, we find nostalgic feelings for a Middle Ages of the nation's history, which people knew nothing or very little about. The poet and scholar of the classics Thomas Gray (1716–1771) published *The Bard: A Pindaric Ode* (1757), which was based on his research into the thirteenth-century wars of King Edward I of England (r. 1272–1307) in Wales as well as his own study of Welsh harp music. The Shakespeare scholar Edward Capell (1713–1781) published *Prolusions, or Select Pieces of Ancient Poetry* (1760), which contained editions of works mainly from the sixteenth century, the selection of which was aimed to contribute to establishing an indigenous English literary tradition. While Grey's *The Bard* was a totally creative work and Capell edited actual sixteenth-century texts in *Prolusions*, trying to be scrupulous about the editing, the *Reliques of Ancient English Poetry* (1765) by Bishop Thomas Percy (1729–1811) falls in between them. Percy based his published collection of English ballads (some thought to date back to the twelfth century) on a manuscript he found in the home of a friend in Shropshire (the maid had been using folios from it to light the fire). Urged by the English writer and lexicographer Samuel Johnson (1709–1784) to publish the text, Percy published 45 heavily redacted works from the manuscript (which has 195 items) and added 135 ballads and metrical poems from other published and unpublished sources, including three anonymous oral tradition tales. Percy would not let scholars examine the manuscript (known as the Percy Folio) during his lifetime. He may have been influenced by the example of Macpherson, who appeared reluctant to share the manuscript or manuscript fragments upon which he said his "translations" were based.

Counter-Responses to the Challenge— Emancipation of Reason or of the Passions? (ca. 1775–ca. 1800)

The third phase was the counter-response to the challenge and runs roughly from 1775 to 1800. This counter-response took two different forms. Since the challenge of the previous phase was to rationalism, one of the lines of response was to try to reassert reason—that is, put reason back in its rightful place in the order of things, to in effect enthrone reason again as the arbiter of all things. The other trend was to subsume reason to the passions. The premise was that emotions are natural and reason is artificial and just gets in the way. Those who followed this line tried to make reason subordinate to the passions rather than the other way around. This last counter-response to the challenge led right into nineteenth-century Romanticism.

During this period, the reaction to the Ossian poems also went in two directions. The first was the skeptical opposition led by Johnson and Hume; the second was the wholehearted embracing of the work as an authentic and a true representation of the Scottish ancient heritage.

Examples of Each of the Enlightenment Phases

I set 1690 as the beginning of the first phase because of the essay by British philosopher John Locke (1632–1704) titled *An Essay concerning Human Understanding*, which was published in 1690). In it, he posited the notion that the human infant when it is born is a blank slate (*tabula rasa*), that it has no knowledge and is dependent entirely on the senses to acquire information. Reason, then, is the crucible that processes those sense perceptions, and the result is the basis of our knowledge. At the time when Locke wrote, the given epistemology was that the infant already has all the knowledge that it will ever have and that it is contained in the soul. The thinking was that the human soul is connected to the divine soul, which is an emanation from the divine intellect. So the ideal forms of the divine intellect are manifested in the divine soul, which our human souls are connected to, and that is our source of true knowledge. Since the infant has a soul, the infant has all of the information that is already contained within it. In that view of things, this world is a world of illusion and deception, and we can only be led astray by knowledge of this world. Locke's epistemology based on empiricism and reason says, instead, that all of our knowledge comes from this world. And that has been the prevailing view of epistemology since the eighteenth century.

A founder of the Scottish Enlightenment was Francis Hutcheson (1694–1746). Born of Scottish Presbyterian parents in Ulster in what is today Northern Ireland, Hutcheson was appointed professor of philosophy at Glasgow University in Scotland. He was clearly part of the first phase of the European Enlightenment, being influenced by, among others, John Locke. In 1726, Hutcheson published *An Inquiry into the Original of Our Ideas of Beauty and Virtue*, in which he came up with a formula for human happiness, part of which reads: $M = (B + S) \times A = BA + SA$; and therefore $BA = M - SA = M - I$, where $M = $ Morality, $B = $ Benevolence, $S = $ Self-love, $A = $ Ability, and $I = $ Interest.[4] Hutcheson was serious about finding out the secret of human happiness and very much interested in laying the groundwork in a scientific sense. His

---

4. Frances Hutcheson, *An Inquiry into the Original of Our Ideas of Beauty and Virtue*, rev. ed. (1726; Indianapolis: Liberty Fund, 2004, 129.

attempts did not work out, but he had an influence on another Scottish philosopher, who was part of the second phase of the Enlightenment—David Hume (1711–1776).

Hume led the challenge to reason and optimism from the side of philosophy. *An Enquiry concerning Human Understanding* was a work that he originally published in 1739, but it did not make much of a splash then except that two reviewers said it was difficult to understand. It was too early for such counter-rational ideas to find much of an audience. The book was reissued in 1748, just in time for the rise of challenges to the notion of reason enthroned. Hume was in revolt against rationalist systems. He questioned all knowledge that we gain from sensory experience. He said that there are two categories of this knowledge—impressions and ideas. An impression, like noise, is a sensation. A knock on the door, in contrast, is an idea. He tried to distinguish between something that our senses detect that we do not quite understand and something that we interpret. So ideas are impressions that are interpreted.

In his twenties, Hume left England and went to France and spent some time at a Jesuit college where he could have access to the library and was under the influence of Jesuits. He wrote his great philosophical work there. When he came back to England, he tried to get his book published but found difficulty because who would want to read a book on philosophy by an unknown philosopher, especially one that challenged the prevailing notions of reason and optimism? He was able to get it published anonymously, so his name is not on the original work but was added when it was republished.

In the spirit of Hutcheson but contrary to his intent, Hume devised a rational proof to prove that reason could not prevail. Of course, the proof failed, because it would have to; if it had succeeded, then reason could prove something. Hume's challenge to reason was in many respects a wakeup call to those who had this great optimism. They had to deal with Hume's challenge, and they did so in various ways.

This early period of optimism also included François-Marie Arouet, who wrote under the pen name Voltaire (1694–1778). Voltaire was initially very much a believer that everything could be figured out. He had a friendship with the French physicist and philosopher Émilie du Chatelet, one of the top mathematicians of the period, who had read Newton's *Principia Mathematica* and who was one of the few people at the time who could understand it. She explained it to Voltaire so he could write a popular version called *Elements of the Philosophy of Newton* (1738). Voltaire strongly believed in the notion of applying the principles of Newton to human endeavor.

In a book published in 1747 called *Zadig, or The Destined One*, Voltaire has a story that is very similar to his later work *Candide*. Zadig is born and raised in isolated circumstances, away from society. People were born good, but it was society that corrupts. So Zadig is uncorrupted, he is an innocent. He reaches late adolescence and then is introduced to society and thinks it is all rather ridiculous. But because of his early upbringing he is not corrupted or corruptible. He goes through certain tribulations, trials, and misfortunes, but he holds on to his natural innocence, and in the end everything turns out well and it has a happy ending. Voltaire is using the theme of the noble savage here—that is, the person raised away from society, such as Tarzan or Crocodile Dundee, develops noble characteristics that people in society do not develop. Such a work had already appeared in the seventeenth century with Hans Jakob Christoffel von Grimmelshausen's novel *Simplicius Simplicissimus* (1668). And it could also be said about Ossian, who though raised in society, is from a time (the third century) that, from a Scottish nationalist viewpoint, elicited simpler and purer characteristics of the true Scottish hero.

On the morning of November 1, 1755, an earthquake hit Lisbon, Portugal, resulting in a fire and tsunami that caused vast destruction and the death of tens of thousands of people. This event triggered a question not only in the mind of Voltaire but also in many of the other *philosophes*. It was not that event alone, but the earthquake was a trip wire because doubts were already creeping in. Are we really going to be able to figure things out, are we on the right track, is this working? The Lisbon earthquake brought it home. No. It is not working. We are not figuring things out. Why did that have to happen?

Voltaire went through a crisis of his former beliefs, and he wrote a poem called "On the Lisbon Disaster, or an Examination of the Axiom 'All Is Well.'" He was quite upset by all of that and part of his working out this crisis was writing *Candide, or Optimism* (1759). It is not the same story, but it is the same theme as *Zadig*. Candide is a young man raised in somewhat isolated circumstances in the castle of Baron Thunder-ten-Tronckh. He falls in love with the baron's daughter Cunégunde, then is cast out of the castle and goes through a lot of trials and tribulations. He encounters his tutor Dr. Pangloss at different times during his journeys. Pangloss keeps assuring him that this is the best of all possible worlds, but Candide has trouble applying Pangloss's view when he sees death and destruction all around him. Many years later he returns to the castle. He finds Cunégunde, but she is no longer the beautiful maiden he remembered. In the end, Candide decides to honor his initial love for Cunégunde, although he does not feel the same attraction for her as he once did. Voltaire closes his tale with the idea that all you can do is tend your own garden.

The third phase, the counter-responses to the challenge, includes Immanuel Kant (1724–1804) because he is the leading light of trying to re-enthrone reason. When Kant read Hume's book, he said it was as though he was awakened from sleepwalking. He realized that the questions Hume raised were fundamental and that one could not proceed any further with philosophy until one had answered them.

Among his formulations was something called the categorical imperative, which sees the individual not as isolated but as part of a species. The development of the individual mirrors the development of the species. Thus, whatever the individual does defines what the species does. If the individual lies, then mankind is defined as also lying. If the individual steals, mankind steals. According to Kant, we have to think in terms of our connection with our communities, our society, and all of humankind. We cannot say, well, everybody does it, because that is a copout. We are then determining our actions by what humankind does rather than determining what humankind does by our actions.

The other optional response was the abandonment of reason to a greater or lesser degree. The Marquis de Sade (1740–1814) promoted the active pursuit of personal pleasure. In *Justine, or The Misfortunes of Virtue* (1791), he reversed the outcome of the usual moral tale of the young woman who maintains her virtue through vicissitudes. Instead of being rewarded in the end, she experiences cosmic punishment. Thus, de Sade was proposing in effect that reason is not a guide to happiness and joy. Although he is not usually thought of as one of the great Enlightenment thinkers, de Sade does represent in a rather extreme way the emancipation of the passions.

Giovanni Jacopo Casanova (1725–1798) left extensive memoirs in which he described his life of libertinism. For him, satisfaction of personal pleasure seemed to be all that there was as a goal to life. De Sade and Casanova are representative of the extreme of denial of reason as a guide to one's personal conduct. Instead, the personal passions are the only guide. Other writers tend to be less extreme.

Johann Wolfgang von Goethe (1749–1832) began writing during the Enlightenment period and became one of the great Romantic period writers. *The Sorrows of Young Werther*, published in 1774, was a kind of milestone in European literature in that he combined a genre, the epistolary novel, with certain gothic novel themes that were usually reserved for what we would call romance fiction. Goethe developed them in a way that was more literarily acceptable to the intelligentsia. The story is a very simple one. Werther is a young man. He falls in love with a woman he cannot have. She marries someone else. He writes long letters pining away for her, and then he goes and kills himself. The book was a great success throughout Europe and started a period of what is called Sentimentalism in European literature—a precursor of and transition to Romanticism. Sentimental novels did necessarily have happy endings, although they might, but the whole idea was for the reader to be caught up in the pathos of it all. This type of novel had been around for some time, even during the optimism and reason phase of the Enlightenment. Jean-Jacques Rousseau (1712–1778) describes in his *Confessions* (completed by 1769; first half published in 1782, second half in 1789) how when he was growing up he and his father (his mother having died in childbirth) would read such novels to each other, sometimes all night until daybreak.[5]

N. M. Karamzin (1766–1826) was a Russian writer who traveled extensively in western Europe. He was in France at the time of the French Revolution. When he returned to Russia, he was caught up in the sentimental literature phase that was going on in western Europe, and in 1792 he wrote a short story called *Poor Liza* (*Bednaia Liza*). It was a great success in Russia at the time. Again it is a simple story, the kind of story that had been around for a long time, but it was his describing of it, his telling of it, that had such a great impact on other writers. Liza is a young peasant woman who lives with her mother. She is befriended by an army officer who promises that he will marry her, but he is called away to maneuvers. He says he will return with the wedding ring and they will get married. He does not return. Liza begins to wonder, thinks maybe he has been killed, and travels to St. Petersburg, where she finds out that he has been back for weeks living it up, partying, and so forth. She is distraught, returns to her farm, and walks into the lake and drowns herself.

Macpherson's Ossian poems and the controversy surrounding them were an integral part of the evolving European and Scottish Enlightenments. The Ossian cycle fits neatly into the second phase of the challenge to reason and optimism. Instead of Lockean epistemology, the Ossian cycle taps into an intuitive understanding of the deep past of Scotland. All "true" Scots should be able to connect in their hearts and souls with their common Gaelic past in a way that non-Scots cannot. Likewise, each national ethnos, according to this line of feeling, requires its own national epic. It also serves as a symbol of rebellion against the tyranny of reason and logic and the blank slate of Lockean epistemology.

Into the Thicket

James Macpherson was born in a small town in northern Scotland called Ruthven in the district of Badenoch. This area was the heart of the Gaelic-speaking part of Scotland. Gaelic had been the standard language of the kingdom of

---

5. *The Confessions of Jean-Jacques Rousseau*, trans. J. M. Cohen (London: Penguin Classics, 1953), 19–20.

Scotland in the eleventh century, but by the eighteenth century, English was replacing Gaelic except in remote Highland areas.

Macpherson attended higher educational institutions that later became the University of Aberdeen. While at college, he began writing poetry, including a six-canto epic poem titled *The Highlander*. After graduating, he went back to Ruthven to teach in the local school. In a conversation with his friend the Scottish minister and playwright John Home (1722–1808) (not to be confused with David Hume) in 1759, he recited some Gaelic verse that he had memorized. He then either told Home about or showed him Gaelic manuscripts in his possession. If he had shown Home manuscripts, we do not know if these were original manuscripts that Macpherson had collected or were merely his own writings on eighteenth-century paper. In later investigations, these supposed manuscripts did not turn up.

In any case, Home was impressed and encouraged Macpherson to publish them. Macpherson, who had a working knowledge of Gaelic, said he would translate them. The next year (1760) Macpherson published these translations from presumed original manuscripts or from oral traditions that he had written down. The full title of the work was *Fragments of Ancient Poetry Collected in the Highlands of Scotland and Translated from the Gaelic and Erse Languages*. The second volume of Ossian poems was titled *Fingal, an Ancient Epic in Six Books* and published in 1762. Fingal was a third-century Scottish king of Morven (northern Scotland) and the father of Ossian. Included in the volume were sixteen poems that dealt with other events involving Fingal, his sons, and Ossian's son, Oscar. Also included was a sixteen-page "Dissertation concerning the Antiquity, etc., of the poems of Ossian, the son of Fingal." The third and final volume was titled *Temora, an Ancient Epic in Eight Books*. It also includes six related poems and Macpherson's "Dissertation," now expanded to thirty-four pages.

According to Macpherson biographer Paul J. deGategno, the "controversy is best understood by viewing the argument in three distinct stages."[6] He defined the first stage as being 1760–1765, when Macpherson published the poems, and people like David Hume, Samuel Johnson, and Horace Walpole raised doubts about Macpherson's claim that he was translating from old Gaelic manuscripts. These doubts were countered by people like the Scottish minister and rhetorician Hugh Blair (1718–1800), who was convinced Macpherson was telling the truth. The second stage deGategno saw as being 1773–1783, which saw Macpherson publishing a complete edition of the three works with "corrections," Johnson's tour of the Scottish Highlands resulting in the publication of *Journey to the Western Islands of Scotland* (1775), and the critical as-

---

6. Paul J. deGategno, *James Macpherson* (Boston: Twayne, 1989), 99.

sessment by Hume "Of the Poems of Ossian," as well as the sponsoring by the Scottish General Sir John MacGregor Murray (1745–1822) of a fund for the publication of Macpherson's Gaelic manuscripts. The third stage deGategno identified was from 1797 to 1805, during which time a committee appointed by the Highland Society of Scotland investigated the matter and published its report. In 1805, two notable events occurred that led deGategno to choose that year as a cutoff. The first was the publication of a critical (in both senses of the word) edition by the Scottish historian Malcolm Laing (1762–1818) of Macpherson's Ossian poems.[7] Laing recreated the intellectual world of the author as demonstrating the influence of "the jargon of the Northern Schools" (i.e., the philosophical views of the scholars at the University of Aberdeen), of the "measured prose" and "inflated diction" typical of the literati of eighteenth-century Edinburgh, of eighteenth-century norms for representing heroes as well as heroines, and of the King James Bible in terms of cadence and meter. As the historian of the Scottish Enlightenment John Dwyer noted, Laing found that the poems' "most common reference points were Homer's *Iliad*, Virgil's *Aeneid*, [John] Milton's *Paradise Lost* [1667] and *Il Penseroso* [1645/46], [Thomas] Gray's *Elegy Written [in a Country Churchyard* (1751)], Robert Blair's *The Grave* [1743], [Edward] Young's *Night Thoughts* [1742–1745], [William] Collins' *Ode to Pity* [1746], and [John] Home's *Douglas* [1756]."[8] With the exception of Homer and Virgil, these "reference points" would not have been available to an early Scottish bard. What Laing considered to be most convincing that the poems were forged in the eighteenth century was the way in which the poems seem to cater to the fashion of the time of sublimity and sentimentality.[9]

This third phase also saw the publication in the *Edinburgh Review* of a review written by Sir Walter Scott (1771–1832) of the Highland Society report and of Laing's edition. Scott was a famed medievalist and writer of historical fiction placed in the Middle Ages. He concluded that the question of authenticity was now settled against Macpherson: "We believe no well-informed person will now pretend that Ossian is to be quoted as historical authority, or that a collection of Gaelic poems does any where exist, of which Macpherson's version can be regarded as a faithful, or even a loose translation."[10] Nonetheless, he

---

7. *The Poems of Ossian, &c. Containing the Poetical Works of James Macpherson*, ed. Malcolm Laing, 2 vols. (Edinburgh: J. Ballantyne, 1805).

8. John Dwyer, "The Melancholy Savage: Text and Context in the *Poems of Ossian*," in *Ossian Revisited*, ed. Howard Gaskill (Edinburgh: Edinburgh University Press, 1991), 166.

9. Laing in *Poems of Ossian, &c.*, vol. 1, 358–360, n. 6.

10. Walter Scott, review of *Report of the Highland Society of Scotland . . . and the Poems of Ossian . . . Works of James Macpherson*, in *Edinburgh Review* 6, no. 12 (July 1805): 429.

acknowledged the poems of Ossian as significant but rejected the assertion that their significance lay in some kind of Scottish nationalism. Instead, he saw Macpherson's creation as the work of a talented Scottish poet:

While we are compelled to renounce the pleasing idea, "that Fingal lived, and that Ossian sung," our national vanity may be equally flattered by the fact that a remote, and almost a barbarous corner of Scotland, produced, in the 18th century, a bard, capable not only of making an enthusiastic impression on every mind susceptible of poetical beauty, but of giving a new tone to poetry throughout all Europe.[11]

Scott's dual solution—condemn the work as historically inauthentic but praise the literary originality of the author—seemed to be a compromise that the scholarly world could accept.

The controversy over its authenticity, however, did not end there, so we may call deGategno's three stages the earliest phase of the controversy. For example, in 1875, the Scottish cleric and writer Peter Hately Waddell (1817–1891) accused Johnson, Laing, and other doubters of Macpherson as propounding "imaginary arguments . . . with studied contempt" and of supplementing their "critical antipathies . . . with insolence and scorn."[12] What Waddell set out to do in his book is show that "The topography of Ossian . . . —which was a mystery to Johnson, to Pinkerton, to Laing, and a wilderness of error to MacPherson [sic] himself—will be found capable of identification at this hour, to its minutest features—in Scotland, in Ireland, in the Orkneys, and even in Iceland, by the light of Ossian's text." If Waddell had succeeded in demonstrating the accuracy of topographical details that would have been unknown to Macpherson, that still would not have absolved him of hearing the names in oral ballads without knowing what they were referring to and including them because he liked the way they sounded. Waddell's argument is similar to the one that Macpherson defenders have made about the personal names in the poems. A number of names that can be found in the Ossian cycle can also be found in the *Book of the Dean of Lismore*, a compilation of forty-four Irish bardic poems along with twenty-one Scottish bardic poems, among other items. The manuscript was compiled mainly by James MacGregor, dean of Lismore, in the first half of the sixteenth century.[13] Again, as with topographical names, it may contribute to the argument that Macpherson was channeling early Scottish

11. Scott, review of *Report of the Highland Society*, 462.

12. Peter Hately Waddell, *Ossian and the Clyde, Fingal in Ireland. Oscar in Iceland, Or Ossian Historical and Authentic* (Glasgow: James MacLehose, 1875), 3.

13. *Heroic Poetry from the Book of the Dean of Lismore*, ed. Neil Ross (Edinburgh: Oliver & Boyd for the Scottish Gaelic Texts Society, 1939).

Gaelic poems and ballads to a certain extent, but it does not in and of itself mean that he was translating from an actual manuscript text.

In 1906, Keith Norman MacDonald, a Scottish doctor, published a work titled *In Defence of Ossian: Being a Summary of the Evidence in Favour of the Authenticity of the Poems*. MacDonald's argument was that only someone who had witnessed the events being described in the poems could have written them. Macpherson, according to MacDonald, deserves credit "for having rescued them from oblivion."[14] The scholarly community was able to dismiss MacDonald's *Defence* as not that of a specialist. It was less easy to do so with the book of the Scottish poet and academic Derick Smith Thomson (1921–2012) titled *Gaelic Sources of Macpherson's Ossian* (1952).[15] In it, Thomson compared Macpherson's Ossian poems with authentic Gaelic ballads both published and unpublished. He found thirty-eight instances of similarities that suggest Macpherson used them as sources. Thomson argued that the oral Gaelic tradition of the Scottish highlands had not changed much over the centuries and posited that those ballads contemporary to Macpherson accurately represented that earlier tradition and were probably known to him. Thus, Thomson turned the plagiarism accusation around to indicate a positive authentic Gaelic influence on Macpherson.

Thomson also defended Macpherson to a certain extent by suggesting that "it seems not unlikely that at one time he was really under the impression that there existed an epic poem, or epic poems, in Gaelic" and that "he may have thought at first that the MS. of the Book of the Dean was such an epic poem."[16] Thomson acknowledged that if Macpherson thought that in the beginning, he did not think it for long. To Macpherson's credit, according to Thomson, "At no time . . . does he insist strongly that such a poem existed in a complete form in MS." Instead, he saw himself as helping "in arranging the parts so as to form the whole."[17] Thomson used as an example *Fingal*, where "he certainly 'combined and brought together some pieces which he found scattered,'" such as his representation of the Battle of Lora, where "he used various versions of the poem *Teanntachd mhór na Féinne*."[18] Thomson did, however, fault Macpherson's work on the ballads as taking them away further from "their prototypes": "Macpherson's refining and bowdlerising pen has

---

14. Keith Norman MacDonald, *In Defence of Ossian: Being a Summary of the Evidence in Favour of the Authenticity of the Poems* (Edinburgh?, 1906), 73.

15. Derick Smith Thomson, *Gaelic Sources of Macpherson's Ossian* (Edinburgh: Published for the University of Aberdeen by Oliver and Boyd, 1952).

16. Thomson, *Gaelic Sources*, 83.

17. Thomson, *Gaelic Sources*, 83.

18. Thomson, *Gaelic Sources*, 84. The quoted words within the quotation from Thomson are from Blair in the *Report of the Highland Society of Scotland*, 61.

often changed the atmosphere of the ballads almost beyond recognition." Thomson concluded that "although much has been found in common between Macpherson's work and the ballads, essentially they are profoundly different." Thomson found the ballads to be "thoroughly native," whereas he saw "Macpherson's work is a blend—and seldom a happy one—of several different cultures." For Thomson, "the 'corrupt copies' of the Gaelic bards [are] more interesting than Macpherson's imposing edifice."[19] Of course, much of what Thomson wrote here is based on his own aesthetic judgment, which to be sure should not be taken lightly. Yet others may and often do have a different view of the value of Macpherson's Ossian cycle, either better or worse. In terms of attribution, the question was becoming one of how much Macpherson "channeled" the ancient Gaelic poems through what he had absorbed in the oral culture, how much of it was based on actual Gaelic poems, and how much of it was derived from Greek, Latin, and English sources.

The American humanities scholar Adam Potkay (b. 1961), in an attempt to explain the popularity of Macpherson's Ossian poetry, pointed to "their distinctly contemporary concerns." In contrast to Percy's ballads "or the genuine Ossianic fragments known to Irish scholars," Potkay saw the Ossian cycle as "in effect, a palimpsest of savage and enlightened knowledge and manners . . . a tale of two consciousness."[20] The "modern" eighteenth-century sensibilities in the heroes of the cycle had been noted previously. Hume, for example, in a letter dated September 1763, to Hugh Blair, one of the supporters of authenticity, wrote that

> I must own, for my part, that though I have had many particular reasons to believe these poems genuine, more than it is possible for any Englishman of letters to have, yet I am not entirely without my scruples on that head. You think that the internal proofs in favor of the poems are very convincing: so they are; but there are also internal reasons against them, particularly from the manners.[21]

Blair, for his part, attributed the "delicacy of sentiment" to bards who had been influenced in a civilizing direction by philosophical Druids. Henry Home, Lord Kames, argued that the perceived modern sentiment in the poems was evidence of their genuineness because a modern author would not have done something so anachronistic as to impose modern sentiments on a savage people:

---

19. Thomson, *Gaelic Sources*, 84.

20. Adam Potkay, "Virtue and Manners in Macpherson's Poems of Ossian," *PMLA* 107, no. 1 (January 1992): 121.

21. *The Letters of David Hume*, 2 vols., vol. 1: *1727–1765*, ed. J. Y. T. Greig (Oxford: Clarendon, 1932), 399.

Whether the work be late, or composed four centuries ago, a man of such talents inventing a historical fable, and laying the scene of action among savages in the hunter-state, would naturally frame a system of manners the best suited in his opinion to that state. What then could tempt him to adopt a system of manners so opposite to any notion he could frame of savage manners? The absurdity is so gross, that we are forced, however reluctantly, to believe, that these manners are not fictitious, but in reality the manners of this country, coloured perhaps, or a little heightened, according to the privilege of an epic poet.[22]

A 1991 collection of scholarly articles, none of which defended the poems' authenticity as having been discovered by Macpherson, does attempt to rehabilitate Macpherson's contribution. The editor of the collection, Howard Gaskill, summarized the main thrust of the articles included therein by raising a number of questions:

How many informed readers were aware of Ossian's importance for, say, Tennyson? . . . How many of the extent to which Macpherson's work really emerges as a product of the Scottish Enlightenment? Or of the questionable premises from which Samuel Johnson and his followers launched their attack on Macpherson? How many of those who ruthlessly consign the impudent forger to the dung-heap of literary history have any idea what an Ossianic ballad actually looks like? Are we not usually guilty of condemning Macpherson for being unfaithful to a tradition of which we ourselves are entirely ignorant? Lastly, how many of us have actually read Ossian?[23]

All the questions that Gaskill raises are worthwhile considering. Perhaps the most relevant for the present investigation and of authorship issues in general is the last question about actually reading the work. That question can be transformed into a principle of authorship attribution—namely, one should, first of all, read the text that is under scrutiny before making any pronouncements about it.[24]

In another essay in the collection, Donald E. Meek pointed to the "singular importance" of Macpherson in "deliberately dr[awing] attention to, and

---

22. Henry Home (Lord Kames), *Sketches of the History of Man*, 2 vols., vol. 1 (London: W. Strahan and T. Cadell; Edinburgh: W. Creech, 1774), 283–284.

23. Howard Gaskill, "Introduction," in *Ossian Revisited*, 2.

24. Richard Rosen used the word *bullcrit* to describe the tendency among the literati to discuss with great authority books they had not read: "Bullcrit is judgmentalism without judgment, familiarity without knowledge, received wisdom without emotional response, informedness without information." Richard Rosen, "Bullcrit: The Reading Disorder of the Literary Fast Lane," *New York*, February 6, 1989, 44.

creatively utiliz[ing], the rich Gaelic ballad tradition of the Highlands."[25] Furthermore, he defended Macpherson against the accusations of his being a fraud: "Macpherson, for all his faults (and he doubtless had some), was not a literary hijacker; he was operating, to a considerable extent, within a tradition which was well rooted in Scotland, and which, down to his own time, had preserved an intrinsic creativity and ability to vary its forms. Macpherson is likely to have been familiar with the conventions of that tradition, much more familiar than those who have sought to blacken his memory in recent years."[26] The last sentence is a bit gratuitous since it attacks as blackeners those who see Macpherson's reputation as already being in disrepute, and it is based on a supposition about what Macpherson may or may not have been familiar with.

One of the culminations of this movement in the scholarship to rehabilitate Macpherson and give "renewed consideration to the poems of Ossian" is the article of Paul F. Moulton published in 2010, in which he argued that the Ossian cycle's "historical weight alone makes casual dismissals unacceptable."[27] As one who initially casually dismissed the inclusion of Macpherson and the Ossian cycle in this book, I take Moulton's point.

The Takeaway

Our discussion of Macpherson's Ossian cycle in the light of authorship controversies has taken us in a different direction from almost all the other cases in this book. There are some similarities with the Secret Gospel controversy. Like Morton Smith, Macpherson was not claiming authorship of the work under scrutiny but claimed that he had discovered it. And like Smith, Macpherson provided a translation of the text into English. Neither Macpherson nor Smith was able to provide the manuscript which they claim to have translated. Yet Smith was able to provide a photograph of the handwritten text, which the skeptics accused him of forging. Macpherson's supporters produced a "transcription" of the text, but it took about a century before scholarly opin-

---

25. Donald E. Meek, "The Gaelic Ballads of Scotland: Creativity and Adaptation," in *Ossian Revisited*, 19.

26. Meek, "The Gaelic Ballads of Scotland," 19. In an endnote, Meek singles out Hugh Trevor-Roper's article "The Invention of Tradition: The Highland Tradition of Scotland," in *The Invention of Tradition*, ed. Eric Hobsbawn and Terence Ranger (Cambridge: Cambridge University Press, 1983), esp. 16–18.

27. Paul F. Moulton, "A Controversy Discarded and *Ossian* Revealed: An Argument for a Renewed Consideration of *The Poems of Ossian*," *College Music Symposium* 49/50 (2009/2010): 392.

ion fully accepted that Macpherson had back-translated from his own English into Gaelic to create the transcribed version. In contrast, scholarly opinion had tended to side with Smith that he did not forge the source text either through back-translation or through some other means. In contrast to the letter of Clement of Alexandria, which has not had that great an influence except in academic circles, the poems of Ossian had huge influence in the world of literature, folklore studies, and national feeling both in Scotland and elsewhere.

In regard to MacDonald's assertion that only someone who had witnessed the events being described in the poems could have written them, if extrapolated to a principle of authorship attribution needs to be explored. We encountered a similar argument in regard to the Italian plays of Shakespeare and will encounter it later in regard to whether the author of *The Quiet Don* directly participated in the World War I battles that are described in the novel. If that assertion is based merely on a feeling because of the vividness and apparent detail involved, then I can testify from personal experience that it does not work as a principle. While reading C. S. Forester's (1899–1966) novel *The African Queen* (1935), I was convinced (or convinced myself) that the author was describing the trip down the "Ulanga River" to Lake Tanganyika (called Lake Wittelsbach in the novel) based on his own personal experience. One problem with that feeling of mine was that although there is a Ulanga River in Tanzania, it flows in the opposite direction, not westward to Lake Tanganyika but eastward to the Indian Ocean. The other problem is that if the "Ulanga River" being described is actually another river (say, the Malagarasi, which does flow into Lake Tanganyika), we have no corroborating evidence that anything described in the novel coincides with that river. In other words, I have to credit the brilliance of the imaginative narrative description of Forester for giving me the feeling that he was describing something he had seen himself. In contrast, when specific details in a description can be corroborated and can most likely only be explained by the author's having seen what he or she is describing, then it can be raised to a level of principle of authorship attribution. In the case of the Ossian cycle, MacDonald's feeling may be strong that the author is describing events the author saw personally, but unless there is corroborating evidence that the author was actually there, we have to relegate that feeling to a status lower than a principle of authorship attribution and more into the category of authorial brilliance of imagination and vividness of description.

Questions concerning how much of the overall work Macpherson fabricated arose from the beginning. He published the work in three volumes over the course of five years (1760 and 1765) as he claimed a new Gaelic manuscript was found. The problem, as the Scottish-born American historian and linguist

George Fraser Black (1866–1948) pointed out, was that while there are ballads in Gaelic and even texts that have the same proper names and describe some similar events that appear in the epic cycle, Macpherson could not produce the manuscripts that he said he had translated from.[28] Other people at the time took the entire work at face value and used it for nationalist enhancement and for artistic, literary, and musical inspiration of the Sentimental and Romantic periods.

A key principle of bird identification is habitat—is the sighted bird in the habitat that is right for that kind of bird? Applying that principle *mutatis mutandis* to Macpherson, we can say he was in the right habitat culturally to have discovered a previously unknown Gaelic manuscript containing a cycle of poems attributed to the ancient bard Ossian. He was also in the right habitat to be influenced in his own creative efforts by Gaelic ballads and poetry. In the second half of the nineteenth century, a Scottish writer and folklorist, Alexander Carmichael (1832–1912) published six volumes of materials that he gathered in the Scottish highlands, including blessings, charms, hymns, folklore, historical stories, linguistic items, observations of the natural world, poems, proverbs, and songs.[29] Subsequently Carmichael was accused of having altered his sources and that the first three volumes should be considered as a literary representation of materials rather than scientifically accurate one. Yet *Carmina Gadelica (Gaelic Songs)*, as his collection was called, continues to be used as a cultural and historical source for the nineteenth-century Scottish Highlands.

Macpherson did something different from what Carmichael later did, but their methods are related. One major difference is that Macpherson claimed to be translating from actual manuscripts, which apparently never existed. If Macpherson had told the truth, perhaps the "casual dismissals" that Moulton mentioned would not have been so prevalent. His case would have been more similar to that of the English teenager Thomas Chatterton, who forged medieval poetry, wrote political diatribes, and even satirized Macpherson's Ossian cycle. But then the Ossian cycle also might not have had the widespread impact that it did. The prevailing assumption is that anything forged or intentionally deceptive is not worth further consideration. With Macpherson's Ossian cycle, we have a separate genre that is meant to deceive but has historical and literary significance anyway.

---

28. George F. Black, *Macpherson's Ossian and the Ossianic Controversy* (New York: New York Public Library, 1926), 8.

29. *Carmina Gadelica: Hymns and Incantations*, 6 vols., ed. and trans. Alexander Carmichael (Edinburgh: Constable, 1900–1971).

CHAPTER 9

Did Mikhail Sholokhov Write *The Quiet Don?*

> "There have been more discussions about *The Quiet Don* than about any other work in the history of Soviet literature."[1]
>
> —Geir Kjetsaa
>
> "The greatest of all twentieth-century epic novels."[2]
>
> —Roy Medvedev

In order to discuss the novel *The Quiet Don* and the controversy over its authorship, we need first to recount briefly some of the relevant events of World War I, the Russian Revolution of 1917, and the Russian Civil War (1918–1921). In August 1914, Tsar Nicholas II ordered the mobilization of the Russian army in response to Austria-Hungary's declaration of war on Serbia. The mobilization order provoked Kaiser Wilhelm II of Germany to declare war on Russia. The war lasted for over four years, until November 1918. During the third year of war, in March 1917, protests in Petrograd (the wartime name for St. Petersburg) led to the abdication of Nicholas and the formation of a provisional government by Duma members. In April, Vladimir Lenin returned from exile in Switzerland and declared the Bolshevik Party's intent to take power. Four months later, in September, the prime minister, Alexander Kerensky, ordered the arrest of the commander-in-chief of the Russian army, General Lavr G. Kornilov, for an attempted coup. This

---

1. Geir Kjetsaa, "The Charge of Plagiarism against Michail Šolochov," in Geir Kjetsaa, Sven Gustavsson, Bengt Beckman, and Steinar Gil, *The Authorship of* The Quiet Don (Oslo: Solum; Atlantic Highlands, NJ: Humanities Press, 1984), 14. Note: Although *Tikhii Don* is usually translated into English as "Quiet Flows the Don," I am following the practice of Kjetsaa and company of translating it as "The Quiet Don" because there is no word "Flows" in the Russian title.

2. Roy A. Medvedev, *Problems in the Literary Biography of Mikhail Sholokhov*, trans. A. D. P. Briggs (Cambridge: Cambridge University Press, 1977), 21.

event, called the Kornilov Affair, is a controversy of its own since Kornilov's defenders say he was acting under Kerensky's orders to move his troops (which included Don Cossack regiments) closer to Petrograd to support the government against a possible Bolshevik takeover. In November 1917, the Bolsheviks overthrew the provisional government and established themselves as the government of Russia. After this event, called the October Revolution because Russia was still operating under the Julian calendar (which was thirteen days behind the Gregorian calendar at that point), the Bolsheviks ended the war with Germany by the Treaty of Brest-Litovsk (March 1918). But they then found themselves besieged on all fronts by various enemies. The Bolsheviks held on to power in large part due to their organization, central location, internal lines of communication, ruthless use of terror, the strong leadership of Lenin and Leon Trotsky, and the lack of coordination of the Bolsheviks' enemies. In the east, former Tsarist troops (the Whites) commanded by Admiral Alexander V. Kolchak (1874–1920) attacked during the spring of 1919 but were defeated by the Bolsheviks (the Reds) by the summer. In the south, White forces under the command of General Anton I. Denikin (1872–1947) began to attack during the summer of 1919 but were defeated by the Bolsheviks by the fall. A major part of this campaign involved the defeat of the Don Cossack forces under General Vladimir Sidorin by the Red Army cavalry under General Semen Budennyi (1883–1973) in October 1919. These are the same Don Cossack forces being described in *The Quiet Don*.

In Ukraine, the Bolshevik forces were sometimes allied with and at other times battling anarchists under Nestor Makhno as well as the peasant-based militias called Greens. In the west during that time, beginning in February 1919, the newly formed government of Poland was at war with the Bolshevik regime and captured much of the territory that the Bolsheviks had given up to the Germans as a result of the Treaty of Brest-Litovsk. The Bolsheviks' defeat of Denikin's forces in the fall of 1919 allowed them to then focus on the Poles starting in the spring of 1920. Within a year, the Poles and Bolsheviks had signed a peace treaty, the Peace of Riga. In the north, British, French, American, and Canadian troops occupied Archangelsk in July 1918, ostensibly to keep munitions from falling into the hands of the Germans. After the German surrender in November 1918, the French and Canadian troops left, but the British and American troops remained until February 1920, apparently to lend their aid to any anti-Bolshevik efforts.

During this period of the Russian Civil War, the Bolsheviks instituted a policy of "war communism," a type of barter system on a national scale. Under war communism, peasants were to deliver their grain to the cities and receive farm equipment in return. When the peasants balked at this policy, the Bolsheviks sent out requisition squads to commandeer the grain. The requisition squads often took the seed grain as well as the food grain, which meant those peasants had no seed to plant. The result was a severe famine in the country-side from 1920 to 1921.

The period 1921 to 1928 saw the implementation of the New Economic Policy (NEP) by the Bolsheviks. The NEP allowed the return of market-based trade and manufacturing at the lower levels of the economy while the Communist government maintained control of the "commanding heights" of heavy industry and mining. In 1928, Joseph Stalin shifted Communist policy away from the market-based NEP toward forced industrialization of the economy and collectivization of the farms. Concomitantly the relative freedom of expression of the NEP period was replaced by increasingly more repression in general and of artistic expression in particular. It was on the cusp of this last change that the first volume of *The Quiet Don* began to appear in serial form.

Context of the Controversy

In 1965, the Nobel Committee awarded its literature prize to the Soviet writer Mikhail Sholokhov (1905–1984). His magnum opus was the four-volume *The Quiet Don (Tikhii Don)* (1928–1940). The novel as well as most of Sholokhov's other writings, such as a collection of short stories (1926) and the two-volume novel *Virgin Soil Upturned (Podniataia tselina)* (1932–1959), deal with the people of the Don River region.[3] Sholokhov himself was born near the village of Vëshenskaia, about halfway between Moscow and Rostov-on-Don. He received four years of formal education before he quit school in 1918 at the age of thirteen. The ages at which he did things are important to note because they turn up as a central consideration among those who question his authorship. Sholokhov became a member of a Bolshevik food requisition squad in the Don region at the age of fifteen. In 1920, he was allegedly captured by the Ukrainian anarchist forces of Nestor Makhno and by his own account expected to be killed. Makhno personally intervened to spare him.[4] In 1922, at the age of seventeen, when he was serving as tax inspector, he was arrested for

---

3. The Don River begins its journey 1,870 kilometers to the sea about 120 kilometers south of Moscow. It initially flows in a southeasterly direction looking as though it intends to join the Volga River, but then near Voronezh turns abruptly to the southwest to flow into the Sea of Azov.

4. Herman Ermolaev, *Mikhail Sholokhov and His Art* (Princeton, NJ: Princeton University Press, 1982), 7. Similarly in Pushkin's novel *The Captain's Daughter*, Petr Grinëv, who was in the tsarist army, was captured by the rebel forces of Emelian Pugachev, who personally intervened to spare him.

overstepping his power and sentenced by the revolutionary tribunal of the district to be shot. After two days, his sentence was rescinded, but he remained in custody. After his father secured his release by means that are still debated, he was sentenced to two years' probation.[5]

That same year, he began writing and moved to Moscow where he worked at various manual labor jobs while he learned to be a journalist. His first published work was a satirical piece titled "The Test," which he published in a newspaper when he was eighteen. He then returned to Vёshenskaia to devote himself entirely to writing. In January 1924, he married Mariia Gromoslavskaia, the daughter of Peter Iakovlevich Gromoslavskii, who was on the White Don Cossack side during the civil war. In 1926, at the age of twenty-one, Sholokhov published his first book, *Tales from the Don*, a collection of short stories about the Don region during World War I and the civil war. In October 1925, according to his own testimony, he first began to write the book that later became *The Quiet Don*, but it was a false start. His working title was *The Don Country (Donshchina)*, and it was to be about the role that the Cossacks played in the Bolshevik revolution. Sholokhov stated that he was intending to open the novel with a description of the Don Cossacks' participation in the Kornilov Affair of September 1917.[6] But he soon found, again according to his own account, that he had to explain in more detail for the reader the reasons the Don Cossacks would be opposed to the Bolsheviks. That required a year's research to gather information prior to resuming the novel toward the end of 1926. This time, he opened the novel before World War I and within a year had completed the first volume. *The Quiet Don* follows the activities of the Don Cossack officer Grigorii Melekhov through this volume and the three subsequent volumes for about ten years, from 1912 to 1922.

Into the Thicket

Sholokhov published the first three volumes of *The Quiet Don* between 1928 and 1932 in serial form in the literary journal *Oktiabr'*. He completed the fourth volume in 1940, in the meantime being published in serial form in the journal *Novyi mir*. Accusations of plagiarism began with publication of the first vol-

5. Ermolaev, *Mikhail Sholokhov and His Art*, 7–8. Sholokhov shares with Fedor Dostoevsky the experience of having been sentenced to be executed, but in both cases the sentence was rescinded, Dostoevsky's in a much more dramatic way.

6. *M. A. Sholokhov. Seminarii*, ed. F. A. Abramovic and V. V. Gura, 2nd ed. (Leningrad: Gosudarstvennoe uchebno-pedagogicheskoe izdatel'stvo ministerstva prosveshcheniia RSFSR, Leningradskoe otdelenie, 1962), 254–255.

ume in 1928. The initial claim was that the book manuscript had been in an officer's map case, which Sholokhov stole.[7] Other versions depicted the officer in question as a member of the (anti-Bolshevik, pro-tsarist) White Guard who had been killed in battle. The publishers of *Oktiabr'* started to receive calls from unknown individuals saying that the "old woman" (*starushka*) could arrive to restore rightful authorship to her son.[8]

By early 1929, the first twelve chapters of volume three were published in *Oktiabr'*. When the April issue of the journal came out without the continuation of the novel and without any explanation why the expected next chapter was not there, it provoked conspiracy theories at the time (and still does). Some forty-six years later, in 1975, the Soviet literary scholar Konstantin I. Priima (1912–1991) noted that the next installment of the novel was to deal with the Vëshenskaia uprising of 1919, an uprising of the Cossacks against the Bolsheviks. Priima asserted that supporters of Trotsky, who had been exiled from the Soviet Union in February 1929, delayed publication because they did not want the truth of the uprising to come out.[9] Trotsky was in charge of the Red Army in 1919 and for all intents and purposes was its founder. Yet, the notion that Trotskyites were conspiring was a standard Stalinist trope and was used to arrest and punish innocent people.

After the posthumous publication in 1929 of a 1917 letter by Leonid Andreev (1871–1919) in which he tells Sergei Gouloushëv that his "Quiet Don," has been rejected by the newspaper he (Andreev) edited, Sholokhov wrote a letter to Alexander Serafimovich about the anonymous accusations. He pointed out that the Gouloushëv article "From the Quiet Don," which was subsequently published in the journal *Narodnyi vestnik* (*People's News*), had nothing in common with his own work; it was travel notes. He thought the accusations against him were the result of "organized envy." Serafimovich, who had written the preface to Sholokhov's collection of short stories two years earlier, concurred. Intermittent waves of plagiarism accusations occurred in 1928–1929 and 1937–1938. At that point, Sholokhov received Stalin's explicit support, and that quieted the accusations for a time.

In 1974, an anonymous author known as D* (subsequently revealed to be Irina Medvedeva-Tomashevskaia, the author of several historical studies

---

7. A[leksandr] I[vanovich] Khvatov, *Khudozhestvennyi mir Sholokhova* (Moscow: Sovetskaia Rossia, 1970), 29.

8. I[saak] G[rigor'evich] Lezhnev, *Put' Sholokhova. Tvorcheskaia biografiia* (Moscow: Sovetskii pisatel', 1958), 214.

9. Konstantin Priima, "Gordost' sovetskoi i mirovoi literatury. Po stranitsam zarubezhnoi progrsivnoi pechati," *Inostrannaia literatura*, no. 5, 1975: 203; Priima, "Velikaia evropeia," *Vechernii Rostov*, May 24, 1978, 3.

devoted to literature and history of the early nineteenth century) wrote that she had done a comparison of selected passages from *The Quiet Don*, Sholokhov's other writings, and writings of Fedor Dmitrievich Kriukov (1870–1920) and concluded that Sholokhov had plagiarized an unpublished manuscript of Kriukov's.[10] D* claimed that in several sections of the novel between 70 and 90 percent of the text of the passages were taken from Kriukov. This three-way comparison became the method of much of the future attempts to corroborate or refute Sholokhov's authorship.

Alexander Solzhenitsyn (1918–2008), who won the Nobel Prize in Literature in 1970, five years after it was awarded to Sholokhov, published a summary of his doubts in 1974.[11] The main basis of his skepticism is that when *The Quiet Don* first began to appear in serial form in 1928, "the reading public found itself confronted with something unprecedented in the history of literature"—that is, that a "twenty-three-year-old beginner had created a work out of material which went far beyond his own experience of life and his level of education."[12] The novel's most impressive quality, according to Solzhenitsyn, was "its deep insight into the way of life and the psychology of the characters it portrayed." He remarked that the ostensible author was not a Cossack and was thus an "outsider"; nonetheless "the emotional force" of the book "was directed against the influence of 'outsiders'. . . ."[13] This message espoused in the novel, Solzhenitsyn noted, was never personally espoused by Sholokhov, who stayed "faithful to this very day to the mentality of those who requisitioned produce from the peasantry by force and served in 'special purpose' units." The scenes of the Great War and the Russian Civil War were "vividly" depicted "and with apparent first-hand knowledge" by someone who "had been far too young to take part." Solzhenitsyn referred to "the kind of literary power which can normally be attained only after many attempts by a practiced and gifted author—yet the finest sections were those which came first." Solzhenitsyn then discussed the speed of production: "The first volume was begun in 1926 and delivered complete to the editors in 1927; the splendid second volume was finished only a year after that; the third volume was ready within even less than a year of the second . . . only not being published immediately as a result of 'proletarian' censorship." He asked, "What are we to

---

10. D*, *Stremia "Tikhogo Dona" (Zagadka romana)* (Paris: YMCA-Press, 1974).

11. Aleksandr Solzhenitsyn, "Preface," in *Stremia "Tikhogo Dona"* by D* [I. N. Medvedeva-Tomashevskaia] (Paris: YMCA-Press, 1974). Solzhenitsyn's preface was reprinted and translated in the *Times Literary Supplement (TLS)* on October 4, 1974, as "Sholokhov and the Riddle of 'The Quiet Don.'" Reprinted in the *TLS*, May 26, 2016. It is the 1974 version that I cite here.

12. Solzhenitsyn, "Sholokhov and the Riddle," 1056.

13. Solzhenitsyn, "Sholokhov and the Riddle," 1056.

conclude" when we realize that "neither the level of achievement nor the rate of production has been confirmed or repeated in the subsequent forty-five years of his career!" Solzhenitsyn declared there to be "too many miracles!"[14] He pointed to the rumors that accompanied the serialized publication of volume one in 1928 that the book Sholokhov put his name to as author was written by "a Cossack officer who had been killed." Solzhenitsyn recalled that, when "only a boy of twelve" and living in Rostov-on-Don, Sholokhov's plagiarizing the novel "was talked of with such assurance among adults that it impressed itself clearly" on him. Solzhenitsyn saw Kriukov as occupying first place among the favorite Cossack writers by people of the region.

As rhetorically persuasive as Solzhenitsyn's argument may appear at first glance, a closer examination reveals a circumstantial subjectivity at its core. There may be something attractive about it all as a whole but nothing compelling about any part of it. One could, for example, argue that the novel does not go far beyond the experience of life or level of education of that particular twenty-three-year-old, not just an average twenty-three-year-old. An example of another twenty-three-year-old publishing a spectacular first novel is Carson McCullers (1917–1967) with *The Heart Is a Lonely Hunter* (1940), which was selected by the Modern Library as number seventeen on the list of the one hundred best English-language novels.[15] Just because someone is an outsider does not mean that person cannot empathize with or take the point of view of an insider, as McCullers did with the down-and-outers of the American South. In *In the First Circle*, Solzhenitsyn himself created a brilliant description of Stalin writing "On Marxism in Linguistics" from inside Stalin's mind. Any number of writers can write vividly of things they have not personally experienced. The novelist C. S. Forester wrote vivid scenes of naval battles during the Napoleonic Wars, yet he was born in 1899, fully 90 to 100 years after the battles he was describing. To be sure, the speed of production of the initial volumes of *The Quiet Don* is unusual but not unprecedented. After all, these were novels. The Russian historian S. M. Solov'ev (1820–1879) was noted for producing a scholarly volume a year of his *History of Russia from the Earliest Times* between 1851 and 1879, a total of twenty-nine volumes. Finally, it is not relevant what people in Rostov-on-Don thought about who the author was or the certainty with which they thought it. People elsewhere in Russia thought just as certainly that Sholokhov did write it.

Solzhenitsyn's assertion that "the Don writer Alexander Serafimovich" knew "the true story of this book" is probably accurate. Serafimovich

---

14. Solzhenitsyn, "Sholokhov and the Riddle," 1056.
15. Modern Library, *100 Best Novels*, http://www.modernlibrary.com/top-100/100-best-novels/.

(1863–1949) was an established writer and took on the role of Sholokhov's patron during this period. Besides writing the preface to Sholokhov's collection of short stories in 1926, he recommended to the editors of the journal *Oktiabr'* that they publish *The Quiet Don*. He always supported the view that Sholokhov wrote all four volumes. Solzhenitsyn was not content with that. In describing Serafimovich as a "Don writer" and "by then well on in years," Solzhenitsyn provided the underpinnings for his contention that Serafimovich was hiding the truth. As Solzhenitsyn saw it, Serafimovich knew that Sholokhov had come into possession of the manuscript of a White Guards officer. Being a proponent of writing about the Don region, Serafimovich wanted the "brilliant novel about the region" published but in the Bolshevik-controlled Soviet Union would have little hope of its being published under the name of Kriukov, who was an enemy of the Bolsheviks. Thus, according to Solzhenitsyn, in order to get the book published, Serafimovich went along with Sholokhov's idea of issuing it as his own work. Serafimovich then favorably reviewed the first chapters in the party newspaper *Pravda*.[16] Almost a year following that review, in 1929 he wrote a letter to the editors of *Pravda* with four other writers—Leopold L. Averbakh, (1903–1937), Alexander A. Fadeev (1901–1956), Vladimir M. Kirshon (1902–1938), and Vladimir P. Stavskii (1900–1943)—attacking those who questioned Sholokhov's authorship as "enemies of the proletarian dictatorship" for "spreading malicious slander."[17] Solzhenitsyn claimed that the appearance of this article "nipped in the bud" any chance that an investigation might have been started.

To be sure, the five cowriters of the letter addressed the question of stylistic comparisons: "Any reader even if they are not experienced in literature, who knows the works of Sholokhov published earlier, can easily notice the common stylistic features, the manner of writing, the approach to depicting people found in those of his early works and for the 'Quiet Don.'"[18] They also claimed that such gossip "acquires a systematic character, accompanying the nomination of almost every new talented proletarian writer." They saw this type of gossip as a sign that proletarian literature was having an impact because "the enemies are forced to fight it with the help of malicious and petty slander." They asked the "literary and Soviet public" to help in "identifying 'specific carriers of evil' in order to bring them to justice,"[19] but they did not indicate

16. A[lexander] Serafimovich, "Tikhii Don," *Pravda*, April 19, 1928, 8.

17. A. Serafimovich, L. Averbakh, V. Kirshon, A. Fadeev, and V. Stavskii, "Pis'mo v redaktsiiu," *Pravda*, March 29, 1929, 4.

18. Serafimovich, Averbakh, Kirshon, Fadeev, and Stavskii, "Pis'mo v redaktsiiu," 4.

19. Serafimovich, Averbakh, Kirshon, Fadeev, and Stavskii, "Pis'mo v redaktsiiu," 4.

whether any formal investigation had been made into the authorship question, only that it was self-evident that Sholokhov wrote *The Quiet Don.*

In contrast to Solzhenitsyn's passionate prosecution of the case against Sholokhov's authorship, and the five cowriters' just as passionate defense of Sholokhov's authorship, the historian Roy Medvedev (b. 1925) analyzed the pros and cons of the evidence and various arguments dispassionately. His arguments are worth considering in more depth because they shaped so many subsequent lines of inquiry. As Medvedev pointed out: "Both the critic 'D' and Solzhenitsyn consider Kryukov to be the main author of *The Quiet Don,* or, more precisely, the most probable author of the epic. Sholokhov they consider to be a co-author who spoiled the novel."[20] Medvedev concluded, nonetheless, that "even if we come to the firm conclusion that he had before him the unfinished novel of another author we must also remain convinced that the part played by Sholokhov in the creation of this epic novel was far more considerable than 'D' and Solzhenitsyn believe."[21]

Medvedev justified doing a profile of the author based on a close reading of the novel. We have become familiar with this profiling technique in the chapters on Rashid-al-Din, Shakespeare, and Kurbskii. Medvedev described "a commentator" who in a letter to him performed a thought experiment in this regard in relation to Leo Tolstoy: "Had *War and Peace* appeared anonymously we should have explained without too much trouble, even proved, that it could not have been written by Nekrasov or Turgenev or any other of the titans of literature at work in the sixties and seventies of the nineteenth century. The process of elimination would probably indicate a man who had taken part in a recent war, a landowner, and so on, in other words, the man from Yasnaya Polyana."[22] Medvedev asked whether we might "imagine for a while that this [novel *The Quiet Don*] . . . appeared anonymously and then, by analyzing the main distinctive features of its author, seek him out among the writers of the first quarter of the twentieth century?"[23] After discussing various objections that have been made to such a method, Medvedev concluded: "The method of determining the author through the various peculiarities of his text is a perfectly legitimate and scholarly one widely used in literary criticism as well as in a number of academic and non-academic institutions quite remote from literature."[24]

---

20. Medvedev, *Problems,* 20.
21. Medvedev, *Problems,* 143.
22. Medvedev, *Problems,* 21.
23. Medvedev, *Problems,* 21.
24. Medvedev, *Problems,* 22.

Medvedev came up with the following eight "distinguishing features" of the author of *The Quiet Don*:

1. "Love for the Cossacks, whose tragedy the author not only comprehended but interpreted as his own"; "a feeling of inseparable attachment to them 'in sickness and in health.'"
2. "Hostility toward 'outsiders.'"
3. "A celebratory attitude to Cossack farm work." An appreciation of "the Cossack peasant at work: joy and celebration" in contrast to "most Russian writers early in the twentieth century [who] depicted peasant work as hard labour, wearisome servitude, a cruel necessity of their existence."
4. "Encyclopedic knowledge of the Don Cossacks and their region."
5. "Craftsmanship of power and originality." Medvedev emphasized the "remarkable artistry and an exceptionally good literary education." Despite there being "quite a lot of badly written pages, even whole chapters, and there are certain freely drawn and unexpressive characters," Medvedev found it "hard to decide where the talent (or, we can say without exaggeration, genius) of the author shows most strongly: in the skilful plot-construction, in the psychological depth and 'visual' impact of the leading heroes and episodic characters alike, in the rich style of the dialogues, in the epic power of the battle scenes, in the love scenes with their obvious passion and yet propriety, in the pictures of nature, or in the unobtrusive humour." He went on to comment: "The portraits of most of the heroes of *The Quiet Don* are unmistakably drawn by the hand of a distinguished master. The author singles out skilfully the most characteristic and enduring features of his heroes and a number of small but appropriate details to complete the image."
6. "Personal involvement," which Medvedev noted as the author's "undoubted personal participation in the events described." In Medvedev's view, the "sensation never leaves the readers" that whoever wrote *The Quiet Don* "has seen the Don clear itself of ice many times over, has saddled a horse, built up stooks of hay, dug and sown the Don Cossack soil, that he knows every nook and cranny of a Cossack hut, merchant's house or landowner's country seat."
7. "The author's political sympathies," which Medvedev described as "sympathy for the political outlook of the Cossack farmer and the idea of Cossack self-government." The author, according to Medvedev, exhibits "disdain, even contempt, for the collapsed Russian monarchy

and for the Provisional Government . . . . decisively against what he considers the senseless imperialist war" opposed to "the ideals of the nobility, the generals and the officers controlling Russia." The author has "no sympathy for the Bolsheviks either." In Medvedev's view, the "author's strongest attachment is to the ideals of the Cossack farming-class and the Cossack commune known as the *obshchina*."

8. "The general philosophy of the author . . . is a humanism which embraces all mankind," which, as Medvedev pointed out, "some Marxist theoreticians . . . call 'abstract humanism.'" Medvedev contrasted this abstract humanism with proletarian humanism and class-conscious humanism, which *The Quiet Don*'s author considers to be "not humanism at all." The author has "an awareness of the contrast between the true lives of real people and any form of dogmatic ideology."[25]

Medvedev devoted the next two chapters of his book to a thought experiment. If *The Quiet Don* had appeared anonymously, would it have been possible to guess the author at that time? He focused specifically on two individuals: (1) consideration of Sholokhov as the possible author and (2) consideration of Kriukov as the possible author.

In regard to Sholokhov, Medvedev asserted that he would probably not have been one of the authors considered by contemporary literary critics. There was little in the content of the stories that Sholokhov had published two years earlier (except that they were about the Don region) that would lead one to connect their author with the author of *The Quiet Don*. Medvedev did not consider this difference to be a mark against Sholokhov's authorship because there are other cases of a well-received book being published by previously relatively unknown writer. Medvedev pointed especially to the novel *Far from Moscow* (1948), which was written by "a hitherto unknown far-eastern writer Vasilii Azhaev." Had it been published anonymously, "it is scarcely possible that any specialist literary critic could have identified him as the author, a modest employee on the journal *Far East* who had so far published nothing more than two quite unremarkable collections of stories."[26]

Medvedev then did a point-by-point comparison of the eight characteristics that he extracted from his profile analysis of the author of *The Quiet Don* and found no coincidence with Sholokhov's previously published work.

---

25. Medvedev, *Problems*, 24, 56, 27, 56, 29, 30, 31, 56, 31, 32, 37, 41, 56, 41, 43, 56, 43, 52, 56, respectively.

26. Medvedev, *Problems*, 23.

Medvedev cited the Soviet writer and literary critic Isaak Grigor'evich Lezhnev (1891–1955), for example, that in the short stories collected in *Tales of the Don*, one finds no Cossacks or peasants with mixed feelings toward the Bolsheviks as one finds in *The Quiet Don*.[27] Medvedev concluded this chapter with this observation: "All things considered, the personality of the twenty-three-year-old Mikhail Sholokhov is strikingly at variance with the author's 'personality-pattern'" as inferred from the novel itself.[28]

Medvedev then performed the same thought experiment in regard to Kriu-kov. One of the paradoxes he highlighted was the "very extensive . . . liter-ary output" of this writer (at least "200 . . . essays, stories and tales" between 1892 and 1919) that "would fill 9 or 10 volumes" and the almost complete ig-noring of him in Soviet literary scholarship of Russian writers, even in ency-clopedias and histories of Russian literature about that time.[29] He also noted that Kriukov's biography included a populist, anti-Bolshevik activism, a stint in the first Duma, and military service in World War I and the Russian Civil War. In going through the "distinguishing features" that he extracted from his analysis of *The Quiet Don*, Medvedev found evidence in Kriukov's writings that matched up with every one of them.

He noticed another point of similarity with Kriukov. According to Sholo-khov's account, after initially starting the novel, he decided that the reader needed more "prehistory" of the Don Cossacks. So he moved the beginning of the novel to before World War I. It had already been pointed out by Sol-zhenitsyn and others that the battle scenes in *The Quiet Don* are written quite vividly, but Sholokhov had not been in battle. The World War I scenes at the front that are described ("the first book . . . ends with a description of events at the front in August and September 1914 and the second book begins with a picture of the front in October 1916") remarkably coincide with the times Kriukov was at the front: "All the events occurring at the front and described in *The Quiet Don* Kryukov could have seen with his own eyes."[30] As a result, Medvedev concluded: "Thus, in our examination of the hypothesis that Kryu-kov could have been the author there can be no doubting his personal involvement."[31] Defenders of Sholokhov would probably respond that this is just a coincidence and that Sholokhov, although too young to take part in these battles, was in the vicinity.

27. Lezhnev, *Put' Sholokhova*, 87.
28. Medvedev, *Problems*, 77.
29. Medvedev, *Problems*, 79.
30. Medvedev, *Problems*, 91.
31. Medvedev, *Problems*, 91.

The Russian literary scholar Herman Ermolaev took issue with Medvedev's assertion that Kriukov could have been involved in the battles described in *The Quiet Don*. Ermolaev cited the "topical sketches" that Kriukov published in "sufficient number . . . to allow us to trace his whereabouts and activities with a great degree of certainty." As an example, Ermolaev focuses on Kriukov's trip with a mobile hospital unit to the Caucuses during the conflict with Turkey: "Kriukov arrived in the battle zone only in February 1915 and stayed there about two weeks" during "a lull in the fighting caused by a period of bad roads" as was the case when he also went to the Galician sector of the front in the winter of 1916." Furthermore, according to Ermolaev, "Kriukov made only occasional visits to the trenches."[32] None of this, of course, would have precluded either Kriukov or Sholokhov from talking with soldiers who were actually in the fighting and gathering information about the battles that way. Ermolaev seemed to be objecting mainly to Medvedev's inference that Kriukov was actually in the battles themselves.

Another point of similarity with Kriukov that Medvedev noted are that several of the scenes described in *The Quiet Don* bear a remarkable closeness to scenes described in Kriukov's writings.[33] For example, in Kriukov's *Autumn Furrows*, Uliana, the wife of a soldier, tells the Cossack Terpug that her father-in-law beats her:

"Just look here . . . ." In one swift movement she undid the buttons and dropped her shirt down over her left shoulder. Her naked young body gleamed milk-white in the moonlight and her small, supple breasts with their dark nipples shone before him . . . . He glanced quickly at two dark marks on her left side and looked away again immediately.[34]

In a similar way, in *The Quiet Don*, Aksinia tells Grigorii Melekhov that her husband beats her:

Wrathfully she tore open the collar of her jacket. On the rosy, girlishly swelling breasts were numerous cherry-blue bruises. "Don't you know? He beats me every day. He is sucking the blood out of me!" She buttoned her jacket with trembling fingers, and . . . glanced at Grigorii, who had turned away.[35]

In both cases, a married woman is being beaten and tells the Cossack man who is in love with her by briskly opening her top to reveal the bruises on her

32. Ermolaev, *Mikhail Sholokhov and His Art*, 279.
33. Medvedev, *Problems*, 102–108.
34. Biblioteka 'Znanie,' Book 27, p. 42, as translated and cited in Medvedev, *Problems*, 102, 214n49.
35. Mikhail Sholokhov, *And Quiet Flows the Don*, trans. Stephen Garry (New York: Knopf, 1934), 60.

breasts. In both cases, the Cossack man turns away. Medvedev went on to point out a number of parallel descriptions of natural scenes on the Don River during various times of the year. Medvedev commented on these parallels: "One can hardly fail to notice the similarities in style and mood of the author, or authors, of these extracts."[36] One could posit that Sholokhov had been inspired by those scenes in reading Kriukov to write something similar. It would, after all, be in the spirit of the T. S. Eliot dictum, "Good writers borrow; great writers steal." Yet the problem with the idea that Sholokhov was inspired by Kriukov's published work is that Sholokhov denied ever having read anything by Kriukov.

Nevertheless, Medvedev saw differences in the literary style between the landscapes: "Kryukov's landscapes are more cloying, more 'literary', less disciplined, less precise than those of *The Quiet Don*."[37] Medvedev then discussed the possibility that the differences could be explained by Kriukov's maturing as a writer and decided that to a certain extent it could but not entirely.[38]

The logic of Medvedev's analysis on the question of authorship of *The Quiet Don* led him to the conclusion that the concerns of those who question Sholokhov's experience, maturity as a writer, and political views are justified. On the other hand, the writing that appears in *The Quiet Don* is similar, although superior, to Kriukov's writings. To make sense of this apparent conundrum, Medvedev conjectured that Sholokhov, who was in command of requisition squads at the time of Kriukov's death, managed to obtain the metal box that contained the manuscripts Kriukov was working on. Furthermore, he could have done so through his father-in-law, the Don Cossack and minor literary figure Peter Gromoslavskii, who worked under Kriukov in 1918–1919 on the newspaper *Donskie vedomosti* (the *Don Gazette*). When Kriukov died, according to Medvedev's sources, Gromoslavskii helped bury him and thus might have had access to any manuscripts that Kriukov was working on. Those manuscripts, again according to Medvedev's speculation, were then edited and refined to become the novel that we know as *The Quiet Don*.[39] In 2011, Medvedev revisited the issue and came to a different conclusion concerning Sholokhov's role in writing the novel: "If it is possible to talk about co-authorship in creating *The Quiet Don*, then undoubtedly the co-author of Mikhail Sholokhov was the popular memory, stories and testimonies of people who went through the most difficult trials of their time and told the young writer every-

---

36. Medvedev, *Problems*, 108.
37. Medvedev, *Problems*, 108.
38. Medvedev, *Problems*, 109.
39. Medvedev, *Problems*, 59–60.

thing that had happened."[40] It was not that he dismissed completely his previous analysis of stylistic and profile characteristics of the author; he just gave that analysis less weight.

Discovery of Manuscripts

The claim of a number of skeptics that Sholokhov found the box containing the manuscript of Kriukov's unpublished novel (or it fell into his hands as the leader of a requisition squad), which then was destroyed, was often supplemented with the related question of where the drafts of *The Quiet Don* were that Sholokhov worked on before publication. Solzhenitsyn, for one, found the absence odd. He focused on the official explanation that Sholokhov's archive was in lost in World War II: "In 1942, when the battlefront came close to the village of Vëshenskaia; Sholokhov, as the most important man in the area, could have obtained transport even before the district Party committee did, and evacuated his precious archives. But through some strange indifference, this was not done. And the whole of his archives, we are now told, were lost in the bombardment."[41] In 1984, the journalist Lev Kolodnyi (b. 1932), after a search that he later described, found the presumed lost working drafts of volumes one and two of *The Quiet Don* in Moscow.[42] It is now generally believed that these are the manuscripts examined by the five writers of the letter defending Sholokhov in 1929. An analysis of the handwriting by the Russian Academy of Sciences in 1999 corroborated that one of the hands was Sholokhov's (the others being his wife and sisters who transcribed parts of the text) and that the manuscripts authentically dated to the 1920s. Skeptics remained doubtful. They still dispute whether these were truly working drafts or are later copies made to look like manuscripts.

Computer-Assisted Stylistic Analysis

The first substantial computer-assisted stylistic analysis of *The Quiet Don* authorship question was performed by the Norwegian team of Geir Kjetsaa (1937–2008), Sven Gustavsson, Bengt Beckman, and Steinar Gil. Each one contributed an essay to the book. Kjetsaa questioned Medvedev's assertion that if

---

40. Roy Medvedev, *"Tikhii Don": zagadki i otkrytiia velikogo romana* (Moscow: AIRO-XXI, 2011), 205.

41. Solzhenitsyn, "Sholokhov and the Riddle," 1056.

42. Lev Kolodnyi, *Kto napisal "Tikhii Don": khronika odnogo poiska* (Moscow: Golos, 1995); Kolodnyi, *Kak ia nashel "Tikhii Don": khronika poiska analiz teksta* (Moscow: Golos, 2000).

The Quiet Don had been published anonymously, Kriukov would have been the choice of having been the likely author. Kjetsaa cited the evaluations of others of Kriukov's work, including "even the most positive articles on Krjukov written by his friends and admirers," do not substantiate Medvedev's assertion.[43] Yet the particular evaluations he cited do not support such a definitive assessment. A. G. Gornfel'd described Kriukov as an engaging "second rank" writer,[44] which is true—he was not of the same rank as Chekhov, Gorkii, or Belyi—without necessarily being a significant knock on the quality of his writing. V. F. Botsianovskii described him as a writer of "small miniatures on themes of everyday life in the style of Chekhov."[45] Being compared with Chekhov does not exclude one from consideration of having authored *The Quiet Don*. M. Rudin described Kriukov as producing "talented sketches from Cossack life."[46] Since *The Quiet Don* is full of such "talented sketches" of the Cossacks' daily life, the assessment hardly seems preclusionary. To his credit, Kjetsaa does cite the assessment of Kriukov in the *Festschrift* volume devoted to his twenty-fifth year as a writer: "the first and most powerful national Don writer,"[47] which would seem to put him on the inside track of possible candidates. Kjetsaa found that he had to explain away that assessment by assigning a political motive to it: "Of course, the evaluations in this book, published in November 1918 [i.e., at the height of the Russian Civil War], are very much coloured by enthusiasm for Kriukov and his fight against the Bolsheviks."[48] One should not forget, however, that *The Quiet Don* has a sympathetic treatment of those Cossacks who are fighting against the Bolsheviks, which, as Medvedev pointed out, places Kriukov's views in alignment with the profile that he drew from the novel.

But it is not Kjetsaa's qualitative arguments against Kriukov's authorship that we are concerned with here—since he makes clear throughout his essay that he favors Sholokhov as the author—but with his computer-assisted stylistic assessment. As we saw with the stylistic analysis of Shakespeare's works, even the most extensive and detailed computer analysis can be faulty if the premises upon which the analysis is conducted are faulty. Unlike the team that did the computer assessment of the Shakespearean canon with writers other than the reputed author, Kjetsaa compared (1) the writing style of Kriukov with (2) that of Sholokhov in his writings other than *The Quiet Don* and both of them with

---

43. Kjetsaa, "The Charge of Plagiarism," 36.

44. A[rkadii] G[eorgievich] Gornfel'd, "Pamiati F. D. Kriukova," *Vestnik literatury* 6, no. 18 (1920): 15.

45. Vl. Botsianovskii, "Iz vospominanii o F. D. Kriukove," *Vestnik literatury* 9, no. 21 (1920): 15.

46. M. Rudin in *Rul'*, April 29 (16), 1921, as translated and cited in Kjetsaa, "The Charge of Plagiarism," 36.

47. *Rodimyi krai. Sbornik, posviashchenyi dvadtstipiatiletiiu literaurnoi deiatel'nosti F. D. Kriukova (1893–1918 g.g.)* (Ust'-Medveditskaia: Sever Dona, 1918), 3.

48. Kjetsaa, "The Charge of Plagiarism," 36, n. 5.

(3) the style of *The Quiet Don* itself. Kjetsaa ran two pilot studies with the aim of "discovering some of the most advantageous parameters for 'measuring' the language and style."[49] In the pilot studies, he chose one thousand sentences from each of the above three categories (two works of Kriukov, two of Sholokhov, and one each from the first two volumes of *The Quiet Don*). To obviate his own bias in choice of sentences in each text, he stated that the

> sentences from each text were taken from pages selected with the aid of a table of random numbers, after a stratification had been carried out that would ensure equal possibilities of selecting pages in the first and second half of the works involved. To reduce as much as possible any context bias in the sentences chosen for analysis, paragraphs containing direct speech, or a report of some character's thought, or any questions, were excluded. In other words, the investigation was concentrated exclusively on each author's own speech.[50]

He tested for the average sentence length, which turned out to favor Sholokhov (Kriukov = 13.9 words per sentence; Sholokhov = 12.9; *The Quiet Don* = 12.4). But Kjetsaa acknowledged that "the difference is no greater than can be found between various texts written by one and the same author and . . . can hardly be used as an argument in our analysis." He was able to reach a different conclusion based on percentage of sentences within word ranges. In the 6–10 word range, the results were Kriukov 26.1 percent, Sholokhov 33.2 percent, *The Quiet Don* 32.8 percent. To get another perspective, he applied the Kolmogorov-Smirnov test "to measure the difference between the accumulated relative frequencies of the sentence length intervals."[51] Kolmogorov-Smirnov is intended to test whether the difference in two data sets is significant. It produces a coefficient (λ) of significance, which allowed Kjetsaa to conclude: "Judging from the parameter of sentence length distribution, we may exclude Krjukov as a candidate for the authorship of *The Quiet Don*, while we are not entitled to exclude Šolochov from being considered the author of the novel."[52] Kjetsaa also found the average word length, correlation of word length with sentence length, and "vocabulary profile" (words used *n* times) in the Sholokhov sample to be closer to those of *The Quiet Don* than the Kriukov sample was.

Kjetsaa also analyzed parts-of-speech distribution, which is based on a smaller sample than the sentence-length analysis, namely ten samples of five

49. Kjetsaa, "The Charge of Plagiarism," 44.
50. Kjetsaa, "The Charge of Plagiarism," 45.
51. Kjetsaa, "The Charge of Plagiarism," 66.
52. Kjetsaa, "The Charge of Plagiarism," 66.

hundred words from each of the six texts (totaling thirty thousand words). In the average use of the seven parts of speech, only adjectives favor Kriukov; the other six favor Sholokhov. He went on to analyze word distributions at the beginnings and ends of sentences and found that "Krjukov has a more varied method of concluding his sentences than Šolochov and the author of *The Quiet Don*" although the beginnings of sentences "showed a fairly equal number of combinations" among the three populations.[53] Finally, Kjetsaa applied Student's t-test to obtain confidence intervals for each of the text samples and once again found the Sholokhov samples to be closer to *The Quiet Don* samples in terms of lower repetitiveness of vocabulary than the Kriukov samples.[54]

Subsequent statistical studies have generally upheld Kjetsaa's conclusions. In 2007, the Norwegian statistician Nils Lid Hjort (b. 1953) used the data that Kjetsaa had reported on sentence lengths and applied a few more statistical tests such as Poisson distribution to them. He "conclude[d] that the sentence length data speak very strongly in Sholokhov's favour."[55]

The Russian statistician Mikhail Iur'evich Mikheev (b. 1957) did a key word in context comparison of samples from Kriukov and Sholokhov. Mikheev concluded that *The Quiet Don* is something Kriukov wrote that was reworked extensively by Sholokhov,[56] which supports Medvedev's conjecture. Mikheev claimed he was using a larger sample than Kjetsaa did, but he does not seem to have specified the sample size.

In 2016, the Russian physicist Sadin Nazirovich Boziev (b. 1960) again subjected to statistical analysis excerpts from the writings of Kriukov, *The Don Tales* of Sholokhov, and *The Quiet Don* and concluded that the style of *The Don Tales* is identical with that of *The Quiet Don*.[57]

The Controversy Continues

Despite the statistical analyses favoring Sholokhov as the author of *The Quiet Don*, accusations of his having plagiarized from Kriukov or other authors continue to be made, especially in Russia. It has also resulted in extensive re-

53. Kjetsaa, "The Charge of Plagiarism," 52.

54. Kjetsaa, "The Charge of Plagiarism," 97.

55. Nils Lid Hjort, "And Quiet Does Not Flow the Don: Statistical Analysis of a Quarrel between Nobel Laureates," https://cas.oslo.no/getfile.php/138668-1461568659/CAS_publications/Seminar_booklets/PDF/Consilience_LidHjort.pdf (2007), 139.

56. Mikhail Iur'evich Mikheev, "Sholokhov ili vse-taki—Kriukov? Neformal'nye protsedury pro ustanovlenie avtorstva 'Tikhogo Dona,'" in *Komp'iuternaia lingvistika i intellektual'nye tekhnologii. Po materialam ezhegodnoi Mezhdunarodnoi konferentsii "Dialog"* no. 11 (2012): 431–442.

57. Sadin Nazirovich Boziev, *Prevratnosti tekstov proizvedenii M. A. Sholokhov i F. D. Kriukova* (Moscow: Vash format, 2016).

search into the history of Russian literature in the twentieth century. A few examples follow.

According to the historian Andrei V. Venkov (b. 1954) in 2000 and again in 2010, the novel was the result of a collective and cumulative effort. The argument in the book is only implicit, in that the reader has to construct what the implications are for Sholokhov's authorship. Venkov referred to the "editorial portfolio" (*redaktorskaia portfel'*).[58] He believes Sholokhov used what he calls "Tatar materials" (*Tatarevskie materialy*) including the papers of Kriukov, of the writer and journalist Roman P. Kumov (1888–1919), and of others. Venkov summed up his main conclusions this way:

> *The Quiet Don* contains a huge amount of historical information. To gather it in such a volume required time and great professional effort [*usiliia*]. . . . The battle, historical, and even quotidian and love [*bytovye i liubovnye*] scenes of the novel were written on the basis of journal and newspaper articles and archival documents of the beginning of the twentieth century. The novel began with the events of the turn of the twentieth century. The novel is saturated with colors, smells, sounds many times [*na poriadok*] more than any contemporary romance of the same size. Is it possible for one person to attract so many colors and create such a number of unique images? . . . A whole series of talented writers took part in the creation of the novel. The names of some of them are still not known to the mass reader.

In 2001, A. G. Makarov and S. E. Makarova claimed that their book "for the first time," provided "a detailed justification for the fact that at the base of *The Quiet Don* was the uncompleted work of . . . Kriukov."[59] This claim, however, overstates the significance of the parallels that they discovered and discuss at length. At best they demonstrated that Sholokhov's declarations of his never having read anything by Kriukov are disingenuous.

In 2005, Feliks Kuznetsov (1931–2016), who was a Russian literary critic and a corresponding member of the Russian Academy of Sciences, wrote a defense of Sholokhov's authorship of *The Quiet Don*.[60] He referred to the "tragic fate" of the novel in being subject to decades of false accusations, and he called Sholokhov "a genius of Russian literature." Kuznetsov discussed the history

---

58. A[ndrei] V[ladimovich] Venkov, *"Tikhii Don. Istochnikovaia baza i problema avtorstva* (Rostov-on-Don: Terra, 2000); rev. ed. (Moscow: AIRO – XXI, 2010). The size of the book increased by 52 percent in ten years, from 584 to 874 pages.

59. A. G. Makarov and S. E. Makarova, *Tsvetok-Tatarnik. V poiskakh avtora "Tikhogo Dona" ot M. Sholokhova k F. Kriukovu* (Moscow: AIRO – XX, 2001).

60. Feliks Kuznetsov, *"Tikhii Don": Sud'ba i Pravda velikogo romana* (Moscow: IMLI RAN, 2005).

of the search for drafts of the novel, which when found were purchased by the Russian Academy of Sciences with the assistance of Vladimir Putin. He concluded that the manuscripts are an indisputable testimony to Sholokhov's authorship of the entire novel. He also investigated the prototype of the heroes of *The Quiet Don*—the Cossacks of the settlement of Vëshenskaia and nearby farms. He found that Kharlampii Ermakov was the prototype for Grigorii Melekhov and that Sholokhov knew the army commander of the Vëshenskaia rebels Pavel Kudinov, who in emigration published articles about the rebellion that confirm the veracity of some incidents depicted in volume three of *The Quiet Don*. Such research into historical evidence that would not otherwise be investigated is a characteristic of genuine authorship controversies.

Other authors, besides Sholokhov and Kriukov, have been proposed as the author, which usually involve some sort of conspiracy. For example, Zeev Bar-Sella, who is a linguist of Russian, Israeli literary scholar, and journalist, speculatively argued in favor of Veniamin Krasnushkin (who wrote under the pseudonym Viktor Sevskii) as being the author.[61] According to Bar-Sella, Krasnushkin owned the manuscript of *The Don Tales* but was part of a conspiracy on the part of the Soviet secret police to enlist a number of Soviet writers in a project to win the Nobel Prize for the Soviet Union. Other books have argued in favor of Serafimovich as the author.[62] In a parallel with the Christopher Marlowe theory of Shakespearean authorship, Aleksei Golovnin argued that the poet Nikolai Gumilev was not executed in St. Petersburg in 1921 but fled to the Don region, became friends with Sholokhov and allowed him to publish his (Gumilev's) works under his own name.[63]

The Takeaway

Accusing a writer of plagiarism (just as accusing someone of forgery) is a serious matter. If the accusations are untrue, then they are also insulting to the writer, whose reputation cannot totally be recovered because the doubt lingers. Ad hominem attacks, such as the one Serafimovich et al. used accusing the skeptics of being enemies of the dominant political ideology in the country, was a type of attack that was all too common in the Soviet Union and equally onerous. Although one can understand the motive behind those who were convinced of Sholokhov's authorship, their lashing out at the accusers

---

61. Zeev Bar-Sella, *Literaturnyi kotlovan. Proekt "Pisatel Sholokhov"* (Moscow: RGGU, 2005).

62. Sergei Koriagin, *"Tikhii Don". Chernye piatna. Kak urodovali istoriiu kazachestva* (Moscow: Iaza, Eksmo, 2006).

63. Aleksei Golovnin, *Za chertoi dvatsat' pervogo* (Russia: Topaz, 1993).

carries (or should carry) no weight in an analytical assessment of the issue of authorship. In defending an author (Sholokhov) who supposedly wrote sympathetically about those who fought against the Bolsheviks, one would think they could be a bit more tolerant of those who doubted Sholokhov's authorship or at least not engage in shaming them publicly. To be sure, some doubters of Sholokhov's authorship of *The Quiet Don* have expressed dismay at Sholokhov's actions while he was a member of the Writer's Union (RAPP) putting other writers in political danger. Yet there is also evidence that he intervened with Stalin directly to protect writers and his home village of Vëshenskaia. In 1966, at the Twenty-Third Party Congress, Sholokhov criticized the dissident writers Iulii Daniel' and Andrei Siniavskii. Once again accusations of his having plagiarized *The Quiet Don* arose in great part as a result. Normatively speaking, in analyzing authorship claims, evidence and arguments are what need to be evaluated, not the person making the claims. It is all too easy to fall into the logical fallacy of questioning the motives of those who disagree with us. Even those with suspect motives can come up with a good argument properly based on evidence.

The fundamental problem that the skeptics focus on is the improbability of a twenty-three-year-old writer, who had no experience with much of what he describes and who showed no great promise to speak of before, writing a monumental classic of world literature. To be sure, Sholokhov was thirty-four when the fourth volume was completed, but the quality of the writing in the first two volumes is generally acknowledged to be better. In addition, the skeptics find it difficult to accept that a leader of a requisition squad for the Bolsheviks during the civil war could demonstrate much if any empathy for the White Cossacks who were fighting them. Yet, the novel treats the Cossack opponents of the Bolsheviks sympathetically. Rumors and then evidence that another writer, Fedor Kriukov, was working on a similar book at the time of his death in 1920 and that the manuscript of that book was in a box with other notes and manuscripts of his led to the speculation that the requisition squad leader Sholokhov came into possession of that box and used the contents to write *The Quiet Don*. Medvedev and others pointed out the similarity in scenes and wording between the novel and Kriukov's other writings.

The accusations of plagiarism began in 1929 before the serialization of the first volume ended. Rather than duck the accusations, Sholokhov provided his notes and drafts to Soviet authorities to show that the work was indeed his. Official Soviet declarations of authenticity made over the decades have been dismissed by the skeptics as disingenuous in great part because the Soviet government lacked any credibility among large segments of the population. Finally, computer-assisted statistical analyses of extensive and randomly chosen excerpts from *The Quiet Don* and two other works by Sholokhov and Kriukov point in the direction of Sholokhov as the author. Yet those same computer analyses do not definitively exclude Kriukov from having been the author. It is just that Sholokhov's style was closer to that of the novel than was Kriukov's. In an attempt to resolve the antithetical directions of the evidence, a number of skeptics have taken up Medvedev's conclusion that Sholokhov did indeed use the manuscript of Kriukov, but that he edited and altered it extensively. He also added material to it, since Kriukov died in 1920 but the novel describes events until 1922.

There are points of similarity of this controversy with the Shakespeare authorship controversy. Like the skeptics' claim that Sholokhov's background, education, and experiences make it improbable that he could have been the author of *The Quiet Don*, so too the Shakespearean skeptics claim that William of Stratford's background, education, and experiences make it improbable that he could have been the author of the Shakespearean canon. Yet, in contrast to the works of Shakespeare, we do have manuscript drafts and notes as well as other writings by Sholokhov. As with the Shakespeare authorship controversy, computer-assisted statistical analyses of style have been done. And in both cases the people doing the analyses concluded in favor of the traditional author. The difference is that in the case of *The Quiet Don* they analyzed other works by the traditional author, which was not the case in relation to the Shakespeare canon. Instead, the statistical analyses of the Shakespeare canon, contrary to what the investigators conclude, point in the direction of the Earl of Oxford, Edward de Vere. The statistical analyses of the most likely authors of *The Quiet Don* point consistently in the direction of Sholokhov.

Medvedev constructed a profile of the author of *The Quiet Don* that seems to correspond much closer to the historical persona of Kriukov than it does to Sholokhov. That raises the question, however, of what kind of person was Sholokhov. I close this section then with the words of Sholokhov's recent biographer Brian Boeck. He presents a nuanced biography of a complex individual, both great writer and plagiarist, both cunning courtier and speaker of truth to power, "a savvy survivor who drank his conscience into submission."[64] At the heart of the mystery of who wrote *The Quiet Don* is the mystery of who Mikhail Sholokhov was.

---

64. Brian J. Boeck, *Stalin's Scribe: Literature, Ambition, Survival: The Life of Mikhail Sholokhov* (London: Pegasus, 2019).

Afterword
Lessons Learned

                In the introduction, I asked you, the reader, to keep an open mind insofar as possible about the controversies within. Likewise, I tried to keep an open mind in researching and writing this book. I think that it is important to emphasize that if one already has a fairly strong opinion about the disputed authorship of a particular text, then one needs to be doubly careful about dismissing outright evidence and arguments that differ from one's own opinion and about drawing parallels with other authorship controversies that seem to favor one's own position. It is all too easy to accept the evidence and similarities if they support one's preconceived notions and concomitantly to overlook or dismiss evidence and dissimilarities if they do not. I tried to avoid taking that easy way myself in the research for this book but found myself time and again beginning to fall into that trap. Research done to prove a point can be valuable, but it can also be inherently flawed by that goal. Research done to find the truth of the matter tends to avoid that flaw. "Let the chips fall where they may" should ideally be the attitude of the researcher, while the human tendency is to try to steer the evidence and the narrative into preconceived channels. It is, after all, how we create our own life narrative (i.e., the story of our lives). Yet, "the truth of the matter" is not such a simple phrase to define. Different people often have different opinions as to what that truth is. I define truth of the matter in research terms as fulfilling three criteria: (1) accurate correspondence to all the relevant evidence,

(2) logical arguments based on that evidence, and (3) conceptual elegance of interpretation—the simplest explanation that conforms to the other two criteria.[1] In other words, it is an analytical definition. Nonetheless, there is still plenty of wiggle room for honest and genuine disagreement over what constitutes fulfillment of each of these criteria.

Perhaps the two most surprising results of my research were the extent to which false (or perhaps one should say, not genuine) attribution without intent to deceive has been made or claimed. I was aware here and there of such a practice previously. Keenan made the claim for those who he thought authored the Kurbskii-Groznyi apocrypha (not forgeries) in the seventeenth century. Yet the extent of the phenomenon either actual or proposed is much larger than I thought. I would now place it as a third category of attribution: (1) genuine attribution, (2) false attribution with intent to deceive, and (3) false attribution without intent to deceive. All three categories are in play when approaching the question of attribution.

In chapter 2, I quoted Alice Cheang as stating: *"Tuoyan*—attribution to a well-known figure—is a common practice in early Chinese texts." The word *tuoyan* means "words ascribed." It was (and has become again) a fairly common practice to add fictional elements to an otherwise journalistic piece. Doing so in modern China has been called "doculiterary." We find such a practice in George Orwell's *Down and Out in Paris and London,* where Orwell defended his book as "mostly true." In that sense, Orwell might find himself agreeing with the quotation that is attributed to Hunter S. Thompson (1937–2005): "Fiction is a bridge to the truth that the mechanics of journalism can't reach."[2] We also find dialogue added to biblical stories and to medieval texts, such as chronicles. One can debate whether that was intended by the author to deceive or to make clearer the truth as the biblical writer or chronicler saw it.

We also find a similar but significantly different practice in historical fiction and in feature films that claim "based on a true story." Adding that phrase allows the filmmakers to use the names of actual people, to have the actors speak words that there is no evidence the historical person spoke, and to add fictional elements to a greater or lesser degree. But then the filmgoer is left to wonder how much corresponds to the historical record and how much is the imaginings of the filmmakers and script writers. It can and does unintentionally de-

---

1. I discuss these criteria more fully in my "Three Criteria of Historical Study," https://donostrowski2.bitbucket.io/RussianCulture/history.pdf.

2. Quoted in Dick Polman, "A New Book Describes Hunter S. Thompson's Prescience," *The Atlantic,* December 28, 2018.

ceive people because often the filmmakers have little or no commitment to staying within the boundaries of the historical record.[3]

We encounter such a practice of attributing entire works that an author writes to an earlier historical figure without intent to deceive in non-Chinese texts as well. In 1992, the Harvard Byzantino-Slavist Ihor Ševčenko wrote a piece in the form of a response by the tenth-century emperor Constantine VII Porphyrogenitus (905–959) to criticism of him by modern-day historians.[4] In 2017, the Byzantinist Leonora Neville wrote a similar piece in the form of a response by the eleventh-century Byzantine princess and historian Anna Komnene to criticism of her by modern-day historians. Neville refers to this technique by the Greek term *ethopoiia* (character representation), which was common in Byzantium itself.[5]

Such a practice—ascribing words to a historical figure without the intent to deceive—occurs in popular culture as well, such as a recent series of quotations ascribed to Abraham Lincoln about the Internet: "The problem with quotes on the Internet is that no one can confirm their authenticity" or "If it is on the Internet, then it must be true; you can't question it" or, my favorite, "Don't believe everything you read on the Internet just because there's a picture with a quote next to it," accompanied by a picture of Abraham Lincoln. In the Soviet Union, a plethora of jokes involve statements, often of an earthy nature, attributed to the Russian Civil War hero Vasilii Ivanovich Chapaev (1887–1919). But there was no intent to deceive anyone that Chapaev had actually said those things. Such joke quotations extend to Confucius: "Confucius say, Man who stands on hill is not on level." There is even a website with the top 100 humorous quotations attributed to "Confucius say." If anyone thinks that Lincoln or Chapaev or Confucius actually said these things, then they are deceiving themselves; there is no forgery.

In chapter 4, I discussed how Deborah Fraioli claimed the letters of Abelard and Heloise are a satire written by someone else to mock them. Likewise, in chapter 5, we saw Alexander Morton posit that the collection of letters attributed to Rashid al-Din were written by someone who intended them to be read as fiction (no intent to deceive). If so, then the respective authors would

---

3. The Alan Alda film *Sweet Liberty* (Universal Pictures, 1986) makes this case very well.

4. Ihor Ševčenko, "Re-reading Constantine Porphyrogenitus," in *Byzantine Diplomacy: Papers of the Twenty-fourth Spring Symposium of Byzantine Studies, Cambridge, March 1990*, ed. Jonathan Shepard and Simon Franklin (Aldershot, UK: Variorum; Brookfield, VT: Ashgate, 1992), 167–195.

5. Leonore Neville, "Anna Komnene: Princess, Historian, and Conspirator?" in *Portraits of Medieval Eastern Europe, 900–1400*, ed. Donald Ostrowski and Christian Raffensberger (London: Routledge, 2018), 82.

have been precursors of satirist Andy Borowitz (b. 1958). But unlike Borowitz, he or she did not head the piece with the words "Not the news."

Another example in our cases may be writing letters in the seventeenth
century under the name of two sixteenth-century figures—Tsar Ivan IV and
Andrei Kurbskii. If Keenan is right, then the authors of the correspondence
did not intend to deceive the reader (i.e., create forgeries), but later readers
were unintentionally deceiving themselves. That would place the Kurbskii-
Groznyi correspondence in the realm of apocrypha, as Keenan asserted, or in
that of *tuoyan*, in the Chinese sense. It would also mean that the correspondence falls into Utechin's third category of sources: "apparently deceptive, that
is, those that are not what they appear to be and were not intended to be taken
as such." It is a common practice in fictional writing to frame the narrative
with an attribution to a person, usually fictional but not always. The most notable example might be *Candide, or Optimism*, at the beginning of which are
the words: "Translated from the German of Doctor Ralph with the additions
which were found in the Doctor's pocket when he died at Minden in the Year
of Our Lord 1759." These words are left off a number of English-language
translations, but they are important as far as authorship studies are concerned,
not because they bring into doubt the authorship of *Candide*, which they don't.
They are important because in the case of *Candide* we know who the author
is, and it is not Doctor Ralph. The reader is in on the joke. But if we did not
know who the real author was, would these words at the beginning of the
novel be thought sufficient to establish that a certain Doctor Ralph was the
author? Even if we determined there was no Doctor Ralph and the book was
not a translation from the German, would we be able to establish Voltaire's
authorship? In the case of *Candide*, probably yes. But are there other works
where someone is identified as the author who is not the author? The answer
again is probably yes. And that brings us back to epistemology. How do we
know who the real author of a written work, musical composition, or paint-
ing is? We have no systematic methodological answer to that.

Another surprise to me was the extent to which profiling (that is, trying to
determine the characteristics of an author from the text) was an accepted procedure. I knew that both Thomas Looney and Edward Keenan had used it.
Looney used it for the Shakespeare canon (chapter 6), while Keenan used it
for the letters attributed to Andrei Kurbskii addressed to Ivan IV (chapter 7).
But I found it also being used by Soudavar in relation to the letters of Rashid
al-Din (chapter 5) and by Medvedev in relation to trying to determine whether
Sholokhov or Kriukov wrote *The Quiet Don* (chapter 9).

On the other hand, as I expected, the most difficult chapter to write and
maintain any degree of neutrality was the chapter on the letter of Clement

of Alexandria and the Secret Gospel of Mark. My preconceived view going into writing the chapter and doing more research was that Morton Smith had indeed discovered an eighteenth-century handwritten copy (in a seventeenth-century printed book) of a letter by late second-century/early third-century Church father Clement of Alexandria and that the extracts from a secret or mystical Gospel of Mark in that letter were genuine. Yet I did my best to try to be fair to the side that had a different point of view. I tried to give the authors of what I read the benefit of the doubt, as I would like to be given it by those who read what I write. When I thought I had found a contradiction in what I was reading, I made sure to look for extenuating circumstances, qualifications, and other possible explanations. In that respect I had in mind the principle of charity as invoked by Alec Fisher in his *The Logic of Real Arguments*.[6] Norman Belagaron defined it as "present[ing] the ideas we are contesting in the most favorable light."[7] I can understand the vehemence of opposition to Smith's discovery—in controversies related to the Bible there are always emotional considerations that well up and can overwhelm critical analysis. And the stated concern by scholars like Francis Watson was that Smith was trying to bring about the downfall of Christianity. Yet, like Hershel Shanks, I continued to be surprised and dismayed by the obvious weaknesses in the arguments of the traditionalists and in their misrepresentations of evidence. One would think that they would be thrilled that the letter of Clement seems to confirm the traditional attribution of the Gospel of Mark to the disciple Mark, not to mention the miracle of the Lazarus story, but they went in a different direction.

Perhaps the easiest chapter for me to write was the one on James Macpherson and the Ossian cycle of poems (chapter 8). Whether I did a good job of it is another matter. In the original proposal for this book and even in early completed drafts, I did not include the Ossian controversy. Mainly I thought it was an issue that had been resolved, so it was not entirely appropriate for this book. Then I discovered there has been, for several decades now, an attempt to revive some legitimacy for Macpherson—that, perhaps, some of his poetry at least was "channeling" early Gaelic ballads. In discussing with a learned colleague of mine the contents of the draft of this book, he immediately asked if I was including a chapter on Macpherson. The more I looked into it, the more I realized that I was wrong to exclude it in the first place. Not only does it help "fill the gap" chronologically between the sixteenth- and seventeenth-century

---

6. Alec Fisher, *The Logic of Real Arguments*, 2nd ed. (Cambridge: Cambridge University Press, 2004), 17–18, 22.

7. Normand Baillargeon, *Petit cours d'autodéfense intellectuelle* (Quebec: Lux Éditeur, 2007), 78.

controversies over Shakespeare and Kurbskii on one side and the twentieth-century controversy regarding Sholokhov on the other, but the substance of the Ossian controversy also provided a much-needed variation on the theme of authorship attribution. Fortunately, the editors at Northern Illinois University Press were open to my late inclusion of that chapter in the book.

In regard to another emotionally visceral controversy, over who wrote the Shakespearean plays and poetry (chapter 6), one also finds both strong and weak arguments and accusations on both sides. I found stronger arguments and better research by some members of the anti-Stratfordian opposition than among the Stratfordian defenders on the question of authorship. In contrast to the traditionalists of the Secret Gospel controversy, who have neither made their case well nor succeeded in denigrating those who support Morton Smith, the Stratfordians have succeeded in belittling the anti-Stratfordians. In part, this difference is the result of the fact that Smith has widespread support among established scholars, whereas only a few established scholars in the field of English literature are anti-Stratfordians; most of the anti-Stratfordians are amateur scholars or specialists in other fields.

Unless one has actually delved into the arguments on both sides, one is most likely to be in favor of William of Stratford as the author of the plays and poems attributed to Shakespeare. It is one of the pillars of the general public's belief system and occurs at a visceral level. To poke at that pillar is to threaten their worldview (I speak from personal experience here), and one risks angry responses. Nonetheless, I encountered a genuine conundrum here. I think it highly unlikely that William of Stratford wrote the plays and poems and highly likely that Edward de Vere wrote or was involved in writing them. But it is odd that no one with personal knowledge of either person or any other person of the time speaks or writes about having met Shakespeare the writer. To this point, Samuel Schoenbaum responded that a great writer does not need to "have lords and ladies in coaches driving up to his door."[8] Was Shakespeare, then, a recluse like J. D. Salinger or Thomas Pynchon, which William of Stratford certainly was not? And the lack of a paper trail, as Price pointed out, is doubly odd, especially in comparison with writers who were his contemporaries. More recent scholarship suggests co-authorships of a number of the plays. It is possible that no single author published under the name William Shakespeare, that the name was used as a generic "Doctor Ralph," and that everyone at the time was in on the joke, but we are not. It could have been a group venture—the Shakespeare syndicate—or random individuals, which

---

8. Samuel Schoenbaum, *Shakespeare's Lives*, new ed. (Oxford: Oxford University Press, 1991), 431.

might help account for the seven plays published under the name William Shakespeare but are not now considered part of the Shakespeare canon.

In that chapter, I chose to ignore the conspiracy theories of the "whacko" Oxfordians, in particular those who advocate for the "Prince Tudor" theory (basically that the 17th Earl of Oxford was the father of his own half-brother). I ignored it because that theory is thoroughly refuted by the evidence. The only way to make it work (somewhat) has been to change the evidence and chronology. As with any conspiracy theory worth its name, those who are proponents of it have to cherry-pick some evidence, modify other evidence, and reject the rest. That is where research with a goal to prove something leads to flawed outcomes. Regrettably, the film *Anonymous* (2011) was based to a large extent on the Prince Tudor conspiracy theory and did the Oxfordian position no favors thereby.

One might also identify the question of whether Moses wrote the Pentateuch (chapter 1) as an emotionally visceral controversy. Challenging that belief can require protective gear. Yet in writing chapter 1, I was helped by the enormous amount (and quality) of scholarship by reputable experts. To be sure, there are vehement disagreements within the scholarship, with accompanying ad hominem attacks, but the field of biblical studies has in general risen above that. Nonetheless, there are still plenty of questions about how the Pentateuch was written that require continued research, especially into the archaeological record.

In chapter 5, I was fortunate to find four articles written specifically on whether Rashid al-Din wrote the correspondence attributed to him—two articles for and two against. That made writing the chapter easier. Nonetheless, the indicators of authorship that the scholars presented point in different directions. If he did write the letters, then why are there so many peculiarities ("dark places") in them? If he did not write them, then who did and why is there so much that is accurate (i.e., confirmable by means of other evidence)? One can only hope that research on the topic is still in its beginning stages and much more evidence will be uncovered and more analysis done.

Finally, in regard to research on the authorship of *The Quiet Don* and the writing of chapter 9, I encountered both vehement arguments and visceral beliefs but also another genuine conundrum. The usual indicators seem to be pointing in different directions. The stylometric evidence points in favor of the traditional attribution to Sholokhov, but the skeptics perceive something awry with attributing the novel solely to Sholokhov.

In the introduction, I quoted the medievalist John Benton to the effect that authorship questions will not be resolved "through discussions of what might be plausible behavior for people . . . but on the basis of the most technical . . . issues, questions of style, dating, sources and so on."[9] Similarly, Ševčenko once told a group of us that if the "short brush strokes" of the historical canvas differ from the "broad brush strokes," he favors the short brush strokes. I think it fair to say that a common practice in scholarship is just the opposite—broad strokes over short strokes. I already pointed out how although Malcolm Laing did some thorough analysis of Macpherson's Ossian poem cycle in identifying reference points in the poems that would not have been available to a medieval bard, Laing was most convinced by the broad strokes of correspondence to eighteenth-century sublimity and sentimentality. Another example might be Isabella de Madariaga's response to Keenan's challenge to the Kurbskii attributions by saying that she was "not qualified in linguistic and textual analysis" (short strokes); yet she found that "as a practicing historian" she could not "accept the validity of Keenan's theories on historical grounds" (broad strokes).

The French historians Charles-Victor Langlois (1863–1929) and Charles Seignobos (1854–1942) describe focusing on a source qua source as preparatory criticism or external criticism. In contrast, they describe focusing on the meaning of a source as higher criticism or internal criticism.[10] This bifurcation approximately coincides with Benton's technical issues/plausible behavior or Ševčenko's short brush strokes/broad brush strokes dichotomy.

The Harvard history professor H. Stuart Hughes (1916–1999) wrote a book titled *History as Art and as Science: Twin Vistas on the Past* (1964). Roughly, the art part of history correlates with higher criticism; the science part with Langlois and Seignobos's lower criticism. The two criticisms go hand in hand, as narrative provides the hypotheses that lower criticism can test against the evidence. The American historian Hayden White (1928–2018) wrote about the pitfalls of narrative when it skews the analysis to fit the narrative.[11] I have applied the term "thick interpretation" to indicate places where the narrative replaces or obscures evidence, and "thin interpretation" where it does not replace or obscure that evidence.[12]

---

9. John F. Benton, "The Correspondence of Abelard and Heloise," in *Fälschungen im Mittelalter. Internationaler Kongress der Monumenta Germaniae Historica, München, 16.–19. September 1986*, vol. 5: *Fingierte Briefe, Frömmigkeit und Fälschung, Realienfälschungen*, MGH Schriften, Bd. 33, V (Hannover: Hahnsche Buchhandlung, 1988), 97.

10. Ch. V. Langlois and Ch. Seignobos, *Introduction to the Study of History*, trans. G. G. Berry (New York: Henry Holt, 1898), 101–122.

11. Hayden White, *Metahistory: The Historical Imagination of Nineteenth-Century Europe* (Baltimore: Johns Hopkins, 1973). See also Donald Ostrowski, "A Metahistorical Analysis: Hayden White and Four Narratives of 'Russian' History," *Clio* 19, no. 3 (1990): 215–236.

12. See my "The Thick and Thin of It: Gary Hamburg's Path toward Enlightenment of Early Modern Russian Political Thought," *Canadian-American Slavic Studies* 53 (2019).

One reader of the book suggested that I conclude with basic principles for authorship studies. The goals of this book were to introduce the readers to nine prominent authorship controversies and to lay the foundation for a field of authorship studies. In that respect, it is meant to open lines of inquiry, and, to do so, the reader thought it might be helpful for me to provide some guidelines that I found applicable in doing my own research on these controversies. Here are those basic principles.

General principles for authorship attribution accompanied by their negative exposition:

1. Read the text in question; don't assume you know what the text says based on what other people say it says.
2. Keep an open mind; avoid premature cognitive closure (especially when you are sure you "know" what the answer is).
3. Follow the evidence; don't try to make the evidence conform to some already existing interpretive framework.
4. Be analytical; avoid unquestioning acceptance of assertions (your own included).
5. When the broad brush strokes and the short brush strokes of historical study are in conflict, favor the short brush strokes; don't depend so much on what is plausible for human behavior as on the technical evidence (forensics).
6. Consider whether an argument or the point one wants to make is applicable to other authorship controversies; otherwise one risks propounding ad hoc arguments/points that are not valid in a more general sense.
7. Be familiar with other authorship attributions and controversies; otherwise one risks engaging in silo scholarship and thereby drawing conclusions that are less than well informed.

These are basically my principles for authorship attribution studies and my conclusion for this book as a whole.

BIBLIOGRAPHY

Abramovic, F. A., and V. V. Gura, eds. *M. A. Sholokhov. Seminarii.* 2nd ed. Leningrad: Gosudarstvennoe uchebno-pedagogicheskoe izdatel'stvo ministerstva prosveshcheniia RSFSR, Leningradskoe otdelenie, 1962.

Albright, William F. "Archaeology and the Date of the Hebrew Conquest of Palestine." *Bulletin of the American Schools of Oriental Research* 58 (April 1935): 10–18.

Alexander, T. D[esmond]. "Are the Wife / Sister Incidents of Genesis Literary Compositional Variants?" *Vetus Testamentum* 42, no. 2 (1992): 145–153.

Alexander, T. Desmond, and David W. Baker, *Dictionary of the Old Testament: Pentateuch.* Downers Grove, IL: InterVarsity Press, 2003.

Allsen, Thomas. *Culture and Conquest in Mongol Eurasia.* Cambridge: Cambridge University Press, 2001.

Ames, Roger T., and Henry Rosemont Jr. "Introduction." *The Analects of Confucius: A Philosophical Translation.* New York: Random House, 1998.

Anderson, Mark. *"Shakespeare" by Another Name: The Life of Edward de Vere, Earl of Oxford, the Man Who Was Shakespeare.* New York: Gotham, 2005.

Andreyev, Nikolay. "The Authenticity of the Correspondence between Ivan IV and Prince Andrey Kurbsky." *Slavonic and East European Review* 53 (1975): 582–588.

Andreyev, Nikolay. "Kurbsky's Letters to Vas'yan Muromtsev." *Slavonic and East European Review* 33 (1955): 414–436.

Anonymous [Joe Klein]. *Primary Colors: A Novel about Politics.* New York: Random House, 1996.

Arends, A. K., trans., A. A. Romaskevich, E. E. Bertel's, and A. Iu. Iakubovskii, eds. *Sbornik letopisei,* vol. 3. Moscow: Akademiia nauk SSSR, 1960.

Arkhangel'skii, A. S. *Ocherki iz istorii zapadno-russkoi literatury XVI–XVII vv.* Moscow, 1888.

Auden, W. H. *The Dyer's Hand, and Other Essays.* New York: Vintage, 1968.

Auerbach, Inge. *Andrej Michajlovič Kurbskij. Leben in osteuropäischen Adelsgesellschaften des 16. Jahrhunderts.* Munich: Otto Sagner, 1985.

Auerbach, Inge. "Ein Analphabet als Schriftsteller? Zur Entstehung und Überlieferug des 'Novyi Margarit.'" In *Andrej Michajlovič Kurbskij Novyj Margarit. Historisch-kritisched Ausgabe auf der Grundlage der Wolfenbütteler Handschrift,* edited by Inge Auerbach, Band 3. Lieferung 11–15 (Bl. 319–466, S. 1–51). Giessen: Wilhelm Schmitz, 1987.

Auerbach, Inge. "Gedanken zur Entstehung von A. M. Kurbskijs 'Istorija o velikom knjaze Moskovskom.'" *Canadian-American Slavic Studies* 13, nos. 1–2 (1979): 166–171.

Auerbach, Inge. "Identity in Exile: Andrei Mikhailovich Kurbskii and National Consciousness in the Sixteenth Century." In *Culture and Identity in Muscovy, 1389–1584*, edited by A. M. Kleimola and G. D. Lenhoff, 11–25. Moscow: ITs-Garant, 1997.

Baillargeon, Normand. *Petit cours d'autodéfense intellectuelle.* Quebec: Lux Éditeur, 2007.

Bar-Sella, Zeev. *Literaturnyi kotlovan. Proekt "Pisatel Sholokhov."* Moscow: RGGU, 2005.

Barber, Ros. *Shakespeare the Evidence: The Authorship Question Clarified* (July 28, 2015), 315–316. https://leanpub.com/Shakespeare.

Barthold, W. W. *Turkestan down to the Mongol Invasion*, 4th ed. London: E. J. Gibb Memorial Trust, 1977.

Beltz, Walter. *God and the Gods: Myths of the Bible.* Translated by Peter Heinegg. New York: Penguin, 1983.

Benton, John F. "The Correspondence of Abelard and Heloise." In *Fälschungen im Mittelalter. Internationaler Kongress der Monumenta Germaniae Historica, München, 16.–19. September 1986. Vol. 5, Fingierte Briefe, Frömmigkeit und Fälschung, Realienfälschungen*, MGH Schriften, Bd. 33, V. 95–120. Hannover: Hahnsche Buchhandlung, 1988.

Benton, John F. "Fraud, Fiction and Borrowing in the Correspondence of Abelard and Heloise." *Pierre Abélard, Pierre le Vénérable: les courants philosophiques, littéraires et artistiques en Occident au milieu du XIIe siècle* [actes et mémoires du colloque international], Abbaye de Cluny, 2 au 9 juillet 1972, 469–506. Paris: Éditions du Centre national de la recherché scientifique, 1975.

Benton, John F. "A Reconsideration of the Authenticity of the Correspondence of Abelard and Heloise." In *Petrus Abaelardus, 1079–1142: Person, Werk und Wirkung*, edited by Rudolf Thomas, 41–52. Trier: Paulinus-Verlag, 1980.

Besters-Dilger, Juliane. *Die Dogmatik des Johannes von Damaskus in der Übersetzung des Fursten Andrej M. Kurbskii (1528–1583).* Freiburg: U. W. Weiher, 1995.

Bietak, Manfred. "Israelites Found in Egypt." *Biblical Archaeology Review* 29 (September/October 2003): 40–47.

Black, George F. *Macpherson's Ossian and the Ossianic Controversy.* New York: New York Public Library, 1926.

Bloom, Harold. *The Book of J.* Translated by David Rosenberg. New York: Grove, Weidenfeld, 1990.

Boeck, Brian J. "Miscellanea Attributed to Kurbskii: The 17th Century in Russia Was More Creative Than We Like to Admit." *Kritika: Explorations in Russian and Eurasian History* 13, no. 4 (Fall 2012): 955–963.

Boeck, Brian J. *Stalin's Scribe: Literature, Ambition, Survival: The Life of Mikhail Sholokhov.* London: Pegasus, 2019.

Botsianovskii, Vl. "Iz vospominanii o F. D. Kriukove." *Vestnik literatury* 9, no. 21 (1920).

Boyle, John A. "Juvayni and Rashīd al-Dīn as Sources on the History of the Mongols." In *Historians of the Middle East*, edited by Bernard Lewis and Peter M. Holt, 133–137. London: Oxford University Press, 1962.

Boyle, John A. "Rashīd al-Dīn: The First World Historian." *Iran* 9 (1971): 19–26.

Boziev, Sadin Nazirovich. *Prevratnosti tekstov proizvedenii M. A. Sholokhov i F. D. Kriukova.* Moscow: Vash format, 2016.

Brazil, Robert Sean. *Edward de Vere and the Shakespeare Printers.* Seattle: Cortical Output, 2010.

Brooks, E. Bruce, and A. Taeko Brooks. *The Original Analects: Sayings of Confucius and His Successors.* New York: Columbia University Press, 1998.

Brown, Pamela Allen. "*Othello* Italicized: Xenophobia and the Erosion of Tragedy." In *Shakespeare, Italy and Intertextuality,* edited by Michele Marrapodi, 145–157. Manchester: Manchester University Press, 2004.

Brown, Scott G. *Mark's Other Gospel: Rethinking Morton Smith's Controversial Discovery.* Waterloo, ONT: Published for the Canadian Corporation for Studies in Religion, 2005.

Browne, Edward G. "The Historians of the Īl-Khání Period." In Edward G. Browne, *A Literary History of Persia.* Cambridge: Cambridge University Press, 1928.

Browne, Edward G. "The Persian Manuscripts of the Late Sir Albert Houtum-Schindler, K.C.I.E." *Journal of the Royal Asiatic Society* 49, no. 4 (October 1917): 657–694.

Burgess, Anthony. *A Clockwork Orange.* New York: Norton, 1963.

Butterworth, G. W., trans. *Origen on First Principles.* London: Society for Promoting Christian Knowledge, 1936.

Camden, William. *Britannia, siue Florentissimorum regnorum Angliæ, Scotiæ, Hiberniæ, et insularum adiacentium ex intima antiquitate chorographica descriptio: nunc postremò recognita, plurimis locis magna accessione adaucta, & chartis chorographicis illustrata.* London: Eliot's Court Press, 1607.

Campbell, Oscar James, ed., and Edward G. Quinn, ass. ed. *The Reader's Encyclopedia of Shakespeare.* New York: Crowell, 1966.

Carmina Gadelica: Hymns and Incantations. 6 vols. Edited and translated by Alexander Carmichael. Edinburgh: Constable, 1900–1971.

Carroll, James. *The Cloister: A Novel.* New York: Random House, 2017.

Casson, John. *Much Ado about Noting: Henry Neville and Shakespeare's Secret Source.* London: Dolman Scott, 2010.

Chambers, E[dmund] K[ercheval]. *William Shakespeare: A Study of Facts and Problems,* 2 vols. Oxford: Clarendon, 1930.

Charrier, Charlotte. *Héloïse dans l'histoire et dans la légende.* Paris: H. Champion, 1933.

Cheang, Alice M. "The Master's Voice: On Reading, Translating and Interpreting the *Analects* of Confucius." *Review of Politics* 62, no. 3 (Summer 2000): 563–581.

Clanchy, Michael. *Abelard: A Medieval Life.* Oxford: Blackwell, 1997.

Clark, Eva Turner. "Lord Oxford's Letters Echoed in Shakespeare's Plays." *Shakespeare Fellowship Quarterly* 7, no. 1 (1946): 10–11.

Clubb, Louise George. "Italian Stories on the Stage." In *The Cambridge Companion to Shakespearean Comedy,* edited by Alexander Leggatt, 43–45. Cambridge: Cambridge University Press, 2002.

Cohen, J. M., trans. *The Confessions of Jean-Jacques Rousseau.* London: Penguin Classics, 1953.

Conner, Robert. *The Secret Gospel of Mark: Morton Smith, Clement of Alexandria and Four Decades of Academic Burlesque.* Oxford: Mandrake of Oxford, 2015.

Constable, Giles. "The Authorship of the *Epistolae duorum amantium*: A Reconsideration." In *Voices in Dialogue: New Problems in Reading Women's Cultural History*, edited by Linda Olson and Kathryn Kerby-Fulton, 167–178. Notre Dame, IN: University of Notre Dame Press, 2005.

D* [Irina Medvedeva-Tomashevskaia]. *Stremia "Tikhogo Dona" (Zagadka romana)*. Paris: YMCA-Press, 1974.

Das, David Hari. "History Writing and Late Muscovite Court Culture: A Study of Andrei Lyzlov's *History of the Scythians*." PhD dissertation, University of Washington, 1991.

Davis, Frank. "Shakspere's Six Accepted Signatures: A Comparison." In *Shakespeare beyond Doubt? Exposing an Industry in Denial*, edited by John M. Shahan and Alexander Waugh, 29–40. Tamarac, FL: Llumina, 2013.

deGategno, Paul J. *James Macpherson*. Boston: Twayne, 1989.

Delektorskii, F. I. "Kritiko-bibliograficheskii obzor drevnerusskikh skazanii o Florentiiskoi unii." *Zhurnal Ministerstva narodnogo prosveshcheniia* 300 (August 1895): 131–183.

Denissoff, Élie. "Une biographie de Maxime le Grec par Kourbski." *Orientalia Christiana Periodica* 20 (1954): 44–84.

Denissoff, Élie. "Maxime le Grec et ses vicissitudes au sein de l'Église Russe." *Revue des études slaves* 31, nos. 1–4 (1954): 7–20.

Dever, William G. *What Did the Biblical Writers Know and When Did They Know It?* Grand Rapids, MI: Eerdmans, 2002.

Dever, William G. "What Remains of the House That Albright Built?" *Biblical Archaeologist* 56, no. 1 (March 1993): 25–35.

Digby, Simon. "The Maritime Trade of India." In *The Cambridge Economic History of India*, vol. 1., edited by Tapan Raychauduri and Irfan Habib, 125–159. Cambridge: Cambridge University Press, 1982.

Dothan, Trude Krakauer, and Moshe Dothan. *People of the Sea: The Search for the Philistines*. New York: Macmillan, 1992.

Dowden, Edward. *Shakespeare: A Critical Study of His Mind and Art*. London: Henry S. King, 1875.

Draya, Ren, and Richard F. Whalen, eds. *Othello, the Moor of Venice*. Truro, MA: Horatio Editions-Llumina, 2010.

Dronke, Peter. "Heloise, Abelard, and Some Recent Discussions." In Peter Dronke, *Intellectuals and Poets in Medieval Europe*. Rome: Edizioni di storia e letteratura, 1992.

Dwyer, John. "The Melancholy Savage: Text and Context in the *Poems of Ossian*." In *Ossian Revisited*, edited by Howard Gaskill, 164–206. Edinburgh: Edinburgh University Press, 1991.

Elliott, Ward E. Y., and Robert J. Valenza. "And Then There Were None: Winnowing the Shakespeare Claimants." *Computers and the Humanities* 30 (1996): 206–207.

Elliott, Ward E. Y., and Robert J. Valenza. "Oxford by the Numbers: What Are the Odds That the Earl of Oxford Could Have Written Shakespeare's Poems and Plays?" *Tennessee Law Review* 72, no. 1 (2004): 323–453.

Elliott, Ward E. Y., and Robert J. Valenza. "The Shakespeare Clinic and the Oxfordians." *The Oxfordian* 12 (2010): 138–167.

Eno, Robert, trans. *The Analects of Confucius: An Online Teaching Translation.* http://www.indiana.edu/~p374/Analects_of_Confucius_(Eno-2015).pdf.

Eno, Robert. "The *Lunyu* as an Accretion Text." In *Confucius and the Analects Revisited,* edited by Michael Hunter and Martin Kern, 39–66. Leiden: Brill, 2018.

Ermolaev, Herman. *Mikhail Sholokhov and His Art.* Princeton, NJ: Princeton University Press, 1982.

Erusalimskii, K[onstantin] Iu. "Ideal'nyi sovet v 'Istorii o velikom kniaze Moskovskom'." In *Tekst v gumanitarnom znanii. Materialy mezhvuzovskoi nauchnoi konferentsii 22–24 aprelia 1997 g.,* edited by O. M. Meduzhevskaia, M. Iu. Rumiantseva, K. Iu. Erusalimskii, and V. V. Zvereva, 73–87. Moscow: Rossiiskii gosudarstvennyi gumanitarnyi universitet, 1997.

Erusalimskii, K[onstantin] Iu. *Sbornik Kurbskogo. Issledovanie knizhnoi kul'tury.* 2 vols. Moscow: Znak, 2009.

Evans, G. Blackmore, ed. *The Riverside Shakespeare.* Boston: Houghton Mifflin, 1974.

Faherty, Teresa J. "*Othello dell' Arte:* The Presence of *Commedia* in Shakespeare's Tragedy." *Theatre Journal* 43 (1991): 179–194.

Fennell, J. L. I., ed. *The Correspondence between Prince A. M. Kurbsky and Tsar Ivan IV of Russia 1564–1579.* Cambridge: Cambridge University Press, 1963.

Fennell, J. L. I., ed. and trans. *Prince A. M. Kurbsky's History of Ivan IV.* Cambridge: Cambridge University Press, 1965.

Fessler, Ignatius Aurelius. *Abälard und Heloise.* 2 vols. Berlin: Friedrich Maurer, 1806–1807.

Filiushkin, A. I. *Andrei Kurbskii.* Moscow: Molodaia gvardiia, 2008.

Filiushkin, A. I. *Andrei Mikhailovich Kurbskii. Prosopograficheskoe issledovanie i germenevticheskii kommentarii k poslaniiam Andreia Kurbskogo Ivanu Groznomu.* St. Petersburg: Izdatel'stvo Sankt-Peterburgskogo universiteta, 2007.

Filiushkin, A. I. *Istoriia odnoi mistifikatsii: Ivan Groznyi i "Izbrannaia Rada."* Moscow: VGU, 1998.

Filiushkin, A. I. "Putting Kurbskii in His Rightful Place." *Kritika: Explorations in Russian and Eurasian History* 13, no. 4 (Fall 2012): 964–974.

Fisher, Alec. *The Logic of Real Arguments.* 2nd ed. Cambridge: Cambridge University Press, 2004.

Floria, B. N. "Novoe o Groznom i Kurbskom." *Istoriia SSSR,* no. 3 (1974): 142–145.

Folkenflik, Robert. "Macpherson, Chatterton, Blake and the Great Age of Literary Forgery." *Centennial Review* 18, no. 4 (1974): 378–391.

Foster, Donald. "Primary Culprit." *New York,* February 26, 1996, 50–57.

Fowler, William Plumer. *Shakespeare Revealed in Oxford's Letters.* Portsmouth, NH: Peter E. Randall, 1986.

Fraioli, Deborah. "The Importance of Satire in Jerome's *Adversus Jovinianum* as an Argument against the Authenticity of the *Historica calamitatum.*" In *Fälschungen im Mittelalter. Internationaler Kongress der Monumenta Germaniae Historica, München, 16.–19. September 1986.* Vol. 5, *Fingierte Briefe, Frömmigkeit und Fälschung, Realienfälschungen,* MGH Schriften, Bd. 33, V, 167–200. Hannover: Hahnsche Buchhandlung, 1988.

Freydank, Dietrich. "A. M. Kurbskij und die Thorie der antiken Historiographiie." In *Orbis mediaevalis. Festgabe für Anton Blaschka zum 75. Geburtstag am 7. Oktober*

1967, edited by Horst Gericke, Manfred Lemmer, and Walter Zöllner, 57–62. Weimar: H. Böhlaus Hachfolger, 1970.

Friedman, Richard Elliott. *The Exodus: How It Happened and Why It Matters.* New York: HarperOne, 2017.

Friedman, Richard Elliott. *Who Wrote the Bible?* New York: Harper & Row, 1987.

Friend, Tad. "Credit Grab," *New Yorker*, October 20, 2003, 160 and following.

Garber, Marjorie. *Shakespeare after All.* New York: Random House, 2004.

Gardner, Daniel K. *Zhu Xi's Reading of the* Analects: *Canon, Commentary, and the Classical Tradition.* New York: Columbia University Press, 2003.

Gaskill, Howard. "Introduction." In *Ossian Revisited*, ed. Howard Gaskill, 1–18. Edinburgh: Edinburgh University Press, 1991.

Geraklitov, A. A. *Filigrani XVII veka na bumage rukopisnykh i pechatnykh dokumentov russkogo proiskhozhdeniia.* Moscow: Akademiia nauk SSSR, 1963.

Gillespie, Stuart. *Shakespeare's Books: A Dictionary of Shakespeare's Sources.* London: Athlone, 2001.

Gilvary, Kevin, ed. *Dating Shakespeare's Plays: A Critical Review of the Evidence.* Tunbridge Wells, UK: Parapress, 2010.

Goldstein, Gary. *Reflections on the True Shakespeare.* Buchholz, DE: Laugwitz Verlag, 2016.

Goldstein, Gary. "Shakespeare's Native Tongue." *Shakespeare Oxford Newsletter*, Fall 1990, 4–8; reprinted in *De Vere Society Newsletter*, November 2009, 28–31.

Golovnin, Aleksei. *Za chertoi dvatsat' pervogo—.* [Russia]: Topaz, 1993.

Gordon, Karen Elizabeth. *The Well-Tempered Sentence: A Punctuation Handbook for the Innocent, the Eager, and the Doomed.* New York: Ticknor and Fields, 1983.

Gornfel'd, A[rkadii] G[eorgievich]. "Pamiati F. D. Kriukova." *Vestnik literatury* 6, no. 18 (1920).

Grant, R. M. "The New Testament Canon." In *The Cambridge History of the Bible.* Vol. 1, *From the Beginnings to Jerome*, edited by Peter R. Ackroyd and C. F. Evans. Cambridge: Cambridge University Press, 1970.

Greig, J. Y. T., ed. *The Letters of David Hume.* 2 vols., vol. 1, *1727–1765.* Oxford: Clarendon Press, 1932.

Greenblatt, Stephen. *Will in the World: How Shakespeare Became Shakespeare.* New York: Norton, 2004.

Grobovsky, Anthony. *The "Chosen Council" of Ivan IV: A Reinterpretation.* Brooklyn, NY: Gaus, 1969.

Halperin, Charles J. "Edward Keenan and the Kurbskii-Groznyi Correspondence in Hindsight." *Jahrbücher für Geschichte Osteuropas* 46, no. 3 (1998): 376–403.

Halpern, Baruch. "Eyewitness Testimony: Parts of Exodus Written within Living Memory of the Event." *Biblical Archaeology Review* 29 (September/October 2003): 50–57.

Hampton-Reeves, Stuart. "The 'Declaration of Reasonable Doubt.'" In *Shakespeare beyond Doubt: Evidence, Argument, Controversy*, edited by Paul Edmondson and Stanley Wells, 201–214. Cambridge: Cambridge University Press, 2013.

Haroutunian, Joseph, and Louise P. Smith, trans. *Calvin: Commentary.* Philadelphia: Westminster, 1958.

Hart, Michael H. *The 100: A Ranking of the Most Influential Persons in History.* New York: Citadel, 1992.

Hayes, John H. "Moses." In *The Oxford Companion to the Bible*, edited by Bruce M. Metzger and Michael D. Coogan, 528–531. Oxford: Oxford University Press, 1993.

Hexter, J. H. *Reappraisals in History: New Views on History and Society in Early Modern Europe.* New York: Harper & Row, 1963.

Hjort, Nils Lid. "And Quiet Does Not Flow the Don: Statistical Analysis of a Quarrel between Nobel Laureates." https://cas.oslo.no/getfile.php/138668 -1461568659/CAS_publications/Seminar_booklets/PDF/Consilience _LidHjort.pdf (2007).

Holinshed, Raphael *The First and Second Volumes of Chronicles*, augmented by John Hooker. London, 1587.

Home, Henry (Lord Kames). *Sketches of the History of Man*. 2 vols. London: W. Strahan and T. Cadell; Edinburgh: W. Creech, 1774.

Honigmann, E. A. J. *Shakespeare: The "Lost Years."* Manchester: Manchester University Press, 1985.

Hopkins, Keith. "Brother-Sister Marriage in Roman Egypt." *Comparative Studies in Society and History* 22, no. 3 (July 1980): 303–354.

Höttemann, Benedikt. *Shakespeare and Italy.* Berlin: Lit Verlag, 2011.

Hunter, Michael. *Confucius beyond the* Analects. Leiden: Brill, 2017.

Hunter, Michael. "Did Mencius Know the *Analects?*" *T'oung Pao* 100, nos. 1/3 (2014): 12.

Hunter, Michael. "The Lunyu as a Western Han Text." In *Confucius and the* Analects *Revisited*, edited by Michael Hunter and Martin Kern, 67–91. Leiden: Brill, 2018.

Hunter, Michael. "Sayings of Confucius Deselected." PhD dissertation, Princeton University, 2012.

Hupfeld, Hermann. *Die Quellen der Genesis und die Art ihrer Zusammensetzung von neuem untersucht.* Berlin: Wiegandt und Grieben, 1853.

Ivanishev, N. D. "Vremennaia Komissiia dlia razbora drevnikh aktov." *Zhizn' kn. Kurbskogo v Litve i na Volyni*, 2 vols. Kiev: I. K. Val'ner, 1849.

Jackson, Peter. "The Mongols and the Delhi Sultanate in the Reign of Muhammad b. Tughluq (1325–1351)." *Central Asiatic Journal* 19, no. 1/2 (1975): 118–157.

Jaeger, C. Stephen. *Ennobling Love: In Search of a Lost Sensibility.* Philadelphia: University of Pennsylvania Press, 1999.

Jaeger, C. Stephen. "*Epistolae duorum amantium* and the Ascription to Heloise and Abelard," In *Voices in Dialogue: New Problems in Reading Women's Cultural History*, edited by Linda Olson and Kathryn Kerby-Fulton, 125–166. Notre Dame, IN: University of Notre Dame Press, 2005.

Jahn, Karl. "Rashīd al-Dīn as World Historian." In *Yádnáme-ye Jan Rypka: Collection of Articles on Persian and Tajik Literature*, edited by J. Bečka, 79–87. Prague: Academia, 1967.

Janson, Tore. "Schools of Cursus in the Twelfth Century and the *Letters* of Heloise and Abelard." In *Retorica e poetica tra i secoli XII e XIV*, edited by Claudio Leonardi and Enrico Menestò, 195–196. Florence: La nuova Italia, 1988.

Jenkins, Philip. *Hidden Gospels: How the Search for Jesus Lost Its Way.* Oxford: Oxford University Press, 2001.

Jensen, Lionel M. *Manufacturing Confucianism: Chinese Traditions and Universal Civilization*. Durham, NC: Duke University Press, 1997.

Jervis, Robert. *Perception and Misperception in International Politics*, new ed. Princeton, NJ: Princeton University Press, 2017 (1st ed., 1976).

Jiménez, Ramón. "The Famous Victories of King Henry the Fifth." In *Dating Shakespeare's Plays: A Critical Review of the Evidence*, edited by Kevin Gilvary, 461–468. Tunbridge Wells, UK: Parapress, 2010.

Johnson, Paul. *A History of the Jews*. New York: Harper & Row, 1987.

Kalugin, V. V. *Andrei Kurbskii i Ivan Groznyi. Teoreticheskie vzgliady i literaturnaia tekhnika drevnerusskogo pisatelia*. Moscow: Iazyki russkoi kul'tury, 1998.

Kalugin, V. V. "Kogda rodilsia kniaz' Andrei Kurbskii." *Arkhiv russkoi istorii* 6 (1995): 241–242.

Kalugin, Vasilii [V. V.]. "Literaturnoe nasledie kniazia Andreia Kurbskogo (Spornye voprosy istochnikov)." *Palaeoslavica* 5 (1997): 83–133.

Kamola, Stefan T. "Rashīd al-Dīn and the Making of History in Mongol Iran." PhD dissertation, University of Washington, 2013.

Karamzin, N. M. *Istoriia gosudarstva Rossiiskogo*. 2nd ed, 12 vols. St. Petersburg: Tip. N. Grecha, 1818–1829.

Keenan, Edward L. *The Kurbskii Groznyi Apocrypha: The Seventeenth-Century Genesis of the "Correspondence" Attributed to Prince A. M. Kurbskii and Tsar Ivan IV*, with an appendix by Daniel C. Waugh. Cambridge, MA: Harvard University Press, 1971.

Keenan, Edward L. "A Landmark of Kurbskii Studies." *Harvard Ukrainian Studies* 10, nos. 1–2 (1986): 241–247.

Keenan, Edward L. "Response to Halperin, 'Edward Keenan and the Kurbskii-Groznyi Correspondence in Hindsight.'" *Jahrbücher für Geschichte Osteuropas* 46, no. 3 (1998): 404–415.

Keenan, Edward L. "Was Andrei Kurbskii a Renaissance Intellectual? Some Marginal Notes on a Central Issue." *Harvard Ukrainian Studies* 27, nos. 1–4 (2004–2005): 25–31.

Khvatov, A[leksandr] I[vanovich]. *Khudozhestvennyi mir Sholokhova*. Moscow: Sovetskaia Rossiia, 1970.

Kieferling, Krystyna. *Jarosław w czasach Anny Ostrogskiej (1594–1635): szkice do portretu miasta i jego właścicielki*. Przemyśl: Archiwum Państwowe: Polskie Towarzystwo Historyczne. Oddział, 2008.

Killebrew, Ann E. *Biblical Peoples and Ethnicity: An Archaeological Study of Egyptians, Canaanites Philistines, and Early Israel, 1300–1100 B.C.E.* Atlanta: Society of Biblical Literature, 2005.

Kim, Tae Hyun, and Mark Csikszentmihalyi. "History and Formation of the *Analects*." In *Dao Companion to the Analects*, edited by Amy Olberding, Dordrecht: Springer, 2013.

Kjetsaa, Geir. "The Charge of Plagiarism against Michail Šolochov." In Geir Kjetsaa, Sven Gustavsson, Bengt Beckman, and Steinar Gil, *The Authorship of The Quiet Don*, 13–99. Oslo: Solum; Atlantic Highlands, NJ: Humanities Press, 1984.

Koch, Klaus. *The Growth of the Biblical Tradition: The Form-Critical Method*. New York: Scribner, 1969.

Koch, Klaus. *Was ist Formgeschichte? Neue Wege de Bibelexegese.* Neukirchen-Vluyn: Neukirchener Verlag des Erzhiehungsvereins, 1964.

Koialovich, M. O. *Litovskaia tserkovnaia uniia.* 2 vols. St. Petersburg, 1859–1861.

Kolodnyi, Lev. *Kak ia nashel "Tikhii Don": khronika poiska analiz teksta.* Moscow: Golos, 2000.

Kolodnyi, Lev. *Kto napisal "Tikhii Don": khronika odnogo poiska.* Moscow: Golos, 1995.

Könsgen, Ewald. *Epistolae duorum amantium. Briefe Abaelards und Heloises?* Mittella-teinisches Studien und Texte 8. Leiden: E. J. Brill, 1974.

Koriagin, Sergei. *"Tikhii Don." Chernye piatna. Kak urodovali istoriiu kazachestva.* Moscow: Iaza, Eksmo, 2006.

Korpela, Jukka. "Feodorit (Theodorit) Kol'skii: Missionary and Princely Agent." In *Religion und Integration im Moskauer Russland: Konzepte und Praktiken, Potentiale und Grenzen 14.–17. Jahrhundert,* edited by Ludwig Steindorff, 201–226. Wiesbaden: Otto Harrassowitz, 2010.

Kotoshikhin, Grigorii. *O Rossii v tsarstvovanie Aleksei Mikhailovicha: Text and Commentary.* Edited by Anne E. Pennington. Oxford: Oxford University Press, 1990.

Kuntz, J. Kenneth. *The People of Ancient Israel: An Introduction to Old Testament Literature, History, and Thought.* New York: Harper & Row, 1974.

Kuznetsov, Feliks. *"Tikhii Don": Sud'ba i Pravda velikogo romana.* Moscow: IMLI RAN, 2005.

Laing, Malcolm, ed. *The Poems of Ossian, &c. Containing the Poetical Works of James Macpherson.* 2 vols. Edinburgh: J. Ballantyne, 1805.

Lalanne, Ludovic. "Quelques doutes sur l'authenticité de la correspondence amoureuse d'Héloise et d'Abailard." *La Correspondance littéraire* 1, no. 2 (November 1856–October 1857): 27–33.

Lambarde, William. *Dictionarium Angliæ topographicum & historicum: An alphabetical description of the chief places in England and Wales; With an account of the most memorable events which have distinguish'd them.* Written 1590s; published 1730 by Fletcher Gyles, over-against Gray's-Inn, Holborne.

Lambin, Georges. *Voyages de Shakespeare en France et en Italie.* Geneva: Droz, 1962.

Langlois, Ch. V., and Ch. Seignobos. *Introduction to the Study of History.* Translated by G. G. Berry. New York: Henry Holt, 1898.

Lau, D. C., trans. *Confucius: The Analects (Lun yü).* London: Penguin, 1979.

Leland, John. *Genethliacon illustrissimi Eäduerdi Principis Cambriae, Ducis Coriniæ, et Comitis Palatini.* London: Reyner Wolfe, 1543.

Leland, John. *Kykneion asma. Cygneia cantio.* London: Reyner Wolfe, 1545.

Levy, Reuben. "The Letters of Rashīd al-Dīn Fadl-Allāh." *Journal of the Royal Asiatic Society of Great Britain and Ireland* 1 (April 1946): 74–78.

Lezhnev, I[saak] G[rigor'evich]. *Put' Sholokhova. Tvorcheskaia biografiia.* Moscow: Sovetskii pisatel', 1958.

Li Si. "Memorial on the Burning of the Books." In *Sources of Chinese Tradition,* vol. 1, compiled by Wm. Theodore de Bary, Wing-tsit Chan, and Burton Watson, 140–141. New York: Columbia University Press, 1964.

Liewehr, Ferdinand. *Kurbskijs "Novyi Margarit."* Prague: Taussig & Taussig, 1928.

Likhachev, D. S. *Tekstologiia. Na materiale russkoi literatury X–XVII vv.* Moscow: Akademiia nauk SSSR, 1962; 2nd ed. Leningrad: Nauka, 1983; 3rd ed. St. Petersburg: Aleteiia, 2001.

Likhachev, D. S., and Ia. S. Lur'e "Arkheograficheskii obzor posanii Ivana Groznogo." In *Poslaniia Ivan Groznogo*, edited by D. S. Likhachev and Ia. S. Lur'e, 495–550. Moscow: Akademiia nauk SSSR, 1951.

Likhachev, N. P. *Paleograficheskoe znachenie bumazhnykh vodianykh znakov*, 3 vols. St. Petersburg: Tip. V. S. Balamev, 1899.

Lindberg, Todd. "The Media's True Colors." *Weekly Standard*, July 29, 1996.

Looney, J. Thomas. *"Shakespeare" Identified in Edward de Vere, the Seventeenth Earl of Oxford.* London: C. Palmer, 1920.

Lur'e, Ia. S. "Voprosy vneshnei i vnutrennei politik v poslaniiakh Ivana IV." In *Poslaniia Ivan Groznogo*, edited by D. S. Likhachev and Ia. S. Lur'e, 456–494. Moscow: Akademiia nauk SSSR, 1951.

Luscombe, D. E. "The *Letters* of Abelard and Heloise since 'Cluny 1972.'" *Petrus Abaelardus, 1079–1142: Person, Werk und Wirkung*, edited by Rudolf Thomas, 19–39. Trier: Paulinus-Verlag, 1980.

MacDonald, Keith Norman. *In Defence of Ossian: Being a Summary of the Evidence in Favour of the Authenticity of the Poems.* Edinburgh(?), 1906.

MacGregor, Arthur. "Swan Rolls and Beak Markings: Husbandry, Exploitation and Regulation of *Cygnus olor* in England, c. 1100–1900." *Anthropozoologica* no. 22 (1996): 39–68.

Madariaga, Isabel de. *Ivan the Terrible: The First Tsar of Russia.* New Haven, CT: Yale University Press, 2005.

Makarii, Bulgakov, Metropolitan. *Istoriia russkoi tserkvi.* 2nd ed. 12 vols. St. Petersburg: P. Golike, 1883–1903.

Makarov, A. G., and S. E. Makarova. *Tsvetok-Tatarnik. V poiskakh avtora "Tikhogo Dona" ot M. Sholokhova k F. Kriukovu.* Moscow: AIRO – XX, 2001.

Malone, Edmond. "An Attempt to Ascertain the Order in Which the Plays Attributed to Shakespeare Were Written." In *The Plays of William Shakespeare in Ten Volumes with the Corrections and Illustrations of Various Commentators*, vol. 1, 2nd ed., edited by Samuel Johnson and George Steevens, 269–346. London, 1778.

Marenbon, John. "Authenticity Revisited." In *Listening to Heloise: The Voice of a Twelfth-Century Woman*, edited by Bonnie Wheeler, 19–33. New York: St. Martin's, 2000.

Marenbon, John. *The Philosophy of Peter Abelard.* Cambridge: Cambridge University Press, 1997.

Martin, Russell E. *A Bride for the Tsar: Bride-Shows and Marriage Politics in Early Modern Russia.* DeKalb: Northern Illinois University Press, 2012.

Maslennikova, N. N. "Ideologicheskaia bor'ba v pskovskoi literature v period obrazovaniia russkogo tsentralizovannogo gosudarstva." *Trudy Otdela drevnerusskoi literatury* 8 (1951): 187–217.

Matus, Irvin Leigh. *Shakespeare, in Fact.* New York: Continuum, 1994.

McCarthy, Dennis, and June Schlueter. *"A Brief Discourse on Rebellion and Rebels" by George North: A Newly Uncovered Manuscript Source for Shakespeare's Plays.* Cambridge: Brewer, 2018.

McNeill, William. *The Rise of the West: The History of the Human Community.* Chicago: University of Chicago Press, 1963.

Medvedev, Roy A. *Problems in the Literary Biography of Mikhail Sholokhov.* Translated by A. D. P. Briggs. Cambridge: Cambridge University Press, 1977.

Medvedev, Roy. *"Tikhii Don": zagadki i otkrytiia velikogo romana.* Moscow: AIRO-XXI, 2011.

Meek, Donald E. "The Gaelic Ballads of Scotland: Creativity and Adaptation." In *Ossian Revisited*, edited by Howard Gaskill, 19–48. Edinburgh: Edinburg University Press, 1991.

Mendonça, Barbara Heliodora C. de. "*Othello*: A Tragedy Built on a Comic Structure." In *Aspects of* Othello: *Articles Reprinted from* Shakespeare Survey, edited by Kenneth Muir and Philip Edwards, 92–99. Cambridge: Cambridge University Press, 1977.

Mews, Constant J. *The Lost Love Letters of Heloise and Abelard: Perceptions of Dialogue in Twelfth-Century France.* New York: Palgrave, 2001.

Mikheev, Mikhail Iur'evich. "Sholokhov ili vse-taki—Kriukov? Neformal'nye protsedury pro ustanovlenie avtorstva 'Tikhogo Dona.'" In *Komp'iuternaia lingvistika i intellektual'nye tekhnologii. Po materialam ezhegodnoi Mezhdunarodnoi konferentsii "Dialog"* (2012), no. 11, 431–442.

Monfrin, Jacques, ed. *Historia calamitatum. Texte critique.* Paris: Vrin, 1959.

Moore, Peter R. *The Lame Storyteller, Poor and Despised.* Edited by Gary Goldstein. Buchholz: Verlag Laugwitz, 2009.

Moos, Peter von. "Die *Epistolae duorum amantium und die säkulare Religion der Liebe*: Methodenkritische Vorüberlegungen zu einem einmaligen Werk mittellateinischer Briefliteratur," *Studi Medievali*, 3rd ser. 44 (2003): 1–115.

Moos, Peter von. *Mittelalterforschung und Ideologiekritik. Der Gelehrtenstreit um Heloise.* Kritische Information, 15. Munich: Wilhelm Fink, 1974.

Moos, Peter von. "*Post festum*—Was kommt nach der Authentizitätsdebatte über die Briefe Abaelards und Heloises?" In *Petrus Abaelardus, 1079–1142: Person, Werk und Wirkung*, edited by Rudolf Thomas, 75–100. Trier: Paulinus-Verlag, 1980.

Morgan, David O. *The Mongols.* Oxford: Basil Blackwell, 1986; 2nd ed. Malden, MA: Blackwell, 2007.

Morgan, David [O]. "Rašid al-din and Ġazan Khan." In *L'Iran face à la domination mongole*, edited by Denise Aigle, 179–188. Tehran: Institut français de recherché en Iran; Louvain: Diffusion, Peeters, 1997.

Morozov, B. N. "Pervoe poslanie Kurbskogo Ivanu Groznomu v sbornike kontsa XVI–nachala XVII v." *Arkheografieheskii ezhegodnik za 1986*, 277–288. Moscow: Nauka, 1987.

Morton, A. H. "The Letters of Rashīd al-Dīn: Īlkhānid Fact or Timurid Fiction?" In *The Mongol Empire and Its Legacy*, edited by Reuven Amitai-Preiss and David O. Morgan, 157–158. Leiden: Brill, 1999.

Moulton, Paul F. "A Controversy Discarded and *Ossian* Revealed: An Argument for a Renewed Consideration of *The Poems of Ossian.*" *College Music Symposium* 49/50 (2009/2010): 392–401.

Muckle, J. T. "Abelard's Letter of Consolation to a Friend (*Historia Calamitatum*)," *Mediaeval Studies* 12, no. 1 (1950): 163–213.

Muckle, J. T. "The Personal Letters between Abelard and Heloise." *Mediaeval Studies* 15, no. 1 (1953): 47–94.

Musumeci, Irene. "Imagining *Othello* as *Commedia dell'arte*" (2002). http://bardolatry .altervista.org/Iago.htm.

Nelson, Alan H. "The Life and Theatrical Interests of Edward de Vere, Seventeenth Earl of Oxford." In *Shakespeare beyond Doubt: Evidence, Argument, Controversy*, edited by Paul Edmondson and Stanley Wells, 39–48. Cambridge: Cambridge University Press, 2013.

Nelson, Alan H. *Monstrous Adversary: The Life of Edward de Vere, 17th Earl of Oxford.* Liverpool: Liverpool University Press, 2003.

Neville, Leonore. "Anna Komnene: Princess, Historian, and Conspirator?" In *Portraits of Medieval Eastern Europe, 900–1400*, edited by Donald Ostrowski and Christian Rafffensberger, 81–90. London: Routledge, 2018.

Newman, Barbara. "Authority, Authenticity, and the Repression of Heloise." *Journal of Medieval and Renaissance Studies* 22 (1992): 121–157.

Niederkorn, William S. "Foreword." In Roger Stritmatter and Lynne Kositsky, *On the Date, Sources and Design of Shakespeare's* The Tempest, 1–6. Jefferson, NC: McFarland, 2013.

Nizami, K. A. "Rashīd al-Dīn Fazl Allah and India." In *Majmūʿa-yi Khaṭāba-hā-yi Taḥqīqī dar bāra-yi Rashīd al-Dīn Faḍlallāh Hamadānī*, edited by S Naṣr, 36–53. Tehran: Dānishgāh-i Ṭihrān, 1971/1972.

Novikoff, Alex J. *The Medieval Culture of Disputation: Pedagogy, Practice, and Performance.* Philadelphia: University of Pennsylvania Press, 2013.

Obolenskii, Mikhail. "O perevode kniazia Kurbskogo sochinenii Ioanna Damaskina." *Bibliograficheskie zapiski* 1858, no. 12, cols. 355–366.

Okolski, Szymon. *Orbis Polonvs, splendoribus caeli: Triumphis mundi: pulchritudine animantium: decore aquatilium: naturae excellentia reptilium, condecoratvs.* 3 vols. Kraków, 1641.

O'Reilly, Edward. "To Investigate the Authenticity of the Poems of Ossian, Both as Given Macpherson's Translation, and as Published in Gaelic, London 1807, under the Sanction of the Highland Society of London; And on the Supposition of Such Poems Not Being of Recent Origin, to Assign the Probable Era and Country of the Original Poet or Poets." *Transactions of the Royal Irish Academy* 16 (1830): 162–336.

Ostrowski, Donald. "Alexander Nevskii's 'Battle on the Ice': The Creation of a Legend." *Russian History* 33, nos. 2–3–4 (Summer-Fall-Winter 2006): 289–312.

Ostrowski, Donald. "Attributions to Andrei Kurbskii and Inferential (Bayesian) Probability." *Canadian-American Slavic Studies* 49, no. 2–3 (2015): 211–233.

Ostrowski, Donald. "'Closed Circles': Edward L. Keenan's Early Textual Work and the Semiotics of Response." *Canadian Slavonic Papers/Revue canadienne des slavistes* 48, no. 3–4 (2006): 269–277.

Ostrowski, Donald. "The *Debate with Iosif* (*Prenie s Iosifom*) as a Fictive Disputation." In *Iosif Volotskii and Eastern Christianity: Essays across Seventeen Centuries*, edited by David Goldfrank, Valeria Nollan, and Jennifer Spock, 183–211. Washington, DC: New Academia, 2017.

Ostrowski, Donald. "A Metahistorical Analysis: Hayden White and Four Narratives of 'Russian' History." *Clio* 19, no. 3 (1990): 215–236.

Ostrowski, Donald. *Muscovy and the Mongols: Cross-Cultural Influences on the Steppe Frontier, 1304–1589.* Cambridge: Cambridge University Press, 1998.

Ostrowski, Donald. "Review of *Dating Shakespeare's Plays: A Critical Review of the Evidence*, edited by Kevin Gilvary." In *Brief Chronicles: An Interdisciplinary Journal of Authorship Studies* 3 (2011): 246–257.

Ostrowski, Donald. "The Thick and Thin of It: Gary Hamburg's Path toward Enlightenment of Early Modern Russian Political Thought," *Canadian-American Slavic Studies* 53 (2019) (forthcoming).

Ostrowski, Donald. "Three Criteria of Historical Study." https://donostrowski2 .bitbucket.io/history.pdf.

Ostrozhskii, Klirik. "Istoriia o razboinich'em florentiiskom sobore." In *Pamiatniki polemicheskoi literatury 3* (1903). *Russkaia istoricheskaia biblioteka* 19 (1903): 433–476.

Partridge, A. C. *Orthography in Shakespeare and Elizabethan Drama: A Study of Colloquial Contractions, Elision, Prosody, and Punctuation.* Lincoln: University of Nebraska Press, 1964.

Partridge, Eric. *A Dictionary of Slang and Unconventional English.* London: Routledge, 2002.

Peacham, Henry. *Minerva Britannia.* 1612.

Petrella. E. D. "Sull'autenticità delle lettere d'Abelardo e Eloisa." *Rendiconti del Reale Istituto Lombardo de scienze e lettere*, 2nd ser., 44 (1911): 554–561, 606–618.

Petrushevkii, I[l'ia] P. "K voprosu o podlinnosti perepiski Rashid ad-Dina." *Vestnik Leningradskogo universiteta* 39 (1948): 124–130.

Petukhov, E. V. "O nekotorykh istoricheskikh i literaturnykh faktakh, sviazannykh s imenem Uspenskogo Pskovo-Pecherskogo monastyria v XVI i XVII vv." Vol. 1, 256–263. *Trudy X Arkheologicheskogo s"ezda.* Riga, 1899.

Petukhov, E. V. *Russkaia literatura. Istoricheskii obzor glavneishikh literaturnikh iavlenii drevnogo i novogo perioda.* 2 vols. 3rd ed. Petrograd: Suvorin, 1916.

Pierce, Frederic Beech. *Pierce Genealogy, Being the Record of the Posterity of Thomas Pierce, an Early Inhabitant of Charlestown, and Afterwards Charlestown Village (Woburn), in New England.* Worcester, MA: Chas. Hamilton, 1882.

Piron, Sylvain. "Heloise's Literary Self-fashioning and the Epistolae duorum amantium." In *Strategies of Remembrance. From Pindar to Hölderlin*, edited by Lucie Doležalová, 102–162. Newcastle upon Tyne, UK: Cambridge Scholars, 2009.

Platonov, S. M. *Ivan Groznyi.* St. Petersburg: Brokgauz-Efron, 1923.

Pointon, A. J. "The Man Who Was Never Shakespeare: The Spelling of William Shakspere's Name." In *Shakespeare beyond Doubt? Exposing an Industry in Denial*, edited by John M. Shahan and Alexander Waugh, 14–28. Tamarac, FL: Llumina, 2013.

Potkay, Adam. "Virtue and Manners in Macpherson's Poems of Ossian," *PMLA* 107, no. 1 (January 1992): 120–130.

Praz, Mario. "Shakespeare and Italy." In *The Flaming Heart: Essays on Crashaw, Machiavelli, and Other Studies of the Relation between Italian and English Literature from Chaucer to T. S. Eliot*, 146–167. New York: Doubleday Anchor, 1958.

Price, Diana. *Shakespeare's Unorthodox Biography: New Evidence of an Authorship Problem.* http://shakespeare-authorship.com/, 2012.

Priima, Konstantin. "Gordost' sovetskoi i mirovoi literatury. Po stranitsam zarubezhnoi progrssivnoi pechati." *Inostrannaia literatura*, no. 5 (1975): 203.

Priima, Konstantin. "Velikaia evropeia." *Vechernii Rostov*, May 24, 1978, 3.

Radice, Betty C., trans. *The Letters of Abelard and Héloïse.* Hammondsworth: Penguin, 1974.

Rashīd al-Dīn. *Letters.* Edited by Muhammad Shafiʿ. Lahore: Published for the University of the Panjab, 1947.

Rashīd al-Dīn. *Perepiska.* Edited and translated by A. I. Falina. Moscow: Nauka, 1971.

Rashīd al-Dīn. *Sawāniḥ al-afkār-i rashīdī.* Edited by Muḥammad Taqi Dānishpazhūh. Tehran: Intishārāt-i Dānishgāh-i Tihrān, 1980.

Rashiduddin Fazlullah [Rashid al-Din]. *Jamiʿuʾt-Tawarikh: Compendium of Chronicles.* Translated by W. M. Thackston. Cambridge, MA: Harvard University Department of Near Eastern Languages, 1999.

Renan, Ernest. *History of the People of Israel: From the Reign of David Up to the Capture of Samaria.* 5 vols. Vol. 1, *Till the Time of King David.* London: Chapman and Hall, 1888.

Robbins, Manuel. *Collapse of the Bronze Age: The Story of Greece, Troy, Israel, Egypt, and the Peoples of the Sea.* iUniverse.com, 2001.

Robertson, D. W., Jr. *Abelard and Heloise.* New York: Dial Press, 1972.

Robinson, Alan. "The Real William Shakespeare." In *Great Oxford: Essays on the Life and Work of Edward de Vere, 17th Earl of Oxford, 1550–1604*, edited by Richard Malim, 237–243. Tunbridge Wells, UK: Parapress, 2004.

Robl, Werner. *Heloisas Herkunft: Hersindis Mater.* Munich: Olzog, 2001.

Rodimyi krai. Sbornik, posviashchenyi dvadtstipiatiletiiu literaurnoi deiatel'nosti F. D. Kriukova (1893–1918 g.g.). Ust'-Medveditskaia: Sever Dona, 1918.

Roe, Richard Paul. *The Shakespeare Guide to Italy: Retracing the Bard's Unknown Travels.* New York: HarperCollins, 2011.

Roscelin de Compiègne, *Epistola ad Abaelardum.* Edited by Joseph Reiners, 63–80. In *Der Nominalismus in der Frühscholastik. Ein Beitrag zur Geschichte der Universalienfrage im Mittelalter*, Beiträge zur Geschichte der Philosophie des Mittelalters. Bd. 8.5. Munster: Aschendorff, 1910.

Rosen, Richard. "Bullcrit: The Reading Disorder of the Literary Fast Lane." *New York*, February 6, 1989, 44–47.

Ross, Neil, ed. *Heroic Poetry from the Book of the Dean of Lismore.* Edinburgh: Oliver and Boyd for the Scottish Gaelic Texts Society, 1939.

Roth, Steve. *Hamlet: The Undiscovered Country.* 2nd ed. Seattle: Open House, 2013.

Rudman, Joseph. "Non-Traditional Authorship Attribution Studies of William Shakespeare's Canon: Some Caveats." *Journal of Early Modern Studies* 5 (2016): 307–328.

Rudman, Joseph. "The State of Authorship Attribution Studies: Some Problems and Solutions," *Computers and Humanities* 31 (1998): 351–365.

Sarkisova, G. I. "Beglyi boiarin Andrei Kurbskii i ego poslaniia." In *Ot Nestora do Fonvizina. Novye metody opredeleniia avtorstva*, edited by L. V. Milov. Moscow: Progress, 1994.

Sasson, Jack M. "Circumcision." In *Harper's Bible Dictionary*, edited by Paul J. Achtemeier. New York: HarperCollins, 2000.

Schaberg, David. "'Sell It! Sell It!': Recent Translations of *Lunyu*." *Chinese Literature: Essays, Articles, Reviews* 23 (2001): 133–137.

Schmeidler, Bernhard. "Der Briefwechsel zwischen Abalard und Heloise eine Fälschung." *Archiv für Kulturgeschichte* 11 (1913): 1–30.

Schmeidler, Bernhard. "Der Briefwechsel zwischen Abaelard und Heloise als eine literarische Fiktion Abaelards." *Zeitschrift für Kirchengeschichte* 54 (1935): 323–338.

Schmeidler, Bernhard. "Der Briefwechsel zwischen Abaelard und Heloise dennoch eine literarische Fiction Abaelards." *Revue Benedictine* 52 (1940): 85–95.

Schoenbaum, Samuel. *Shakespeare's Lives*. Oxford: Oxford University Press, 1991.

Schweitzer, Albert. *The Quest of the Historical Jesus: A Critical Study of Its Progress from Reimarus to Wrede*. Translated by W. Montgomery. London: Adam and Charles Black, 1910.

Scott, Walter. "Review of *Report of the Highland Society of Scotland . . . and the Poems of Ossian . . . Works of James Macpherson*." *Edinburgh Review* 6, no. 12 (July 1805): 429–462.

Searle, Leroy. "New Criticism." In *The Johns Hopkins Guide to Literary Theory*, 2nd ed., 691–698. Baltimore: Johns Hopkins University Press, 2005.

Ševčenko, Ihor. "Re-reading Constantine Porphyrogenitus." In *Byzantine Diplomacy: Papers of the Twenty-fourth Spring Symposium of Byzantine Studies, Cambridge, March 1990*, edited by Jonathan Shepard and Simon Franklin, 167–195. Aldershot, UK: Variorum, 1992.

Shanks, Hershel. "'Secret Mark': Morton Smith – Forger." *Biblical Archaeology Review* 35, no. 6 (2009): 49.

Shanks, Hershel. "'Secret Mark': Restoring a Dead Scholar's Reputation." *Biblical Archaeology Review* 35, no. 6 (2009): 60.

Shapiro, James. *Contested Will: Who Wrote Shakespeare?* New York: Simon & Schuster, 2010.

Shevyrev, S. P. "Novye izvestie o Florentiiskom sobore, izvlecheniie iz Vatikanskoi rukopisi." *Zhurnal Ministerstva narodnogo prosveshchenie*, 1841, bk. 1, 60–78.

Sholokhov, Mikhail. *And Quiet Flows the Don*. Translated by Stephen Garry. New York: Knopf, 1934.

Silvestre, Hubert. "Die Liebesgischichte zwischen Abaelard und Heloise: der Anteil des Romans." In *Fälschungen im Mittelalter. Internationaler Kongress der Monumenta Germaniae Historica, München, 16.–19. September 1986*. Vol. 5, *Fingierte Briefe, Frömmigkeit und Fälschung, Realienfälschungen*, MGH Schriften, Bd. 33, V, 121–165. Hannover: Hahnsche Buchhandlung, 1988.

Skantze, P. A. "Making It Up: Improvisation as Cultural Exchange between Shakespeare and Italy." In *Shakespeare and Intertextuality: The Tradition of Cultures between Italy and England in the Early Modern Period*, edited by Michele Marrapodi, 257–269. Rome: Bulzoni Editore, 2000.

Skrynnikov, R. G. "Kurbskii i ego pis'ma v Pskovo-Pecherskii monastyr'." *Trudy Otdela drevnerusskoi literatury* 18 (1962): 99–116.

Skrynnikov, R. G. "On the Authenticity of the Kurbskii-Groznyi Correspondence: A Summary of the Discussion." *Slavic Review* 37, no. 1 (March 1978): 107–115.

Skrynnikov, R. G. *Perepiska Groznogo i Kurbskogo: Paradoksy Edvarda Kinana.* Leningrad: Nauka, 1973.

Slater, Gilbert. *Seven Shakespeares: A Discussion of the Evidence for Various Theories with Regard to Shakespeare's Identity.* Oxford: Cecil Palmer, 1931.

Slingerland, Edward. *Analects: With Selections from Traditional Commentaries.* Indianapolis: Hackett 2003.

Slingerland, Edward. "Why Philosophy Is Not 'Extra' in Understanding the *Analects." Philosophy East and West* 50, no. 1 (January 2000): 137–141.

Smart, J[ohn] S[emple]. *James Macpherson: An Episode in Literature.* London: David Nutt, 1905.

Smith, Morton. *Clement of Alexandria and a Secret Gospel according to Mark.* Cambridge, MA: Harvard University Press, 1973.

Smith, Morton. *The Secret Gospel: The Discovery and Interpretation of the Secret Gospel According to Mark.* Clearlake, CA: Dawn Horse, 1973.

Smith, Sarah. *Chasing Shakespeares.* New York: Atria, 2003.

Smith, Sarah. "A Reattribution of Munday's 'The Paine of Pleasure.'" *The Oxfordian* 5 (2002): 70–99.

Solovetskii paterik. Moscow: Sinodal'naia biblioteka, 1991.

Solzhenitsyn, Aleksandr. "Sholokhov and the Riddle of 'The Quiet Don.'" *Times Literary Supplement (TLS),* October 4, 1974.

Soudavar, Abolala. "In Defense of Rašid-od-Din and His Letters." *Studica Iranica* 32 (2003): 77–120.

Southern, R. W. *Medieval Humanism and Other Studies.* Oxford: Basil Blackwell, 1970.

Stein, Jean. "William Faulkner: The Art of Fiction, no. 12." *Paris Review,* no. 12 (Spring 1956).

Stritmatter, Roger A. *The Marginalia of Edward De Vere's Geneva Bible: Providential Discovery, Literary Reasoning, and Historical Consequence.* Northampton, MA: Oxenford Press, 2001.

Stroumsa, Guy C., ed. *Morton Smith and Gershom Scholem, Correspondence 1945–1982.* Leiden: Brill, 2008.

Sunstein, Cass R., and Adrian Vermeule. "Conspiracy Theories." Harvard University Law School Public Law & Legal Theory Research Paper Series, 2008.

Szövérffy, Joseph. *Secular Latin Lyrics and Minor Poetic Forms of the Middle Ages: A Historical Survey and Literary Repertory from the Tenth to the Late Fifteenth Century,* 4 vols. Concord, NH: Classical Folia Editions, 1993–1995.

Taylor, Gary, John Howett, Terri Bourus, and Gabriel Egan, eds. *New Oxford Shakespeare: Complete Works. Critical Edition.* Oxford: Oxford University Press, 2016.

Thomas, Rudolf, ed. *Petrus Abaelardus, 1079–1142: Person, Werk und Wirkung.* Trier: Paulinus-Verlag, 1980.

Thomson, Derick Smith. *Gaelic Sources of Macpherson's Ossian.* Edinburgh: Published for the University of Aberdeen by Oliver and Boyd, 1952.

Thomson, Francis J. "The Corpus of Slavonic Translation Available in Muscovy: The Cause of Old Russia's Intellectual Silence and a Contributory Factor to Muscovite Autarky." In *Christianity and the Eastern Slavs.* Vol. 1, *Slavic Cultures in the Middle Ages,* edited by Boris Gasparov and Olga Raevsky-Hughes, 179–214. Berkeley: University of California Press, 1993.

Tsedaka, Benyamin, and Sharon Sullivan, eds. *The Israelite Samaritan Version of the Torah: First English Translation Compared with the Masoretic Version.* Grand Rapids, MI: Eerdmans, 2013.

Twain, Mark. *The Innocents Abroad.* Hartford, CT: American Publishing, 1869.

Ustrialov, N. G. *Skazaniia kniazia Kurbskogo.* 2 vols. St. Petersburg: Tipografiia Imperatorskoi Akademii nauk, 1833; 2nd ed. St. Petersburg: Tipografiia Imperatorskoi Akademii nauk, 1842; 3rd ed. St. Petersburg: Tipografiia Imperatorskoi Akademii nauk, 1868.

Utechin, S. V. *Russian Political Thought: A Concise History.* New York: Praeger, 1963.

Van Els, Paul. "Confucius's Sayings Entombed: On Two Han Dynasty Bamboo *Analects* Manuscripts." In *Confucius and the Analects Revisited: New Perspectives on the Dating on Dating, Composition, and Authorship,* edited by Michael Hunter and Martin Kern, 157–186. Leiden: Brill, 2018.

Van Els, Paul. *The Wenzi: Creativity and Intertextuality in Early Chinese Philosophy.* Leiden: Brill, 2018.

Van Norden, Bryan W. "Introduction." In *Confucius and the Analects: New Essays,* edited by Bryan W. Van Norden. Oxford: Oxford University Press, 2002.

Vendler, Helen. *The Art of Shakespeare's Sonnets.* Cambridge, MA: Harvard University Press, 1997.

Venkov, A[ndrei] V[ladimovich]. *"Tikhii Don." Istochnikovaia baza i problema avtorstva.* Rostov-on-Don: Terra, 2000. Rev. ed., Moscow: AIRO – XXI, 2010.

Vostokov, Aleksandr. *Opisanie russkikh i slovenskikh rukopisei Rumiantsovskogo muzeuma.* St. Petersburg: V tip. Imp. akademii nauk, 1842.

Waddell, Peter Hately. *Ossian and the Clyde, Fingal in Ireland. Oscar in Iceland, Or Ossian Historical and Authentic.* Glasgow: James MacLehose, 1875.

Waley, Arthur. "Introduction." *The Analects of Confucius,* edited and annotated by Arthur Waley. New York: Macmillan, 1938.

Ward, B. M. *The Seventeenth Earl of Oxford, 1550–1604: From Contemporary Documents.* London: John Murray, 1928.

Watson, Burton, trans. *The Complete Works of Chuang Tzu.* New York: Columbia University Press, 1968.

Watson, Francis. "Beyond Suspicion: On the Authorship of the Mar Saba Letter and Secret Gospel of Mark." *Journal of Theological Studies* 61 (2010): 128–170.

Waugh, Alexander. "The True Meaning of Ben Jonson's Phrase: 'Sweet Swan of Avon.'" *The Oxfordian* 14 (2014): 97–103.

Wellhausen, Julius. *Prolegomena to the History of Ancient Israel.* Translated by J. Sutherland Black and Allan Menzies. Edinburgh: Adam and Charles Black, 1885.

Whalen, Richard F. *"Commedia dell'arte* in *Othello,* a Satiric Comedy Ending in Tragedy." *Brief Chronicles* 3 (2011): 71–106.

White, Hayden. *Metahistory: The Historical Imagination of Nineteenth-Century Europe.* Baltimore: Johns Hopkins, 1973.

Wilkinson, Endymion. *Chinese History: A New Manual.* 5th ed. Cambridge, MA: Harvard University Asia Center, 2012.

Yan, Andrew Zhongyu. *An Existential Reading of the Confucian Analects.* Amherst, NY: Cambria, 2011.

Yellin, Jean Fagan. *Harriet Jacobs: A Life.* Cambridge, MA: Basic Civitas, 2004.

Yellin, Jean Fagan. "'Texts and Contexts of Harriet Jacobs's Incidents in the Life of a Slave Girl: Written by Herself." In *The Slave's Narrative*, edited by Charles T. Davis and Henry Louis Gates Jr., 262–282. New York: Oxford University Press, 1985.

Zema, Valerii. "Sprava viry." *Kyivs'ka starovyna*, no. 3 (2001): 190–199.

Zimin, A. A. "Kogda Kurbskii napisal 'Istoriiu o velikom kniaze Moskovskom'?" *Trudy Otdela drevnerusskoi literatury* 18 (1962): 305–308.

Ziolkowski, Jan M. "Lost and Not Yet Found: Heloise, Abelard, and the *Epistolae duorum amantium*." *Journal of Medieval Latin* 14 (2004): 171–202.

Ziolkowski, Jan M. *Letters of Peter Abelard: Beyond the Personal*. Washington, DC: Catholic University Press of America, 2008.

INDEX

CPSIA information can be obtained
at www.ICGtesting.com
Printed in the USA
LVHW090813310520
657034LV00003B/22

9 781501 750823